空知英秋（銀玉）

Hideaki Sorachi(Silver Balls)

Thanks to everyone, we made
it to our first anniversary.
Sometimes I nearly miss my
deadlines, but I'm okay

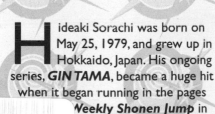

Hideaki Sorachi was born on
May 25, 1979, and grew up in
Hokkaido, Japan. His ongoing
series, *GIN TAMA*, became a huge hit
when it began running in the pages
of *Weekly Shonen Jump* in
GIN TAMA animated series
soon after, premiering on
TV in April 2006. Sorachi
manga debut with the
ot story *DANDELION*!

GIN TAMA VOL. 5
SHONEN JUMP ADVANCED Manga Edition

STORY & ART BY HIDEAKI SORACHI

Translation/Matthew Rosin, Honyaku Center Inc.
English Adaptation/Drew Williams
Touch-up Art & Lettering/Avril Averill
Cover & Interior Design/Sean Lee
Editors/Annette Roman & Mike Montesa

Printed in the U.S.A.

Published by VIZ Media, LLC
P.O. Box 77010
San Francisco, CA 94107

10 9 8 7 6 5 4 3 2
First printing, March 2008
Second printing, May 2014

www.viz.com

THE WORLD'S MOST
CUTTING-EDGE MANGA
SHONEN JUMP
ADVANCED
www.shonenjump.com

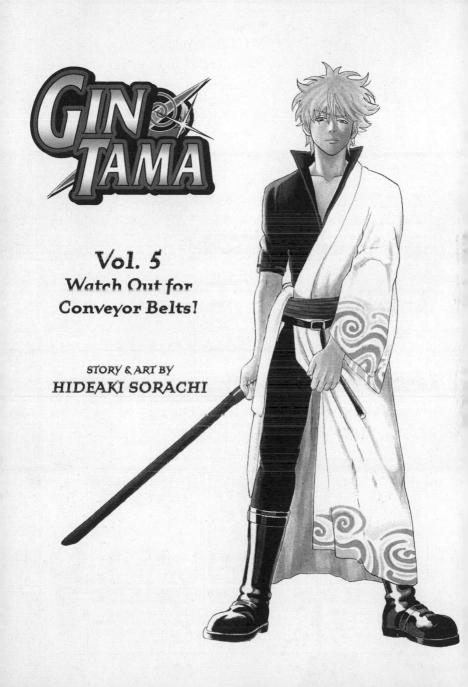

GIN TAMA

Vol. 5
Watch Out for
Conveyor Belts!

STORY & ART BY
HIDEAKI SORACHI

Cast of Characters

Yorozuya Members

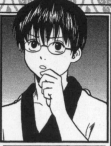

Shinpachi Shimura

Works under Gintoki in an attempt to learn about the samurai spirit, but has been regretting his decision recently. Also president of idol singer Tsu Terakado's fan club.

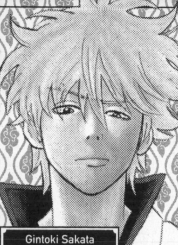

Gintoki Sakata

The hero of our story. He needs to eat something sweet periodically or he gets cranky. He commands a powerful sword arm but is one step away from diabetes. A former member of the exclusionist faction which seeks to eliminate the space aliens and protect the nation.

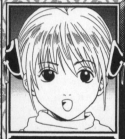

Kagura

A member of the "Yato Clan," the most powerful warrior race in the universe. Her voracious appetite and often inadvertent comic timing are unrivalled.

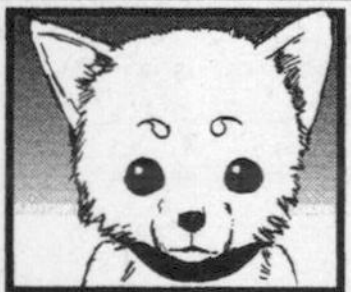

Sadaharu/animal

A giant space creature kept as a pet in the Yorozuya office. Likes to bite people (especially Gintoki).

Shinsengumi Soldiers

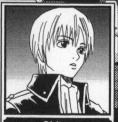

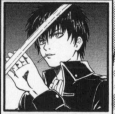

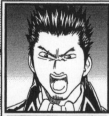

Kondo

Chief of the Shinsengumi, and trusted by all its soldiers. Also stalking Shinpachi's elder sister Otae.

Hijikata

Vice-Chief of the Shinsengumi, Edo's elite Delta Force police unit. His cool demeanor turns to rage the moment he draws his sword. The pupils of his eyes always seem a bit dilated.

Okita

The most formidable swordsman in the Shinsengumi. His jovial attitude hides an utterly black heart. He wants to take over as the Vice-Chief.

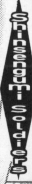

Other Characters

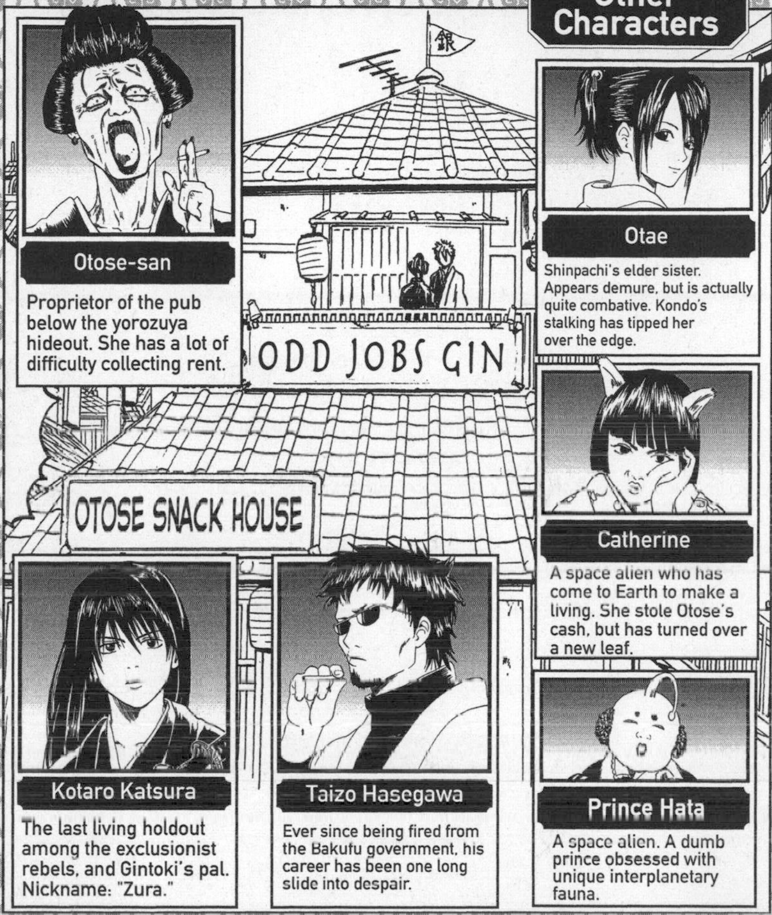
ODD JOBS GIN
OTOSE SNACK HOUSE
Otose-san
Proprietor of the pub below the yorozuya hideout. She has a lot of difficulty collecting rent.
Otae
Shinpachi's elder sister. Appears demure, but is actually quite combative. Kondo's stalking has tipped her over the edge.
Catherine
A space alien who has come to Earth to make a living. She stole Otose's cash, but has turned over a new leaf.
Kotaro Katsura
The last living holdout among the exclusionist rebels, and Gintoki's pal. Nickname: "Zura."
Taizo Hasegawa
Ever since being fired from the Bakufu government, his career has been one long slide into despair.
Prince Hata
A space alien. A dumb prince obsessed with unique interplanetary fauna.

The story thus far

In an alternate-universe Edo (Tokyo), extraterrestrials land in Japan and the new government issues an order outlawing swords. The samurai, who have reached the pinnacle of power and prosperity, fall into rapid decline.

Twenty years hence, only one samurai has managed to hold on to his fighting spirit: a somewhat eccentric fellow named Gintoki "Odd Jobs Gin" Sakata. A lover of sweets and near diabetic, our hero sets up shop as a *yorozuya*—an expert at managing trouble and handling the oddest jobs.

Joining "Gin" in his business is Shinpachi Shimura, whose sister Gin saved from the clutches of nefarious debt collectors. After a series of unexpected circumstances, the trio meet a powerful alien named Kagura, who becomes—after some arm-twisting—a part-time team member.

Recently, the Yorozuya gang has played hooky with a princess, saved Catherine from nasty former associates, gotten spaceshipwrecked during an all-expenses paid cruise, captured a panty thief, and prevented a homicidal robot designer from avenging his son's murder. What in the world will they get into next...?!

WHAT THIS MANGA'S FULL OF vol. 5

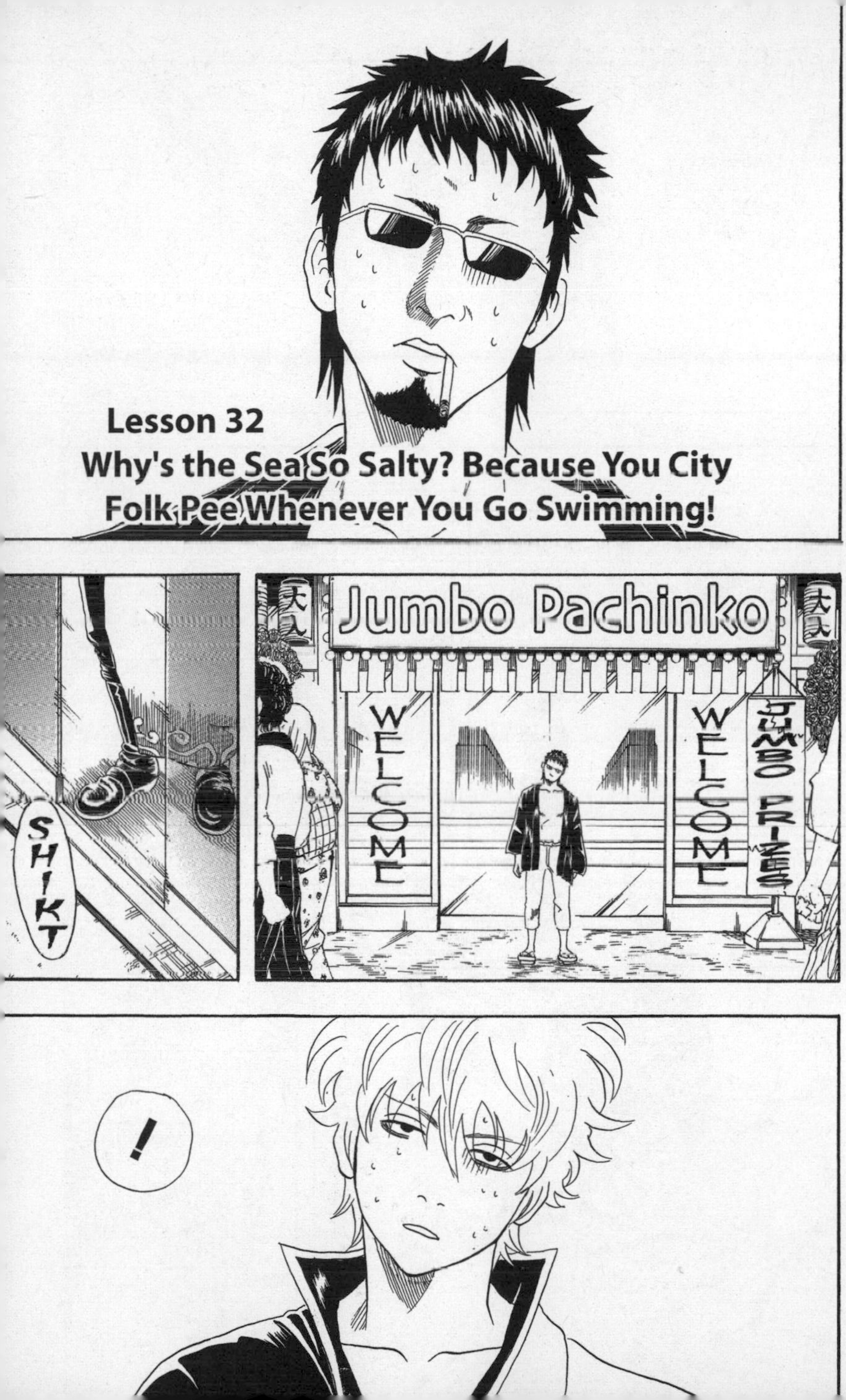
Lesson 32
Why's the Sea So Salty? Because You City Folk Pee Whenever You Go Swimming!
大入
Jumbo Pachinko
大入
WELCOME
WELCOME
JUMBO PRIZES
SHIKT
!

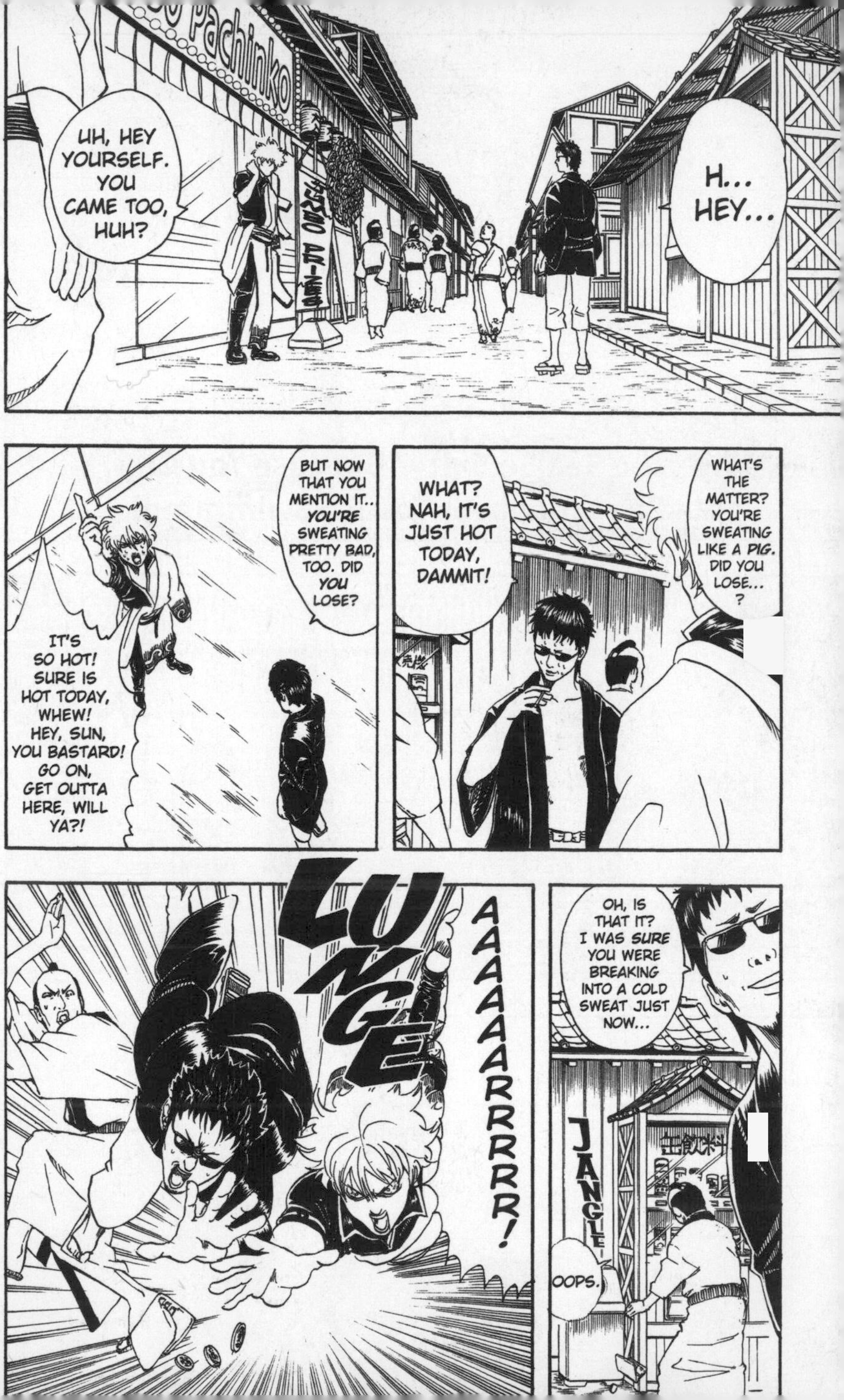
Pachinko
JUMBO PRIZES
H... HEY...
UH, HEY YOURSELF. YOU CAME TOO, HUH?
WHAT'S THE MATTER? YOU'RE SWEATING LIKE A *PIG*. DID YOU LOSE... ?
WHAT? NAH, IT'S JUST HOT TODAY, DAMMIT!
BUT NOW THAT YOU MENTION IT.. *YOU'RE* SWEATING PRETTY BAD, TOO. DID *YOU* LOSE?
IT'S SO HOT! SURE IS HOT TODAY, WHEW! HEY, SUN, YOU BASTARD! GO ON, GET OUTTA HERE, WILL YA?!
OH, IS THAT IT? I WAS *SURE* YOU WERE BREAKING INTO A COLD SWEAT JUST NOW...
JANGLE
OOPS.
LUNGE
AAAAAARRRRR!

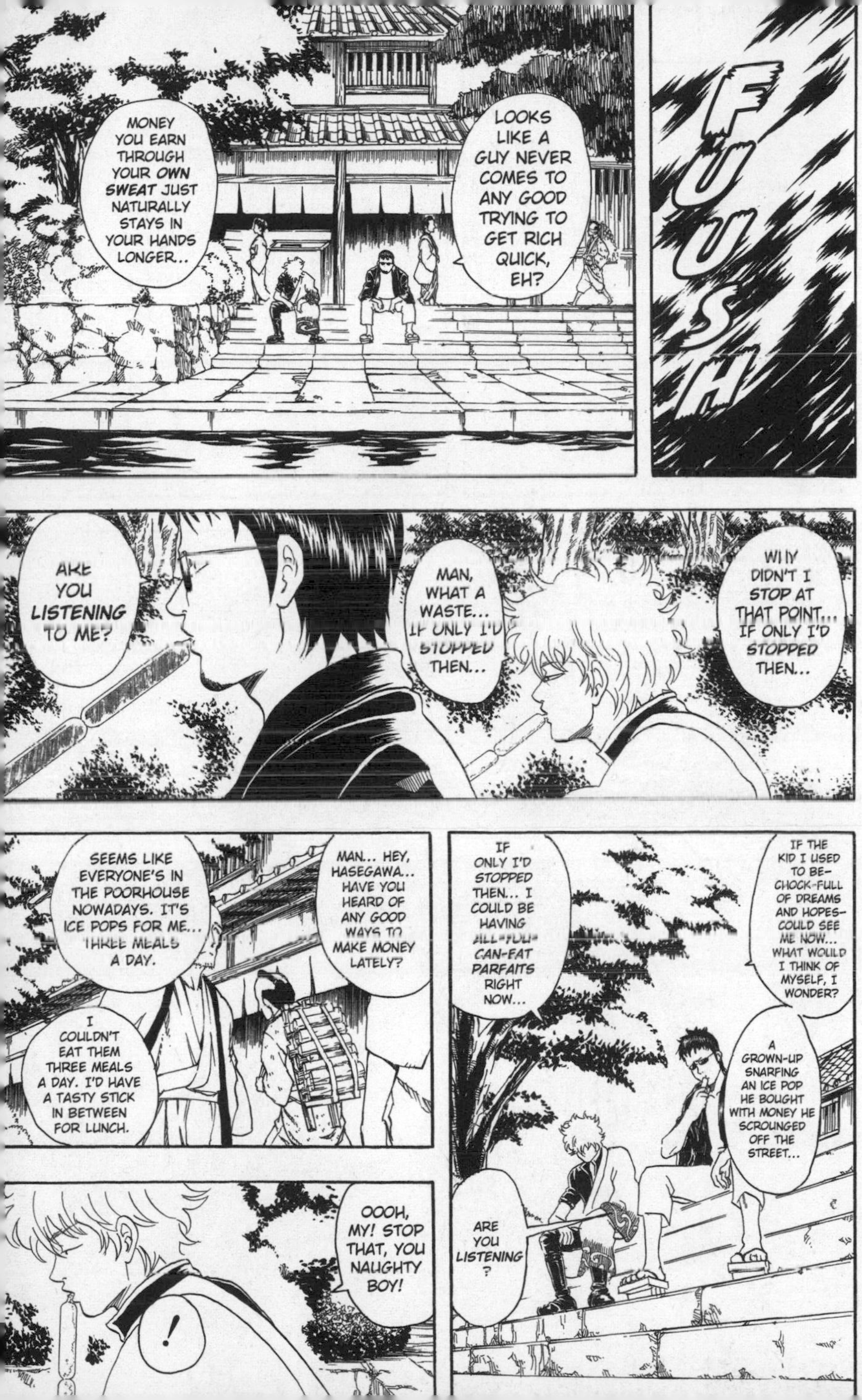
FUUSH
LOOKS LIKE A GUY NEVER COMES TO ANY GOOD TRYING TO GET RICH QUICK, EH?
MONEY YOU EARN THROUGH YOUR OWN SWEAT JUST NATURALLY STAYS IN YOUR HANDS LONGER...
WHY DIDN'T I STOP AT THAT POINT... IF ONLY I'D STOPPED THEN...
MAN, WHAT A WASTE... IF ONLY I'D STOPPED THEN...
ARE YOU LISTENING TO ME?
IF THE KID I USED TO BE—CHOCK-FULL OF DREAMS AND HOPES—COULD SEE ME NOW... WHAT WOULD I THINK OF MYSELF, I WONDER?
IF ONLY I'D STOPPED THEN... I COULD BE HAVING ALL-YOU-CAN-EAT PARFAITS RIGHT NOW...
A GROWN-UP SNARFING AN ICE POP HE BOUGHT WITH MONEY HE SCROUNGED OFF THE STREET...
ARE YOU LISTENING?
MAN... HEY, HASEGAWA... HAVE YOU HEARD OF ANY GOOD WAYS TO MAKE MONEY LATELY?
SEEMS LIKE EVERYONE'S IN THE POORHOUSE NOWADAYS. IT'S ICE POPS FOR ME... THREE MEALS A DAY.
I COULDN'T EAT THEM THREE MEALS A DAY. I'D HAVE A TASTY STICK IN BETWEEN FOR LUNCH.
OOOH, MY! STOP THAT, YOU NAUGHTY BOY!
!

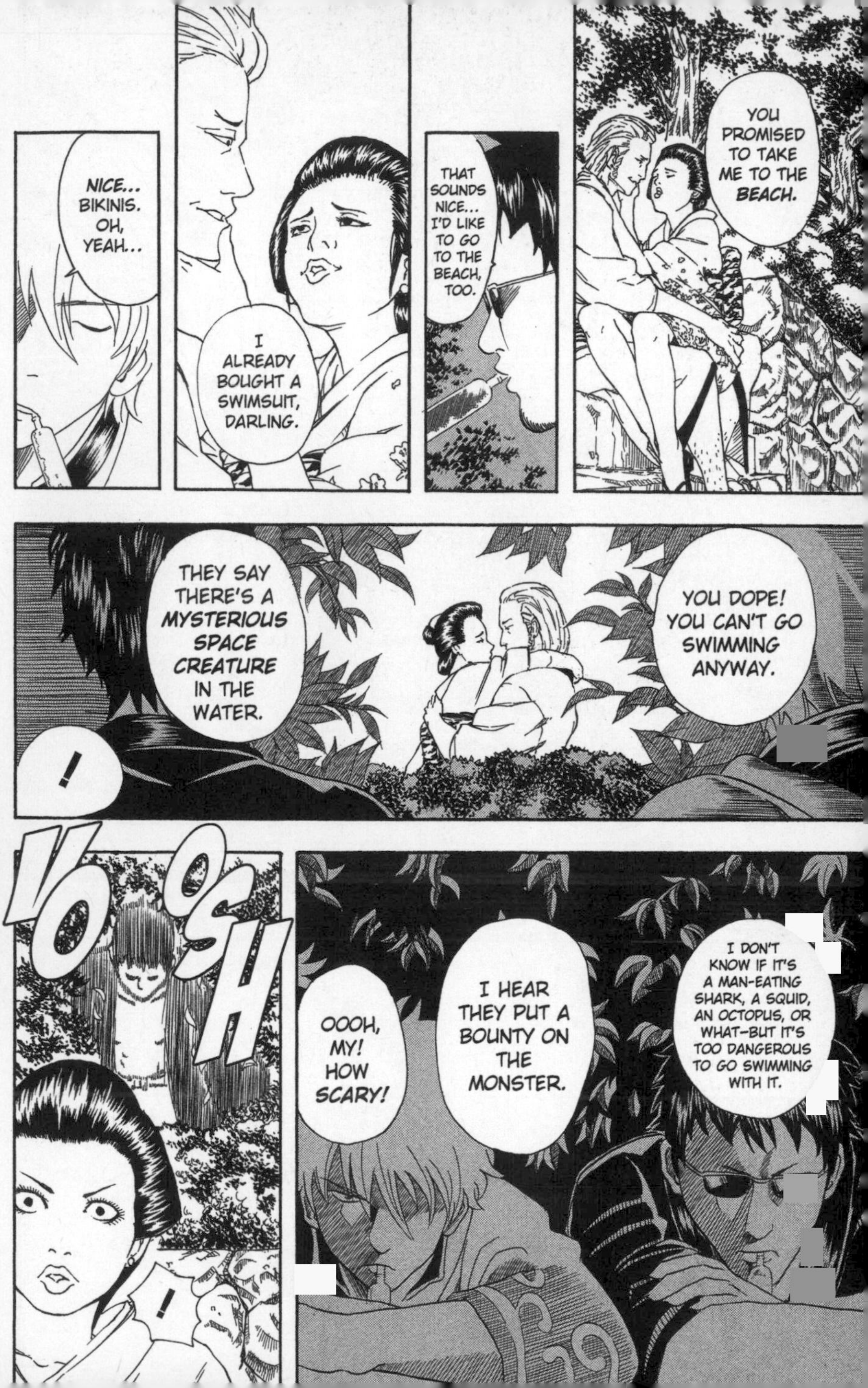
YOU PROMISED TO TAKE ME TO THE BEACH.
THAT SOUNDS NICE... I'D LIKE TO GO TO THE BEACH, TOO.
I ALREADY BOUGHT A SWIMSUIT, DARLING.
NICE... BIKINIS. OH, YEAH...
YOU DOPE! YOU CAN'T GO SWIMMING ANYWAY.
THEY SAY THERE'S A MYSTERIOUS SPACE CREATURE IN THE WATER.
!
I DON'T KNOW IF IT'S A MAN-EATING SHARK, A SQUID, AN OCTOPUS, OR WHAT—BUT IT'S TOO DANGEROUS TO GO SWIMMING WITH IT.
I HEAR THEY PUT A BOUNTY ON THE MONSTER.
OOOH, MY! HOW SCARY!
VOOSH
!

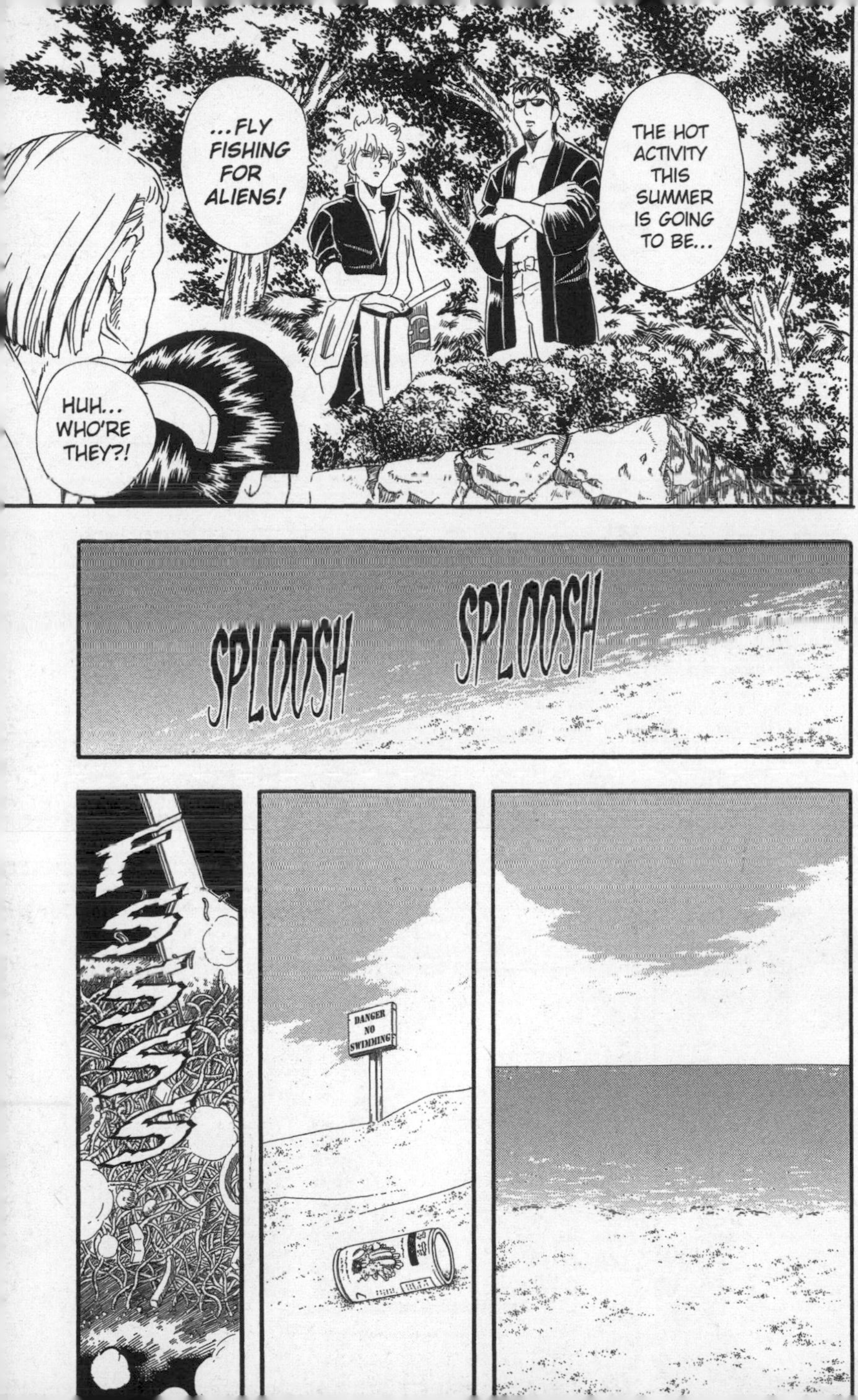
THE HOT ACTIVITY THIS SUMMER IS GOING TO BE...
...FLY FISHING FOR ALIENS!
HUH... WHO'RE THEY?!
SPLOOSH
SPLOOSH
DANGER NO SWIMMING

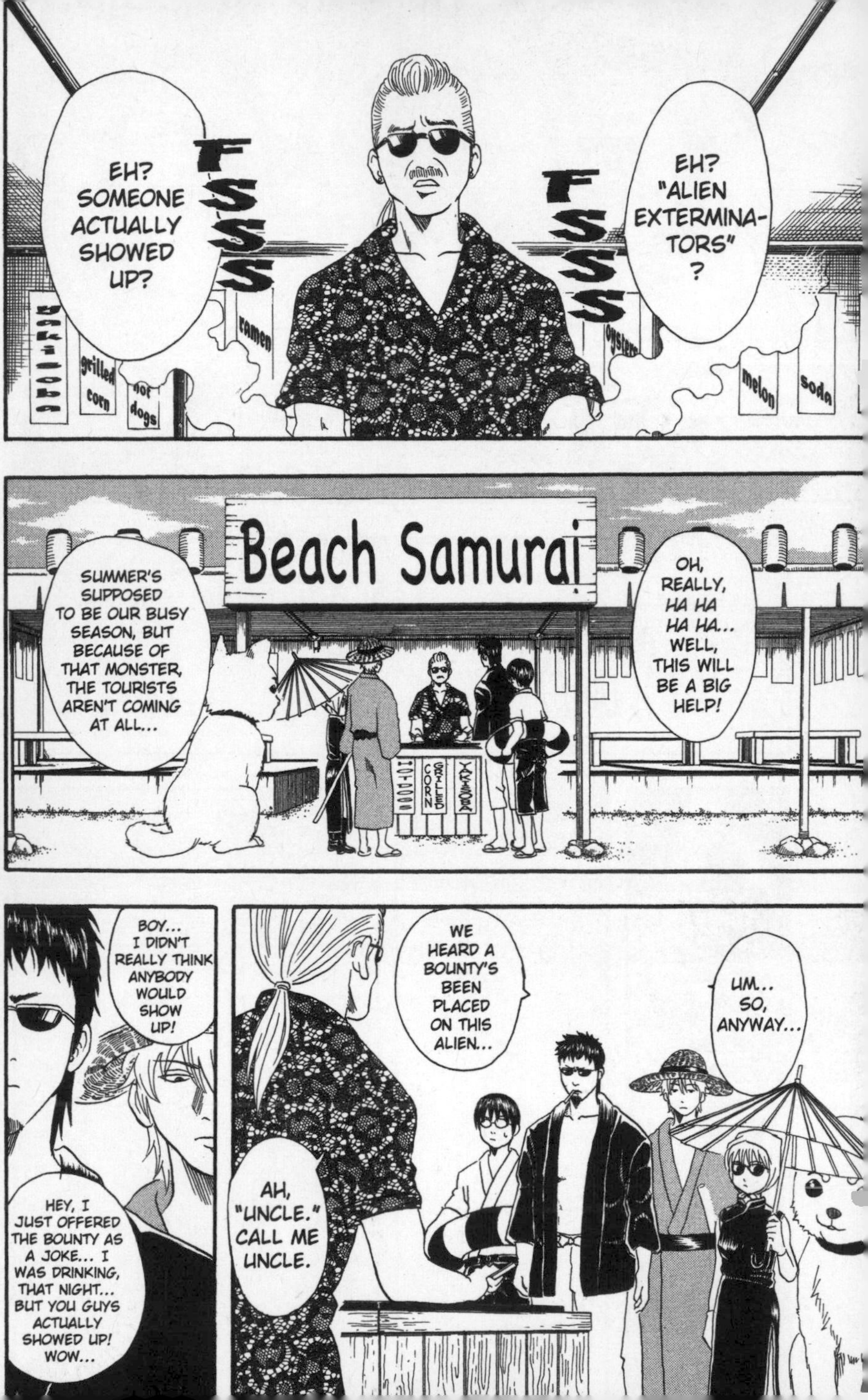
EH? "ALIEN EXTERMINATORS" ?
FSS
FSS
EH? SOMEONE ACTUALLY SHOWED UP?
soda
melon
oysters
ramen
hot dogs
grilled corn
Beach Samurai
OH, REALLY, HA HA HA HA... WELL, THIS WILL BE A BIG HELP!
SUMMER'S SUPPOSED TO BE OUR BUSY SEASON, BUT BECAUSE OF THAT MONSTER, THE TOURISTS AREN'T COMING AT ALL...
YAKISOBA
GRILLED CORN
HOT DOGS
UM... SO, ANYWAY...
WE HEARD A BOUNTY'S BEEN PLACED ON THIS ALIEN...
AH, "UNCLE." CALL ME UNCLE.
BOY... I DIDN'T REALLY THINK ANYBODY WOULD SHOW UP!
HEY, I JUST OFFERED THE BOUNTY AS A JOKE... I WAS DRINKING, THAT NIGHT... BUT YOU GUYS ACTUALLY SHOWED UP! WOW...

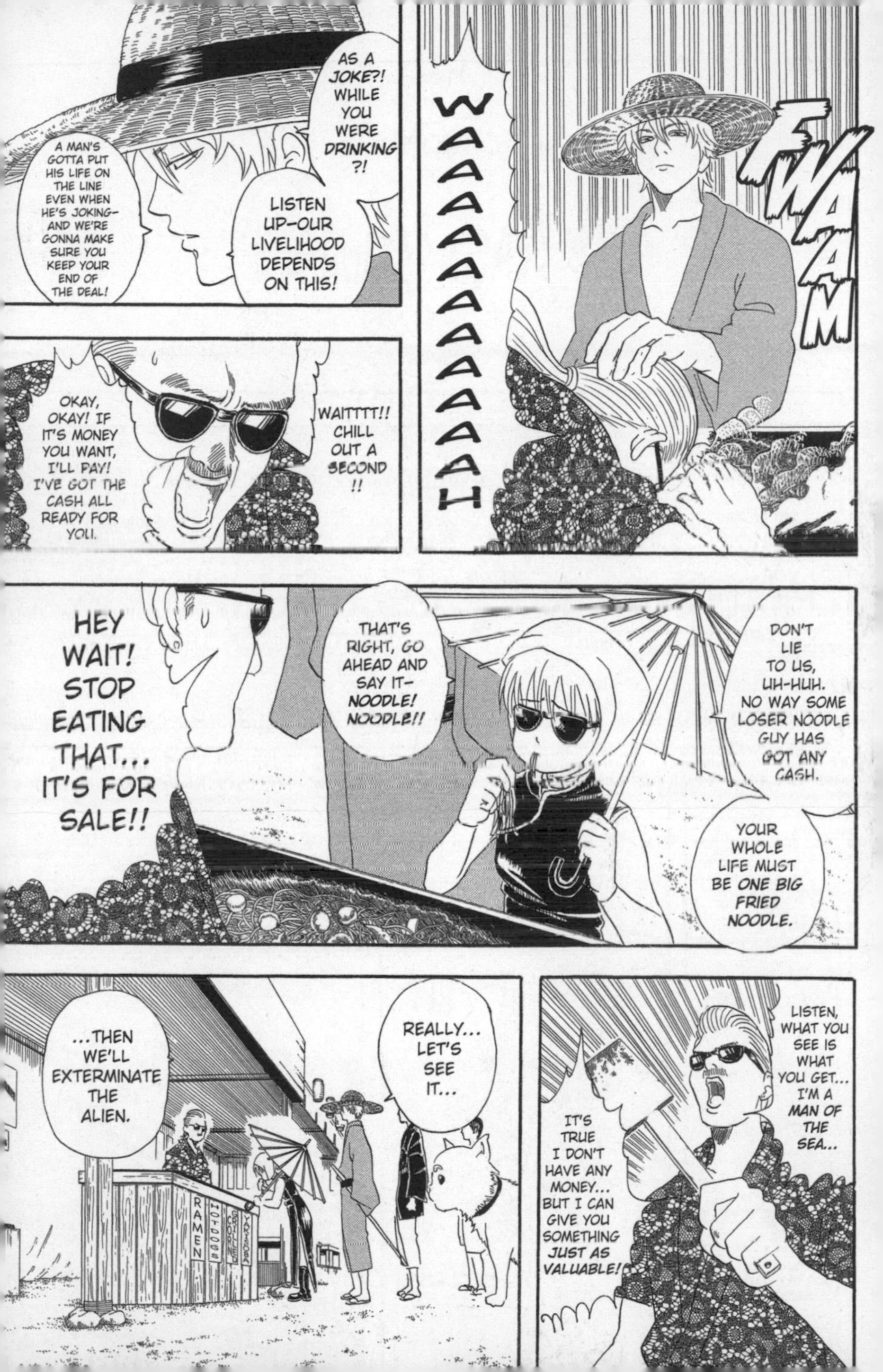
WAAAAAAAAAAAH
FWAAM
AS A JOKE?! WHILE YOU WERE DRINKING?!
LISTEN UP—OUR LIVELIHOOD DEPENDS ON THIS!
A MAN'S GOTTA PUT HIS LIFE ON THE LINE EVEN WHEN HE'S JOKING—AND WE'RE GONNA MAKE SURE YOU KEEP YOUR END OF THE DEAL!
WAITTTT!! CHILL OUT A SECOND!!
OKAY, OKAY! IF IT'S MONEY YOU WANT, I'LL PAY! I'VE GOT THE CASH ALL READY FOR YOU.
DON'T LIE TO US, UH-HUH. NO WAY SOME LOSER NOODLE GUY HAS GOT ANY CASH.
YOUR WHOLE LIFE MUST BE ONE BIG FRIED NOODLE.
THAT'S RIGHT, GO AHEAD AND SAY IT—NOODLE! NOODLE!!
HEY WAIT! STOP EATING THAT... IT'S FOR SALE!!
LISTEN, WHAT YOU SEE IS WHAT YOU GET... I'M A MAN OF THE SEA...
IT'S TRUE I DON'T HAVE ANY MONEY... BUT I CAN GIVE YOU SOMETHING JUST AS VALUABLE!
REALLY... LET'S SEE IT...
...THEN WE'LL EXTERMINATE THE ALIEN.
RAMEN
HOTDOGS
YAKISOBA

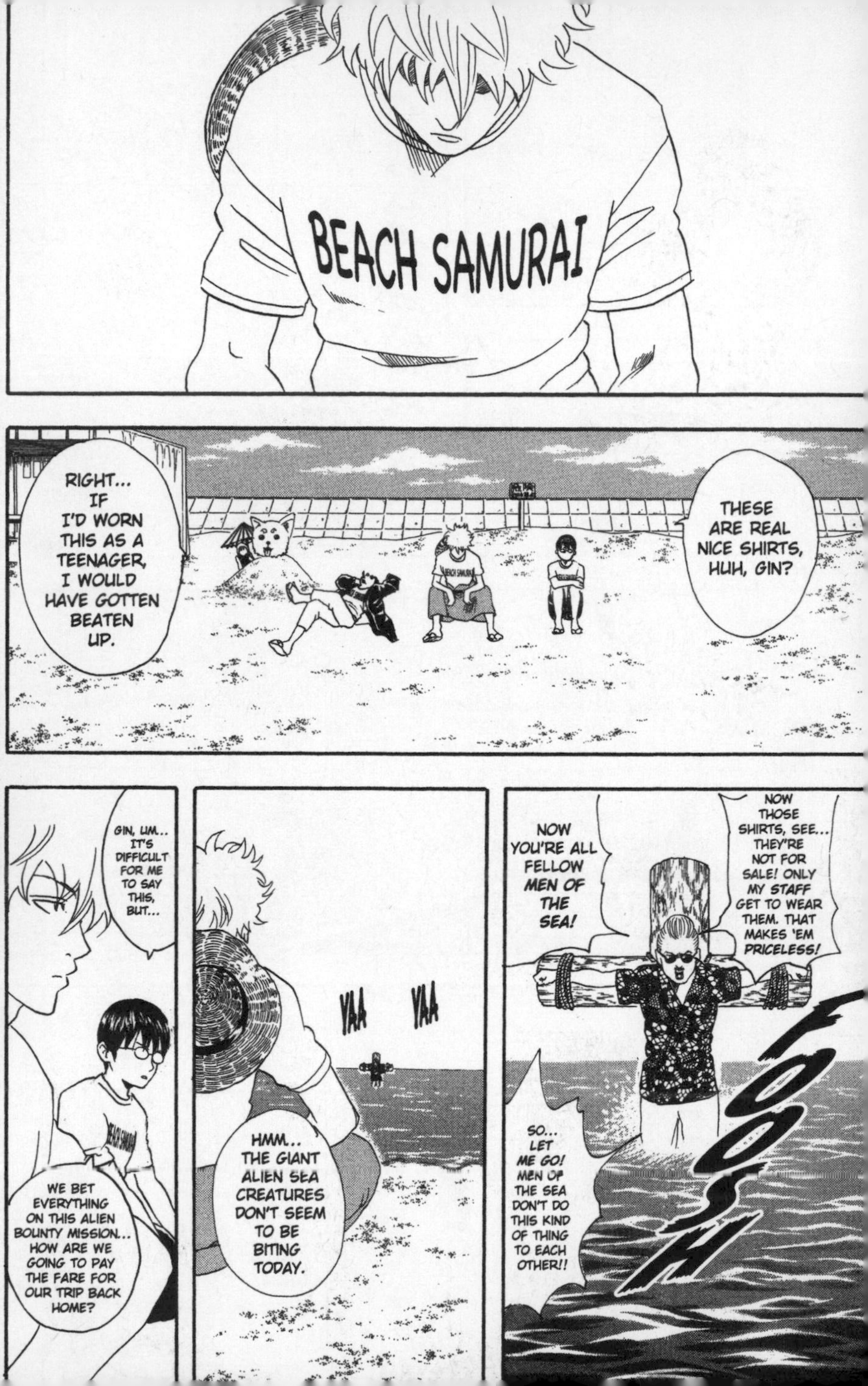
BEACH SAMURAI
THESE ARE REAL NICE SHIRTS, HUH, GIN?
RIGHT... IF I'D WORN THIS AS A TEENAGER, I WOULD HAVE GOTTEN BEATEN UP.
NOW THOSE SHIRTS, SEE... THEY'RE NOT FOR SALE! ONLY MY STAFF GET TO WEAR THEM. THAT MAKES 'EM PRICELESS!
NOW YOU'RE ALL FELLOW MEN OF THE SEA!
SO... LET ME GO! MEN OF THE SEA DON'T DO THIS KIND OF THING TO EACH OTHER!!
YAA YAA
HMM... THE GIANT ALIEN SEA CREATURES DON'T SEEM TO BE BITING TODAY.
GIN, UM... IT'S DIFFICULT FOR ME TO SAY THIS, BUT...
WE BET EVERYTHING ON THIS ALIEN BOUNTY MISSION... HOW ARE WE GOING TO PAY THE FARE FOR OUR TRIP BACK HOME?

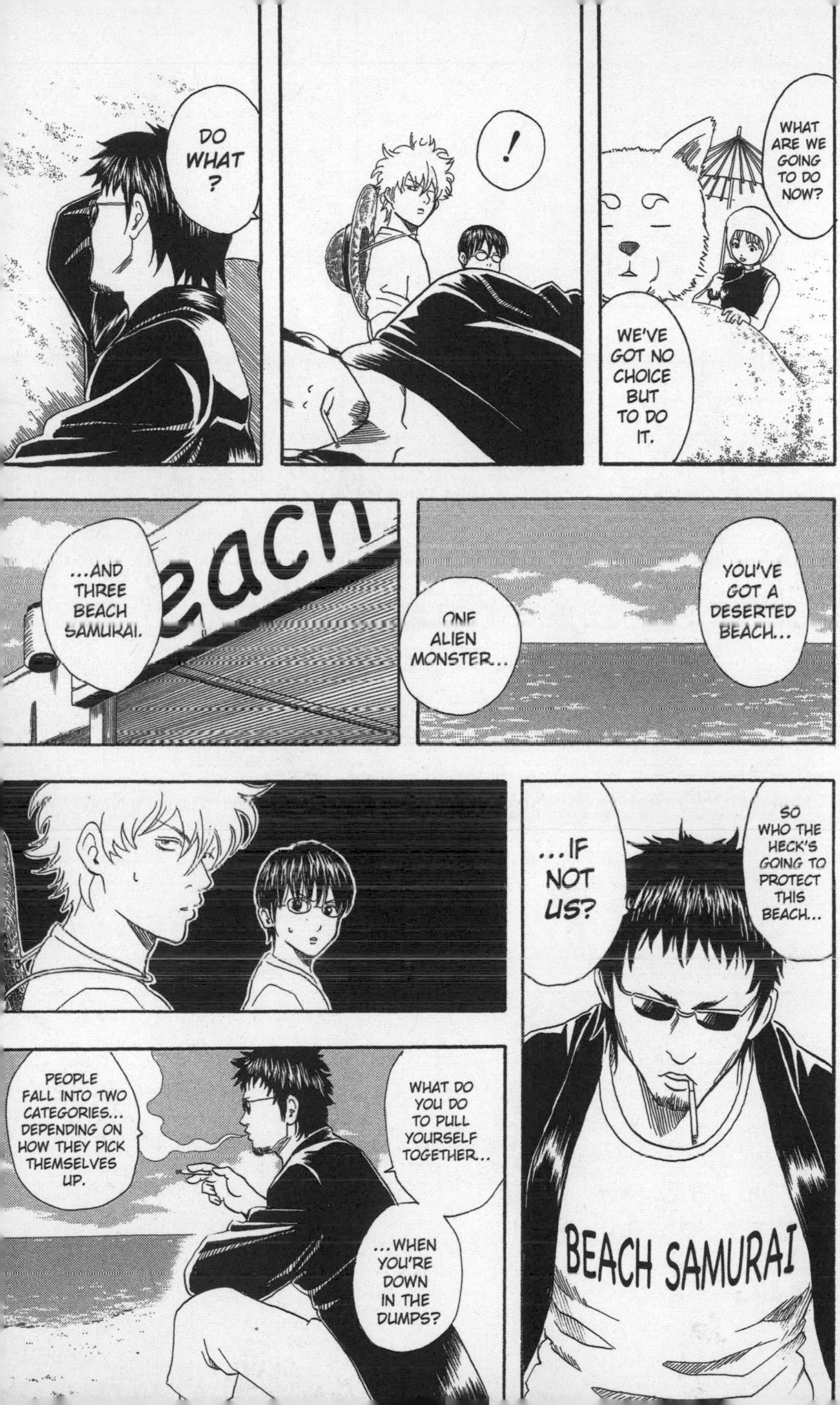
WHAT ARE WE GOING TO DO NOW?
WE'VE GOT NO CHOICE BUT TO DO IT.
!
DO WHAT?
YOU'VE GOT A DESERTED BEACH...
ONE ALIEN MONSTER...
...AND THREE BEACH SAMURAI.
SO WHO THE HECK'S GOING TO PROTECT THIS BEACH...
...IF NOT US?
BEACH SAMURAI
WHAT DO YOU DO TO PULL YOURSELF TOGETHER...
...WHEN YOU'RE DOWN IN THE DUMPS?
PEOPLE FALL INTO TWO CATEGORIES... DEPENDING ON HOW THEY PICK THEMSELVES UP.

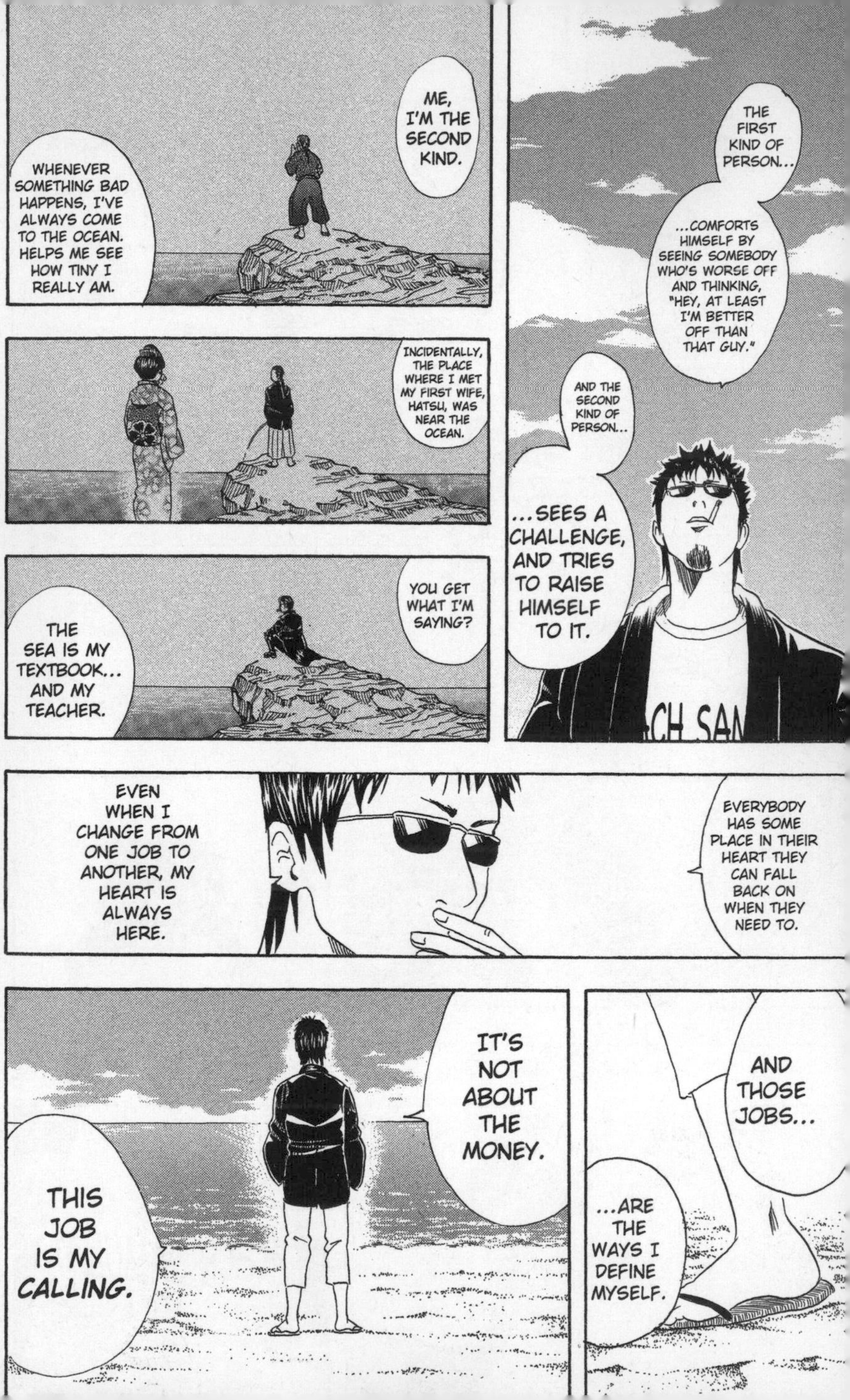
THE FIRST KIND OF PERSON...
...COMFORTS HIMSELF BY SEEING SOMEBODY WHO'S WORSE OFF AND THINKING, "HEY, AT LEAST I'M BETTER OFF THAN THAT GUY."
AND THE SECOND KIND OF PERSON...
...SEES A CHALLENGE, AND TRIES TO RAISE HIMSELF TO IT.
ME, I'M THE SECOND KIND.
WHENEVER SOMETHING BAD HAPPENS, I'VE ALWAYS COME TO THE OCEAN. HELPS ME SEE HOW TINY I REALLY AM.
INCIDENTALLY, THE PLACE WHERE I MET MY FIRST WIFE, HATSU, WAS NEAR THE OCEAN.
YOU GET WHAT I'M SAYING?
THE SEA IS MY TEXTBOOK... AND MY TEACHER.
EVERYBODY HAS SOME PLACE IN THEIR HEART THEY CAN FALL BACK ON WHEN THEY NEED TO.
EVEN WHEN I CHANGE FROM ONE JOB TO ANOTHER, MY HEART IS ALWAYS HERE.
AND THOSE JOBS...
...ARE THE WAYS I DEFINE MYSELF.
IT'S NOT ABOUT THE MONEY.
THIS JOB IS MY CALLING.

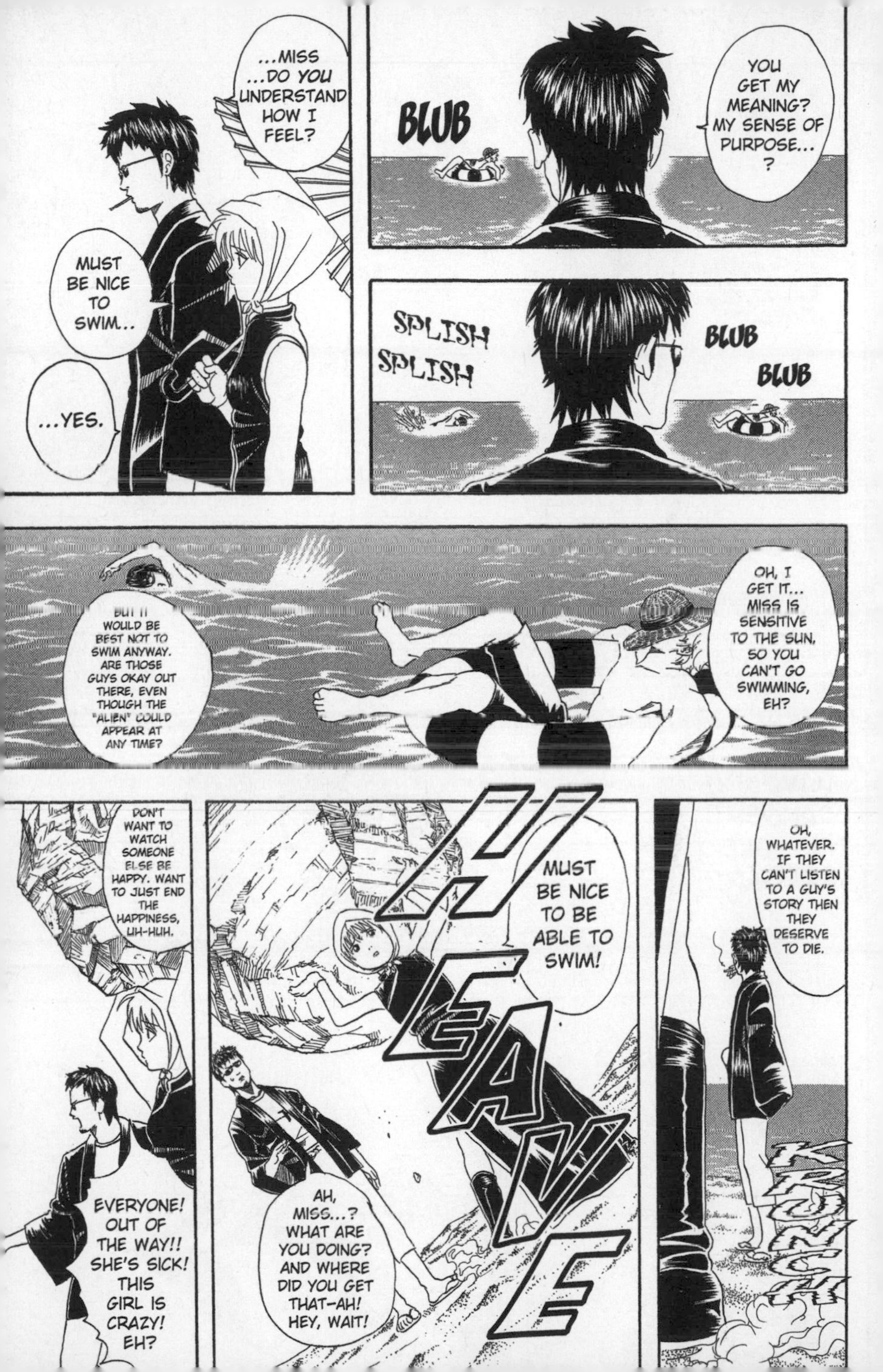
YOU GET MY MEANING? MY SENSE OF PURPOSE...?
BLUB
BLUB
BLUB
SPLISH
SPLISH
...MISS ...DO YOU UNDERSTAND HOW I FEEL?
MUST BE NICE TO SWIM...
...YES.
OH, I GET IT... MISS IS SENSITIVE TO THE SUN, SO YOU CAN'T GO SWIMMING, EH?
BUT IT WOULD BE BEST NOT TO SWIM ANYWAY. ARE THOSE GUYS OKAY OUT THERE, EVEN THOUGH THE "ALIEN" COULD APPEAR AT ANY TIME?
OH, WHATEVER. IF THEY CAN'T LISTEN TO A GUY'S STORY THEN THEY DESERVE TO DIE.
KRUNCH
HEAVE
MUST BE NICE TO BE ABLE TO SWIM!
AH, MISS...? WHAT ARE YOU DOING? AND WHERE DID YOU GET THAT–AH! HEY, WAIT!
DON'T WANT TO WATCH SOMEONE ELSE BE HAPPY. WANT TO JUST END THE HAPPINESS, UH-HUH.
EVERYONE! OUT OF THE WAY!! SHE'S SICK! THIS GIRL IS CRAZY! EH?

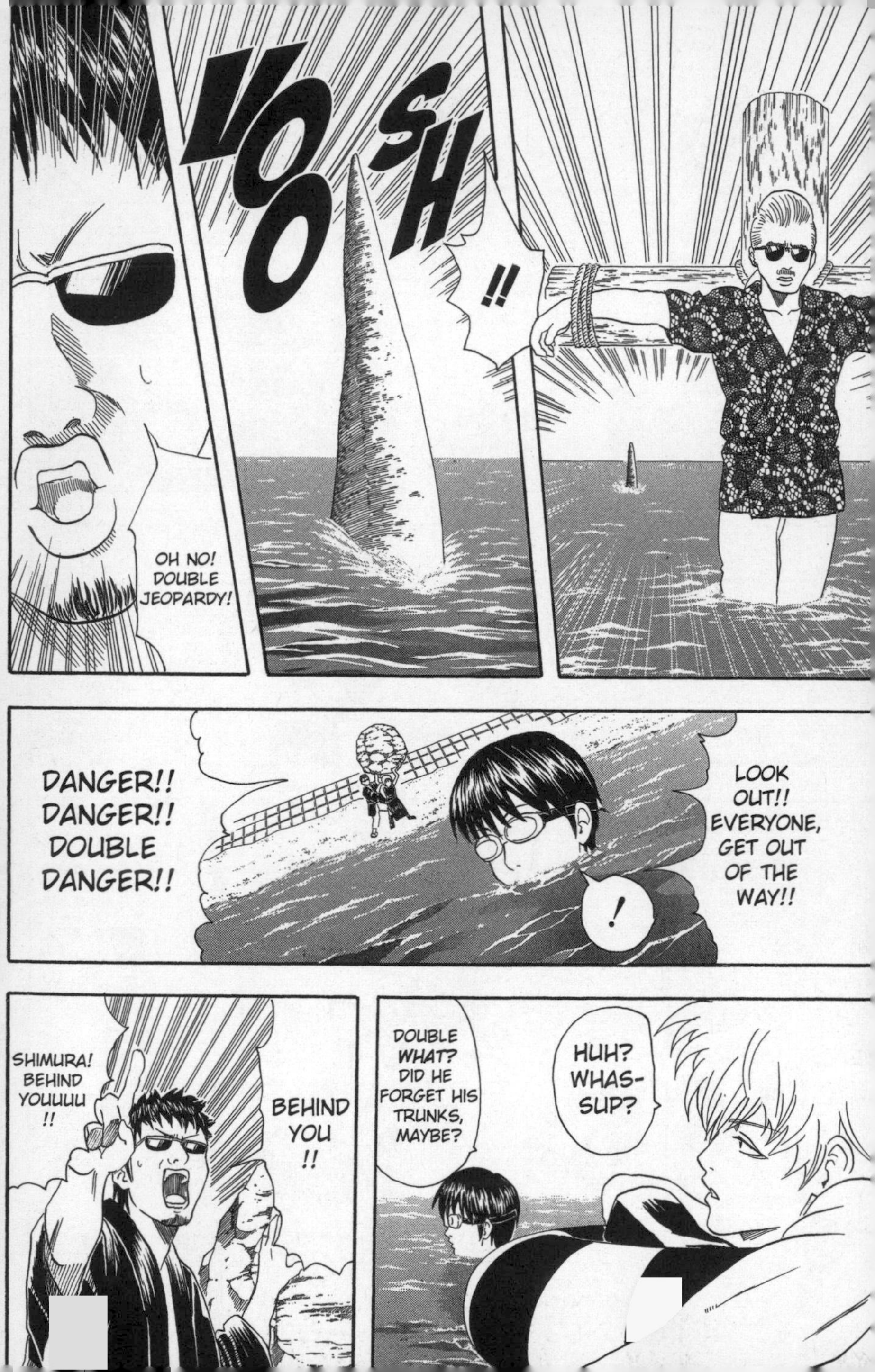
VOOSH
!!
OH NO! DOUBLE JEOPARDY!
LOOK OUT!! EVERYONE, GET OUT OF THE WAY!!
!
DANGER!! DANGER!! DOUBLE DANGER!!
HUH? WHAS-SUP?
DOUBLE WHAT? DID HE FORGET HIS TRUNKS, MAYBE?
BEHIND YOU !!
SHIMURA! BEHIND YOUUUU !!

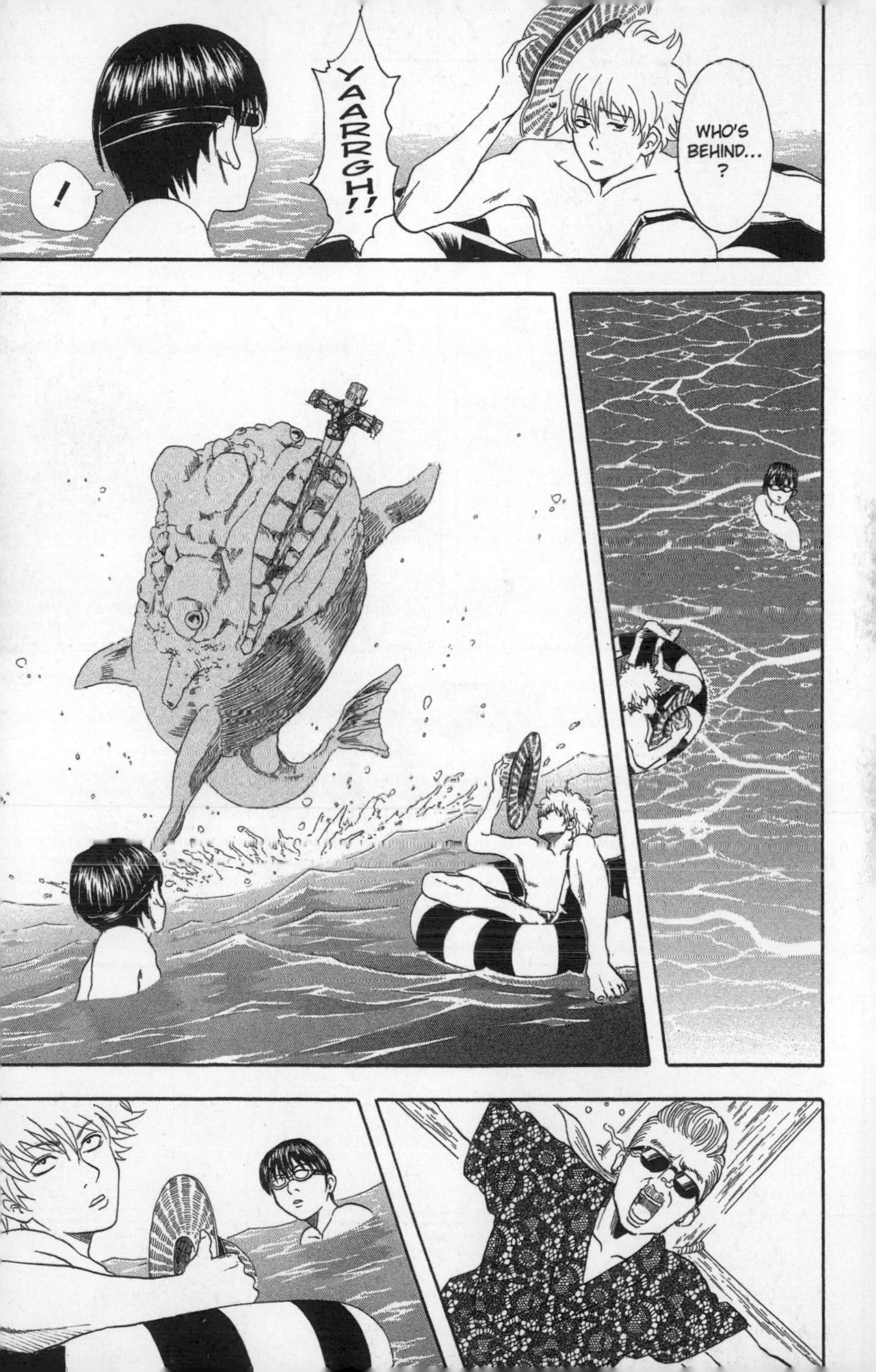
WHO'S BEHIND...?
YAARRGH!!
!

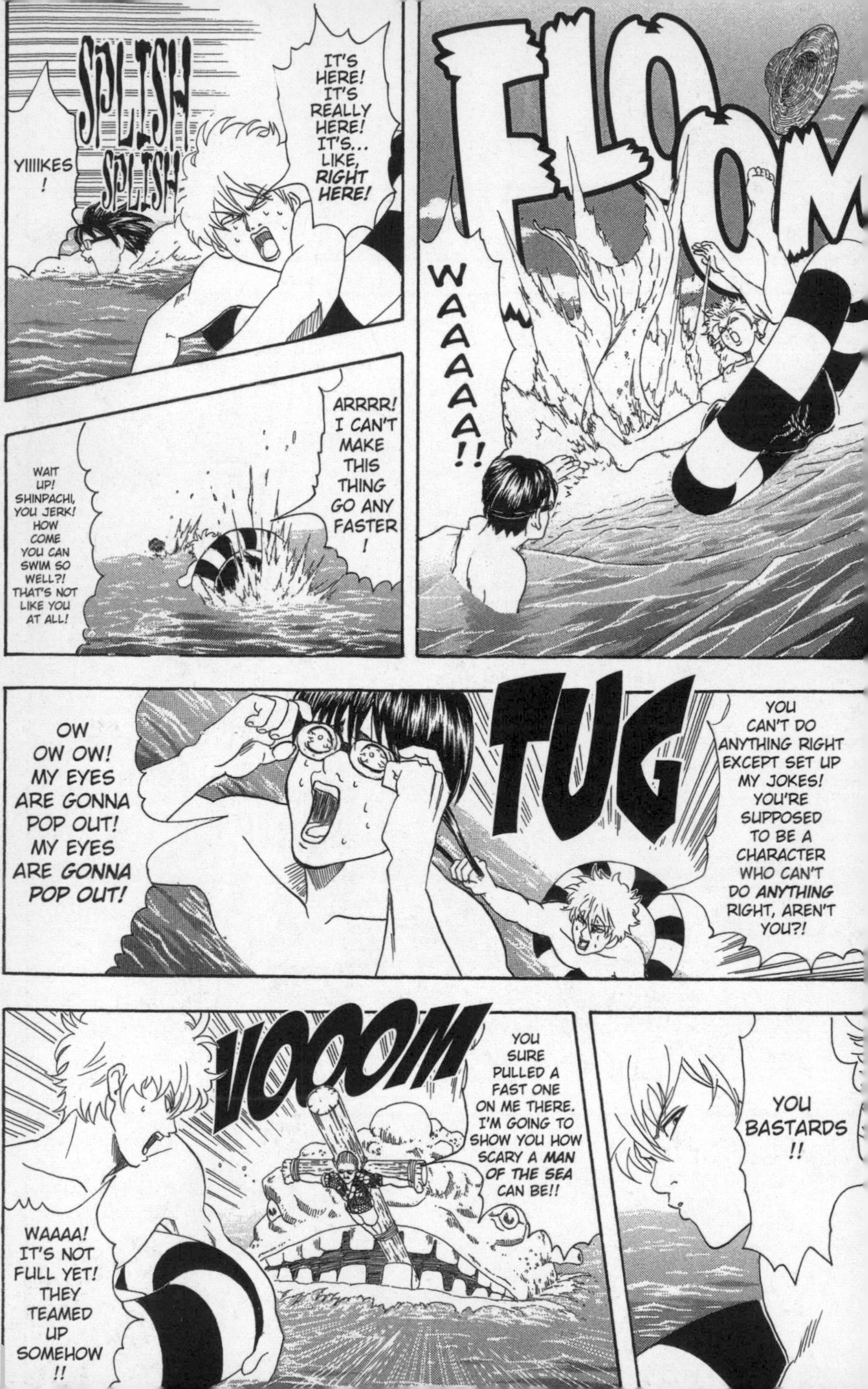
FLOOM
WAAAAAA!!
IT'S HERE! IT'S REALLY HERE! IT'S... LIKE, RIGHT HERE!
SPLISH SPLISH
YIIIIKES!
ARRRR! I CAN'T MAKE THIS THING GO ANY FASTER!
WAIT UP! SHINPACHI, YOU JERK! HOW COME YOU CAN SWIM SO WELL?! THAT'S NOT LIKE YOU AT ALL!
YOU CAN'T DO ANYTHING RIGHT EXCEPT SET UP MY JOKES! YOU'RE SUPPOSED TO BE A CHARACTER WHO CAN'T DO ANYTHING RIGHT, AREN'T YOU?!
TUG
OW OW OW! MY EYES ARE GONNA POP OUT! MY EYES ARE GONNA POP OUT!
YOU BASTARDS!!
YOU SURE PULLED A FAST ONE ON ME THERE. I'M GOING TO SHOW YOU HOW SCARY A MAN OF THE SEA CAN BE!!
VOOOM
WAAAA! IT'S NOT FULL YET! THEY TEAMED UP SOMEHOW!!

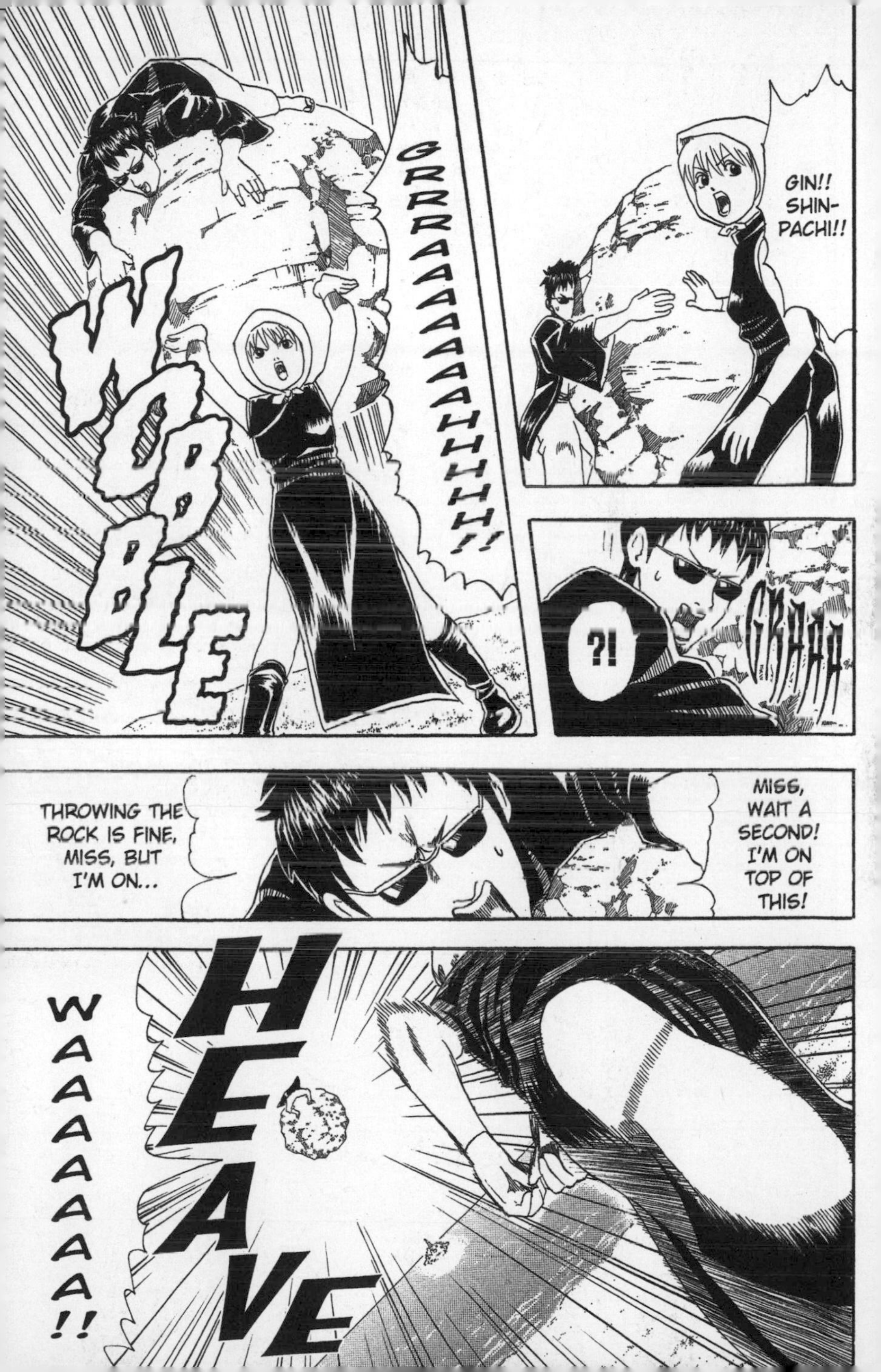
GIN!! SHIN-PACHI!!
?!
GRAAA
GRRRAAAAAAHHHHH!!
WOBBLE
MISS, WAIT A SECOND! I'M ON TOP OF THIS!
THROWING THE ROCK IS FINE, MISS, BUT I'M ON...
HEAVE
WAAAAAAAAA!!

AAAAAAAAAAAA!!

HUH
?

HEY,
THAT'S
...

FOOSH

OOPS.
MY
BAD.

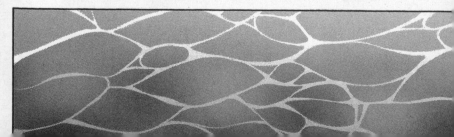

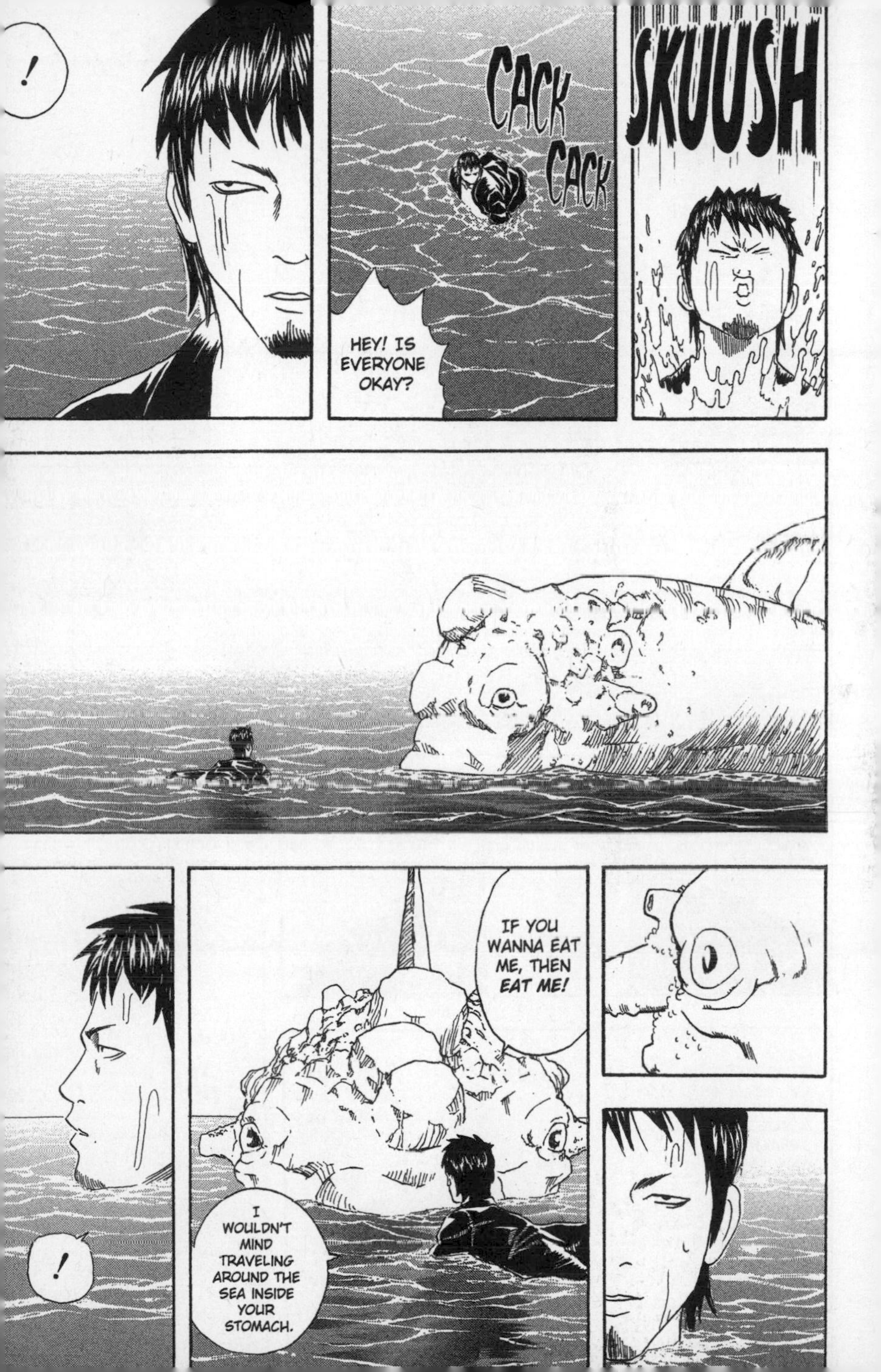
SKUUSH
CACK CACK
HEY! IS EVERYONE OKAY?
!
IF YOU WANNA EAT ME, THEN EAT ME!
I WOULDN'T MIND TRAVELING AROUND THE SEA INSIDE YOUR STOMACH.
!

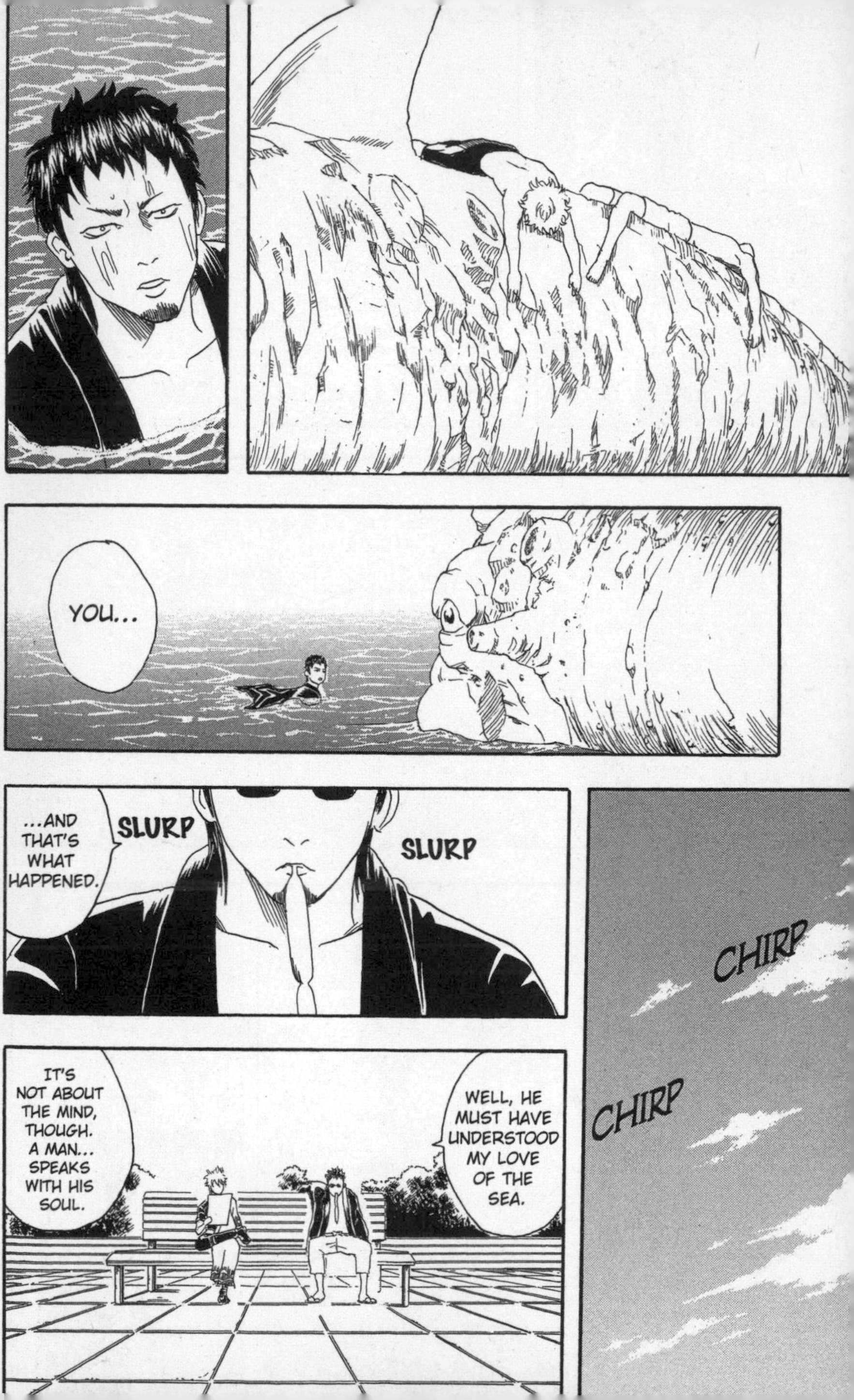
YOU...
CHIRP
CHIRP
SLURP
SLURP
...AND THAT'S WHAT HAPPENED.
WELL, HE MUST HAVE UNDERSTOOD MY LOVE OF THE SEA.
IT'S NOT ABOUT THE MIND, THOUGH. A MAN... SPEAKS WITH HIS SOUL.

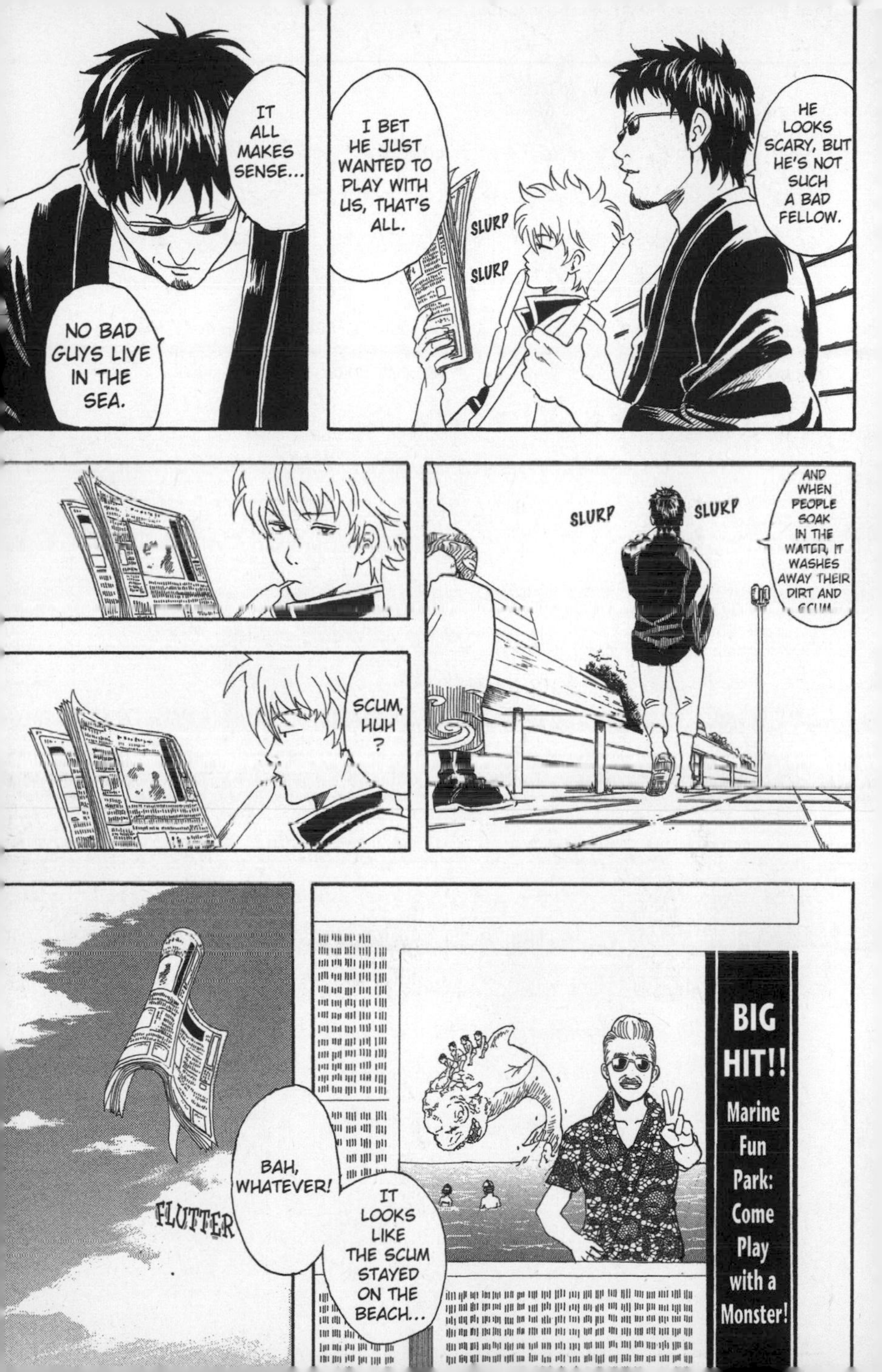
HE LOOKS SCARY, BUT HE'S NOT SUCH A BAD FELLOW.
SLURP
SLURP
I BET HE JUST WANTED TO PLAY WITH US, THAT'S ALL.
IT ALL MAKES SENSE...
NO BAD GUYS LIVE IN THE SEA.
SLURP
SLURP
AND WHEN PEOPLE SOAK IN THE WATER, IT WASHES AWAY THEIR DIRT AND SCUM
SCUM, HUH?
BIG HIT!!
Marine Fun Park: Come Play with a Monster!
IT LOOKS LIKE THE SCUM STAYED ON THE BEACH...
BAH, WHATEVER!
FLUTTER

Thank you very much for buying <u>Gin Tama</u> Volume 5.

Just when Volume 4 had come out in November, Volume 5 went on sale in December. Are you trying to kill me? Everyone's wallets are bulging at the end of the year, so apparently they were aiming for that. Everyone, please be careful not to get hoodwinked into buying it. Um, so this time we have a big Q&A corner, again. It got terrible reviews last time, and I'm just getting clobbered from every direction by letters. Everybody's sending in protests.

Ha, ha, ha, ha.

Someone asked if I was actually trying very hard.

Ha, ha, ha, ha.

Wasn't it a bit harsh to accuse me of acting like a devil, though?

Ha, ha, ha, ha.

That page, see, was finished at the last minute, so this time I had a fight with the editor who was telling me to go with blank pages...so this is literally the result of sweat and tears, okay?!

Well I gotta tell you... Ha, ha, ha, ha.

After that, there was some bad blood between me and the editor.

Ha, ha, ha, ha, ha, ha, ha, ha.

By the way, this page was scheduled at the last minute, too.

Ha, ha, ha, ha, ha, ha, ha, ha.

What am I going to do?

Ha, ha, ha, ha, ha, ha, ha.

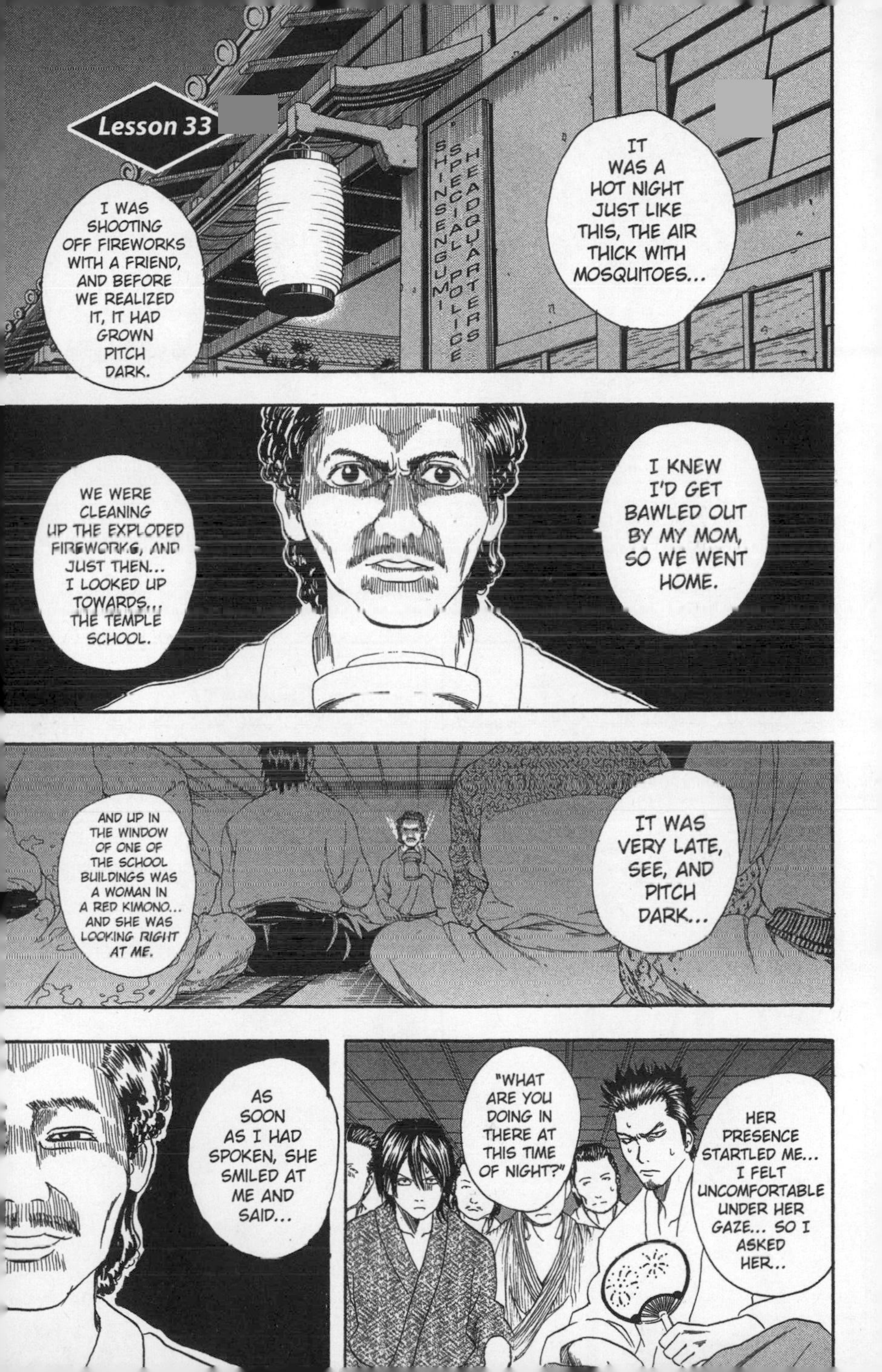
Lesson 33
SHINSENGUMI SPECIAL POLICE HEADQUARTERS
IT WAS A HOT NIGHT JUST LIKE THIS, THE AIR THICK WITH MOSQUITOES...
I WAS SHOOTING OFF FIREWORKS WITH A FRIEND, AND BEFORE WE REALIZED IT, IT HAD GROWN PITCH DARK.
I KNEW I'D GET BAWLED OUT BY MY MOM, SO WE WENT HOME.
WE WERE CLEANING UP THE EXPLODED FIREWORKS, AND JUST THEN... I LOOKED UP TOWARDS... THE TEMPLE SCHOOL.
IT WAS VERY LATE, SEE, AND PITCH DARK...
AND UP IN THE WINDOW OF ONE OF THE SCHOOL BUILDINGS WAS A WOMAN IN A RED KIMONO... AND SHE WAS LOOKING RIGHT AT ME.
HER PRESENCE STARTLED ME... I FELT UNCOMFORTABLE UNDER HER GAZE... SO I ASKED HER...
"WHAT ARE YOU DOING IN THERE AT THIS TIME OF NIGHT?"
AS SOON AS I HAD SPOKEN, SHE SMILED AT ME AND SAID...

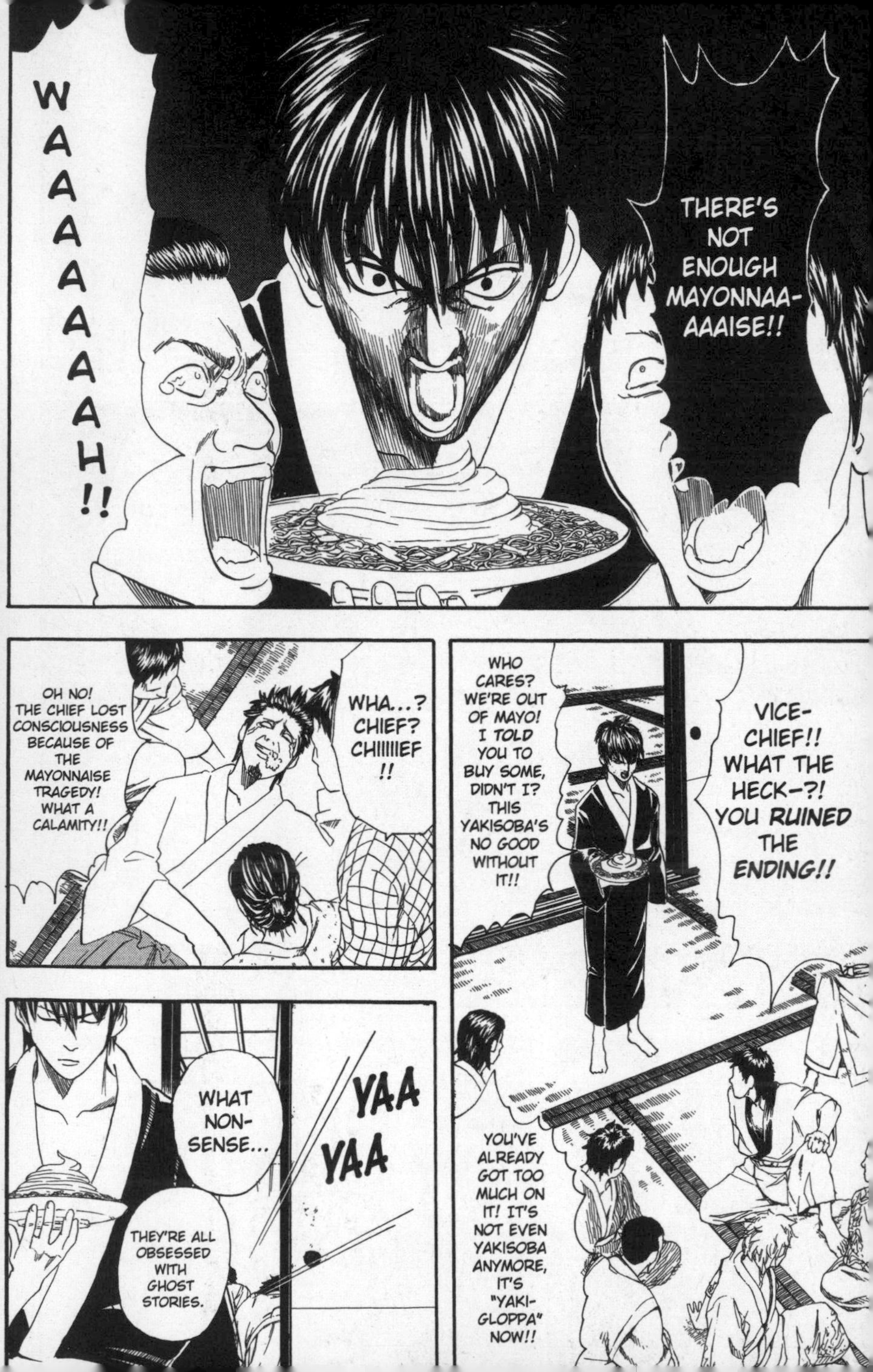
THERE'S NOT ENOUGH MAYONNAA-AAAISE!!
WAAAAAAAH!!
VICE-CHIEF!! WHAT THE HECK-?! YOU RUINED THE ENDING!!
WHO CARES? WE'RE OUT OF MAYO! I TOLD YOU TO BUY SOME, DIDN'T I? THIS YAKISOBA'S NO GOOD WITHOUT IT!!
YOU'VE ALREADY GOT TOO MUCH ON IT! IT'S NOT EVEN YAKISOBA ANYMORE, IT'S "YAKI-GLOPPA" NOW!!
WHA...? CHIEF? CHIIIIIEF!!
OH NO! THE CHIEF LOST CONSCIOUSNESS BECAUSE OF THE MAYONNAISE TRAGEDY! WHAT A CALAMITY!!
YAA YAA
WHAT NON-SENSE...
THEY'RE ALL OBSESSED WITH GHOST STORIES.

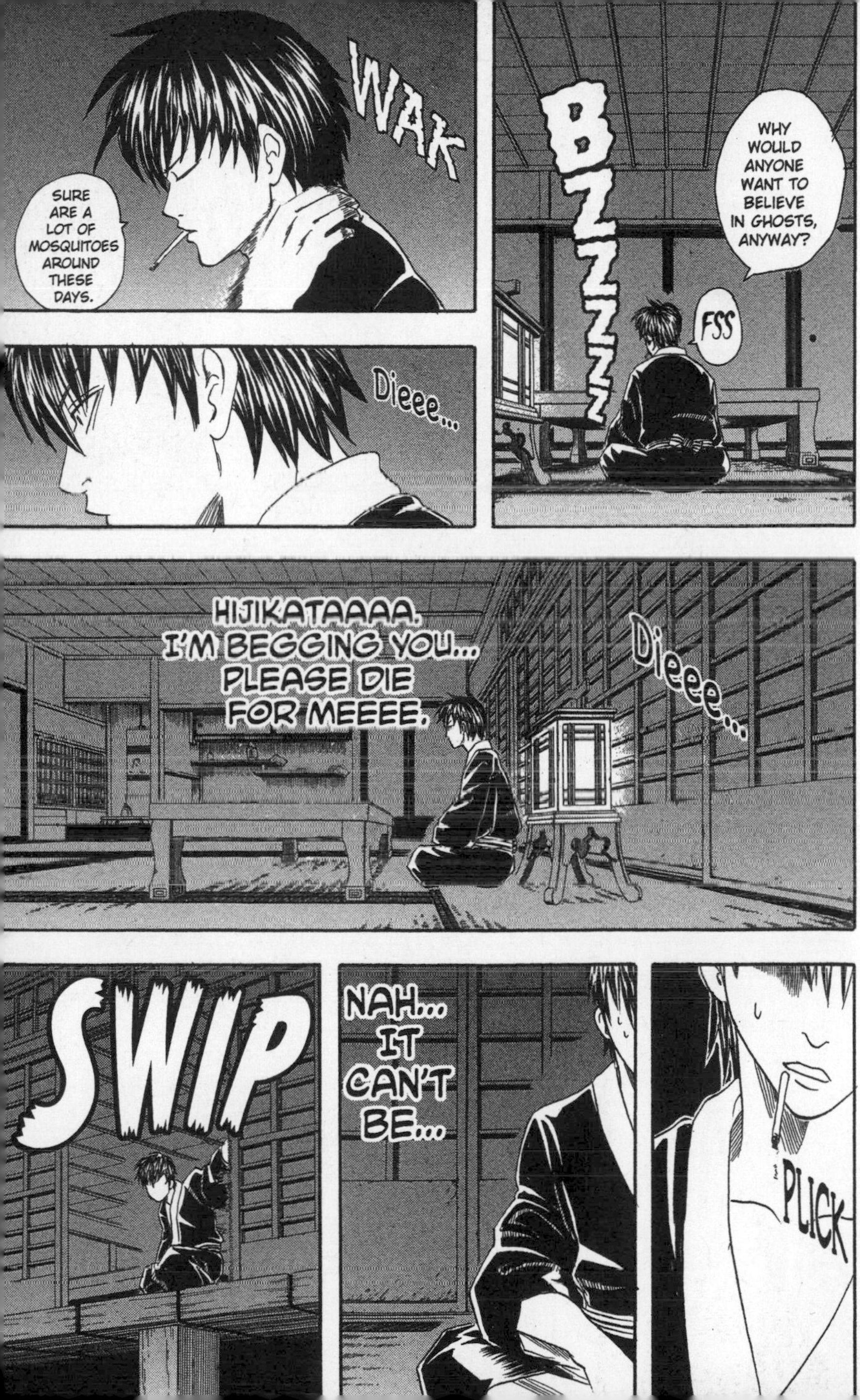
WHY WOULD ANYONE WANT TO BELIEVE IN GHOSTS, ANYWAY?
BZZZZZ
FSS
WAK
SURE ARE A LOT OF MOSQUITOES AROUND THESE DAYS.
Dieee...
Dieeee...
HIJIKATAAAA. I'M BEGGING YOU... PLEASE DIE FOR MEEEE.
PLICK
NAH... IT CAN'T BE...
SWIP

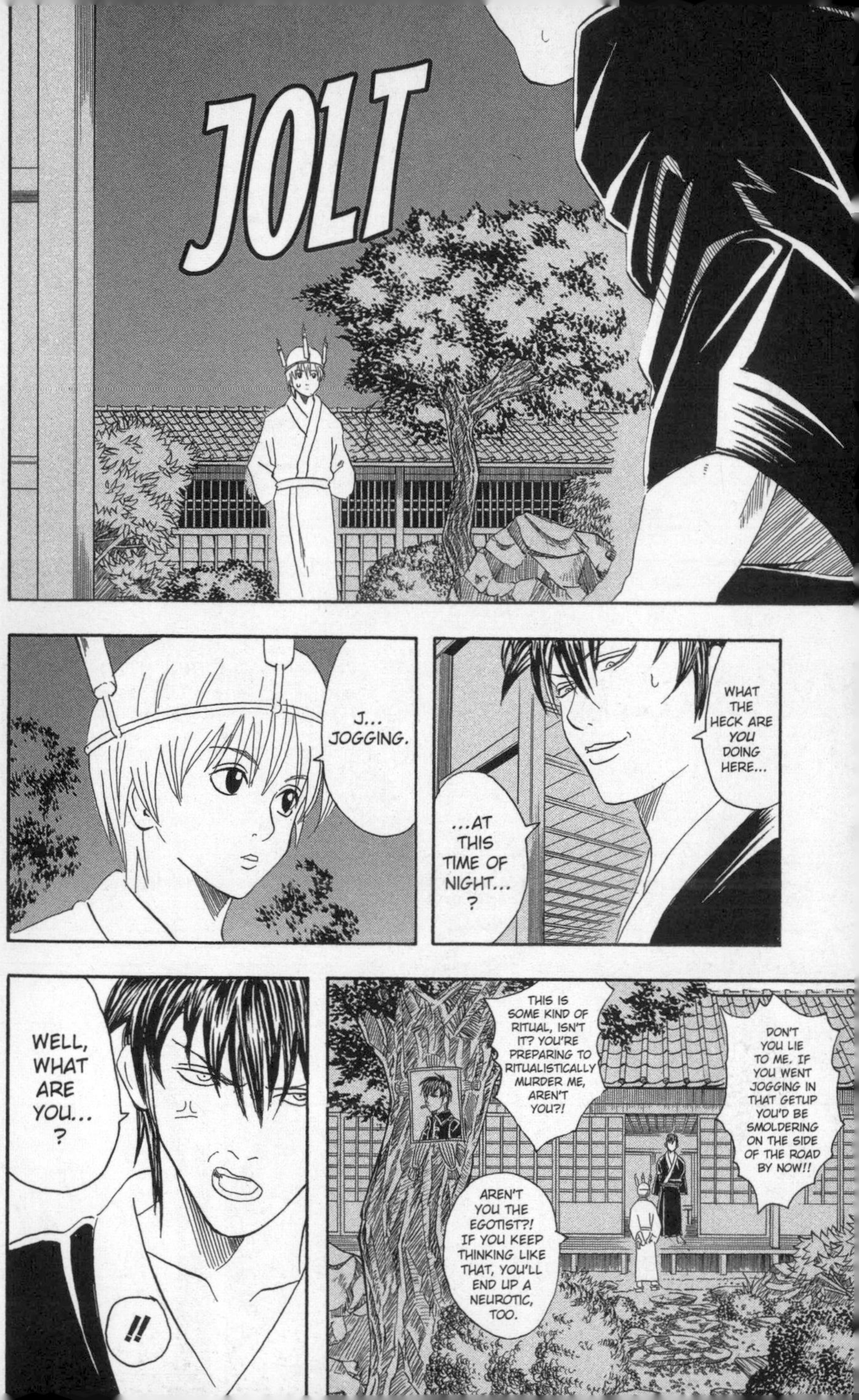
JOLT
WHAT THE HECK ARE YOU DOING HERE...
...AT THIS TIME OF NIGHT...?
J... JOGGING.
DON'T YOU LIE TO ME. IF YOU WENT JOGGING IN THAT GETUP YOU'D BE SMOLDERING ON THE SIDE OF THE ROAD BY NOW!!
THIS IS SOME KIND OF RITUAL, ISN'T IT? YOU'RE PREPARING TO RITUALISTICALLY MURDER ME, AREN'T YOU?!
AREN'T YOU THE EGOTIST?! IF YOU KEEP THINKING LIKE THAT, YOU'LL END UP A NEUROTIC, TOO.
WELL, WHAT ARE YOU...?
!!

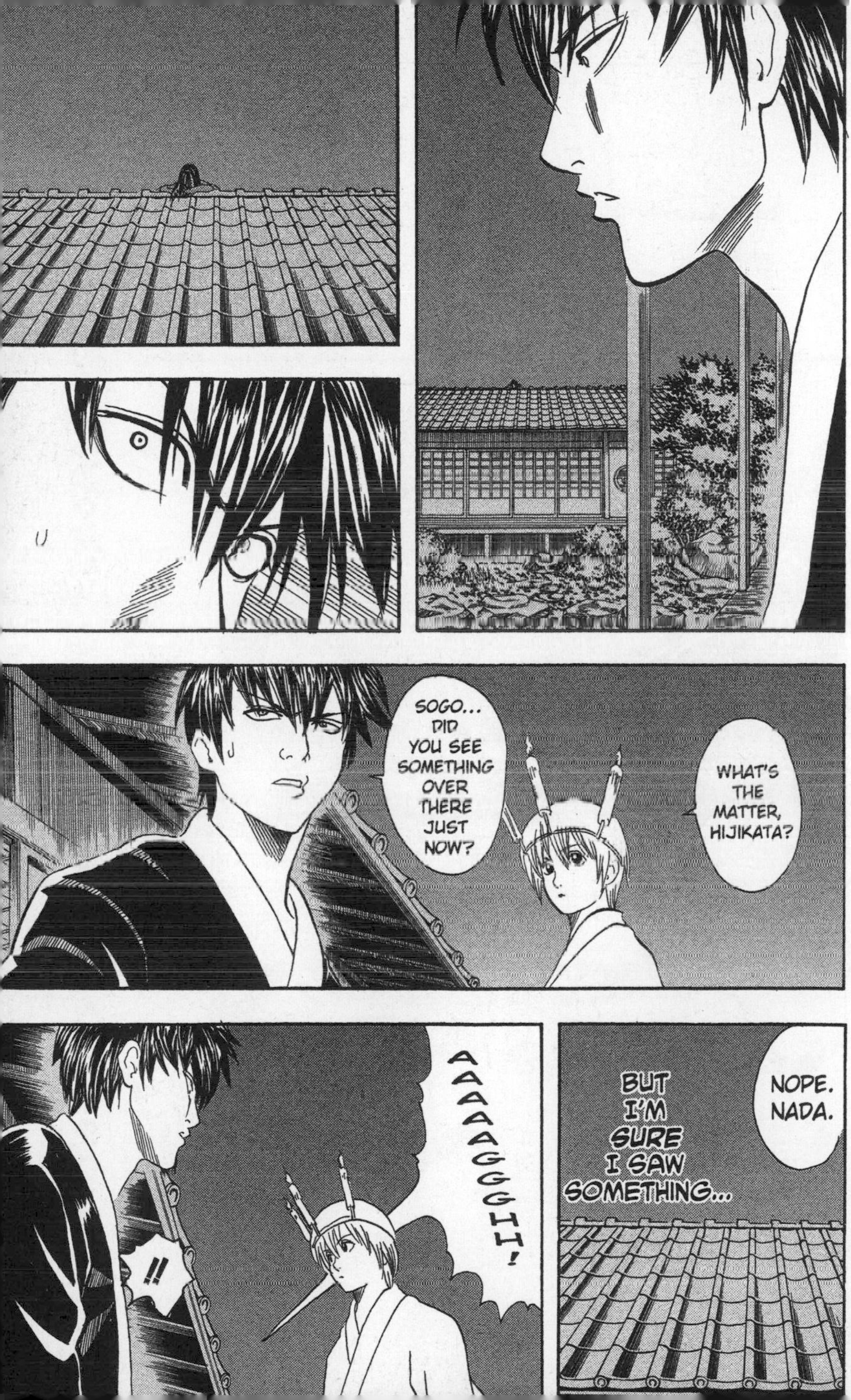
WHAT'S THE MATTER, HIJIKATA?
SOGO... DID YOU SEE SOMETHING OVER THERE JUST NOW?
NOPE. NADA.
BUT I'M SURE I SAW SOMETHING...
AAAAAGGGHH!
!!

Lesson 33: Watch Out for Conveyor Belts!

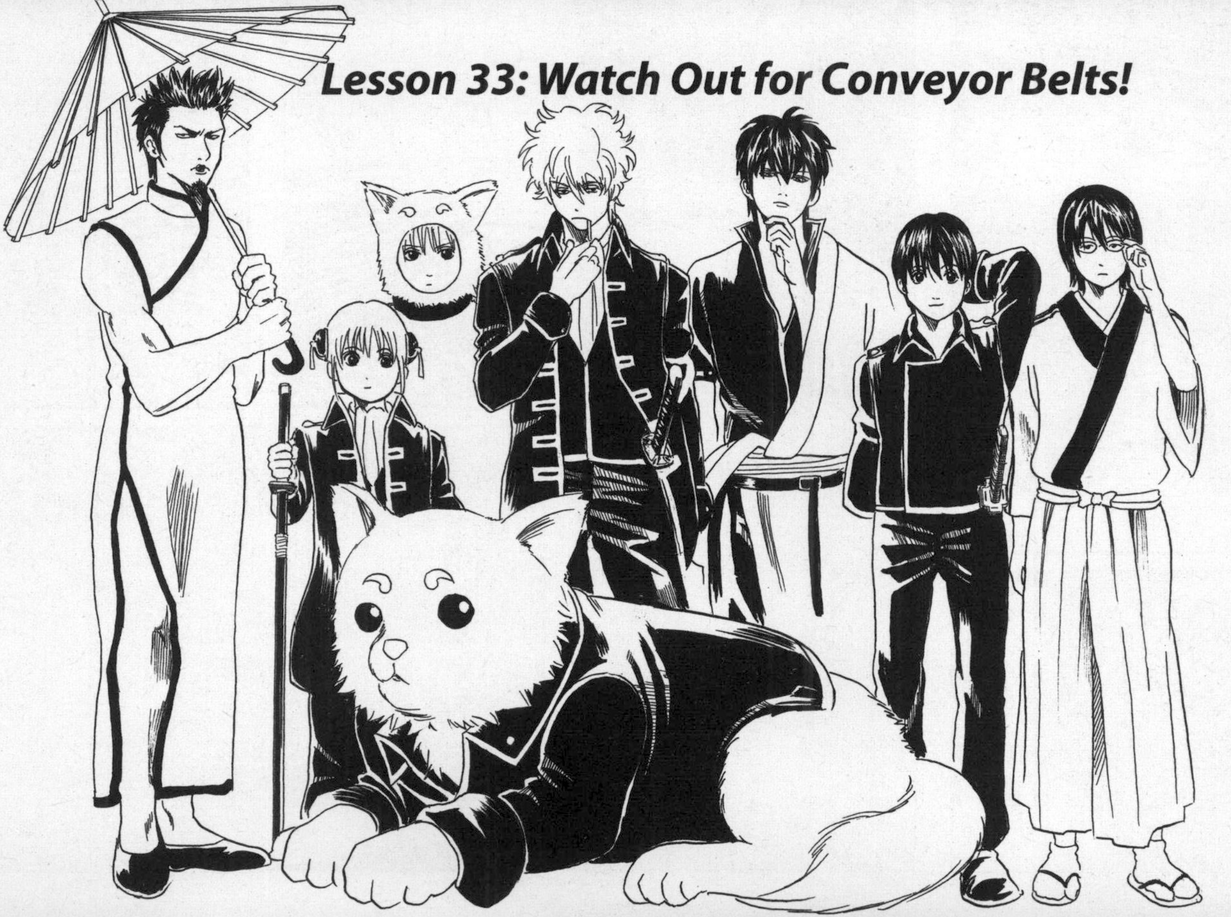

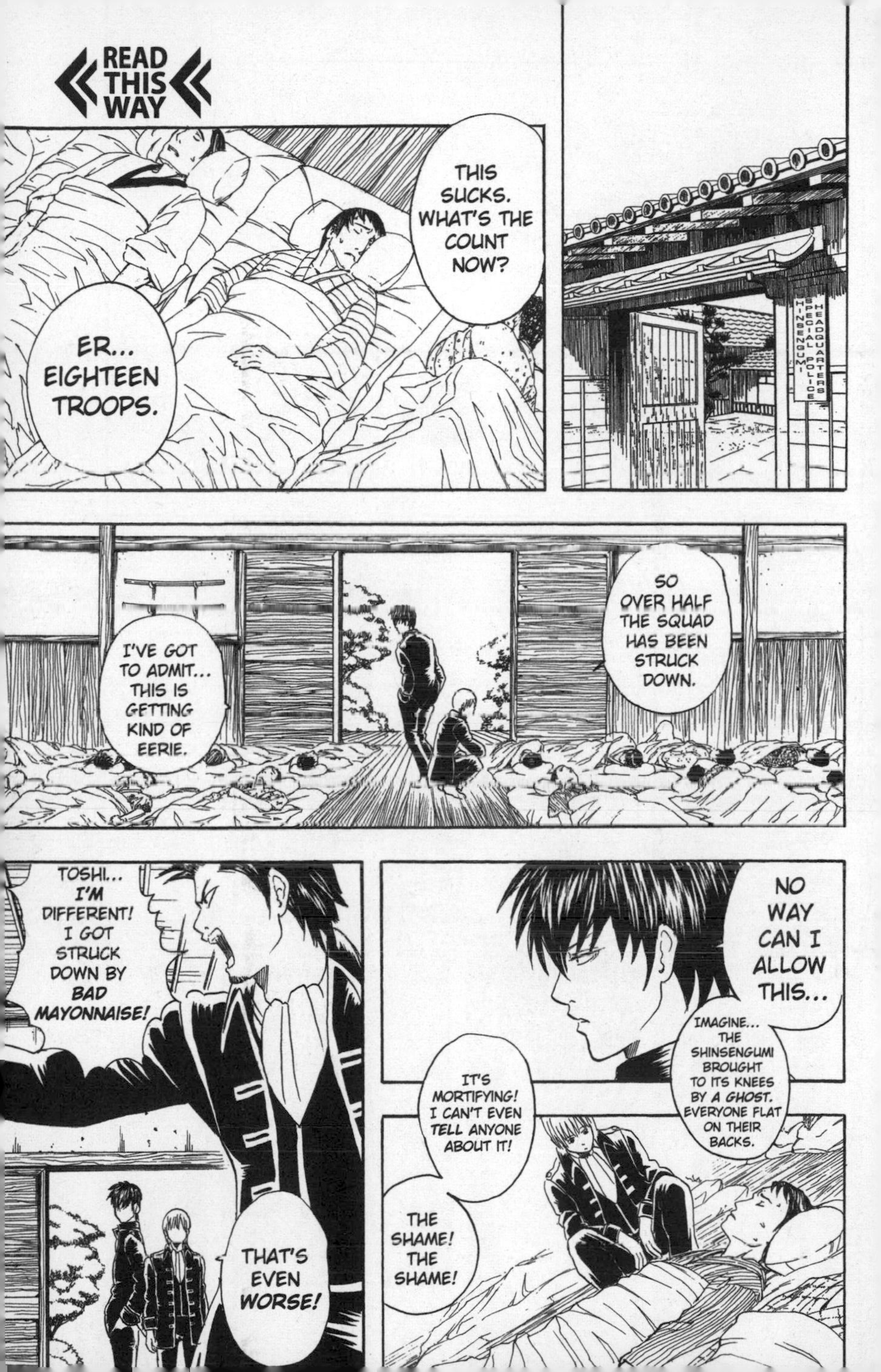
READ THIS WAY
HEADQUARTERS SPECIAL POLICE SHINSENGUMI
THIS SUCKS. WHAT'S THE COUNT NOW?
ER... EIGHTEEN TROOPS.
SO OVER HALF THE SQUAD HAS BEEN STRUCK DOWN.
I'VE GOT TO ADMIT... THIS IS GETTING KIND OF EERIE.
NO WAY CAN I ALLOW THIS...
IMAGINE... THE SHINSENGUMI BROUGHT TO ITS KNEES BY A *GHOST*. EVERYONE FLAT ON THEIR BACKS.
IT'S MORTIFYING! I CAN'T EVEN *TELL* ANYONE ABOUT IT!
THE SHAME! THE SHAME!
TOSHI... *I'M* DIFFERENT! I GOT STRUCK DOWN BY *BAD MAYONNAISE!*
THAT'S EVEN *WORSE!*

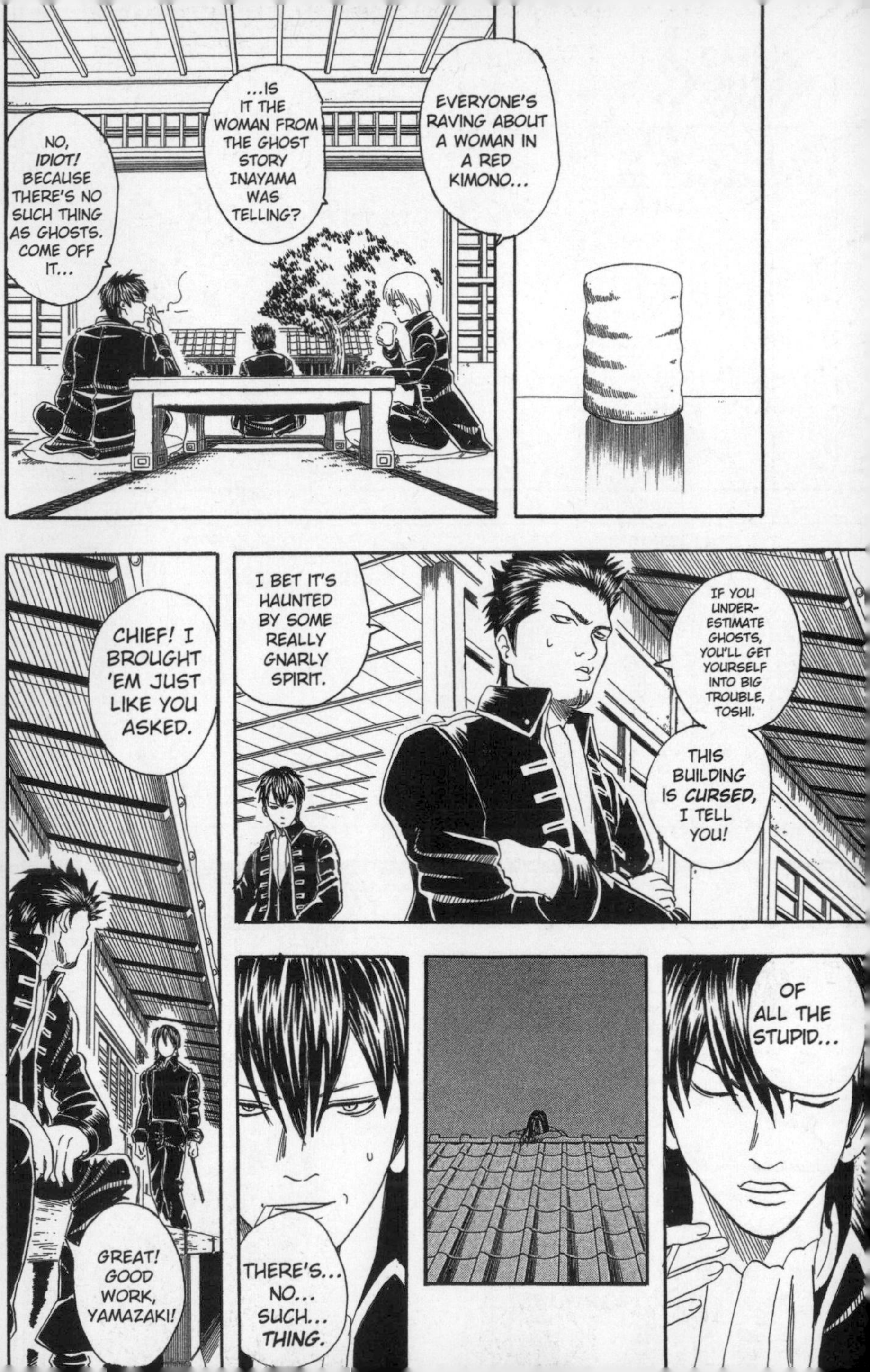
EVERYONE'S RAVING ABOUT A WOMAN IN A RED KIMONO...
...IS IT THE WOMAN FROM THE GHOST STORY INAYAMA WAS TELLING?
NO, IDIOT! BECAUSE THERE'S NO SUCH THING AS GHOSTS. COME OFF IT...
IF YOU UNDER-ESTIMATE GHOSTS, YOU'LL GET YOURSELF INTO BIG TROUBLE, TOSHI.
THIS BUILDING IS CURSED, I TELL YOU!
I BET IT'S HAUNTED BY SOME REALLY GNARLY SPIRIT.
OF ALL THE STUPID...
THERE'S... NO... SUCH... THING.
CHIEF! I BROUGHT 'EM JUST LIKE YOU ASKED.
GREAT! GOOD WORK, YAMAZAKI!

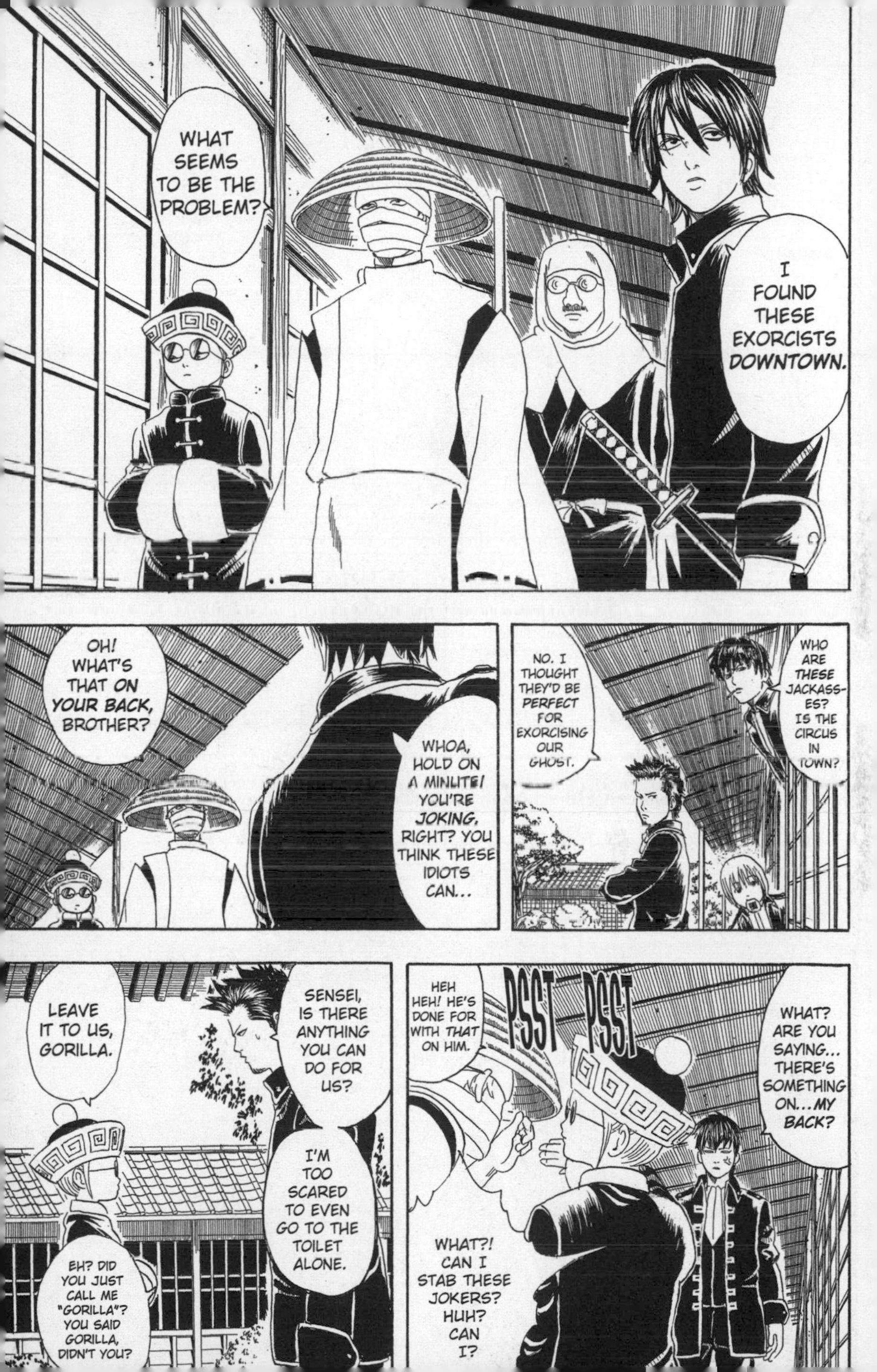
I FOUND THESE EXORCISTS DOWNTOWN.
WHAT SEEMS TO BE THE PROBLEM?
WHO ARE THESE JACKASSES? IS THE CIRCUS IN TOWN?
NO. I THOUGHT THEY'D BE PERFECT FOR EXORCISING OUR GHOST.
WHOA, HOLD ON A MINUTE! YOU'RE JOKING, RIGHT? YOU THINK THESE IDIOTS CAN...
OH! WHAT'S THAT ON YOUR BACK, BROTHER?
WHAT? ARE YOU SAYING... THERE'S SOMETHING ON... MY BACK?
PSST PSST
HEH HEH! HE'S DONE FOR WITH THAT ON HIM.
WHAT?! CAN I STAB THESE JOKERS? HUH? CAN I?
SENSEI, IS THERE ANYTHING YOU CAN DO FOR US?
LEAVE IT TO US, GORILLA.
I'M TOO SCARED TO EVEN GO TO THE TOILET ALONE.
EH? DID YOU JUST CALL ME "GORILLA"? YOU SAID GORILLA, DIDN'T YOU?

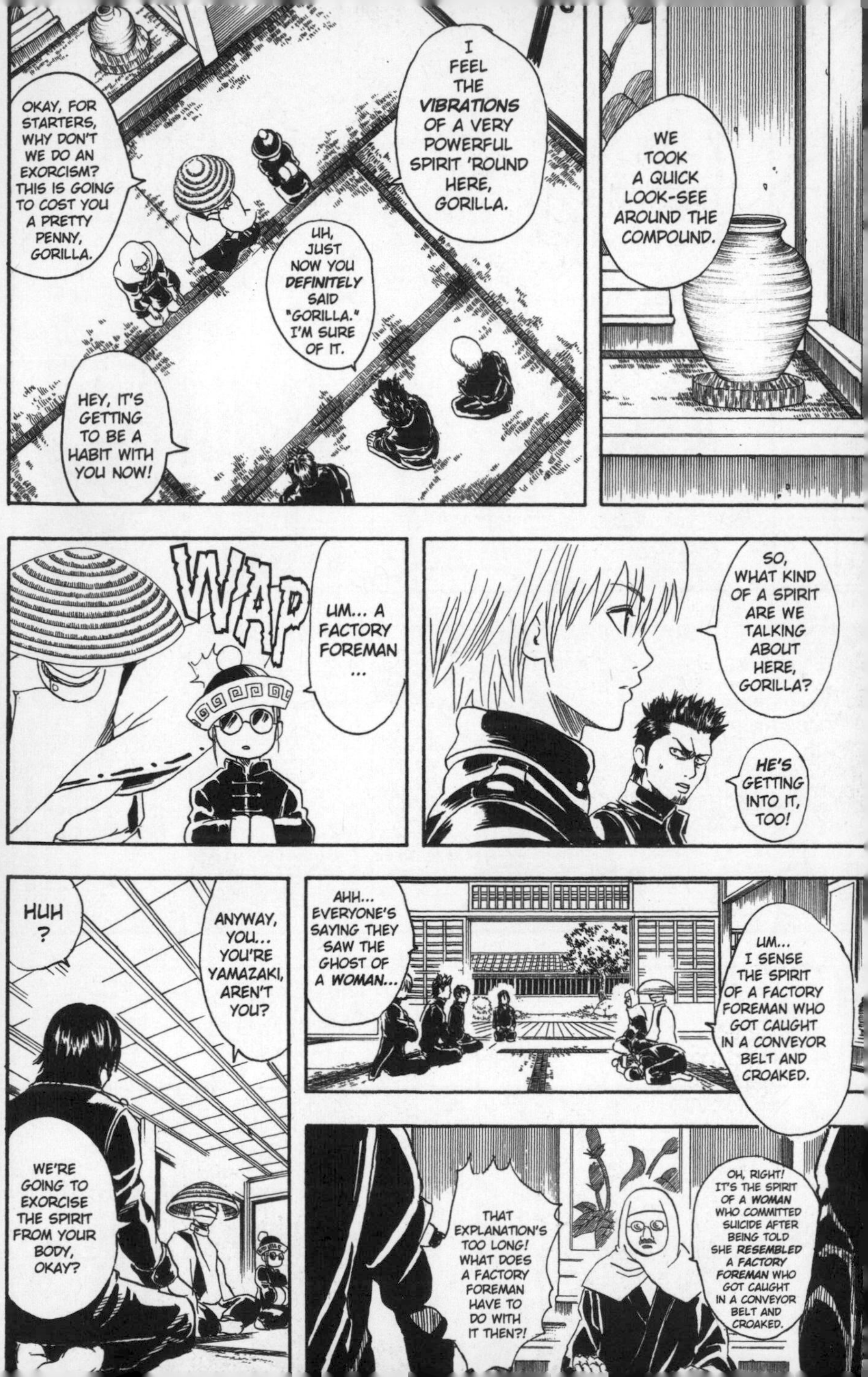
WE TOOK A QUICK LOOK-SEE AROUND THE COMPOUND.
I FEEL THE *VIBRATIONS* OF A VERY POWERFUL SPIRIT 'ROUND HERE, GORILLA.
OKAY, FOR STARTERS, WHY DON'T WE DO AN EXORCISM? THIS IS GOING TO COST YOU A PRETTY PENNY, GORILLA.
UH, JUST NOW YOU *DEFINITELY* SAID "GORILLA." I'M SURE OF IT.
HEY, IT'S GETTING TO BE A HABIT WITH YOU NOW!
SO, WHAT KIND OF A SPIRIT ARE WE TALKING ABOUT HERE, GORILLA?
HE'S GETTING INTO IT, TOO!
WAP
UM... A FACTORY FOREMAN ...
AHH... EVERYONE'S SAYING THEY SAW THE GHOST OF A *WOMAN*...
UM... I SENSE THE SPIRIT OF A FACTORY FOREMAN WHO GOT CAUGHT IN A CONVEYOR BELT AND CROAKED.
OH, RIGHT! IT'S THE SPIRIT OF A *WOMAN* WHO COMMITTED SUICIDE AFTER BEING TOLD SHE *RESEMBLED A FACTORY FOREMAN* WHO GOT CAUGHT IN A CONVEYOR BELT AND CROAKED.
THAT EXPLANATION'S TOO LONG! WHAT DOES A FACTORY FOREMAN HAVE TO DO WITH IT THEN?!
ANYWAY, YOU... YOU'RE YAMAZAKI, AREN'T YOU?
HUH ?
WE'RE GOING TO EXORCISE THE SPIRIT FROM YOUR BODY, OKAY?

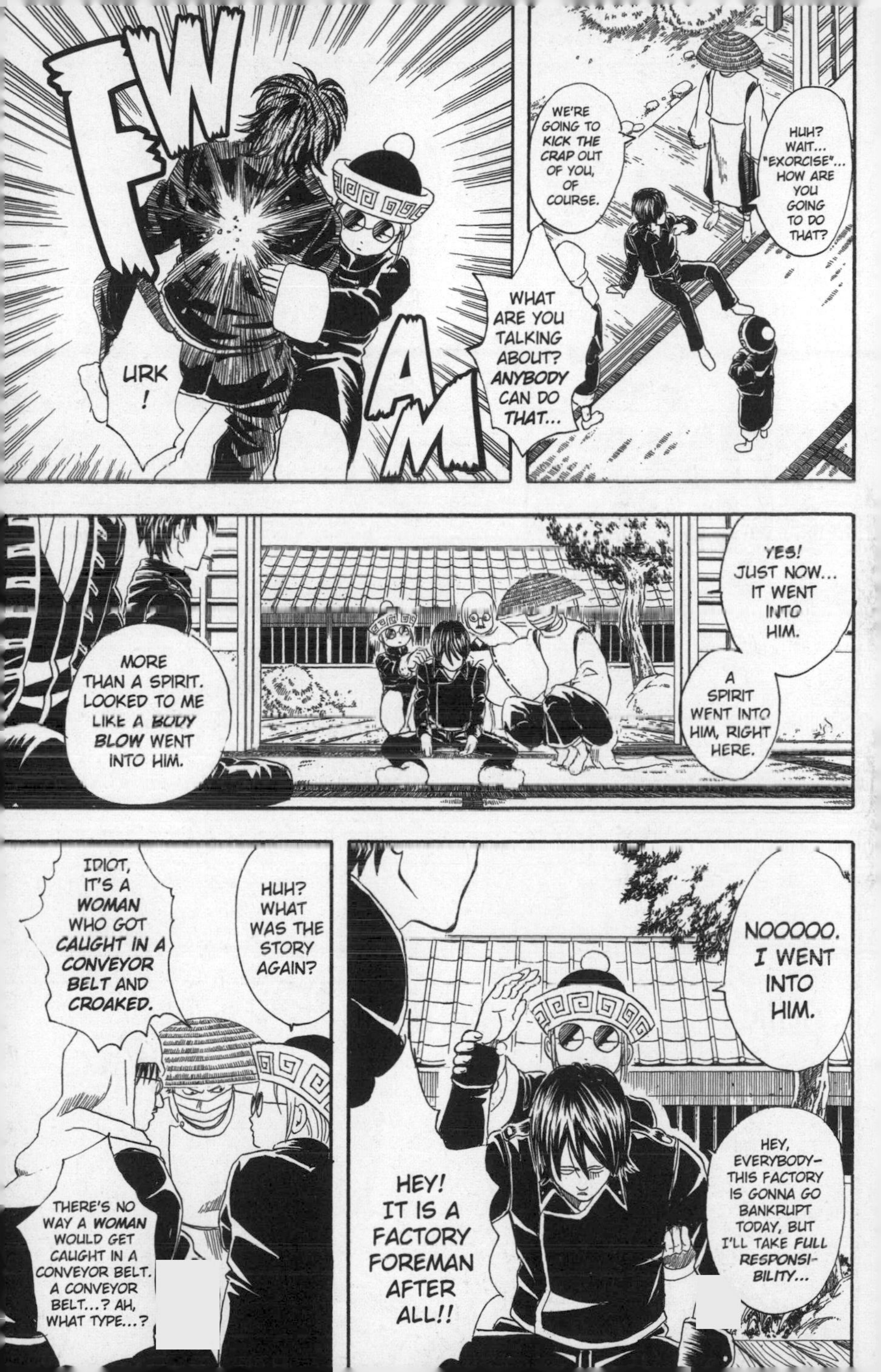
HUH? WAIT... "EXORCISE"... HOW ARE YOU GOING TO DO THAT?
WE'RE GOING TO KICK THE CRAP OUT OF YOU, OF COURSE.
WHAT ARE YOU TALKING ABOUT? ANYBODY CAN DO THAT...
FWAM
URK!
YES! JUST NOW... IT WENT INTO HIM.
A SPIRIT WENT INTO HIM, RIGHT HERE.
MORE THAN A SPIRIT. LOOKED TO ME LIKE A BODY BLOW WENT INTO HIM.
NOOOOO. I WENT INTO HIM.
HEY, EVERYBODY— THIS FACTORY IS GONNA GO BANKRUPT TODAY, BUT I'LL TAKE FULL RESPONSI-BILITY...
HEY! IT IS A FACTORY FOREMAN AFTER ALL!!
HUH? WHAT WAS THE STORY AGAIN?
IDIOT, IT'S A WOMAN WHO GOT CAUGHT IN A CONVEYOR BELT AND CROAKED.
THERE'S NO WAY A WOMAN WOULD GET CAUGHT IN A CONVEYOR BELT. A CONVEYOR BELT...? AH, WHAT TYPE...?

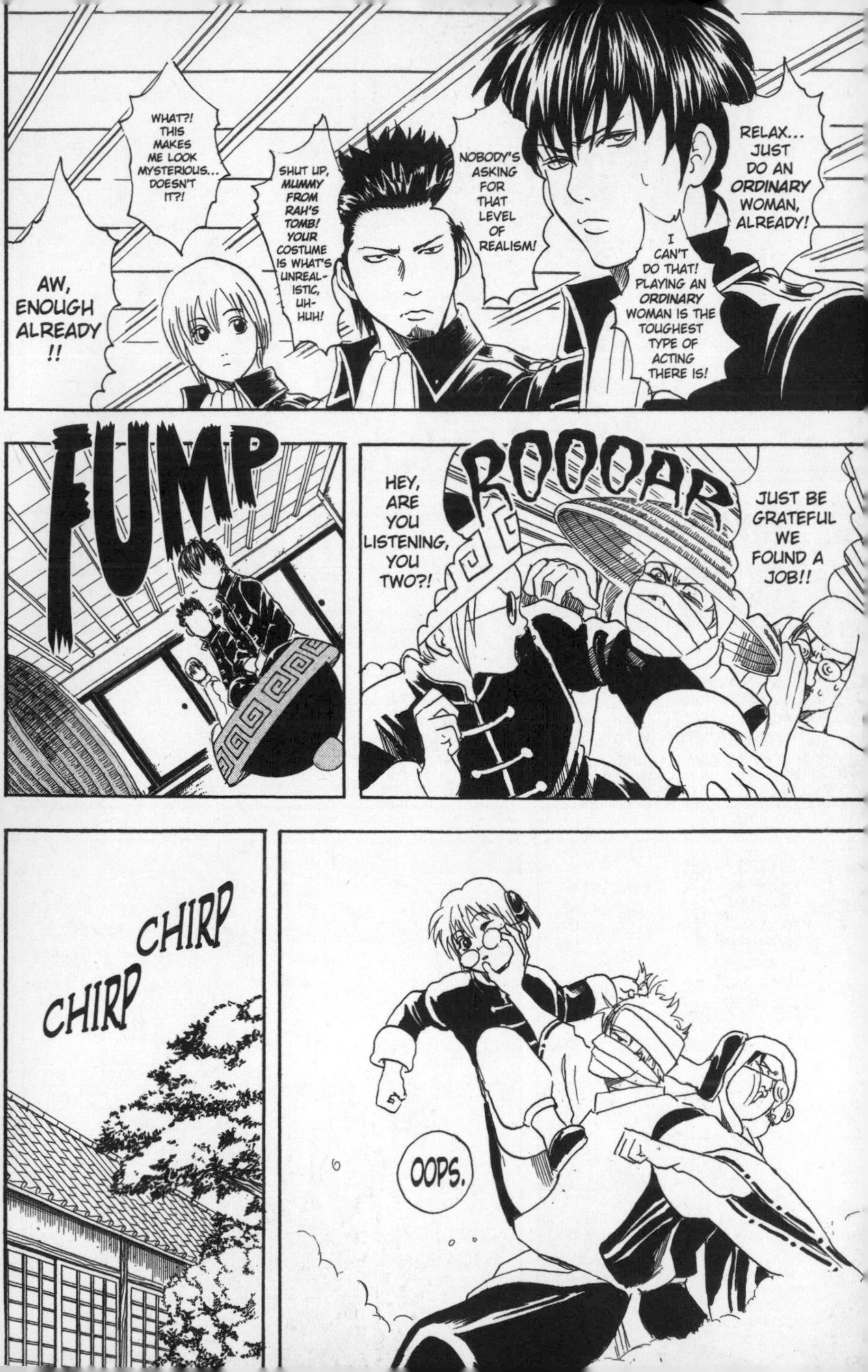
RELAX... JUST DO AN ORDINARY WOMAN, ALREADY!
I CAN'T DO THAT! PLAYING AN ORDINARY WOMAN IS THE TOUGHEST TYPE OF ACTING THERE IS!
NOBODY'S ASKING FOR THAT LEVEL OF REALISM!
SHUT UP, MUMMY FROM RAH'S TOMB! YOUR COSTUME IS WHAT'S UNREAL-ISTIC, UH-HUH!
WHAT?! THIS MAKES ME LOOK MYSTERIOUS... DOESN'T IT?!
AW, ENOUGH ALREADY!!
JUST BE GRATEFUL WE FOUND A JOB!!
ROOOAR
HEY, ARE YOU LISTENING, YOU TWO?!
FUMP
OOPS.
CHIRP
CHIRP

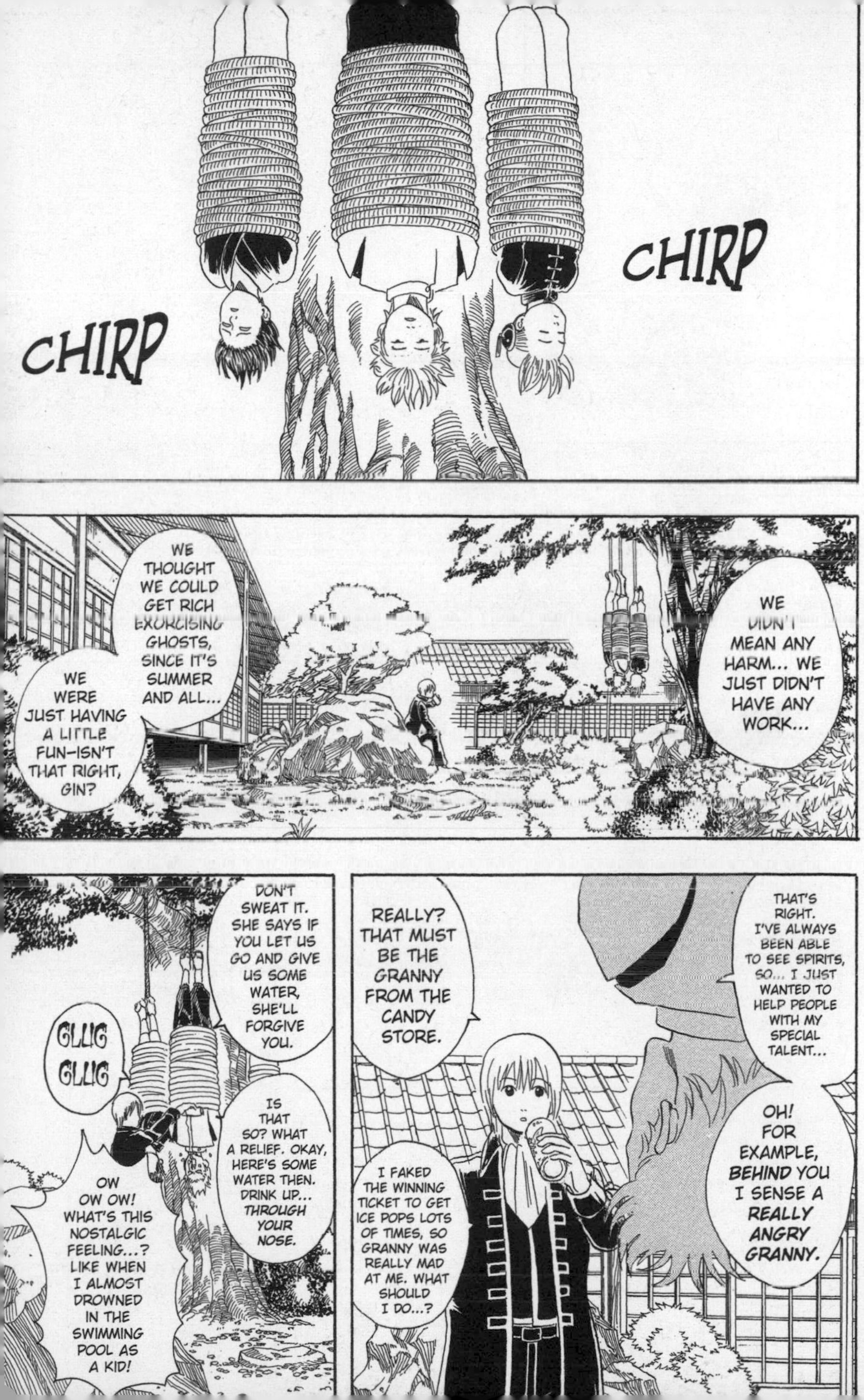
CHIRP
CHIRP
WE DIDN'T MEAN ANY HARM... WE JUST DIDN'T HAVE ANY WORK...
WE THOUGHT WE COULD GET RICH EXORCISING GHOSTS, SINCE IT'S SUMMER AND ALL...
WE WERE JUST HAVING A LITTLE FUN—ISN'T THAT RIGHT, GIN?
THAT'S RIGHT. I'VE ALWAYS BEEN ABLE TO SEE SPIRITS, SO... I JUST WANTED TO HELP PEOPLE WITH MY SPECIAL TALENT...
REALLY? THAT MUST BE THE GRANNY FROM THE CANDY STORE.
OH! FOR EXAMPLE, BEHIND YOU I SENSE A REALLY ANGRY GRANNY.
I FAKED THE WINNING TICKET TO GET ICE POPS LOTS OF TIMES, SO GRANNY WAS REALLY MAD AT ME. WHAT SHOULD I DO...?
DON'T SWEAT IT. SHE SAYS IF YOU LET US GO AND GIVE US SOME WATER, SHE'LL FORGIVE YOU.
GLUG GLUG
IS THAT SO? WHAT A RELIEF. OKAY, HERE'S SOME WATER THEN. DRINK UP... THROUGH YOUR NOSE.
OW OW OW! WHAT'S THIS NOSTALGIC FEELING...? LIKE WHEN I ALMOST DROWNED IN THE SWIMMING POOL AS A KID!

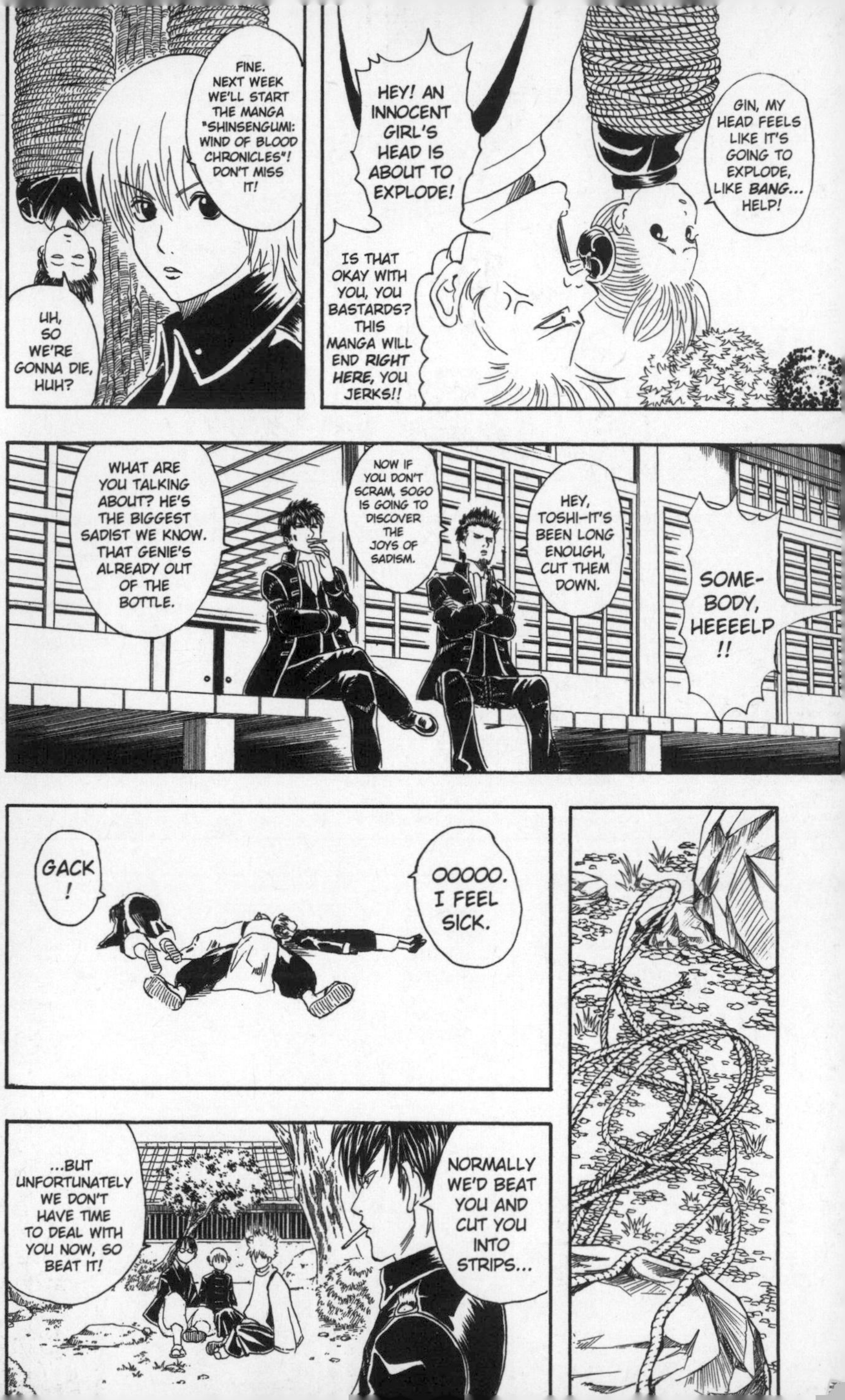
GIN, MY HEAD FEELS LIKE IT'S GOING TO EXPLODE, LIKE BANG... HELP!
HEY! AN INNOCENT GIRL'S HEAD IS ABOUT TO EXPLODE!
IS THAT OKAY WITH YOU, YOU BASTARDS? THIS MANGA WILL END RIGHT HERE, YOU JERKS!!
FINE. NEXT WEEK WE'LL START THE MANGA "SHINSENGUMI: WIND OF BLOOD CHRONICLES"! DON'T MISS IT!
UH, SO WE'RE GONNA DIE, HUH?
SOME-BODY, HEEEELP !!
HEY, TOSHI—IT'S BEEN LONG ENOUGH, CUT THEM DOWN.
NOW IF YOU DON'T SCRAM, SOGO IS GOING TO DISCOVER THE JOYS OF SADISM.
WHAT ARE YOU TALKING ABOUT? HE'S THE BIGGEST SADIST WE KNOW. THAT GENIE'S ALREADY OUT OF THE BOTTLE.
OOOOO. I FEEL SICK.
GACK !
NORMALLY WE'D BEAT YOU AND CUT YOU INTO STRIPS...
...BUT UNFORTUNATELY WE DON'T HAVE TIME TO DEAL WITH YOU NOW, SO BEAT IT!

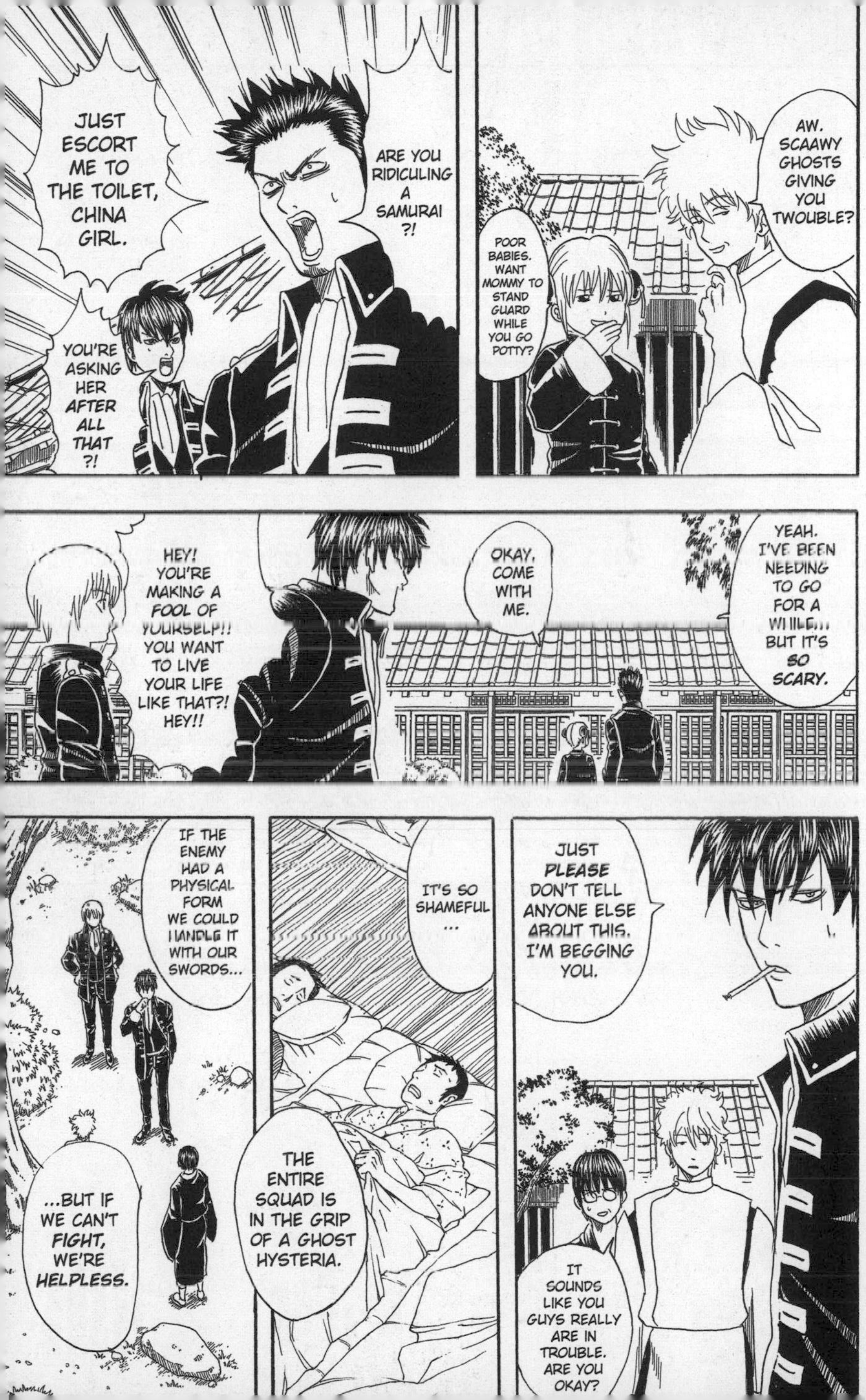
AW. SCAAWY GHOSTS GIVING YOU TWOUBLE?
POOR BABIES. WANT MOMMY TO STAND GUARD WHILE YOU GO POTTY?
ARE YOU RIDICULING A SAMURAI ?!
JUST ESCORT ME TO THE TOILET, CHINA GIRL.
YOU'RE ASKING HER AFTER ALL THAT ?!
YEAH. I'VE BEEN NEEDING TO GO FOR A WHILE... BUT IT'S SO SCARY.
OKAY, COME WITH ME.
HEY! YOU'RE MAKING A FOOL OF YOURSELF!! YOU WANT TO LIVE YOUR LIFE LIKE THAT?! HEY!!
JUST PLEASE DON'T TELL ANYONE ELSE ABOUT THIS. I'M BEGGING YOU.
IT SOUNDS LIKE YOU GUYS REALLY ARE IN TROUBLE. ARE YOU OKAY?
IT'S SO SHAMEFUL ...
THE ENTIRE SQUAD IS IN THE GRIP OF A GHOST HYSTERIA.
IF THE ENEMY HAD A PHYSICAL FORM WE COULD HANDLE IT WITH OUR SWORDS...
...BUT IF WE CAN'T FIGHT, WE'RE HELPLESS.

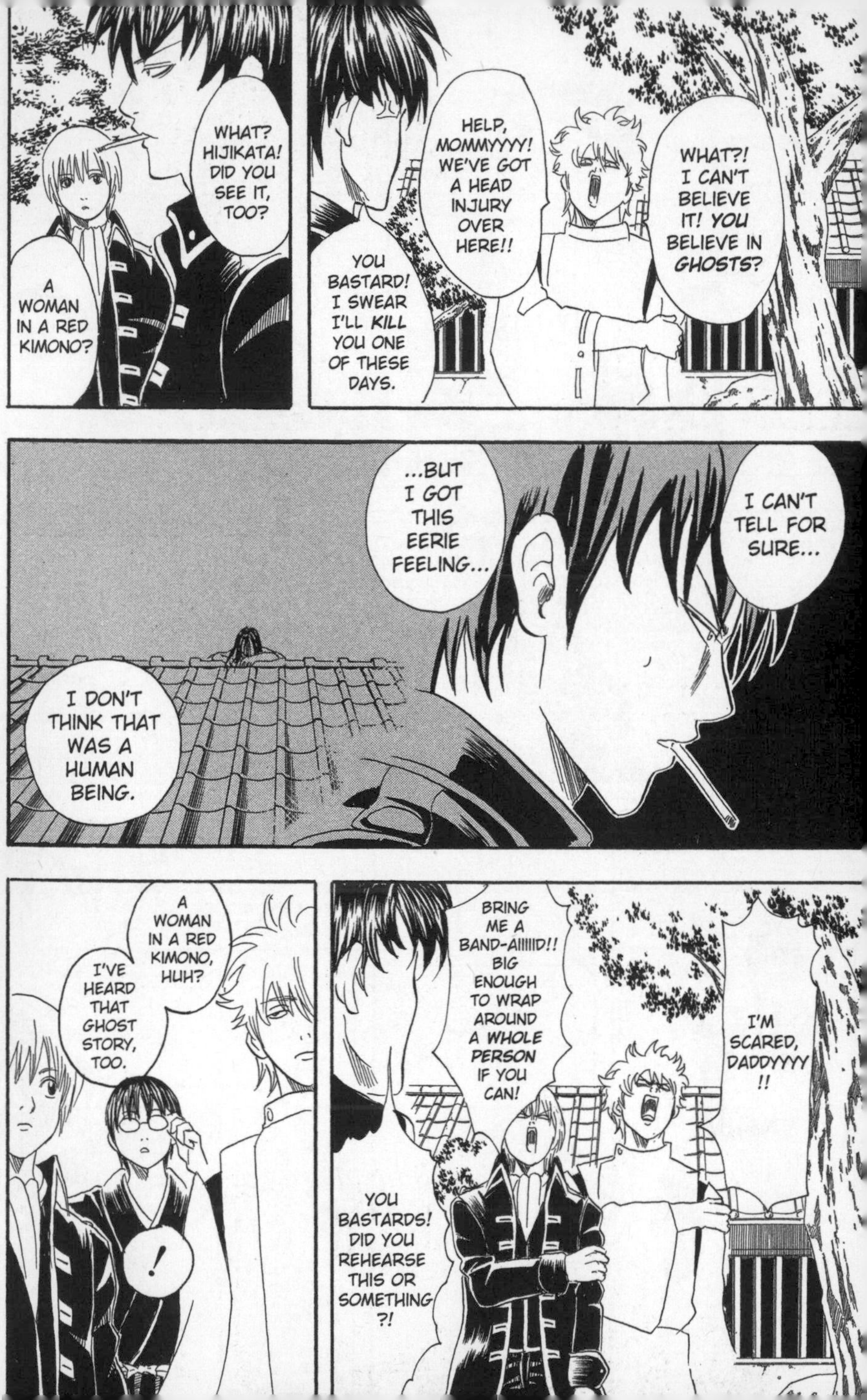
WHAT?! I CAN'T BELIEVE IT! YOU BELIEVE IN GHOSTS?
HELP, MOMMYYYY! WE'VE GOT A HEAD INJURY OVER HERE!!
YOU BASTARD! I SWEAR I'LL KILL YOU ONE OF THESE DAYS.
WHAT? HIJIKATA! DID YOU SEE IT, TOO?
A WOMAN IN A RED KIMONO?
I CAN'T TELL FOR SURE...
...BUT I GOT THIS EERIE FEELING...
I DON'T THINK THAT WAS A HUMAN BEING.
I'M SCARED, DADDYYYY!!
BRING ME A BAND-AIIIIID!! BIG ENOUGH TO WRAP AROUND A WHOLE PERSON IF YOU CAN!
YOU BASTARDS! DID YOU REHEARSE THIS OR SOMETHING?!
A WOMAN IN A RED KIMONO, HUH?
I'VE HEARD THAT GHOST STORY, TOO.
!

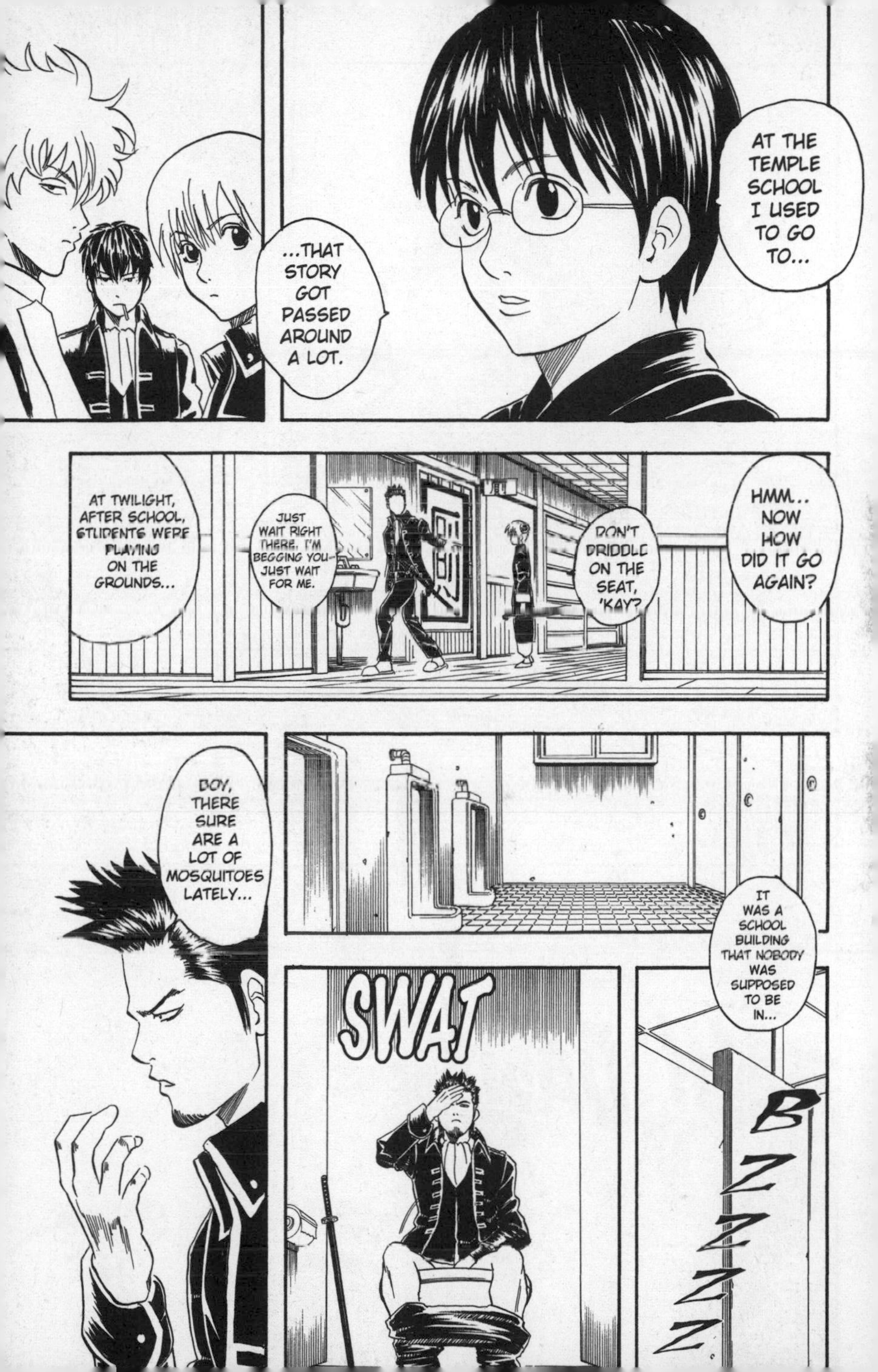
AT THE TEMPLE SCHOOL I USED TO GO TO...
...THAT STORY GOT PASSED AROUND A LOT.
HMM... NOW HOW DID IT GO AGAIN?
DON'T DRIDDLE ON THE SEAT, 'KAY?
JUST WAIT RIGHT THERE, I'M BEGGING YOU. JUST WAIT FOR ME.
AT TWILIGHT, AFTER SCHOOL, STUDENTS WERE PLAYING ON THE GROUNDS...
IT WAS A SCHOOL BUILDING THAT NOBODY WAS SUPPOSED TO BE IN...
BZZZZZZ
SWAT
BOY, THERE SURE ARE A LOT OF MOSQUITOES LATELY...

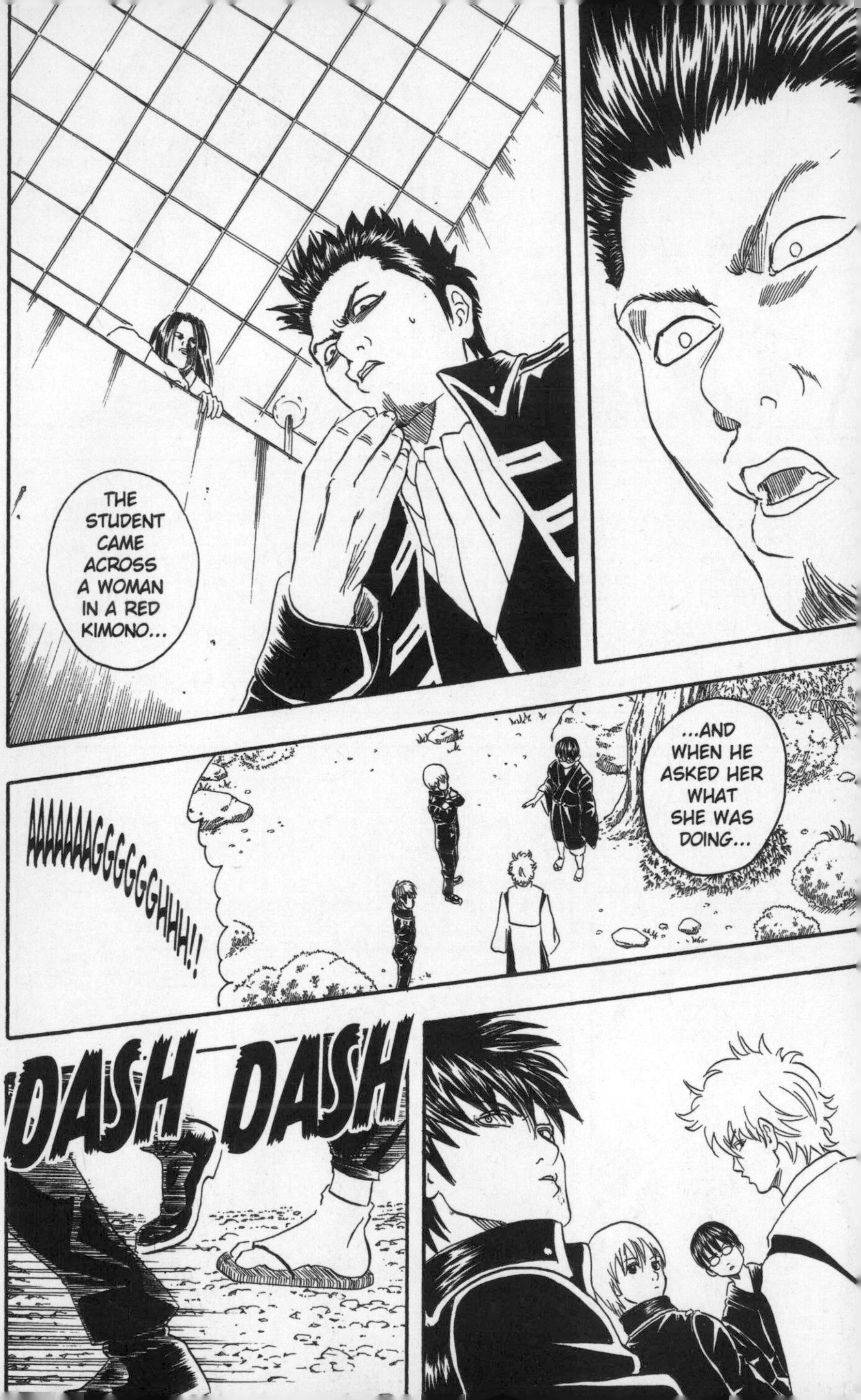
THE STUDENT CAME ACROSS A WOMAN IN A RED KIMONO...
...AND WHEN HE ASKED HER WHAT SHE WAS DOING...
AAAAAAAGGGGGGHHHH!!
DASH DASH

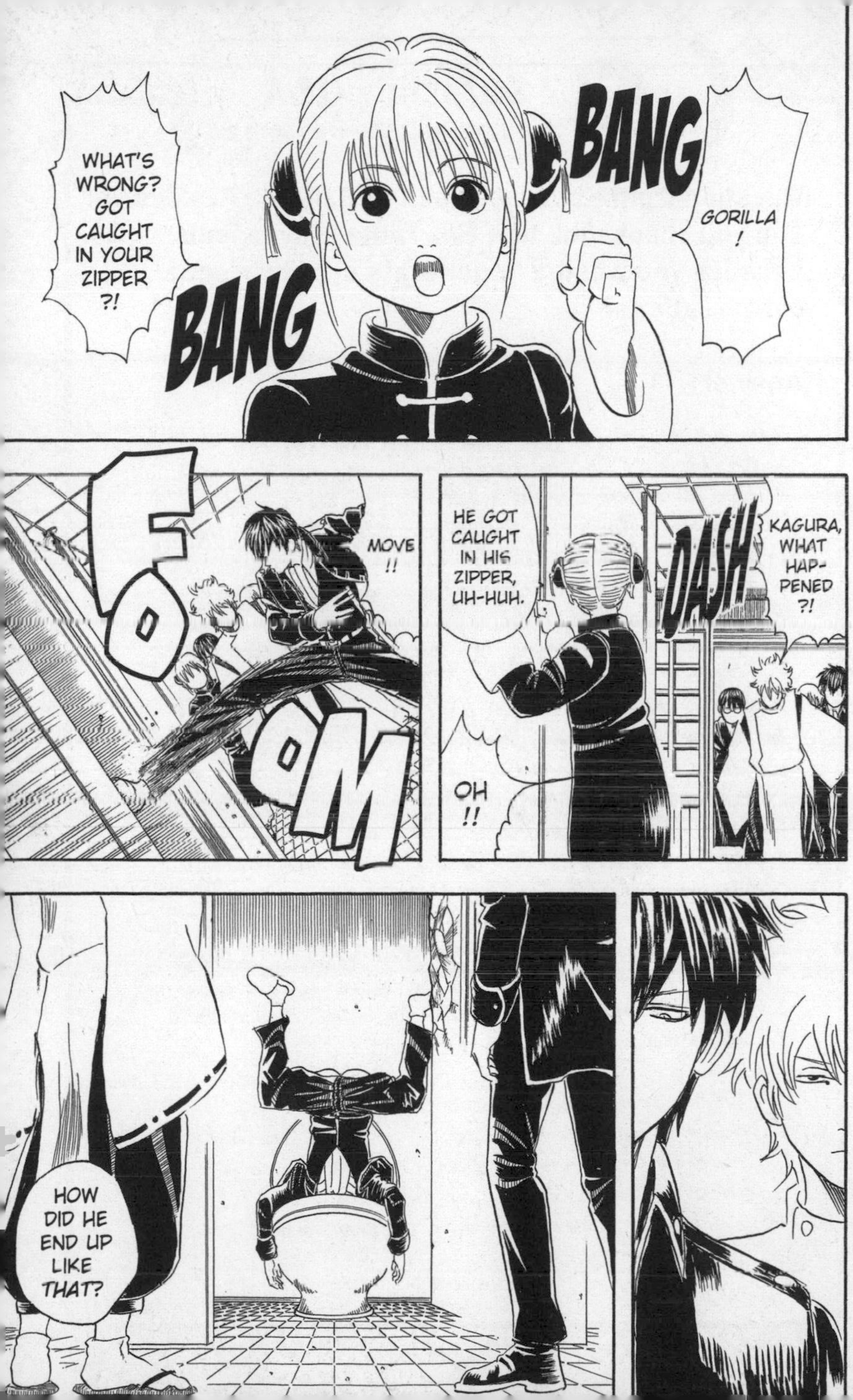
BANG
GORILLA!
WHAT'S WRONG? GOT CAUGHT IN YOUR ZIPPER?!
BANG
KAGURA, WHAT HAP-PENED?!
DASH
HE GOT CAUGHT IN HIS ZIPPER, UH-HUH.
OH!!
MOVE!!
FOOM
HOW DID HE END UP LIKE THAT?

Sorachi's Q&A
Hanging with the Readers #6

(Question from Kobayashi-san of Saitama Prefecture)
Did you choose the title *Gin Tama* (Silver Balls) because you wanted to generate slightly risqué conversations?

(Answer)

The short answer is that I wanted to have a title with impact. In the beginning, when we talked about it in the series meeting, the title was "Yorozuya Gin-san," but since that didn't have any impact at all I discussed alternate ideas with the editor. I was totally disgusted by the editor's lack of sense when he said, "How about Silver Samurai or something like that? Isn't that cool?" So I told him, "Give me a little time to think." After I graduated from college, I went back home to my parents' house for a brief time, and we held a family meeting, where we decided to use Gin Tama. After that, the editor said, "Gin Tama? Great! That'll be popular!" and was all enthusiastic, but only the editor and I were happy with it, and it got terrible feedback from the editorial department. However, Editor Onishi was a real man and got the proposal pushed through by saying, "I got the people upstairs to shut up so we'll go with Gin Tama, okay?" I dunno, was it worth it to make so many enemies?

* Other proposed titles:
"Dashing Gin-san" by Dad   That's boring!
"Carefree Gin-san" by Dad   You stole it!
"Gin-chan goes forth" by Sorachi
           You're stealing it, too, aren't you!

(Q&A #7 is on page 66)

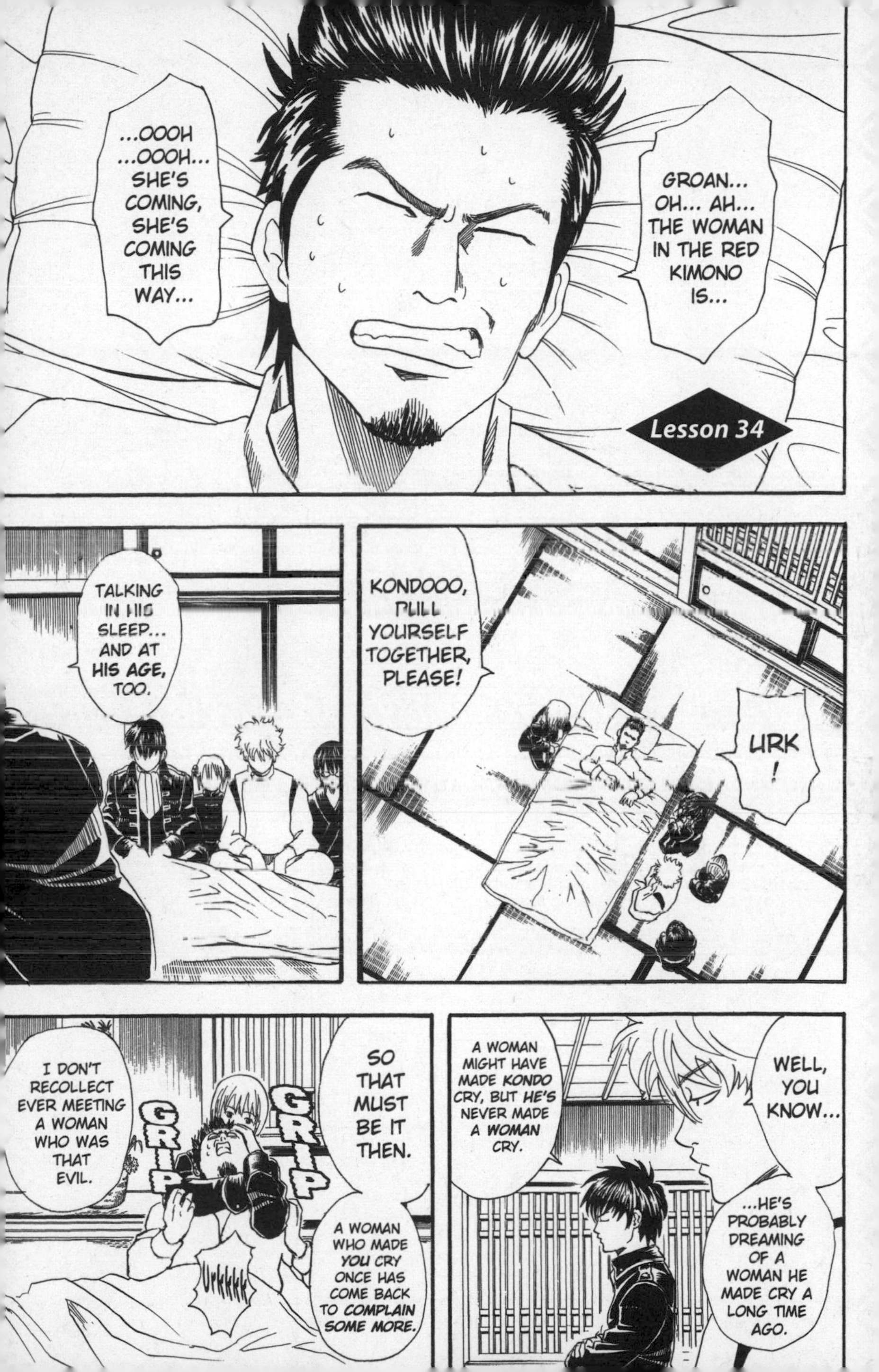
GROAN... OH... AH... THE WOMAN IN THE RED KIMONO IS...
...OOOH ...OOOH... SHE'S COMING, SHE'S COMING THIS WAY...
Lesson 34
URK!
KONDOOO, PULL YOURSELF TOGETHER, PLEASE!
TALKING IN HIS SLEEP... AND AT HIS AGE, TOO.
WELL, YOU KNOW...
...HE'S PROBABLY DREAMING OF A WOMAN HE MADE CRY A LONG TIME AGO.
A WOMAN MIGHT HAVE MADE KONDO CRY, BUT HE'S NEVER MADE A WOMAN CRY.
SO THAT MUST BE IT THEN.
A WOMAN WHO MADE YOU CRY ONCE HAS COME BACK TO COMPLAIN SOME MORE.
GRIP
GRIP
Urkkkk
I DON'T RECOLLECT EVER MEETING A WOMAN WHO WAS THAT EVIL.

Lesson 34: Guys with Inferiority Complexes Get Big Jobs Done

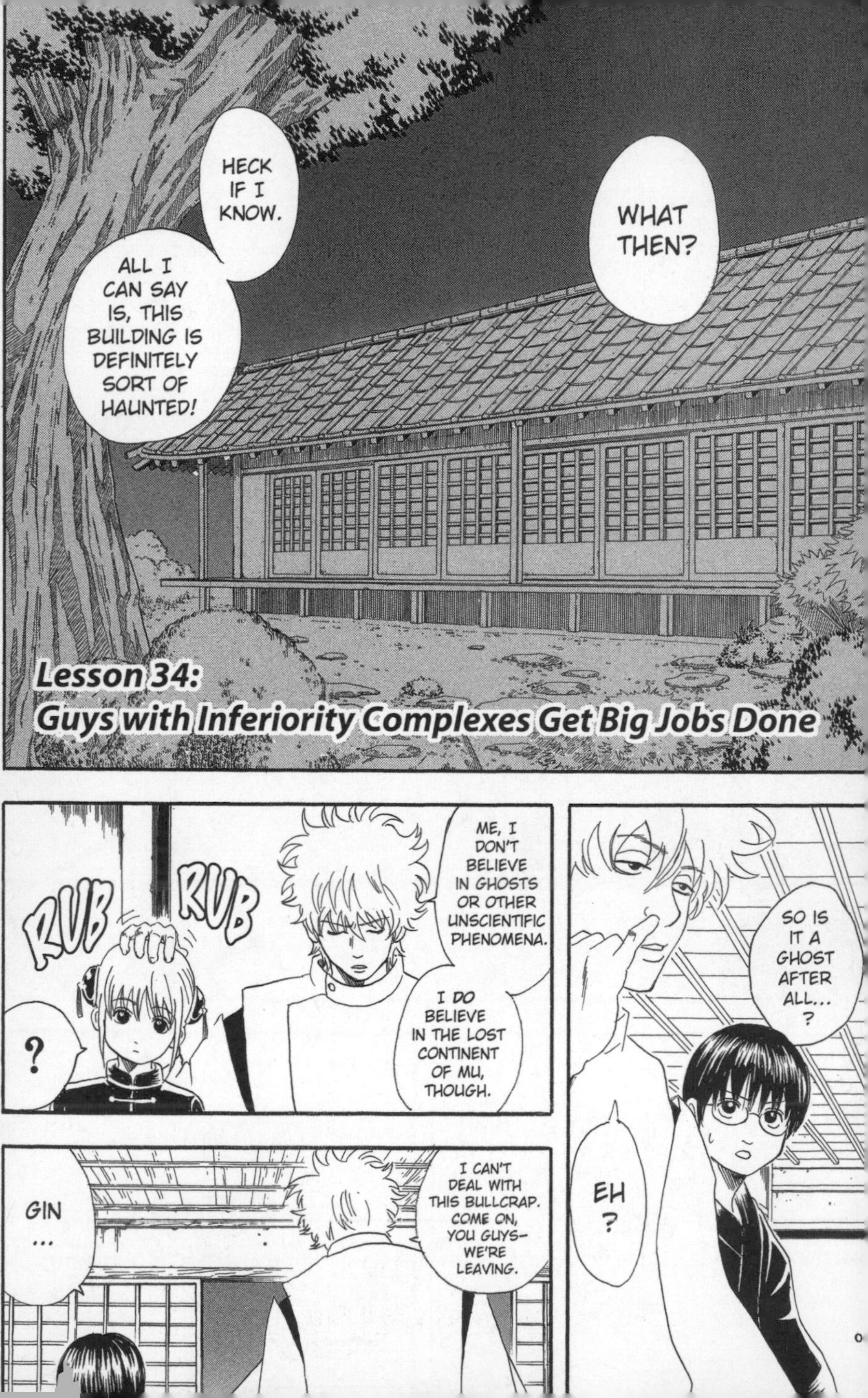
WHAT THEN?
HECK IF I KNOW.
ALL I CAN SAY IS, THIS BUILDING IS DEFINITELY SORT OF HAUNTED!
SO IS IT A GHOST AFTER ALL...?
EH?
ME, I DON'T BELIEVE IN GHOSTS OR OTHER UNSCIENTIFIC PHENOMENA.
RUB RUB
I DO BELIEVE IN THE LOST CONTINENT OF MU, THOUGH.
?
I CAN'T DEAL WITH THIS BULLCRAP. COME ON, YOU GUYS- WE'RE LEAVING.
GIN...

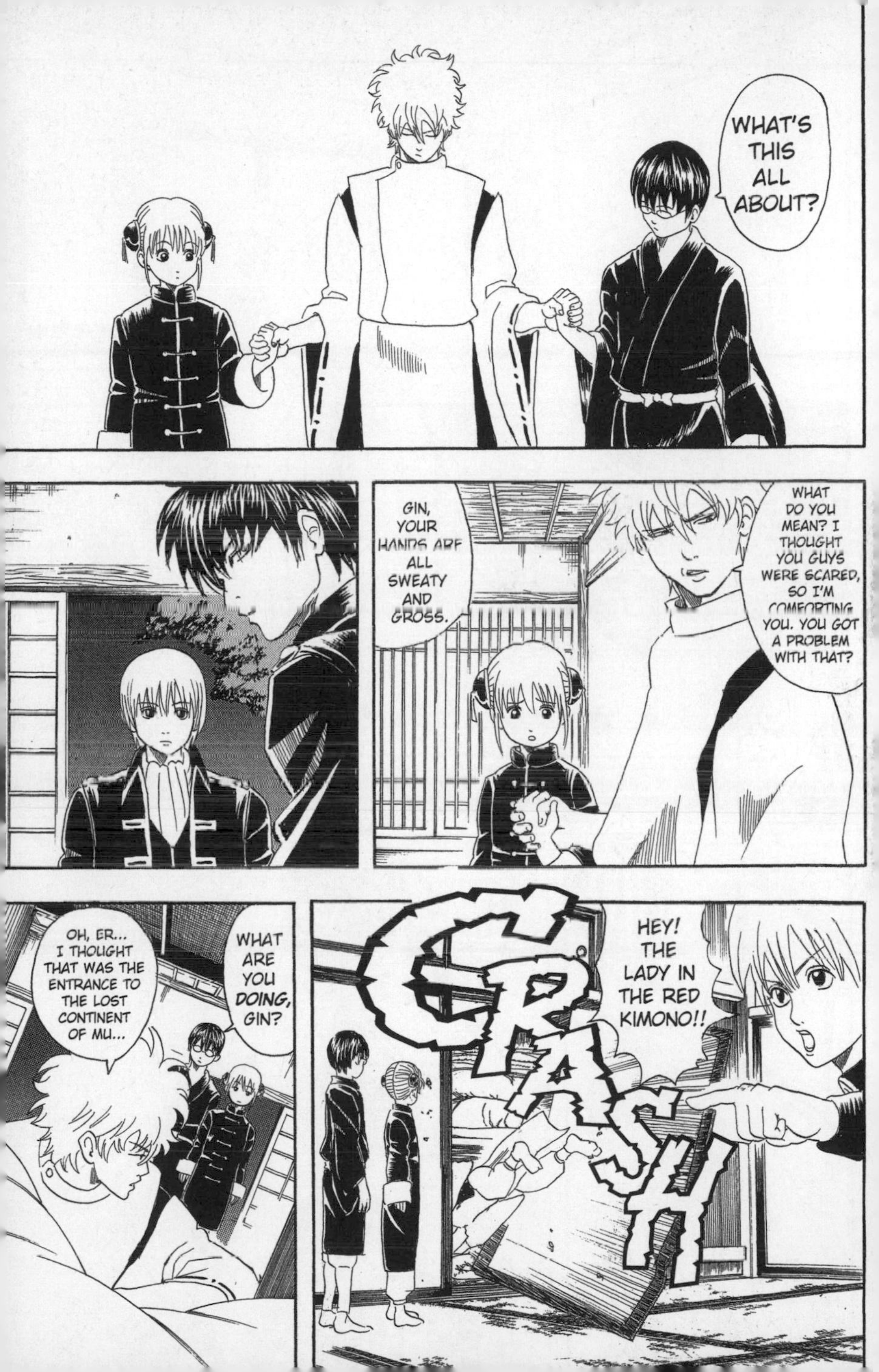
WHAT'S THIS ALL ABOUT?
WHAT DO YOU MEAN? I THOUGHT YOU GUYS WERE SCARED, SO I'M COMFORTING YOU. YOU GOT A PROBLEM WITH THAT?
GIN, YOUR HANDS ARE ALL SWEATY AND GROSS.
HEY! THE LADY IN THE RED KIMONO!!
CRASH
WHAT ARE YOU DOING, GIN?
OH, ER... I THOUGHT THAT WAS THE ENTRANCE TO THE LOST CONTINENT OF MU...

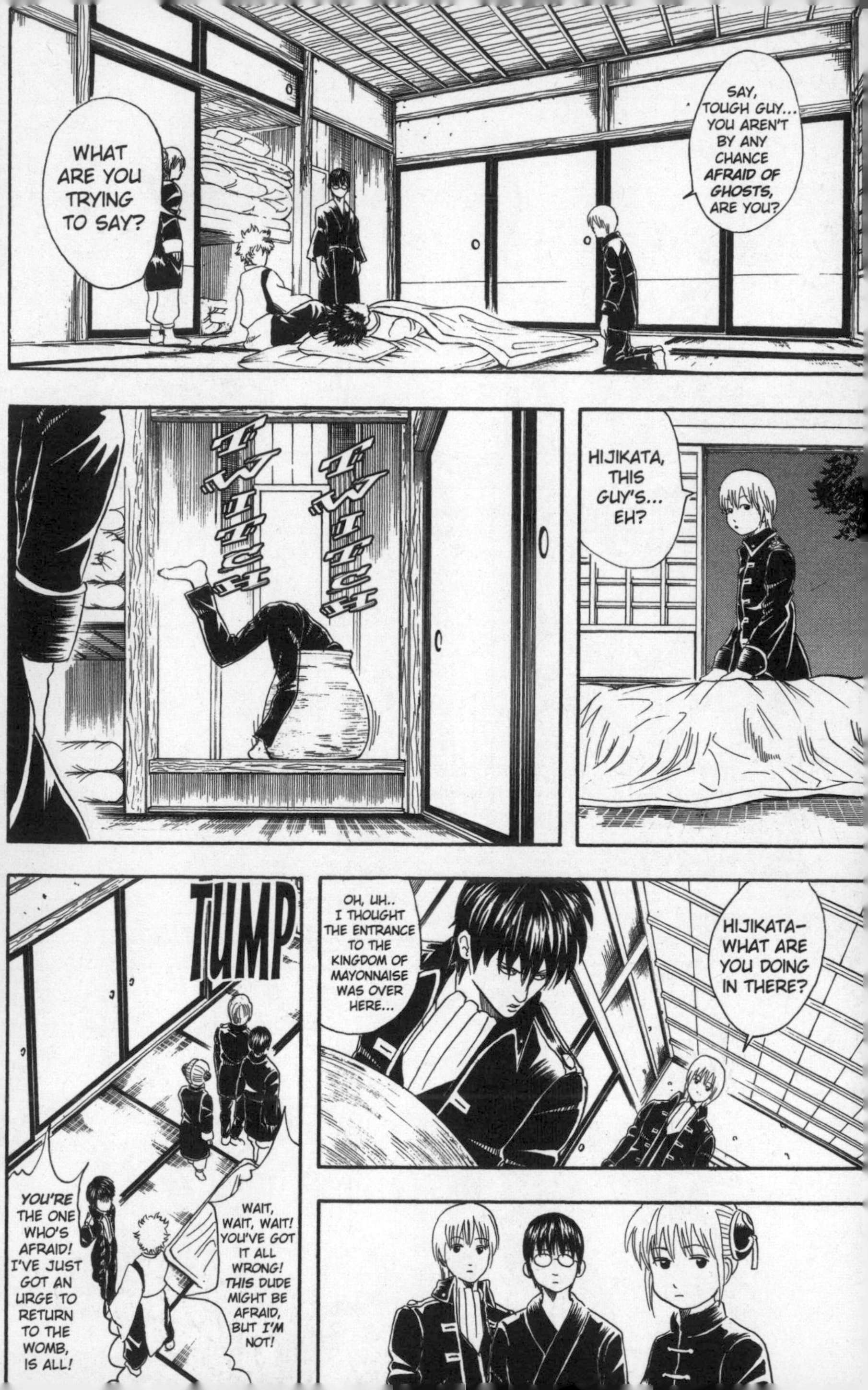
SAY, TOUGH GUY... YOU AREN'T BY ANY CHANCE AFRAID OF GHOSTS, ARE YOU?
WHAT ARE YOU TRYING TO SAY?
HIJIKATA, THIS GUY'S... EH?
TWITCH
TWITCH
HIJIKATA- WHAT ARE YOU DOING IN THERE?
OH, UH.. I THOUGHT THE ENTRANCE TO THE KINGDOM OF MAYONNAISE WAS OVER HERE...
TUMP
WAIT, WAIT, WAIT! YOU'VE GOT IT ALL WRONG! THIS DUDE MIGHT BE AFRAID, BUT I'M NOT!
YOU'RE THE ONE WHO'S AFRAID! I'VE JUST GOT AN URGE TO RETURN TO THE WOMB, IS ALL!

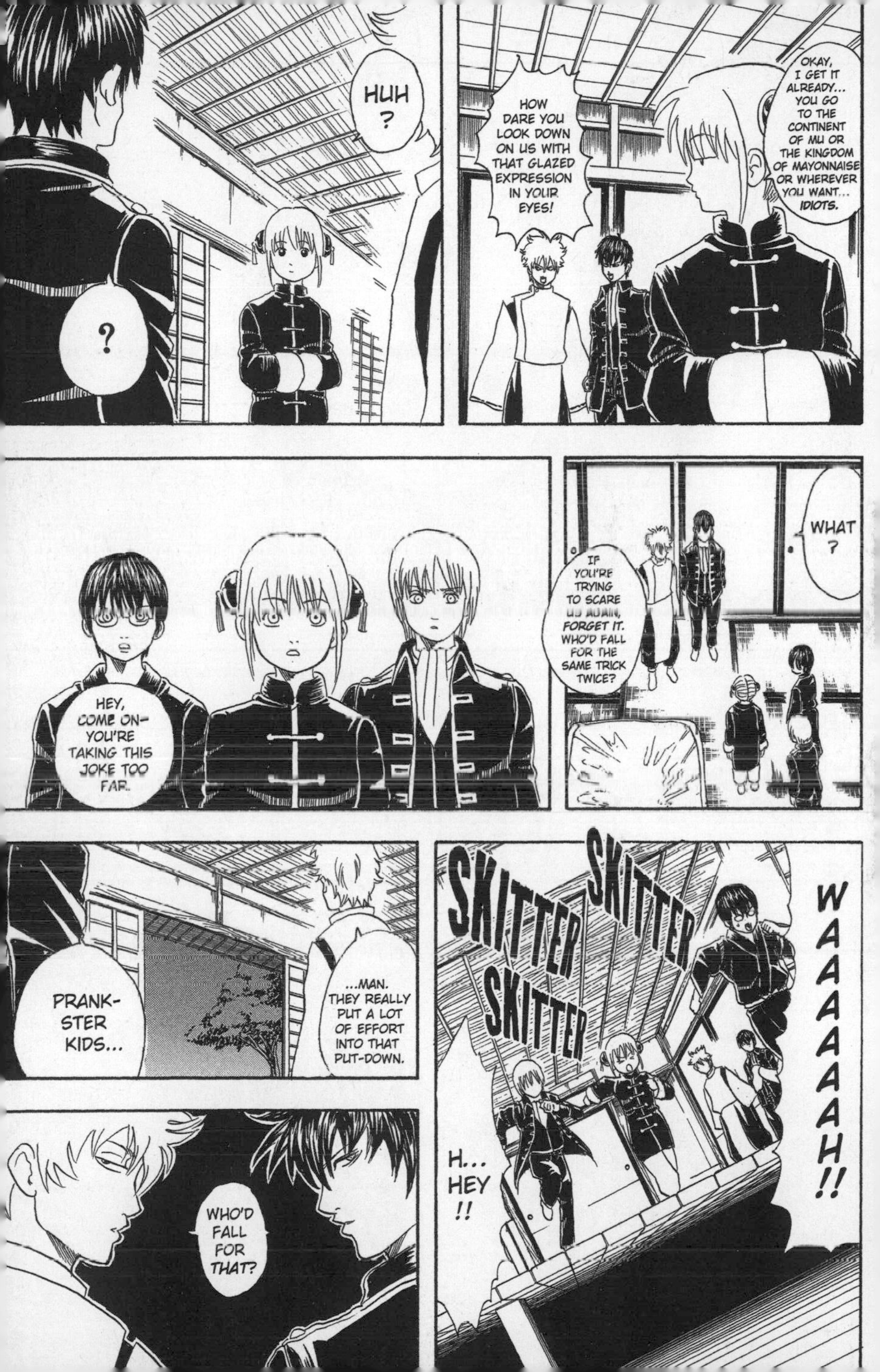
OKAY, I GET IT ALREADY... YOU GO TO THE CONTINENT OF MU OR THE KINGDOM OF MAYONNAISE OR WHEREVER YOU WANT... IDIOTS.
HOW DARE YOU LOOK DOWN ON US WITH THAT GLAZED EXPRESSION IN YOUR EYES!
HUH ?
?
WHAT ?
IF YOU'RE TRYING TO SCARE US AGAIN, FORGET IT. WHO'D FALL FOR THE SAME TRICK TWICE?
HEY, COME ON— YOU'RE TAKING THIS JOKE TOO FAR.
WAAAAAAAH!!
SKITTER
SKITTER
SKITTER
H... HEY !!
...MAN. THEY REALLY PUT A LOT OF EFFORT INTO THAT PUT-DOWN.
PRANK-STER KIDS...
WHO'D FALL FOR THAT?

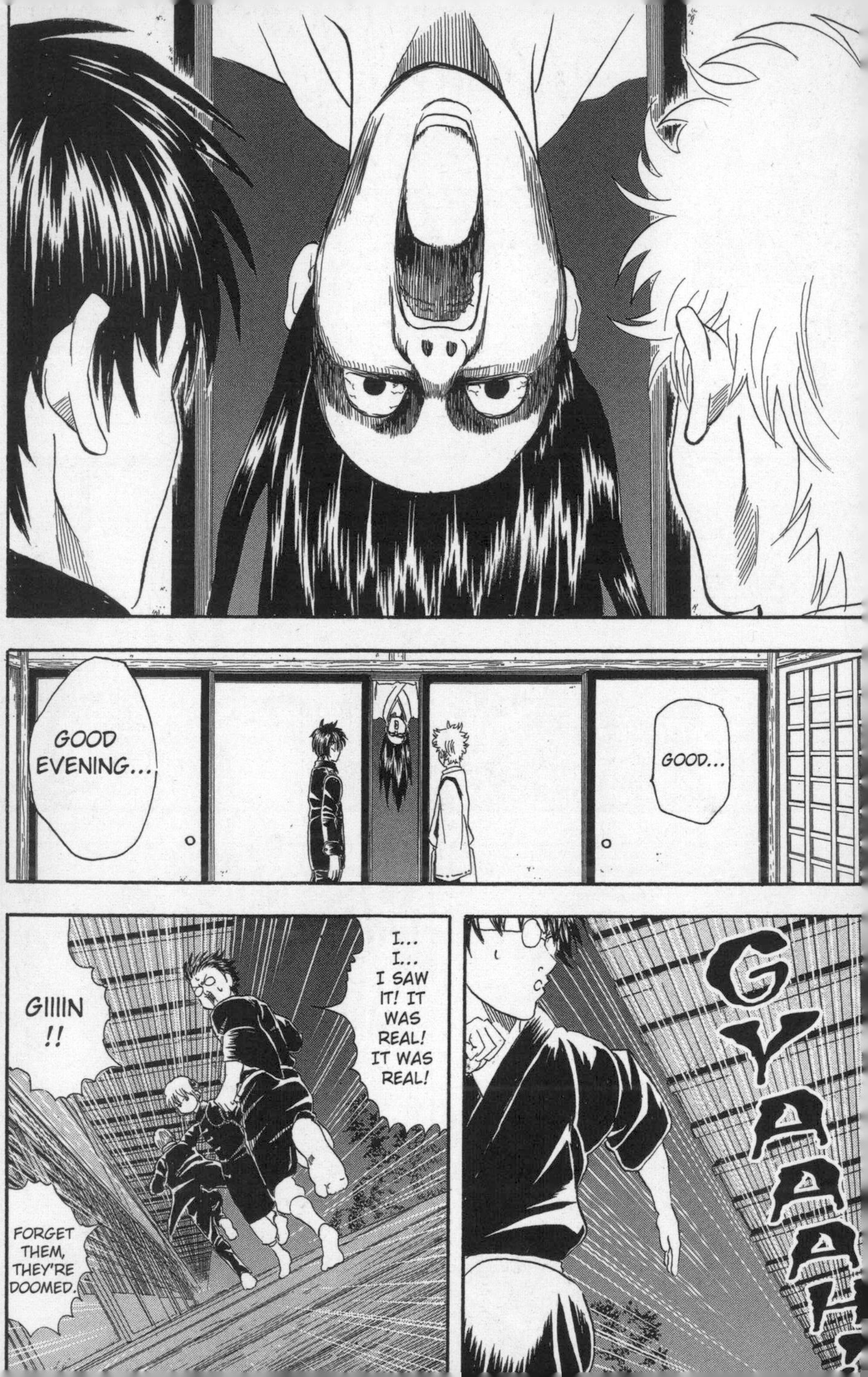
GOOD...
GOOD EVENING...
GYAAAAH
I... I... I SAW IT! IT WAS REAL! IT WAS REAL!
GIIIIN !!
FORGET THEM, THEY'RE DOOMED.

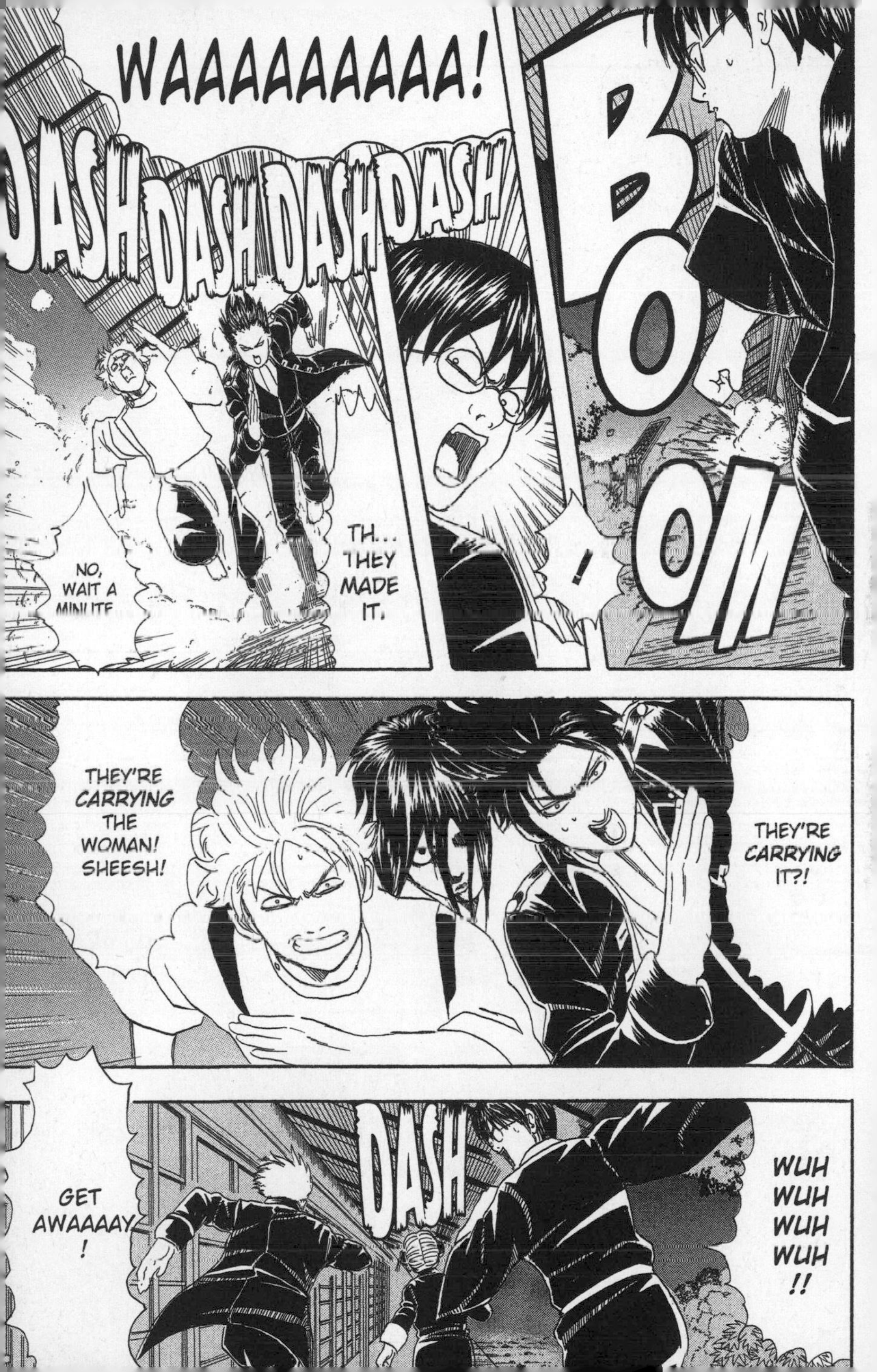
BOOM
!
WAAAAAAAAA!
DASH DASH DASH DASH
TH... THEY MADE IT.
NO, WAIT A MINUTE
THEY'RE CARRYING IT?!
THEY'RE CARRYING THE WOMAN! SHEESH!
WUH WUH WUH WUH!!
DASH
GET AWAAAAY!

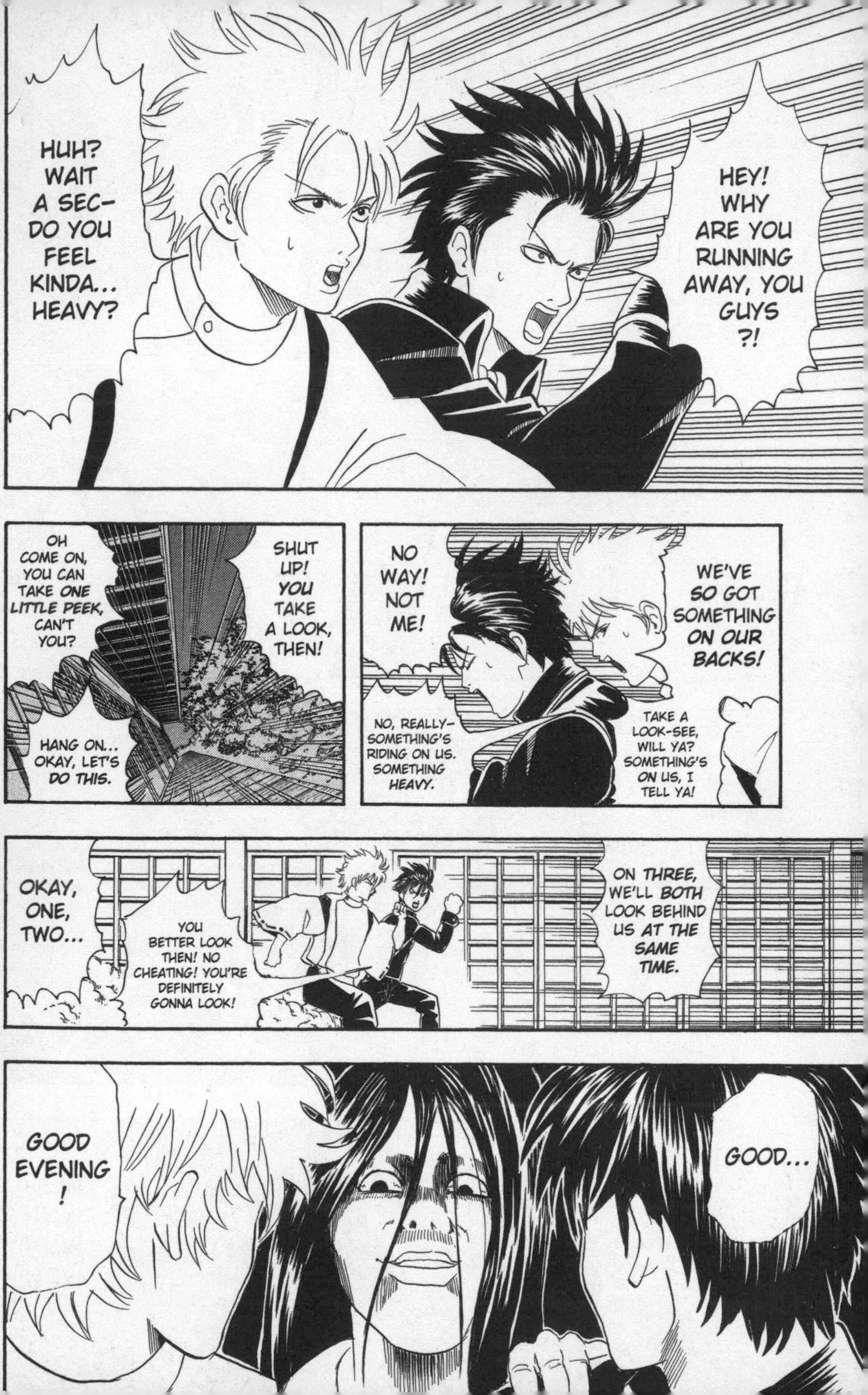
HEY! WHY ARE YOU RUNNING AWAY, YOU GUYS?!
HUH? WAIT A SEC— DO YOU FEEL KINDA... HEAVY?
WE'VE SO GOT SOMETHING ON OUR BACKS!
NO WAY! NOT ME!
TAKE A LOOK-SEE, WILL YA? SOMETHING'S ON US, I TELL YA!
NO, REALLY— SOMETHING'S RIDING ON US. SOMETHING HEAVY.
SHUT UP! YOU TAKE A LOOK, THEN!
OH COME ON, YOU CAN TAKE ONE LITTLE PEEK, CAN'T YOU?
HANG ON... OKAY, LET'S DO THIS.
ON THREE, WE'LL BOTH LOOK BEHIND US AT THE SAME TIME.
YOU BETTER LOOK THEN! NO CHEATING! YOU'RE DEFINITELY GONNA LOOK!
OKAY, ONE, TWO...
GOOD...
GOOD EVENING!

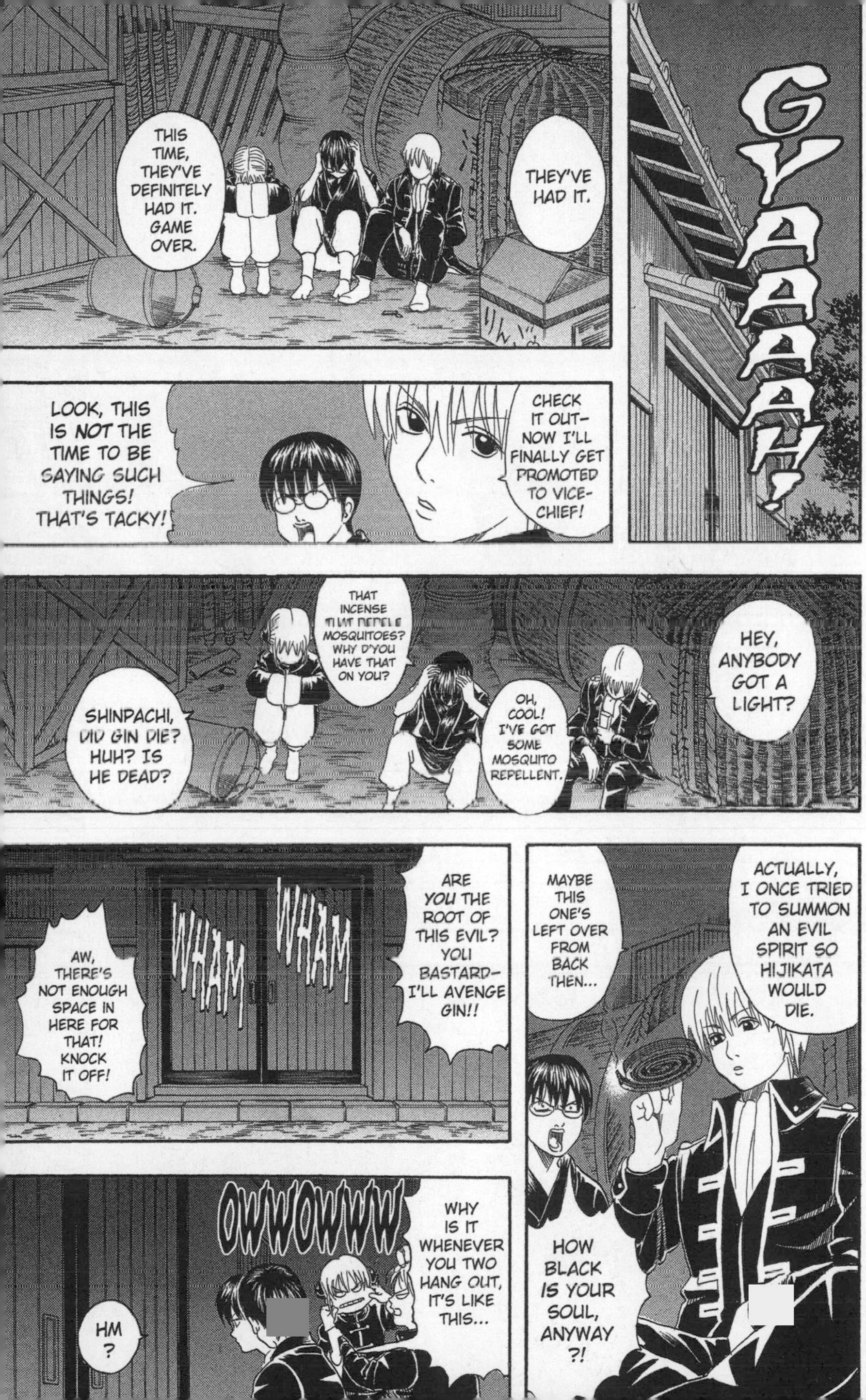
GYAAAAAH!
THEY'VE HAD IT.
THIS TIME, THEY'VE DEFINITELY HAD IT. GAME OVER.
CHECK IT OUT— NOW I'LL FINALLY GET PROMOTED TO VICE-CHIEF!
LOOK, THIS IS NOT THE TIME TO BE SAYING SUCH THINGS! THAT'S TACKY!
HEY, ANYBODY GOT A LIGHT?
OH, COOL! I'VE GOT SOME MOSQUITO REPELLENT.
THAT INCENSE THAT REPELS MOSQUITOES? WHY D'YOU HAVE THAT ON YOU?
SHINPACHI, DID GIN DIE? HUH? IS HE DEAD?
ACTUALLY, I ONCE TRIED TO SUMMON AN EVIL SPIRIT SO HIJIKATA WOULD DIE.
MAYBE THIS ONE'S LEFT OVER FROM BACK THEN...
HOW BLACK IS YOUR SOUL, ANYWAY?!
WHAM
WHAM
ARE YOU THE ROOT OF THIS EVIL? YOU BASTARD— I'LL AVENGE GIN!!
AW, THERE'S NOT ENOUGH SPACE IN HERE FOR THAT! KNOCK IT OFF!
OWWOWWW
WHY IS IT WHENEVER YOU TWO HANG OUT, IT'S LIKE THIS...
HM?

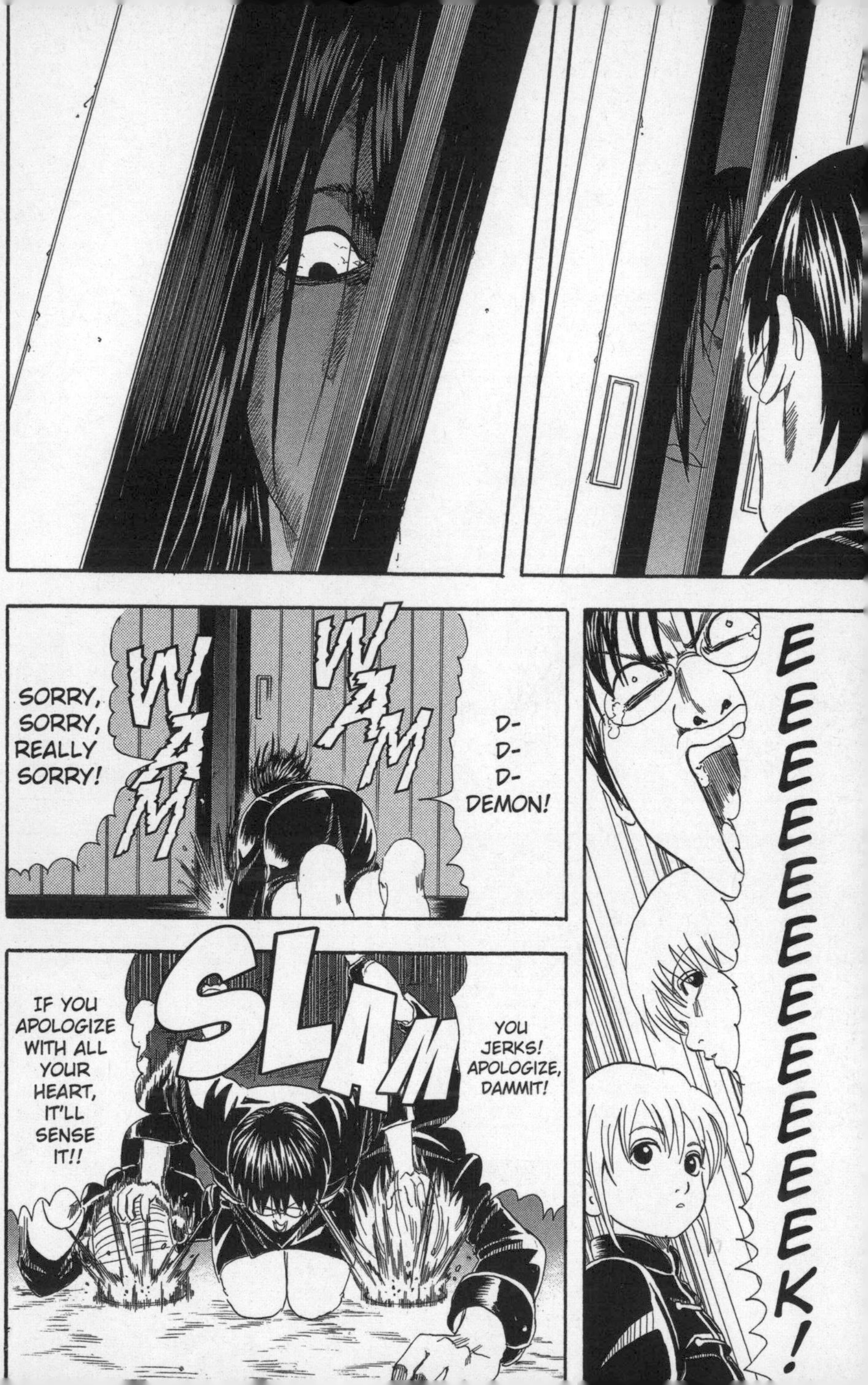
EEEEEEEEEEEEEEK!
D-
D-
D-
DEMON!
WAM
WAM
SORRY, SORRY, REALLY SORRY!
YOU JERKS! APOLOGIZE, DAMMIT!
SLAM
IF YOU APOLOGIZE WITH ALL YOUR HEART, IT'LL SENSE IT!!

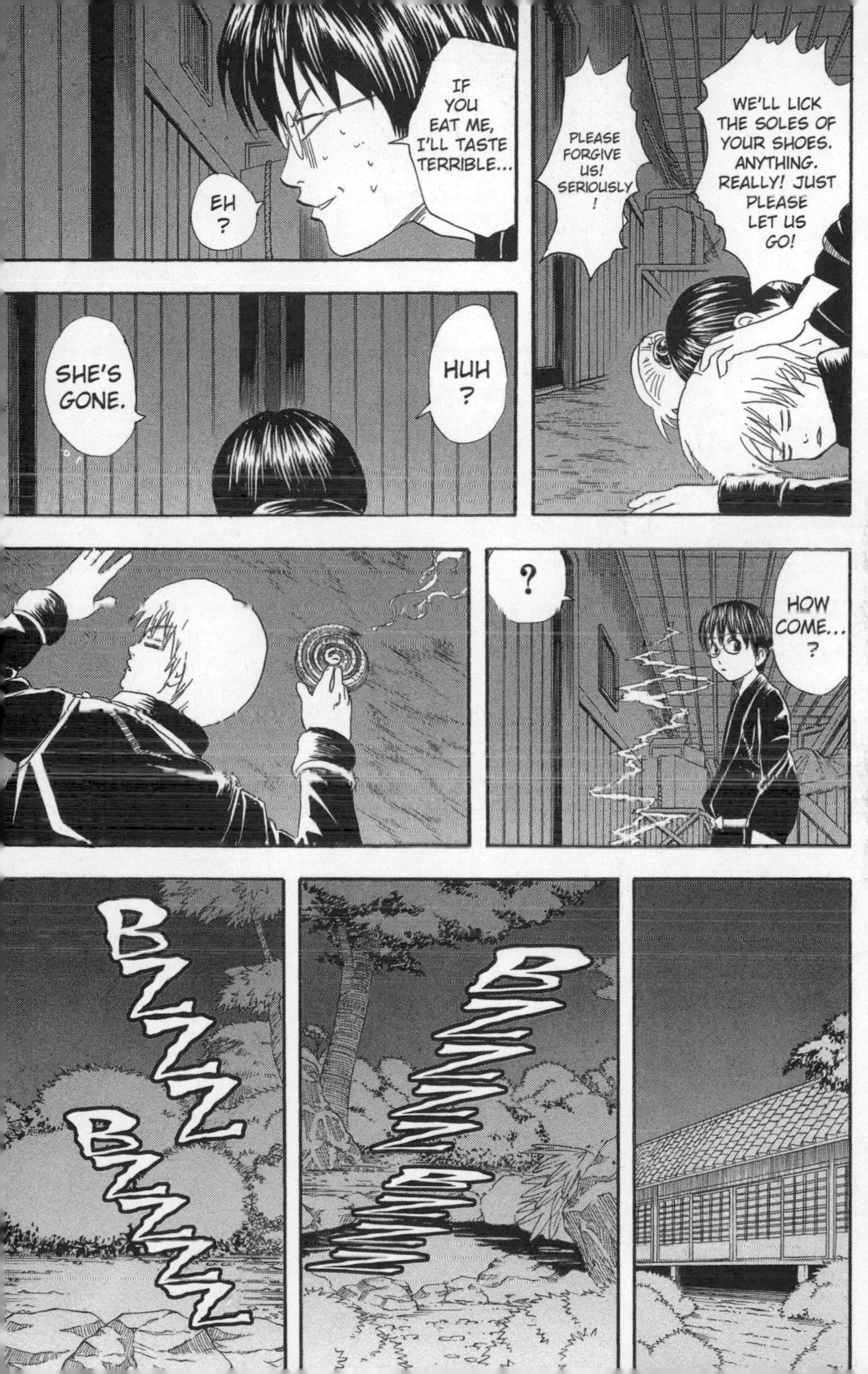
WE'LL LICK THE SOLES OF YOUR SHOES. ANYTHING. REALLY! JUST PLEASE LET US GO!
PLEASE FORGIVE US! SERIOUSLY!
IF YOU EAT ME, I'LL TASTE TERRIBLE...
EH?
HUH?
SHE'S GONE.
HOW COME...?
?
BZZZZZ
BZZZZZ
BZZZZ
BZZZZZ

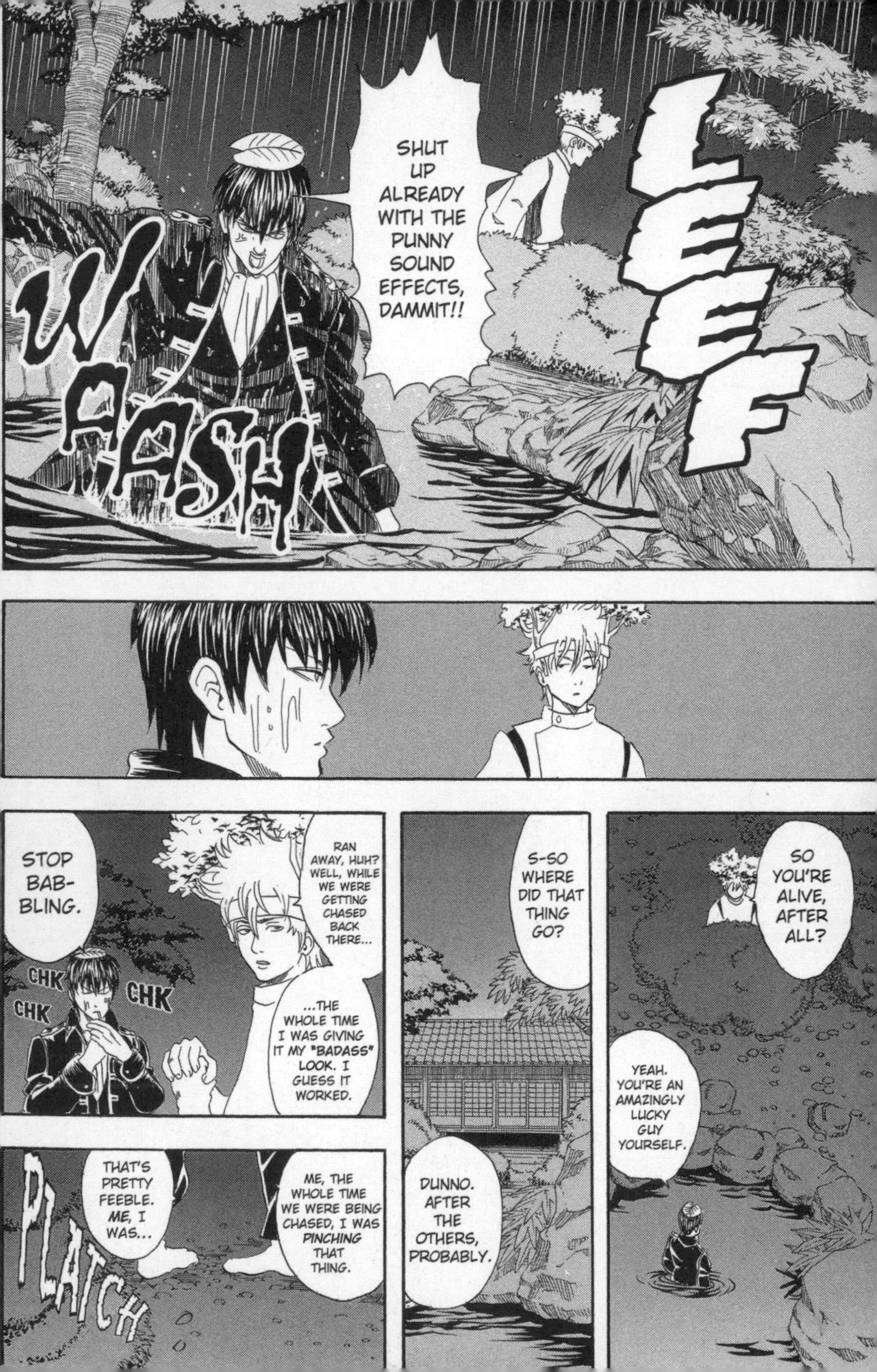
LEEEF
SHUT UP ALREADY WITH THE PUNNY SOUND EFFECTS, DAMMIT!!
WAASH
SO YOU'RE ALIVE, AFTER ALL?
YEAH. YOU'RE AN AMAZINGLY LUCKY GUY YOURSELF.
S-SO WHERE DID THAT THING GO?
DUNNO. AFTER THE OTHERS, PROBABLY.
RAN AWAY, HUH? WELL, WHILE WE WERE GETTING CHASED BACK THERE...
...THE WHOLE TIME I WAS GIVING IT MY "BADASS" LOOK. I GUESS IT WORKED.
STOP BAB-BLING.
CHK
CHK
CHK
ME, THE WHOLE TIME WE WERE BEING CHASED, I WAS PINCHING THAT THING.
THAT'S PRETTY FEEBLE. ME, I WAS...
PLATCH

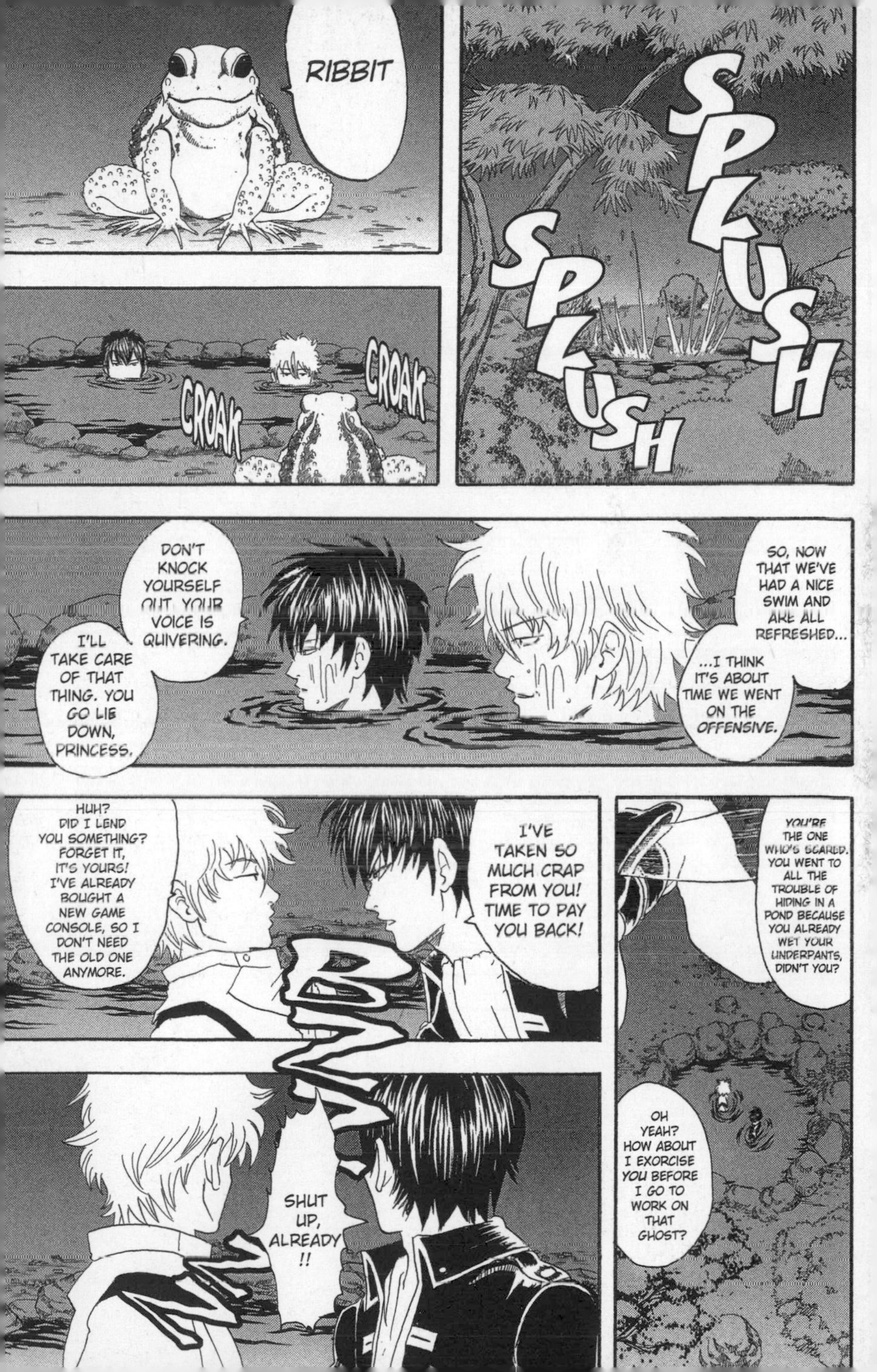
SPLUSH
SPLUSH
RIBBIT
CROAK
CROAK
SO, NOW THAT WE'VE HAD A NICE SWIM AND ARE ALL REFRESHED...
...I THINK IT'S ABOUT TIME WE WENT ON THE OFFENSIVE.
DON'T KNOCK YOURSELF OUT. YOUR VOICE IS QUIVERING.
I'LL TAKE CARE OF THAT THING. YOU GO LIE DOWN, PRINCESS.
YOU'RE THE ONE WHO'S SCARED. YOU WENT TO ALL THE TROUBLE OF HIDING IN A POND BECAUSE YOU ALREADY WET YOUR UNDERPANTS, DIDN'T YOU?
OH YEAH? HOW ABOUT I EXORCISE YOU BEFORE I GO TO WORK ON THAT GHOST?
I'VE TAKEN SO MUCH CRAP FROM YOU! TIME TO PAY YOU BACK!
HUH? DID I LEND YOU SOMETHING? FORGET IT, IT'S YOURS! I'VE ALREADY BOUGHT A NEW GAME CONSOLE, SO I DON'T NEED THE OLD ONE ANYMORE.
SHUT UP, ALREADY!!

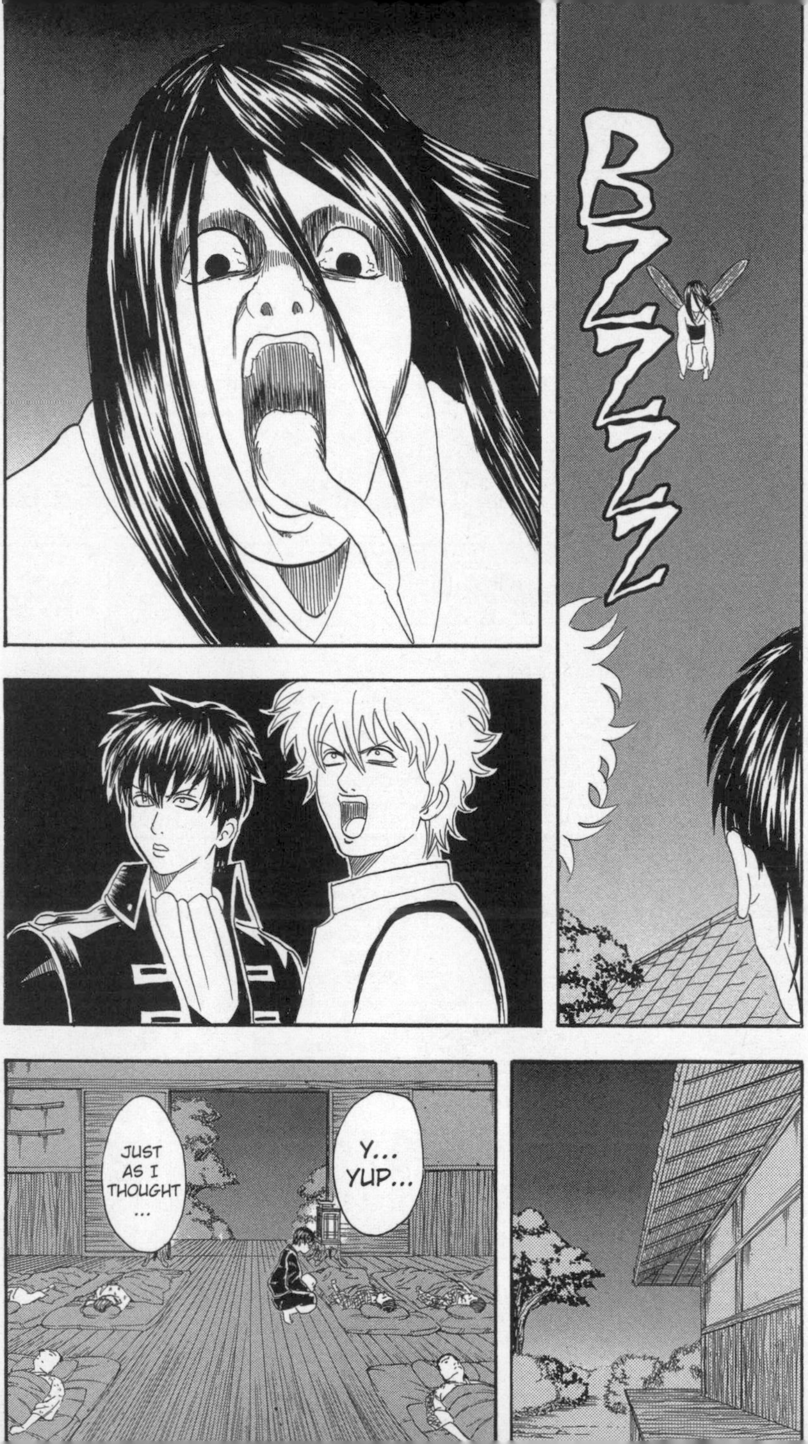
BZZZZ
Y... YUP...
JUST AS I THOUGHT ...

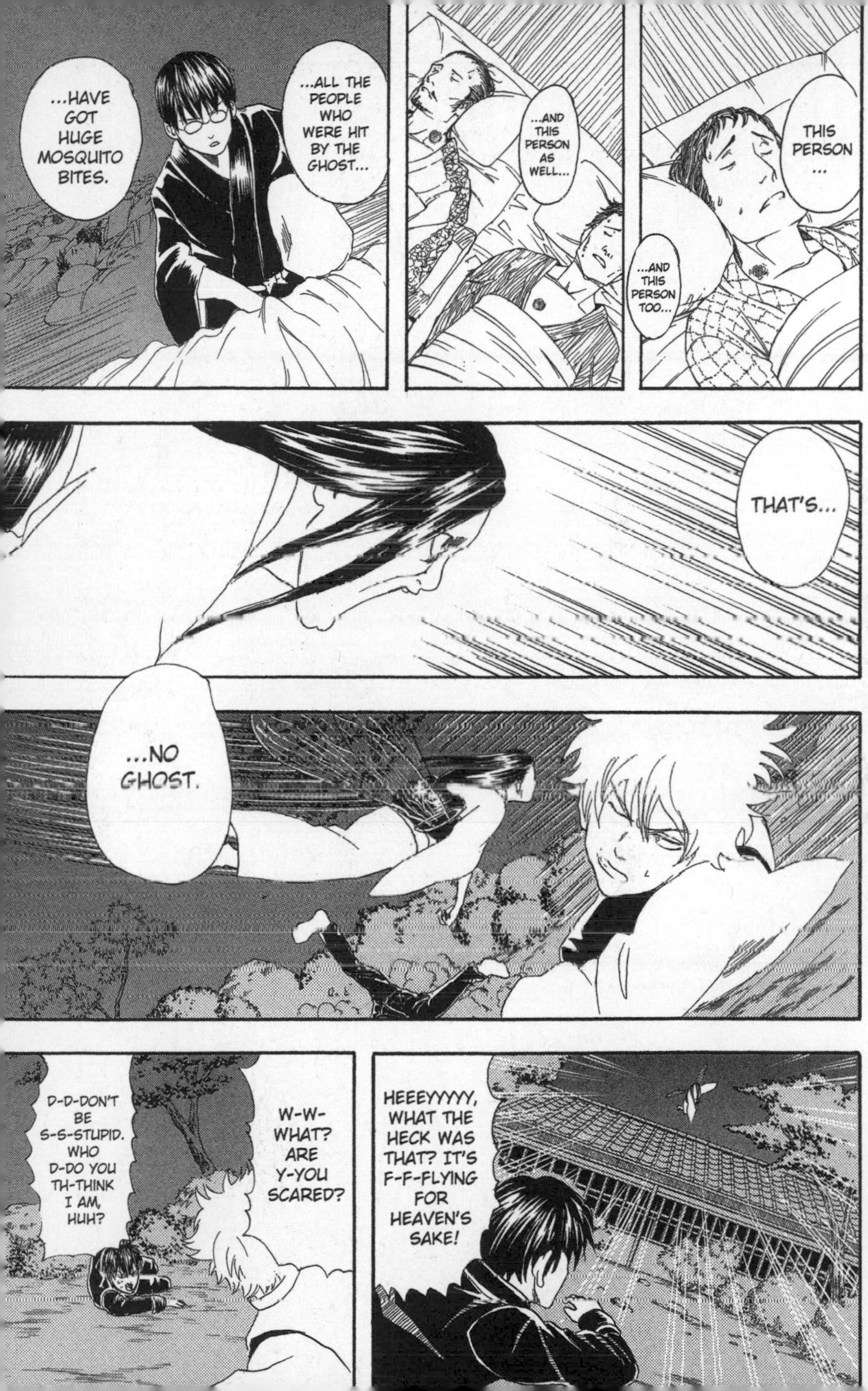
THIS PERSON ...
...AND THIS PERSON TOO...
...AND THIS PERSON AS WELL...
...ALL THE PEOPLE WHO WERE HIT BY THE GHOST...
...HAVE GOT HUGE MOSQUITO BITES.
THAT'S...
...NO GHOST.
HEEEYYYYY, WHAT THE HECK WAS THAT? IT'S F-F-FLYING FOR HEAVEN'S SAKE!
W-W-WHAT? ARE Y-YOU SCARED?
D-D-DON'T BE S-S-STUPID. WHO D-DO YOU TH-THINK I AM, HUH?

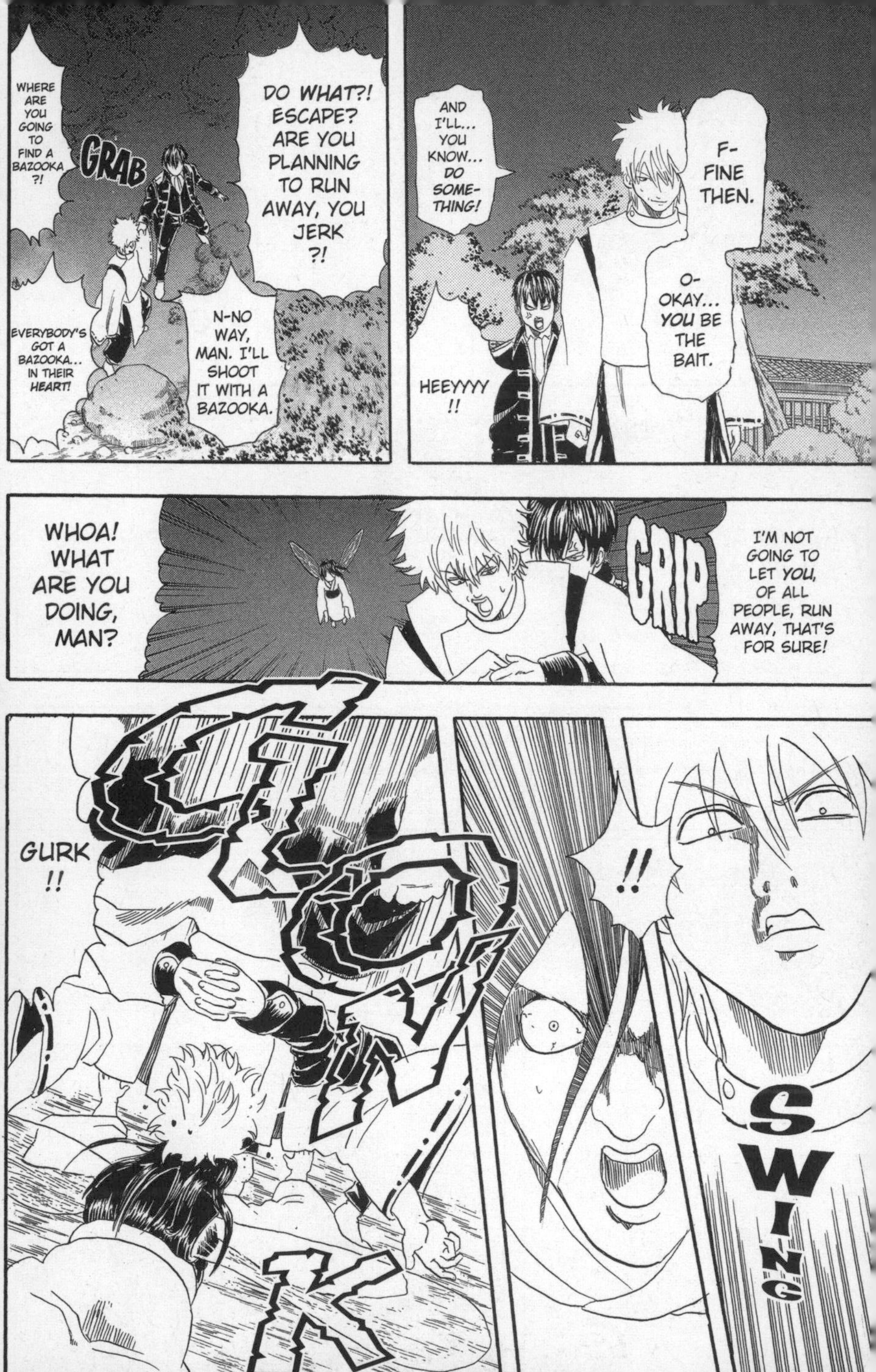
F-FINE THEN.
AND I'LL... YOU KNOW... DO SOMETHING!
O-OKAY... YOU BE THE BAIT.
HEEYYYY!!
DO WHAT?! ESCAPE? ARE YOU PLANNING TO RUN AWAY, YOU JERK?!
WHERE ARE YOU GOING TO FIND A BAZOOKA?!
GRAB
N-NO WAY, MAN. I'LL SHOOT IT WITH A BAZOOKA.
EVERYBODY'S GOT A BAZOOKA... IN THEIR HEART!
I'M NOT GOING TO LET YOU, OF ALL PEOPLE, RUN AWAY, THAT'S FOR SURE!
GRIP
WHOA! WHAT ARE YOU DOING, MAN?
SWING
!!
GURK!!

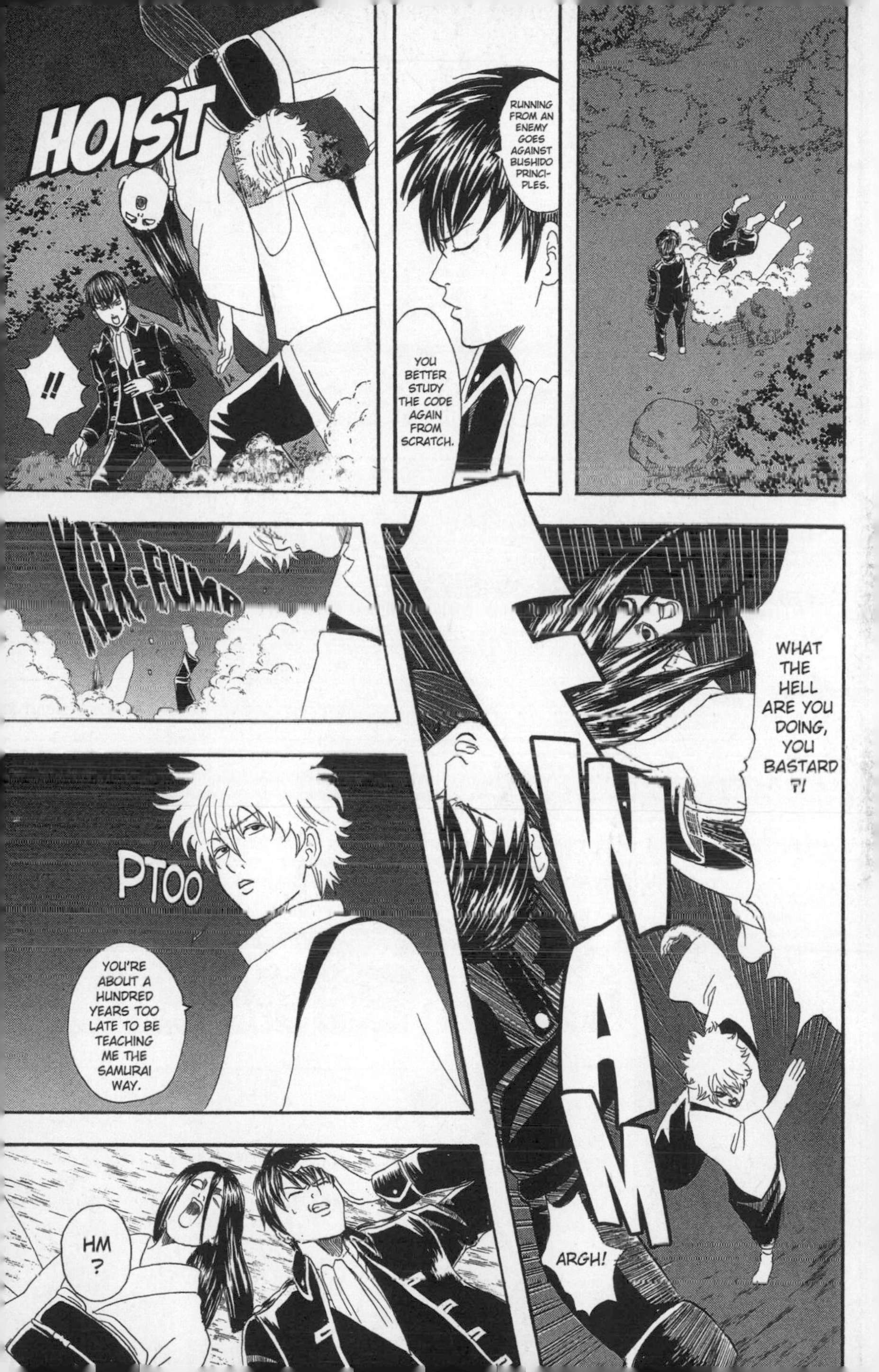
RUNNING FROM AN ENEMY GOES AGAINST BUSHIDO PRINCI-PLES.
YOU BETTER STUDY THE CODE AGAIN FROM SCRATCH.
HOIST
!!
WHAT THE HELL ARE YOU DOING, YOU BASTARD ?!
WHAM
ARGH!
KER-FUMP
PTOO
YOU'RE ABOUT A HUNDRED YEARS TOO LATE TO BE TEACHING ME THE SAMURAI WAY.
HM ?

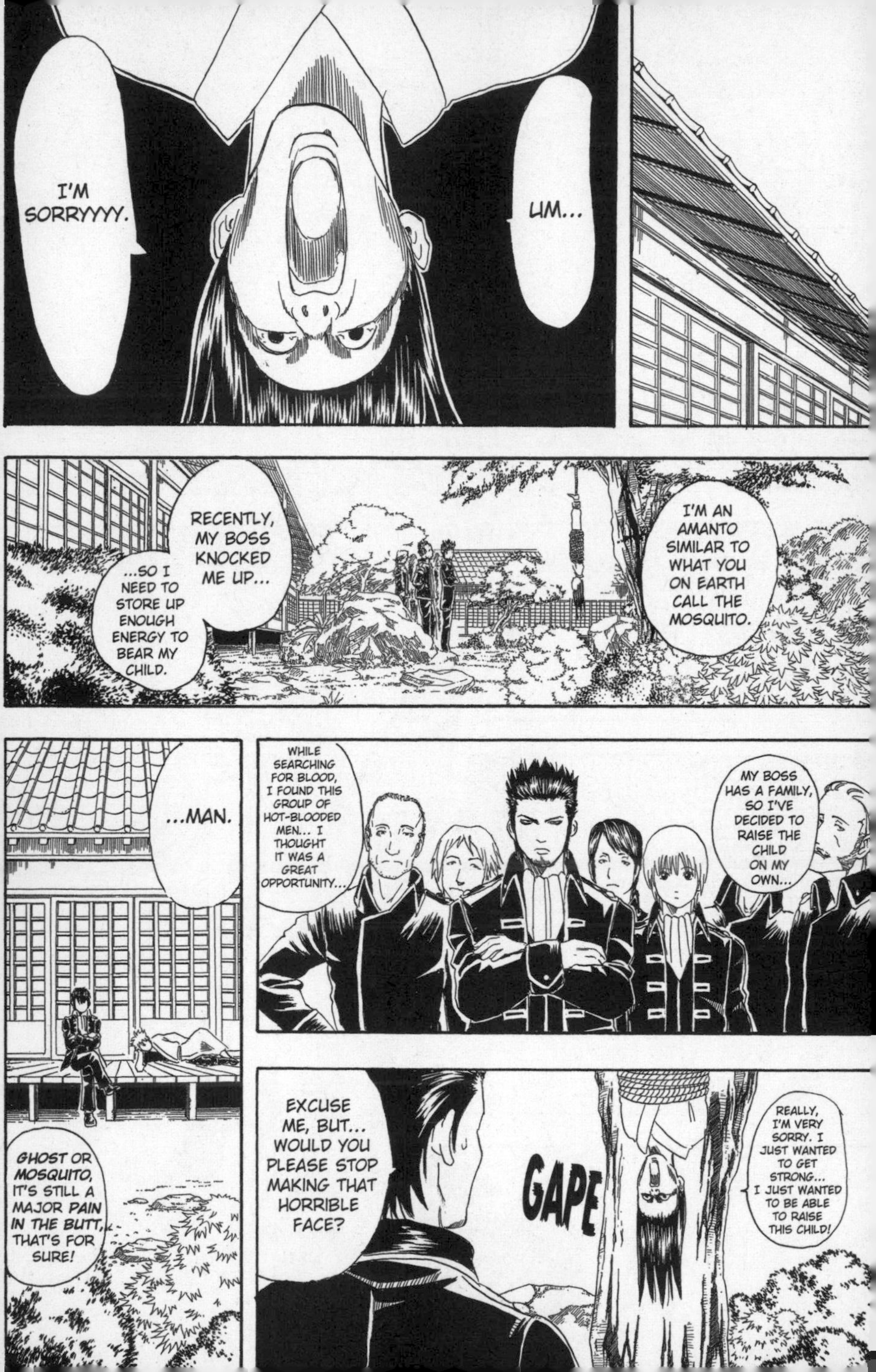
UM...
I'M SORRYYYY.
I'M AN AMANTO SIMILAR TO WHAT YOU ON EARTH CALL THE MOSQUITO.
RECENTLY, MY BOSS KNOCKED ME UP...
...SO I NEED TO STORE UP ENOUGH ENERGY TO BEAR MY CHILD.
MY BOSS HAS A FAMILY, SO I'VE DECIDED TO RAISE THE CHILD ON MY OWN...
WHILE SEARCHING FOR BLOOD, I FOUND THIS GROUP OF HOT-BLOODED MEN... I THOUGHT IT WAS A GREAT OPPORTUNITY...
REALLY, I'M VERY SORRY. I JUST WANTED TO GET STRONG... I JUST WANTED TO BE ABLE TO RAISE THIS CHILD!
GAPE
EXCUSE ME, BUT... WOULD YOU PLEASE STOP MAKING THAT HORRIBLE FACE?
...MAN.
GHOST OR MOSQUITO, IT'S STILL A MAJOR PAIN IN THE BUTT, THAT'S FOR SURE!

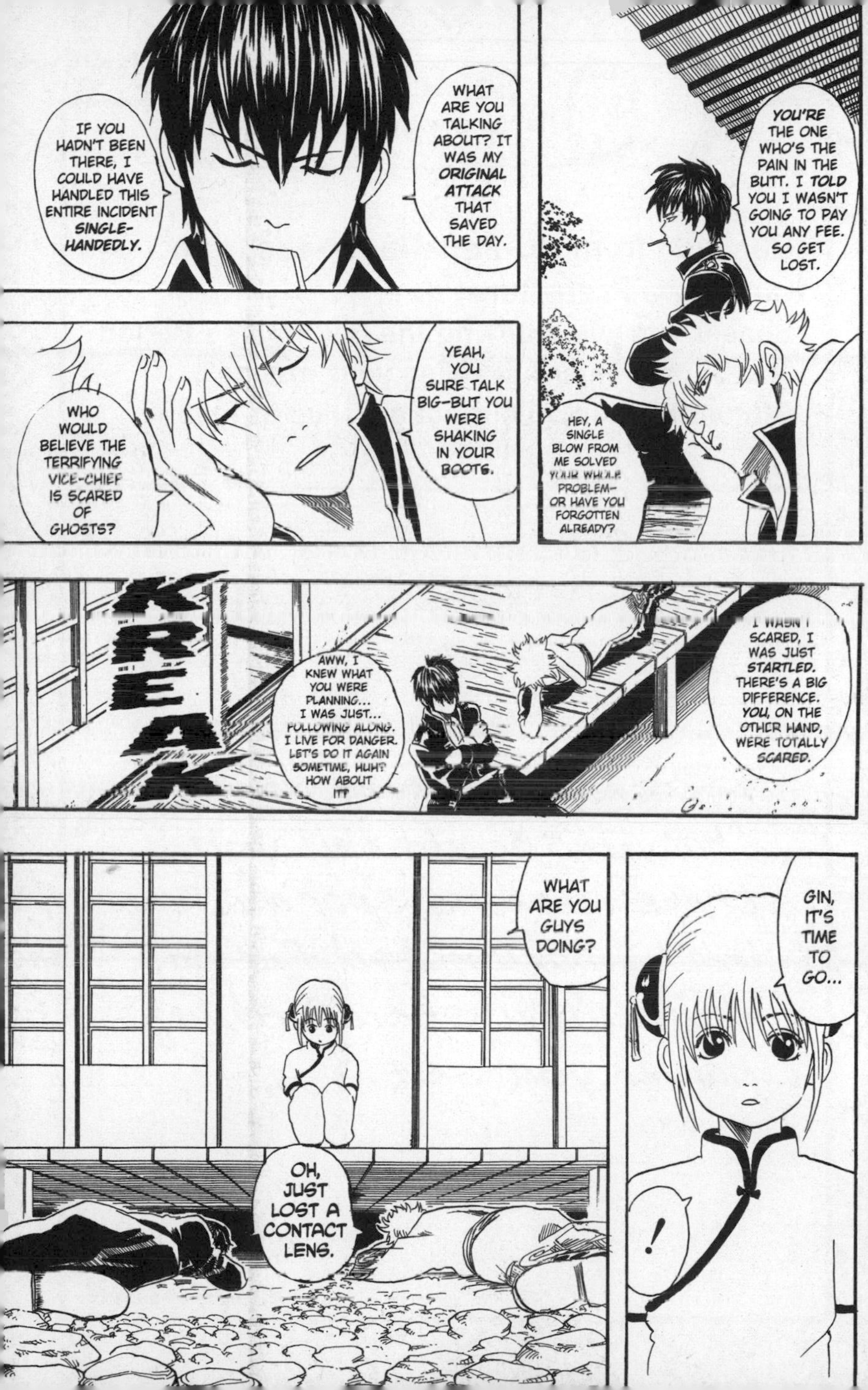
YOU'RE THE ONE WHO'S THE PAIN IN THE BUTT. I TOLD YOU I WASN'T GOING TO PAY YOU ANY FEE. SO GET LOST.
HEY, A SINGLE BLOW FROM ME SOLVED YOUR WHOLE PROBLEM— OR HAVE YOU FORGOTTEN ALREADY?
WHAT ARE YOU TALKING ABOUT? IT WAS MY ORIGINAL ATTACK THAT SAVED THE DAY.
IF YOU HADN'T BEEN THERE, I COULD HAVE HANDLED THIS ENTIRE INCIDENT SINGLE-HANDEDLY.
YEAH, YOU SURE TALK BIG—BUT YOU WERE SHAKING IN YOUR BOOTS.
WHO WOULD BELIEVE THE TERRIFYING VICE-CHIEF IS SCARED OF GHOSTS?
I WASN'T SCARED, I WAS JUST STARTLED. THERE'S A BIG DIFFERENCE. YOU, ON THE OTHER HAND, WERE TOTALLY SCARED.
AWW, I KNEW WHAT YOU WERE PLANNING... I WAS JUST... FOLLOWING ALONG. I LIVE FOR DANGER. LET'S DO IT AGAIN SOMETIME, HUH? HOW ABOUT IT?
KREAK
GIN, IT'S TIME TO GO...
!
WHAT ARE YOU GUYS DOING?
OH, JUST LOST A CONTACT LENS.

Sorachi's Q&A
Hanging with the Readers #7

(Question from No-Pen-Name-san from Kanagawa Prefecture)
Sensei, are you studying the Bakumatsu Period thoroughly before drawing your manga?
Munemitsu Mutsu did not grow up in Tosa.

(Answer:)

Before you worry about that, I should tell you there were no space aliens in the Bakumatsu Period, either. You should study harder yourself.

(Q&A #8 is on page 86)

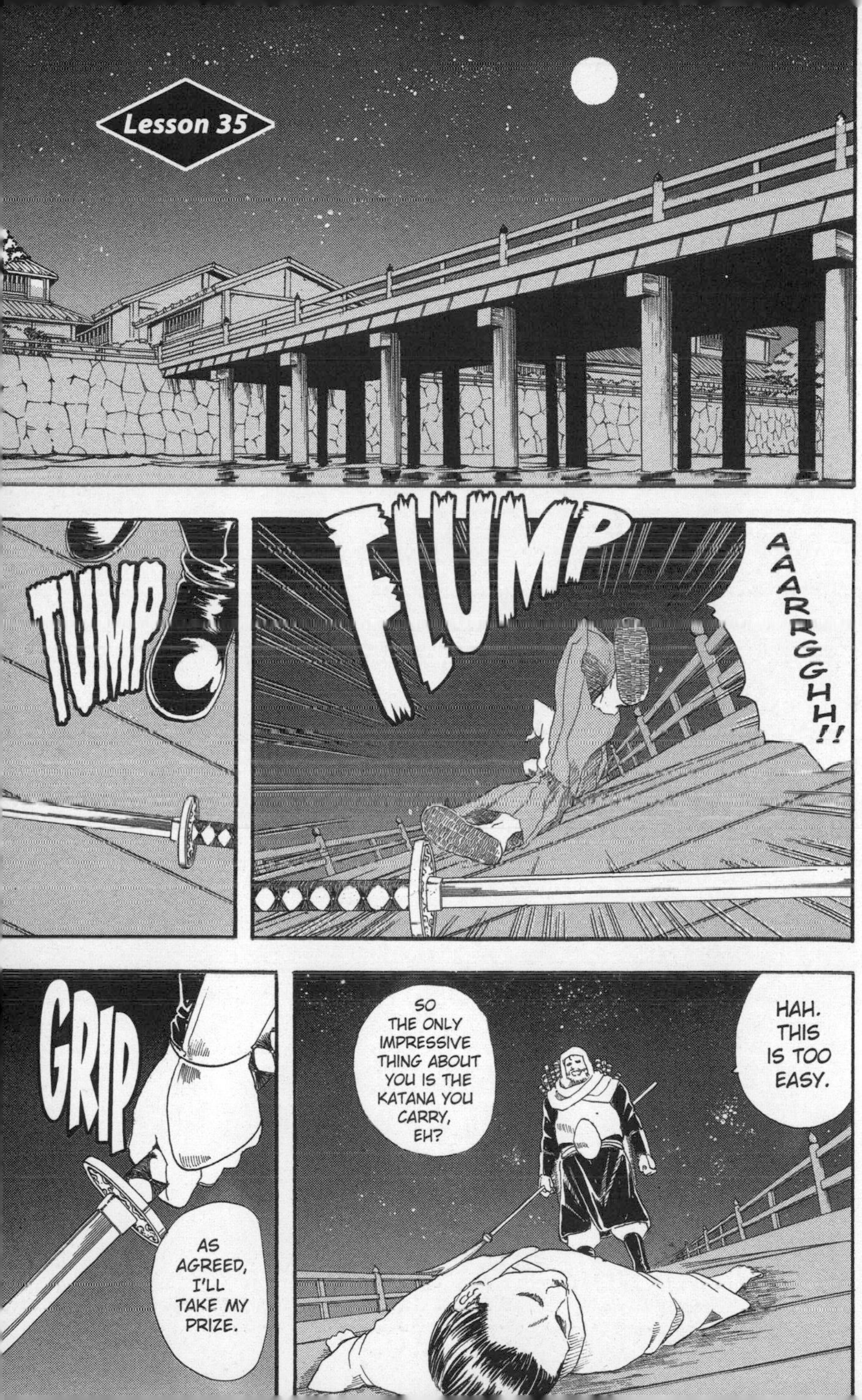
Lesson 35
AAARRGGHH!!
FLUMP
TUMP
HAH. THIS IS TOO EASY.
SO THE ONLY IMPRESSIVE THING ABOUT YOU IS THE KATANA YOU CARRY, EH?
GRIP
AS AGREED, I'LL TAKE MY PRIZE.

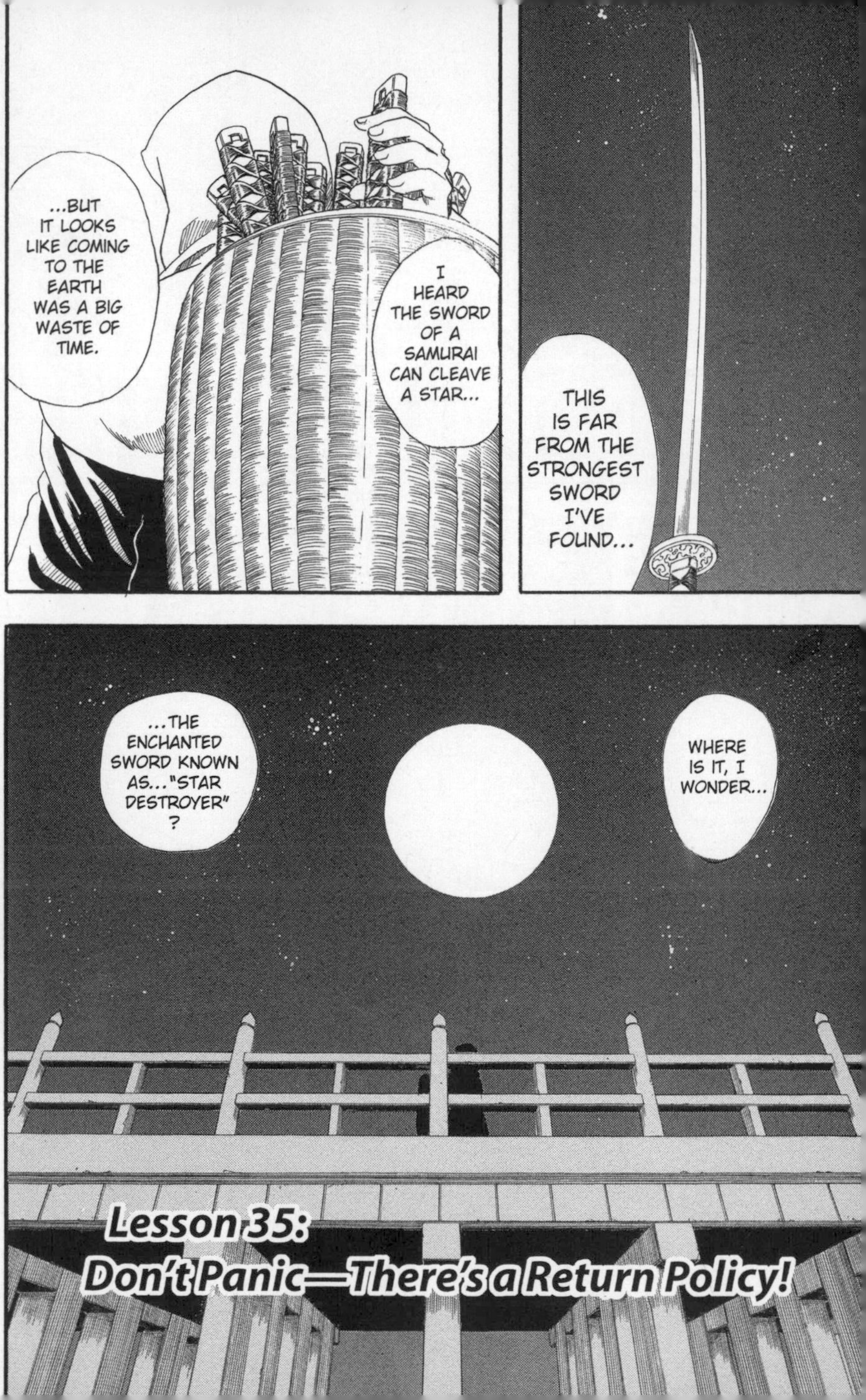
THIS IS FAR FROM THE STRONGEST SWORD I'VE FOUND...
I HEARD THE SWORD OF A SAMURAI CAN CLEAVE A STAR...
...BUT IT LOOKS LIKE COMING TO THE EARTH WAS A BIG WASTE OF TIME.
WHERE IS IT, I WONDER...
...THE ENCHANTED SWORD KNOWN AS..."STAR DESTROYER" ?

Lesson 35: Don't Panic—There's a Return Policy!

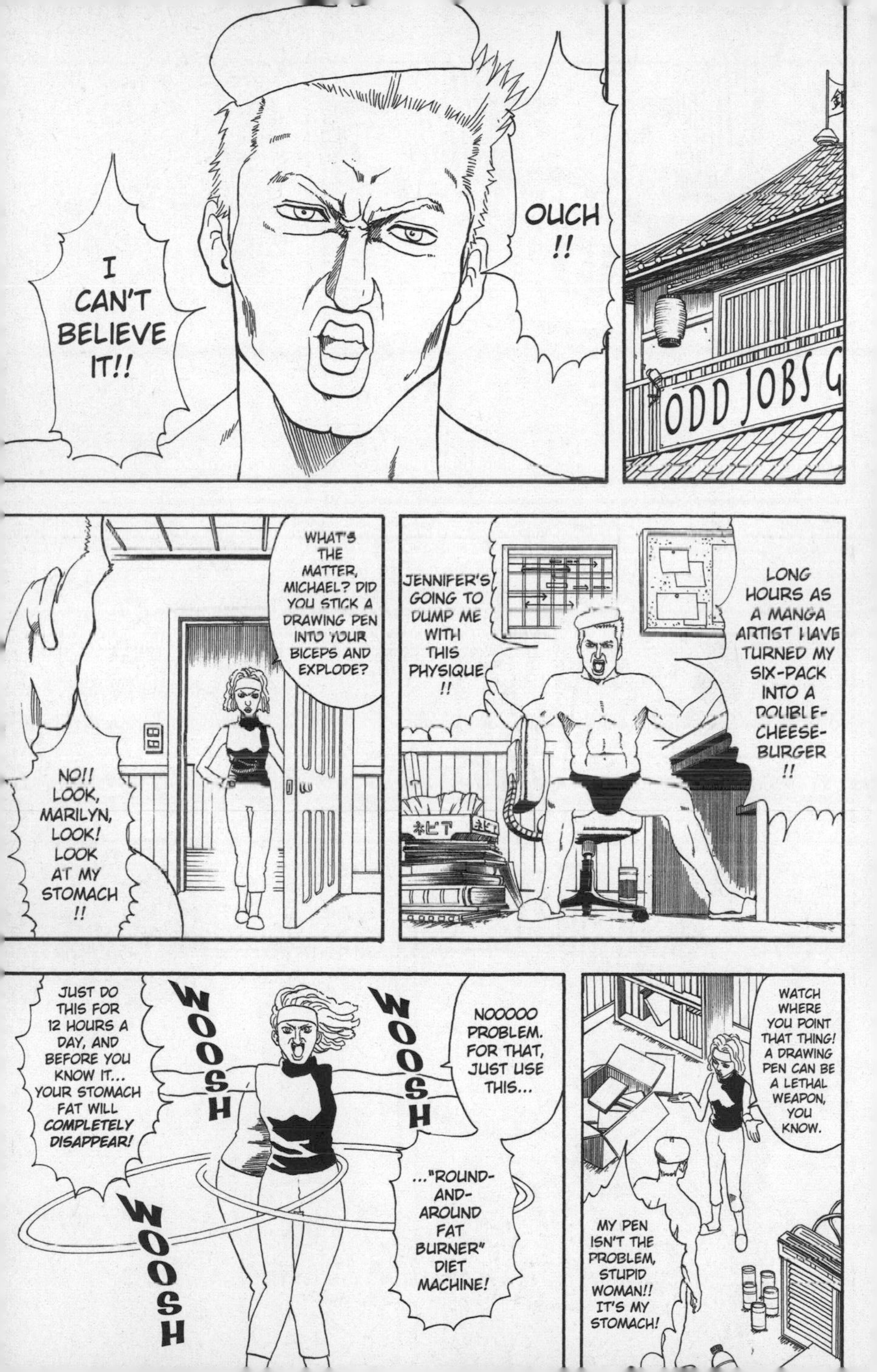
ODD JOBS G
OUCH!!
I CAN'T BELIEVE IT!!
LONG HOURS AS A MANGA ARTIST HAVE TURNED MY SIX-PACK INTO A DOUBLE-CHEESE-BURGER!!
JENNIFER'S GOING TO DUMP ME WITH THIS PHYSIQUE!!
WHAT'S THE MATTER, MICHAEL? DID YOU STICK A DRAWING PEN INTO YOUR BICEPS AND EXPLODE?
NO!! LOOK, MARILYN, LOOK! LOOK AT MY STOMACH!!
WATCH WHERE YOU POINT THAT THING! A DRAWING PEN CAN BE A LETHAL WEAPON, YOU KNOW.
MY PEN ISN'T THE PROBLEM, STUPID WOMAN!! IT'S MY STOMACH!
WOOSH
NOOOOO PROBLEM. FOR THAT, JUST USE THIS...
..."ROUND-AND-AROUND FAT BURNER" DIET MACHINE!
WOOSH
JUST DO THIS FOR 12 HOURS A DAY, AND BEFORE YOU KNOW IT... YOUR STOMACH FAT WILL COMPLETELY DISAPPEAR!
WOOSH

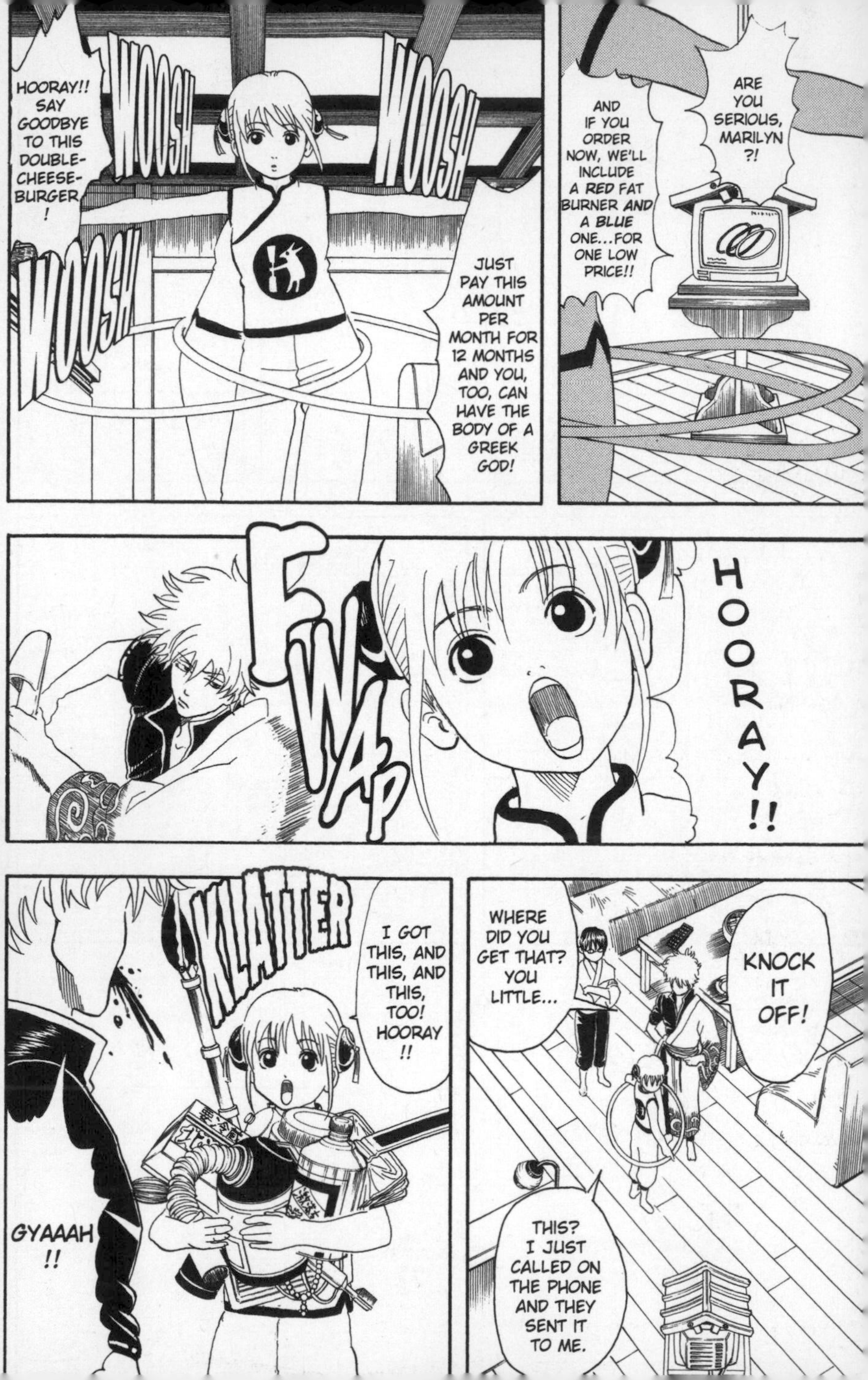
ARE YOU SERIOUS, MARILYN?!
AND IF YOU ORDER NOW, WE'LL INCLUDE A RED FAT BURNER AND A BLUE ONE...FOR ONE LOW PRICE!!
WOOSH
JUST PAY THIS AMOUNT PER MONTH FOR 12 MONTHS AND YOU, TOO, CAN HAVE THE BODY OF A GREEK GOD!
WOOSH
HOORAY!! SAY GOODBYE TO THIS DOUBLE-CHEESE-BURGER!
WOOSH
HOORAY!!
FWAP
KNOCK IT OFF!
WHERE DID YOU GET THAT? YOU LITTLE...
THIS? I JUST CALLED ON THE PHONE AND THEY SENT IT TO ME.
I GOT THIS, AND THIS, AND THIS, TOO! HOORAY!!
KLATTER
GYAAAH!!

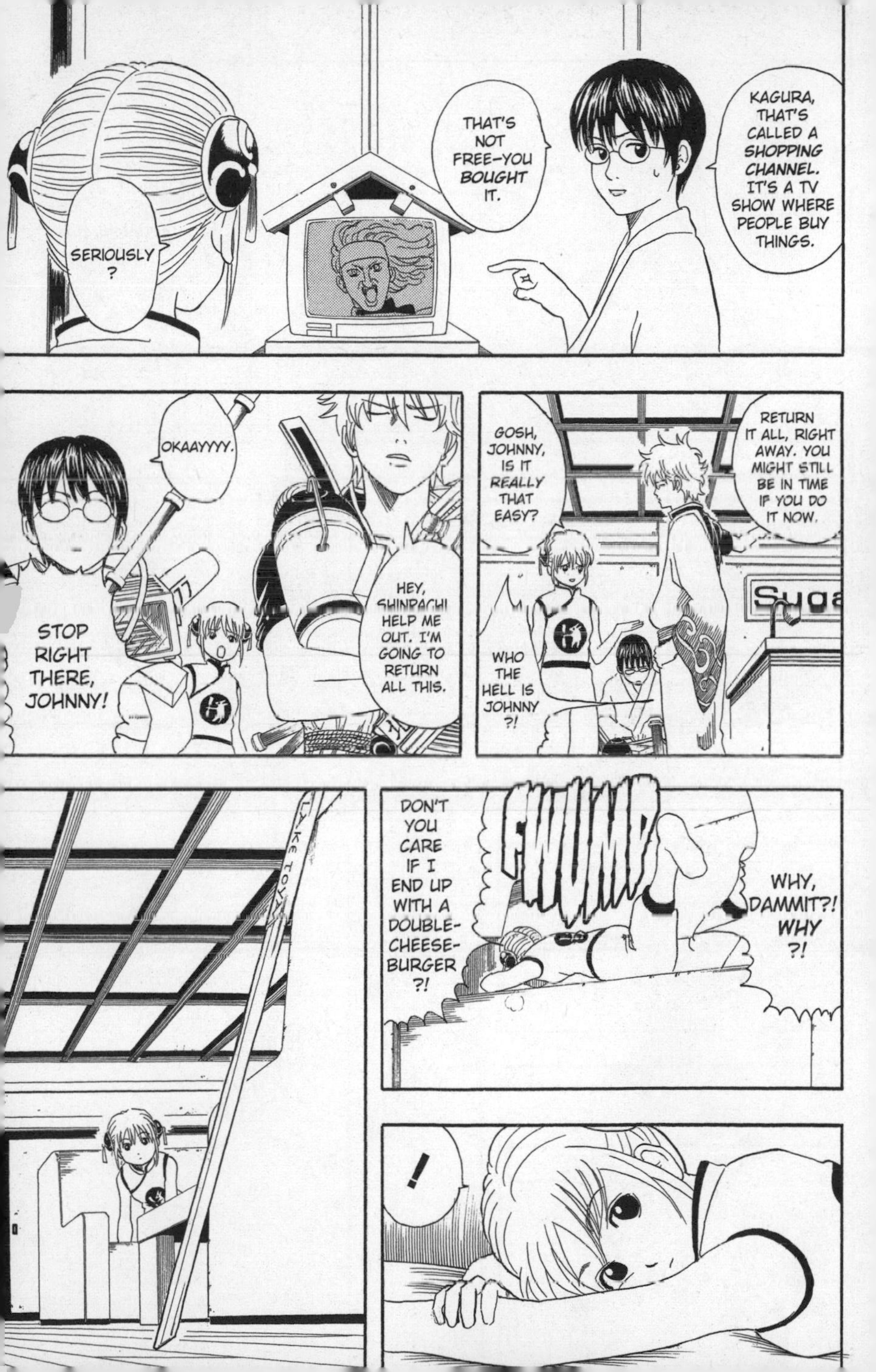
KAGURA, THAT'S CALLED A SHOPPING CHANNEL. IT'S A TV SHOW WHERE PEOPLE BUY THINGS.
THAT'S NOT FREE—YOU BOUGHT IT.
SERIOUSLY?
RETURN IT ALL, RIGHT AWAY. YOU MIGHT STILL BE IN TIME IF YOU DO IT NOW.
GOSH, JOHNNY, IS IT REALLY THAT EASY?
WHO THE HELL IS JOHNNY?!
Suga
HEY, SHINPACHI HELP ME OUT. I'M GOING TO RETURN ALL THIS.
OKAAYYYY.
STOP RIGHT THERE, JOHNNY!
WHY, DAMMIT?! WHY?!
FWUMP
DON'T YOU CARE IF I END UP WITH A DOUBLE-CHEESEBURGER?!
!
LAKE TOYA

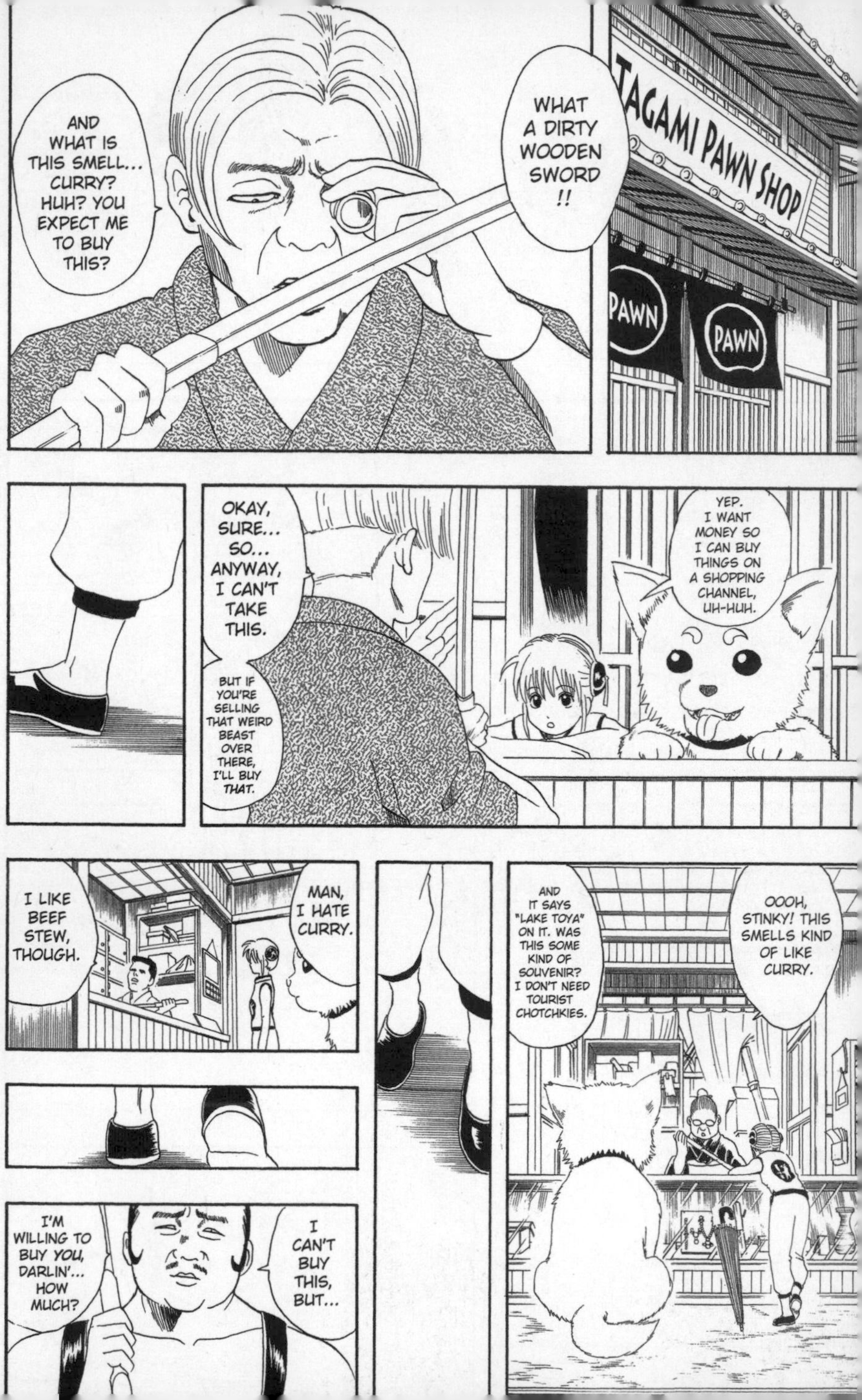
TAGAMI PAWN SHOP
PAWN
PAWN
WHAT A DIRTY WOODEN SWORD !!
AND WHAT IS THIS SMELL... CURRY? HUH? YOU EXPECT ME TO BUY THIS?
YEP. I WANT MONEY SO I CAN BUY THINGS ON A SHOPPING CHANNEL, UH-HUH.
OKAY, SURE... SO... ANYWAY, I CAN'T TAKE THIS.
BUT IF YOU'RE SELLING THAT WEIRD BEAST OVER THERE, I'LL BUY *THAT*.
OOOH, STINKY! THIS SMELLS KIND OF LIKE CURRY.
AND IT SAYS "LAKE TOYA" ON IT. WAS THIS SOME KIND OF SOUVENIR? I DON'T NEED TOURIST CHOTCHKIES.
MAN, I HATE CURRY.
I LIKE BEEF STEW, THOUGH.
I CAN'T BUY THIS, BUT...
I'M WILLING TO BUY *YOU*, DARLIN'... HOW MUCH?

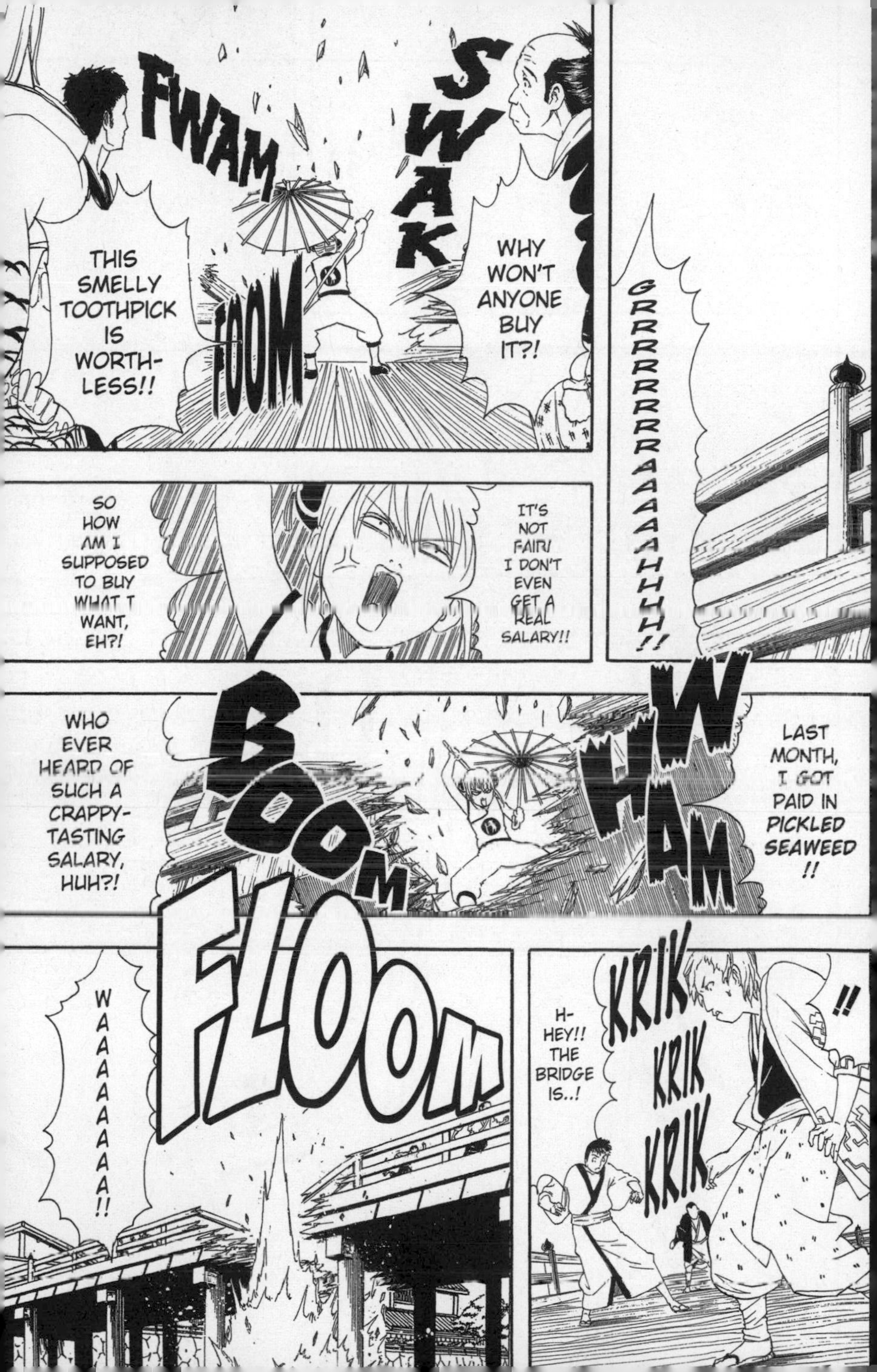
GRRRRRRRAAAAAHHHH!!
SWAK
WHY WON'T ANYONE BUY IT?!
FWAM
FOOM
THIS SMELLY TOOTHPICK IS WORTH-LESS!!
IT'S NOT FAIR! I DON'T EVEN GET A REAL SALARY!!
SO HOW AM I SUPPOSED TO BUY WHAT I WANT, EH?!
LAST MONTH, I GOT PAID IN PICKLED SEAWEED!!
WHAM
BOOM
WHO EVER HEARD OF SUCH A CRAPPY-TASTING SALARY, HUH?!
!!
KRIK KRIK KRIK
H-HEY!! THE BRIDGE IS..!
FLOOM
WAAAAAAAAAAAA!!

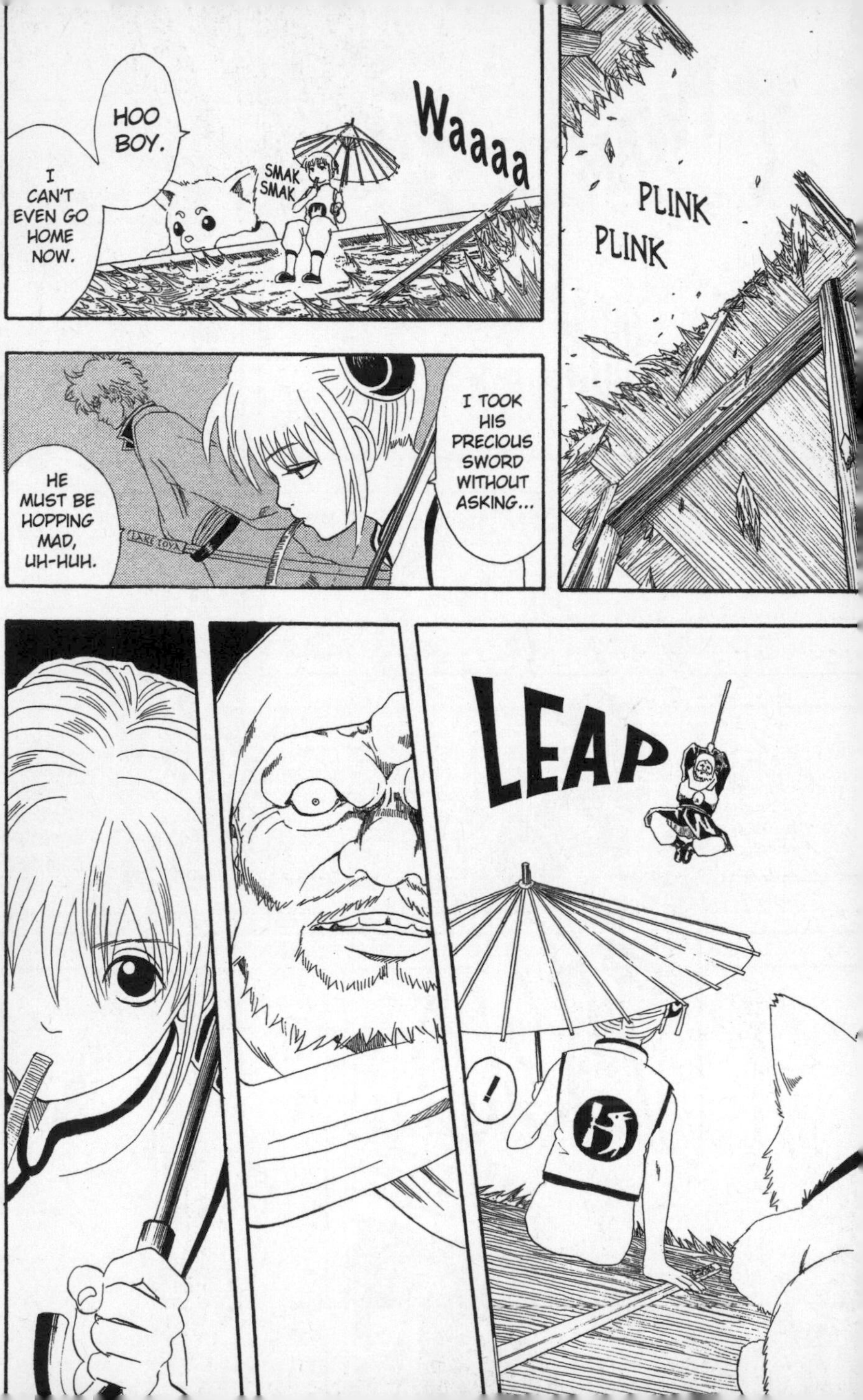
PLINK
PLINK
Waaaa
SMAK SMAK
HOO BOY.
I CAN'T EVEN GO HOME NOW.
I TOOK HIS PRECIOUS SWORD WITHOUT ASKING...
HE MUST BE HOPPING MAD, UH-HUH.
LAKE TOYA
LEAP
!

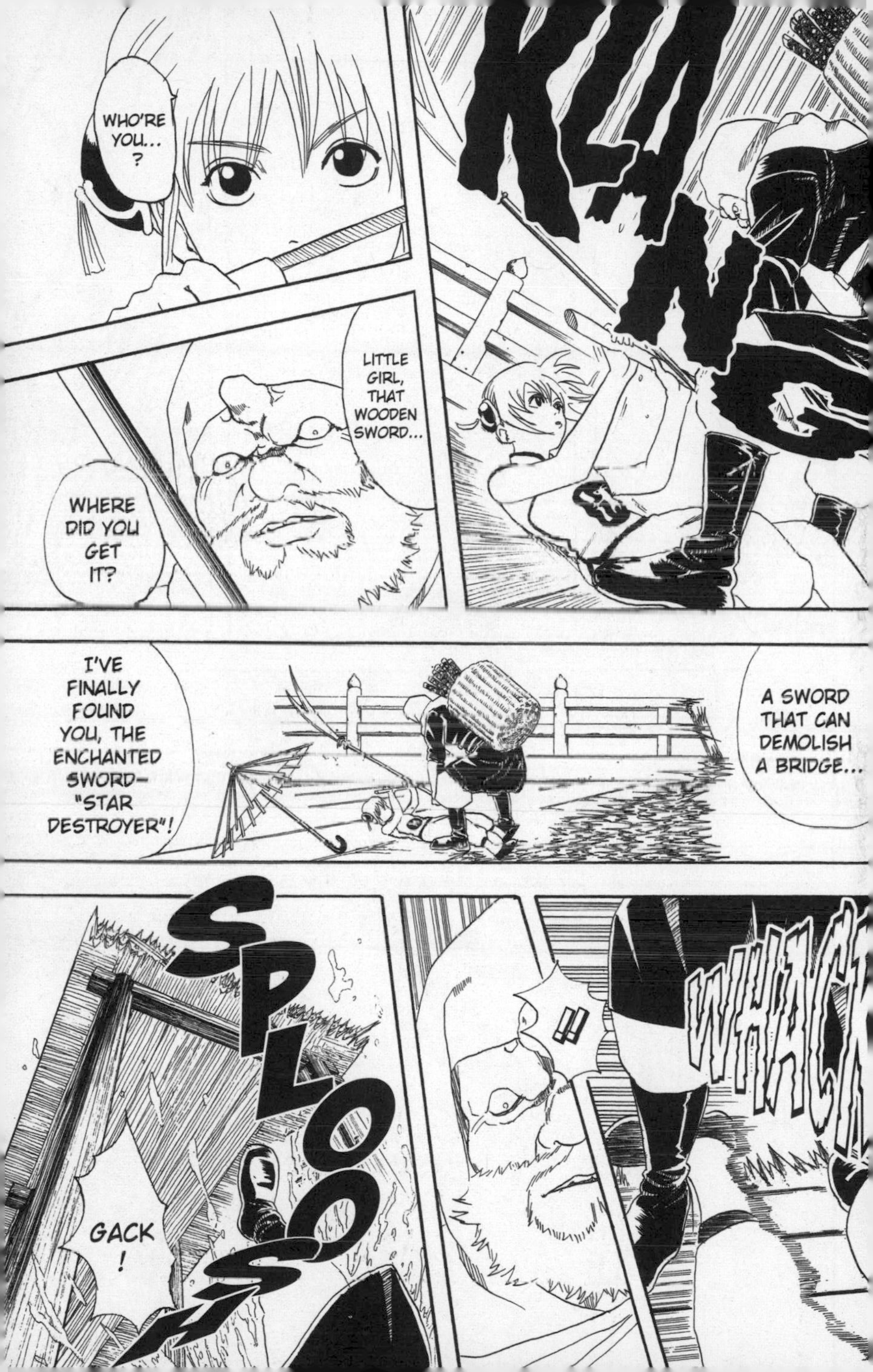
KANG
WHO'RE YOU...?
LITTLE GIRL, THAT WOODEN SWORD...
WHERE DID YOU GET IT?
A SWORD THAT CAN DEMOLISH A BRIDGE...
I'VE FINALLY FOUND YOU, THE ENCHANTED SWORD—"STAR DESTROYER"!
!!
WHACK
SPLOOSH
GACK!

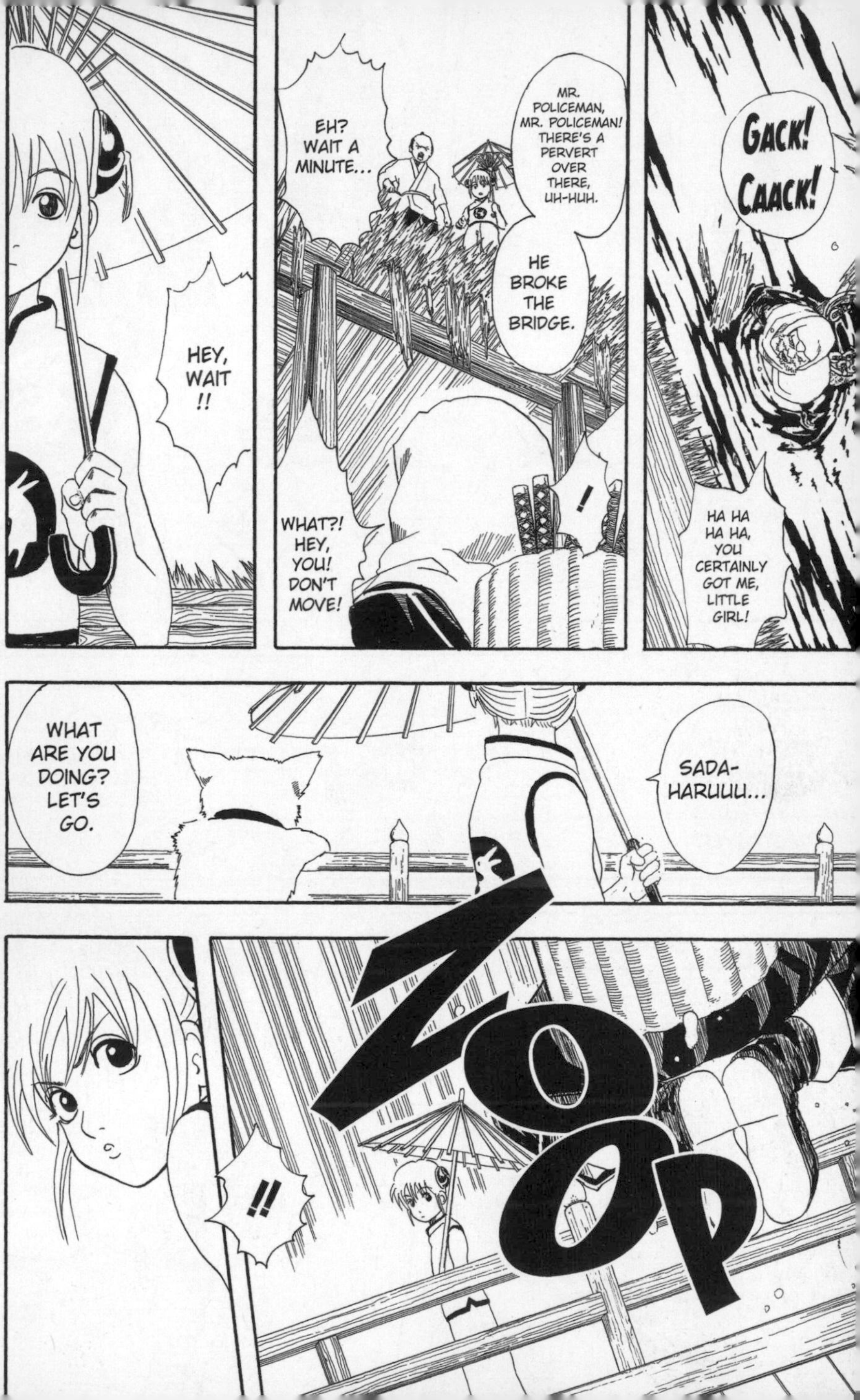
GACK! CAACK!
HA HA HA HA, YOU CERTAINLY GOT ME, LITTLE GIRL!
MR. POLICEMAN, MR. POLICEMAN! THERE'S A PERVERT OVER THERE, UH-HUH.
HE BROKE THE BRIDGE.
EH? WAIT A MINUTE...
!
WHAT?! HEY, YOU! DON'T MOVE!
HEY, WAIT !!
SADA-HARUUU...
WHAT ARE YOU DOING? LET'S GO.
ZOOP
!!

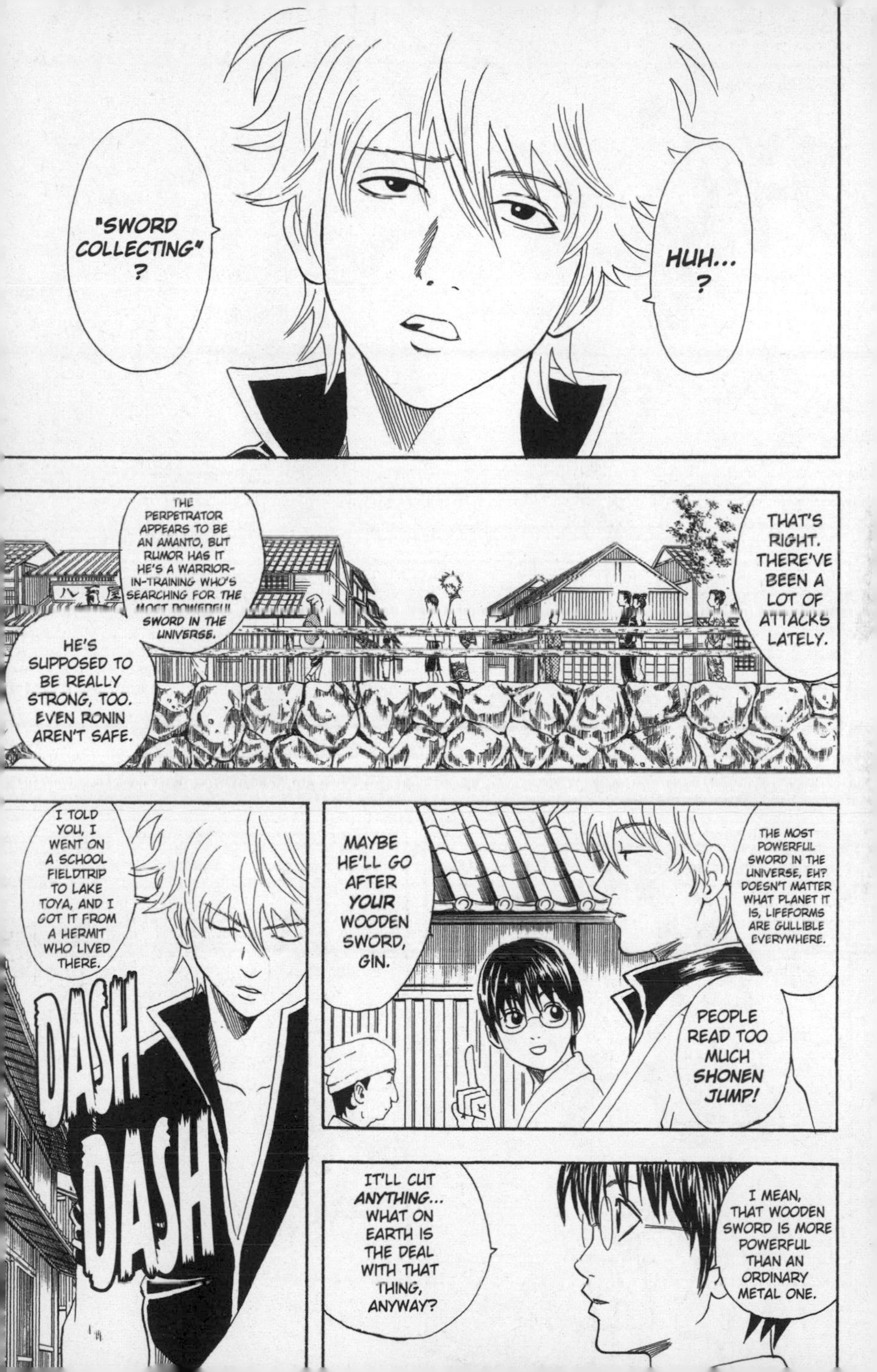
HUH... ?
"SWORD COLLECTING" ?
THAT'S RIGHT. THERE'VE BEEN A LOT OF ATTACKS LATELY.
THE PERPETRATOR APPEARS TO BE AN AMANTO, BUT RUMOR HAS IT HE'S A WARRIOR-IN-TRAINING WHO'S SEARCHING FOR THE MOST POWERFUL SWORD IN THE UNIVERSE.
HE'S SUPPOSED TO BE REALLY STRONG, TOO. EVEN RONIN AREN'T SAFE.
THE MOST POWERFUL SWORD IN THE UNIVERSE, EH? DOESN'T MATTER WHAT PLANET IT IS, LIFEFORMS ARE GULLIBLE EVERYWHERE.
PEOPLE READ TOO MUCH SHONEN JUMP!
MAYBE HE'LL GO AFTER YOUR WOODEN SWORD, GIN.
I MEAN, THAT WOODEN SWORD IS MORE POWERFUL THAN AN ORDINARY METAL ONE.
IT'LL CUT ANYTHING... WHAT ON EARTH IS THE DEAL WITH THAT THING, ANYWAY?
I TOLD YOU, I WENT ON A SCHOOL FIELDTRIP TO LAKE TOYA, AND I GOT IT FROM A HERMIT WHO LIVED THERE.
DASH
DASH

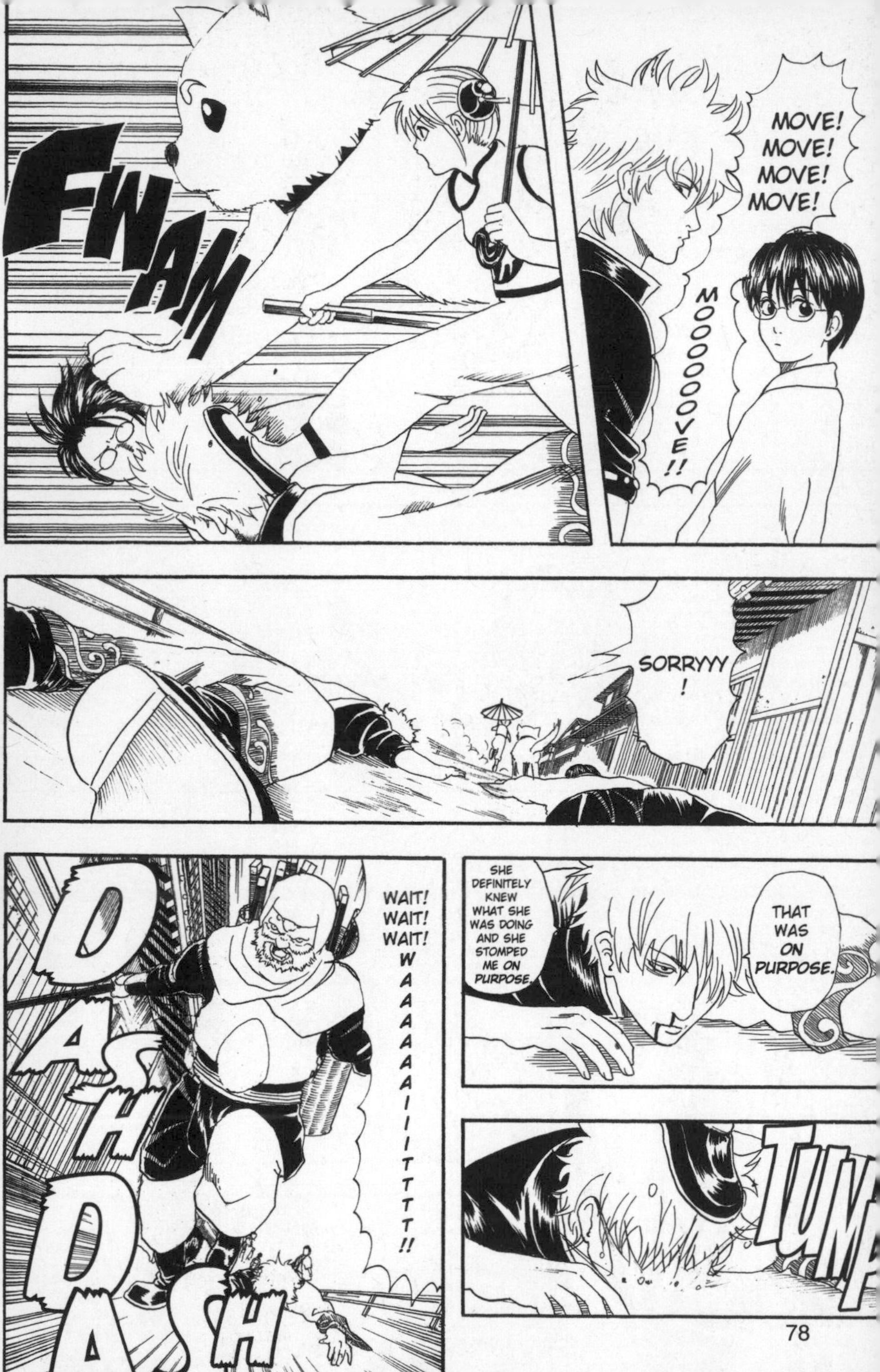
MOVE! MOVE! MOVE! MOVE!
MOOOOOOOVE!!
FWAM
SORRYYY!
THAT WAS ON PURPOSE.
SHE DEFINITELY KNEW WHAT SHE WAS DOING AND SHE STOMPED ME ON PURPOSE.
TUMP
WAIT! WAIT! WAIT! WAAAAAAIIITTTT!!
DASH
DASH

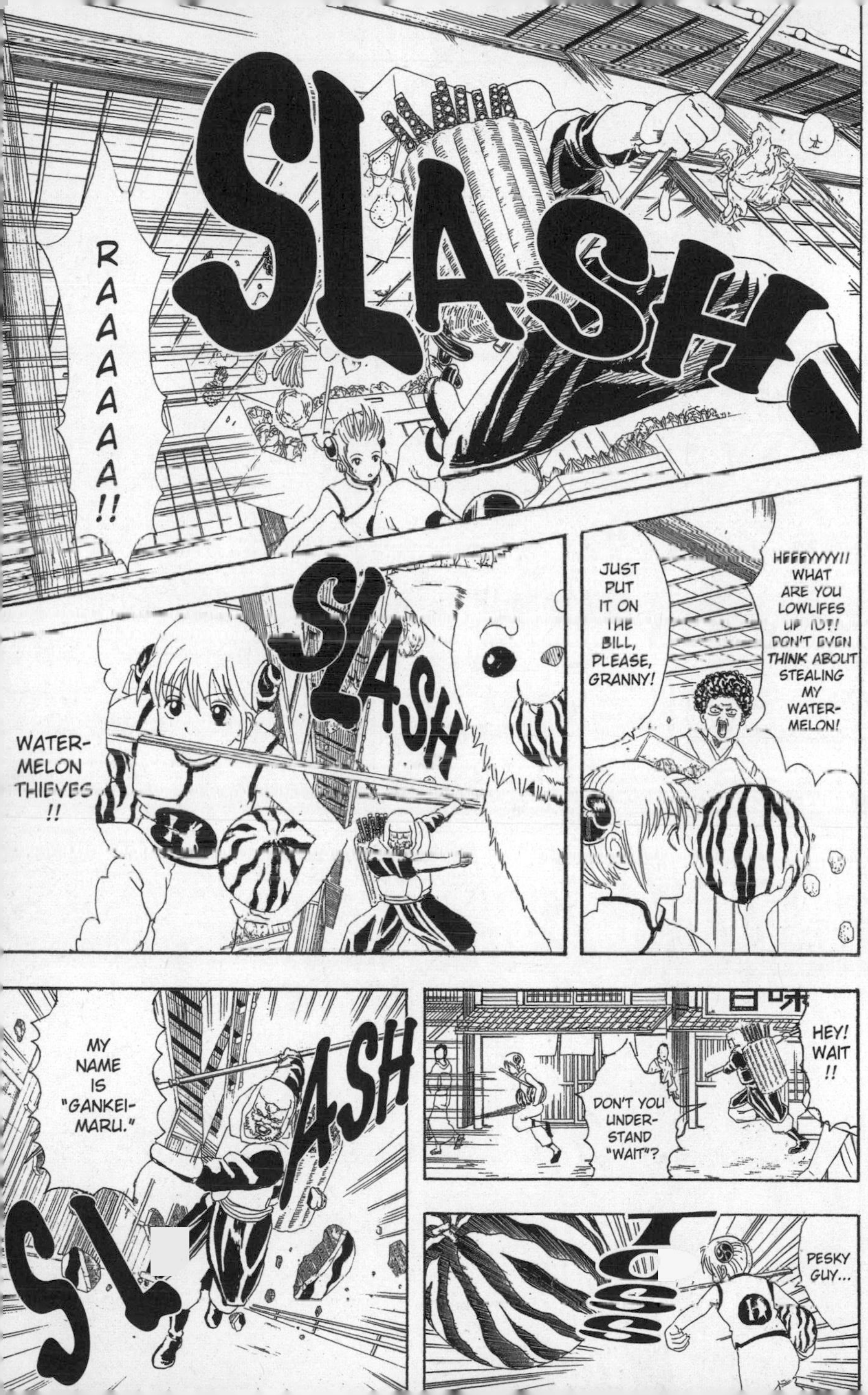
SLASH
RAAAAAAAAA!!
HEEEYYYYY!! WHAT ARE YOU LOWLIFES UP TO?! DON'T EVEN THINK ABOUT STEALING MY WATER-MELON!
JUST PUT IT ON THE BILL, PLEASE, GRANNY!
SLASH
WATER-MELON THIEVES!!
HEY! WAIT!!
DON'T YOU UNDER-STAND "WAIT"?
PESKY GUY...
TOSS
ASH
SL
MY NAME IS "GANKEI-MARU."

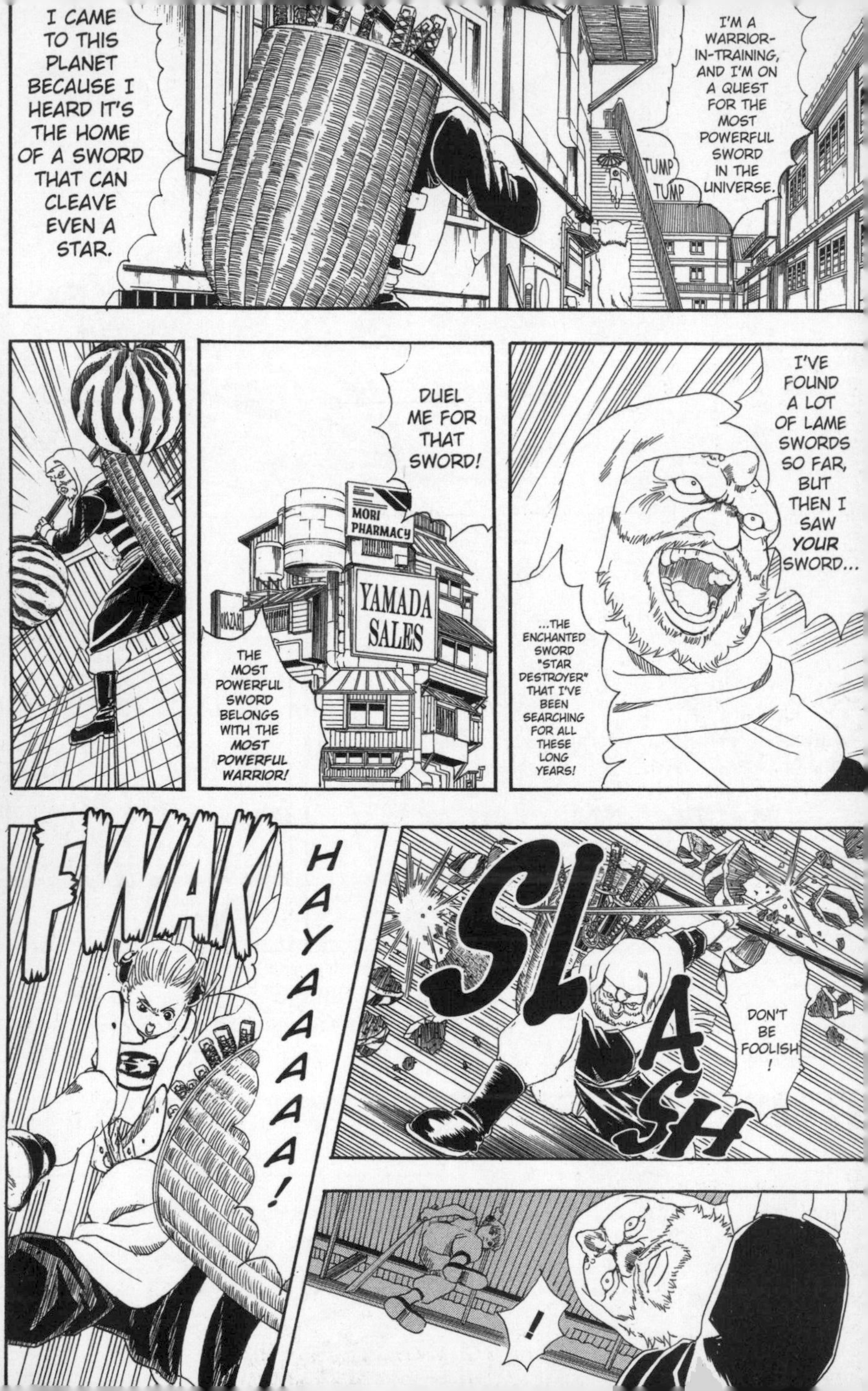
I'M A WARRIOR-IN-TRAINING, AND I'M ON A QUEST FOR THE MOST POWERFUL SWORD IN THE UNIVERSE.
TUMP
TUMP
I CAME TO THIS PLANET BECAUSE I HEARD IT'S THE HOME OF A SWORD THAT CAN CLEAVE EVEN A STAR.
I'VE FOUND A LOT OF LAME SWORDS SO FAR, BUT THEN I SAW *YOUR* SWORD...
...THE ENCHANTED SWORD "STAR DESTROYER" THAT I'VE BEEN SEARCHING FOR ALL THESE LONG YEARS!
DUEL ME FOR THAT SWORD!
MORI PHARMACY
YAMADA SALES
THE MOST POWERFUL SWORD BELONGS WITH THE *MOST POWERFUL WARRIOR!*
SLASH
DON'T BE FOOLISH!
!
FWAK
HAYAAAAAA!

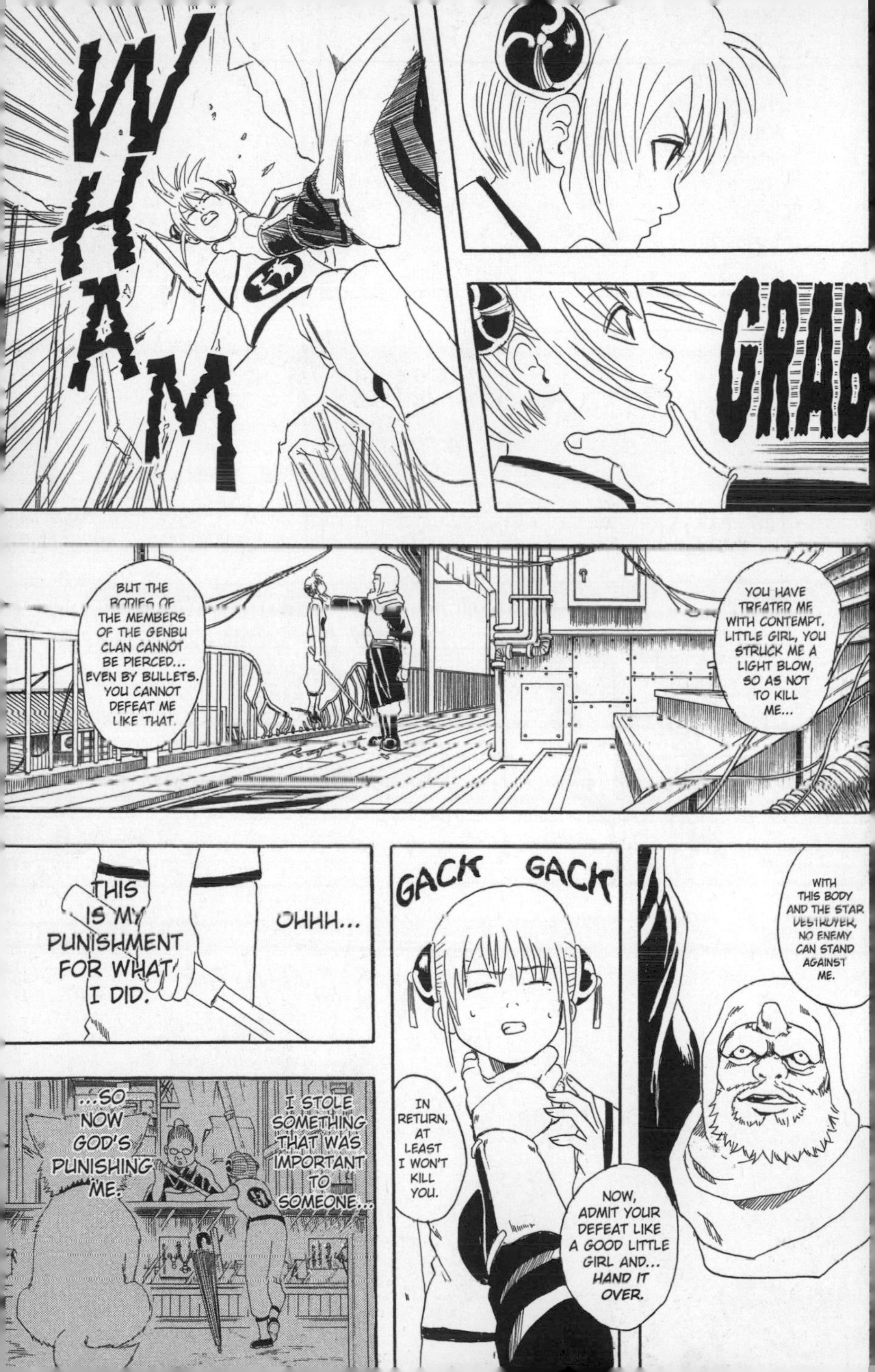
GRAB
WHAM
YOU HAVE TREATED ME WITH CONTEMPT. LITTLE GIRL, YOU STRUCK ME A LIGHT BLOW, SO AS NOT TO KILL ME...
BUT THE BODIES OF THE MEMBERS OF THE GENBU CLAN CANNOT BE PIERCED... EVEN BY BULLETS. YOU CANNOT DEFEAT ME LIKE THAT.
WITH THIS BODY AND THE STAR DESTROYER, NO ENEMY CAN STAND AGAINST ME.
GACK GACK
IN RETURN, AT LEAST I WON'T KILL YOU.
NOW, ADMIT YOUR DEFEAT LIKE A GOOD LITTLE GIRL AND... HAND IT OVER.
OHHH...
THIS IS MY PUNISHMENT FOR WHAT I DID.
I STOLE SOMETHING THAT WAS IMPORTANT TO SOMEONE...
...SO NOW GOD'S PUNISHING ME.

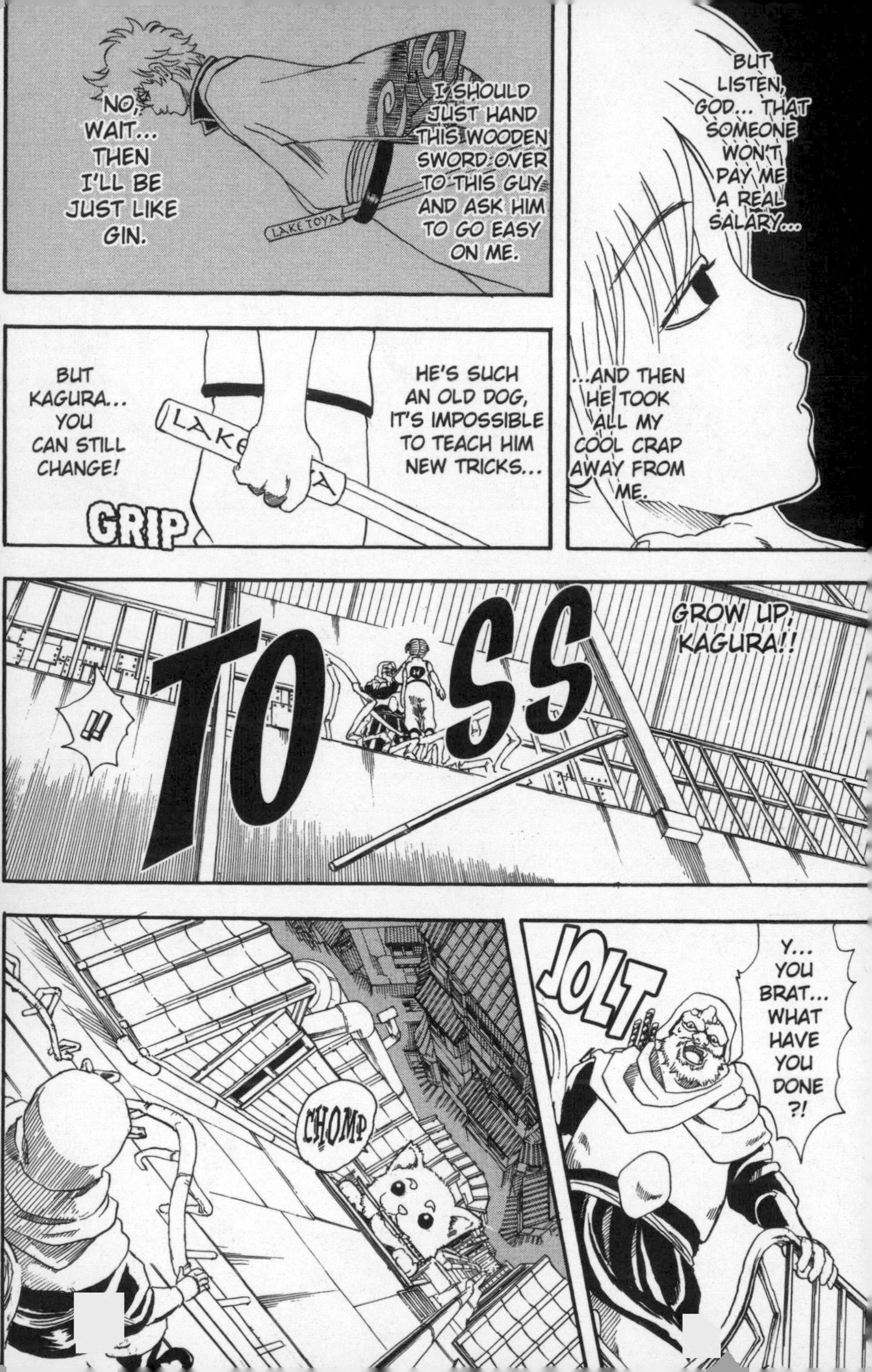
BUT LISTEN, GOD... THAT SOMEONE WON'T PAY ME A REAL SALARY...
...AND THEN HE TOOK ALL MY COOL CRAP AWAY FROM ME.
I SHOULD JUST HAND THIS WOODEN SWORD OVER TO THIS GUY AND ASK HIM TO GO EASY ON ME.
LAKE TOYA
NO, WAIT... THEN I'LL BE JUST LIKE GIN.
HE'S SUCH AN OLD DOG, IT'S IMPOSSIBLE TO TEACH HIM NEW TRICKS...
BUT KAGURA... YOU CAN STILL CHANGE!
GRIP
GROW UP, KAGURA!!
TOSS
!!
JOLT
Y... YOU BRAT... WHAT HAVE YOU DONE?!
CHOMP

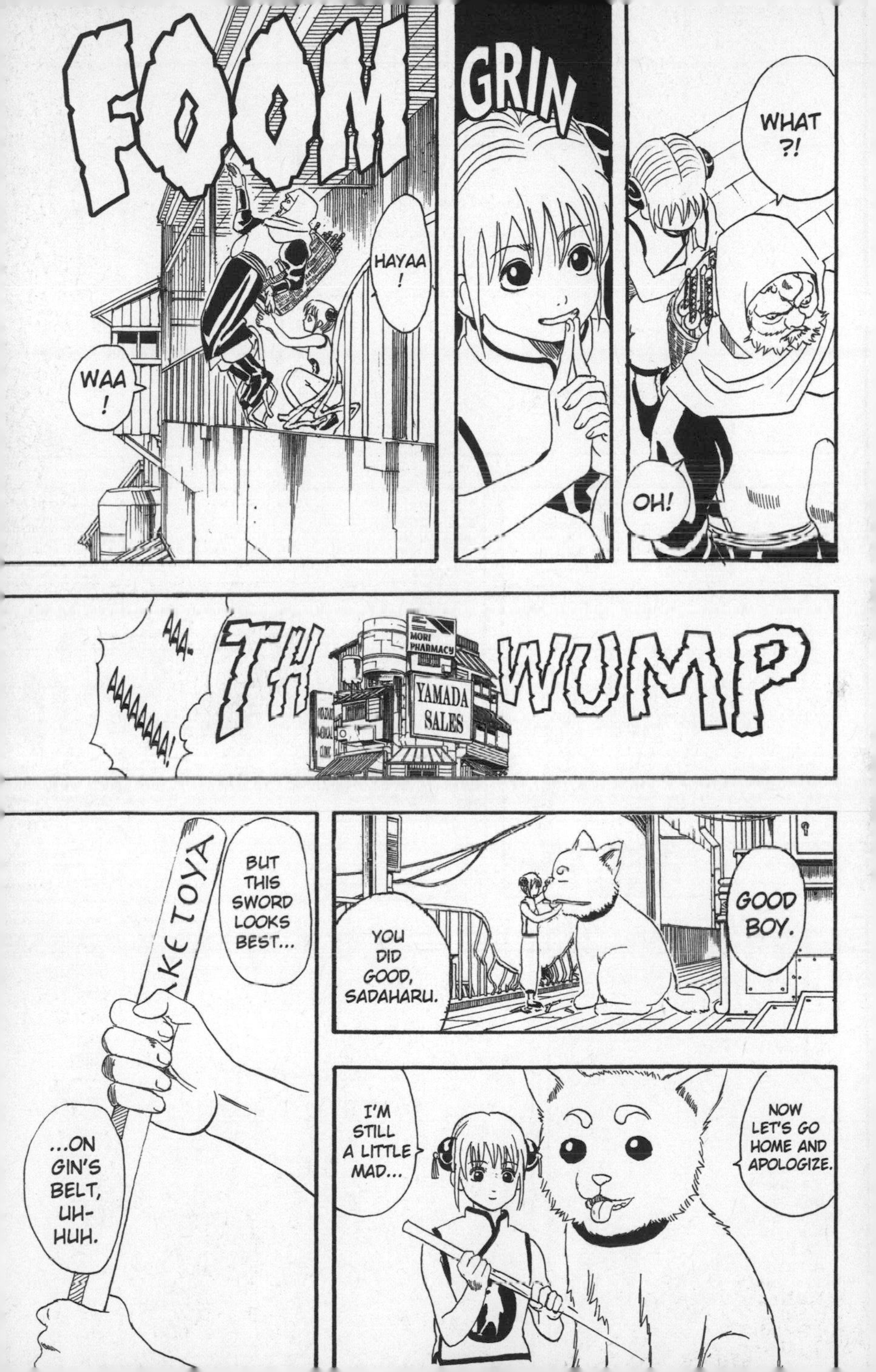
WHAT ?!
OH!
GRIN
FOOM
HAYAA !
WAA !
THWUMP
MORI PHARMACY
YAMADA SALES
AAA-AAAAAAAAA!
GOOD BOY.
YOU DID GOOD, SADAHARU.
NOW LET'S GO HOME AND APOLOGIZE.
I'M STILL A LITTLE MAD...
KE TOYA
BUT THIS SWORD LOOKS BEST...
...ON GIN'S BELT, UH-HUH.

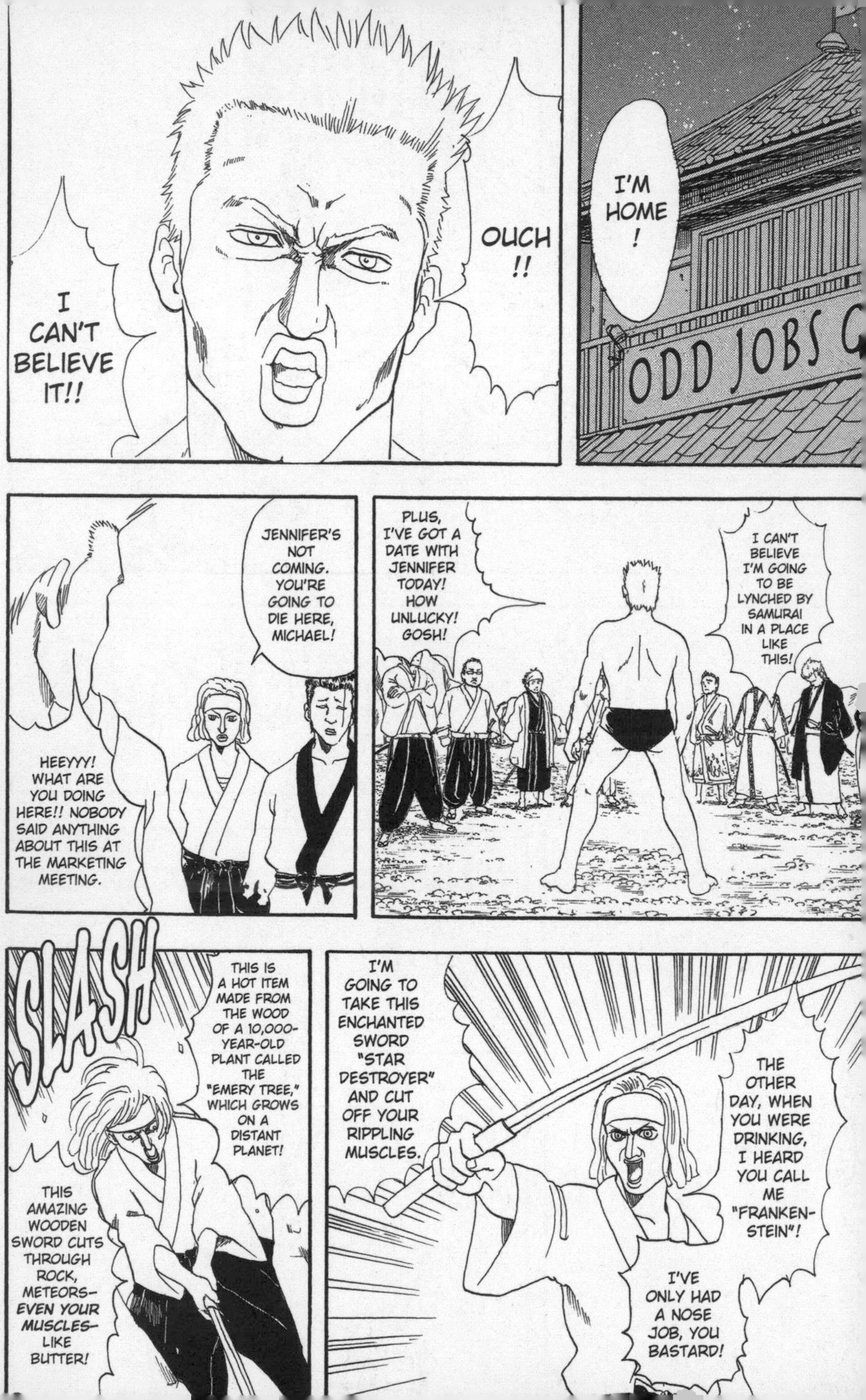
I'M HOME!
ODD JOBS
OUCH!!
I CAN'T BELIEVE IT!!
I CAN'T BELIEVE I'M GOING TO BE LYNCHED BY SAMURAI IN A PLACE LIKE THIS!
PLUS, I'VE GOT A DATE WITH JENNIFER TODAY! HOW UNLUCKY! GOSH!
JENNIFER'S NOT COMING. YOU'RE GOING TO DIE HERE, MICHAEL!
HEEYYY! WHAT ARE YOU DOING HERE!! NOBODY SAID ANYTHING ABOUT THIS AT THE MARKETING MEETING.
THE OTHER DAY, WHEN YOU WERE DRINKING, I HEARD YOU CALL ME "FRANKEN-STEIN"!
I'VE ONLY HAD A NOSE JOB, YOU BASTARD!
I'M GOING TO TAKE THIS ENCHANTED SWORD "STAR DESTROYER" AND CUT OFF YOUR RIPPLING MUSCLES.
SLASH
THIS IS A HOT ITEM MADE FROM THE WOOD OF A 10,000-YEAR-OLD PLANT CALLED THE "EMERY TREE," WHICH GROWS ON A DISTANT PLANET!
THIS AMAZING WOODEN SWORD CUTS THROUGH ROCK, METEORS- EVEN YOUR MUSCLES- LIKE BUTTER!

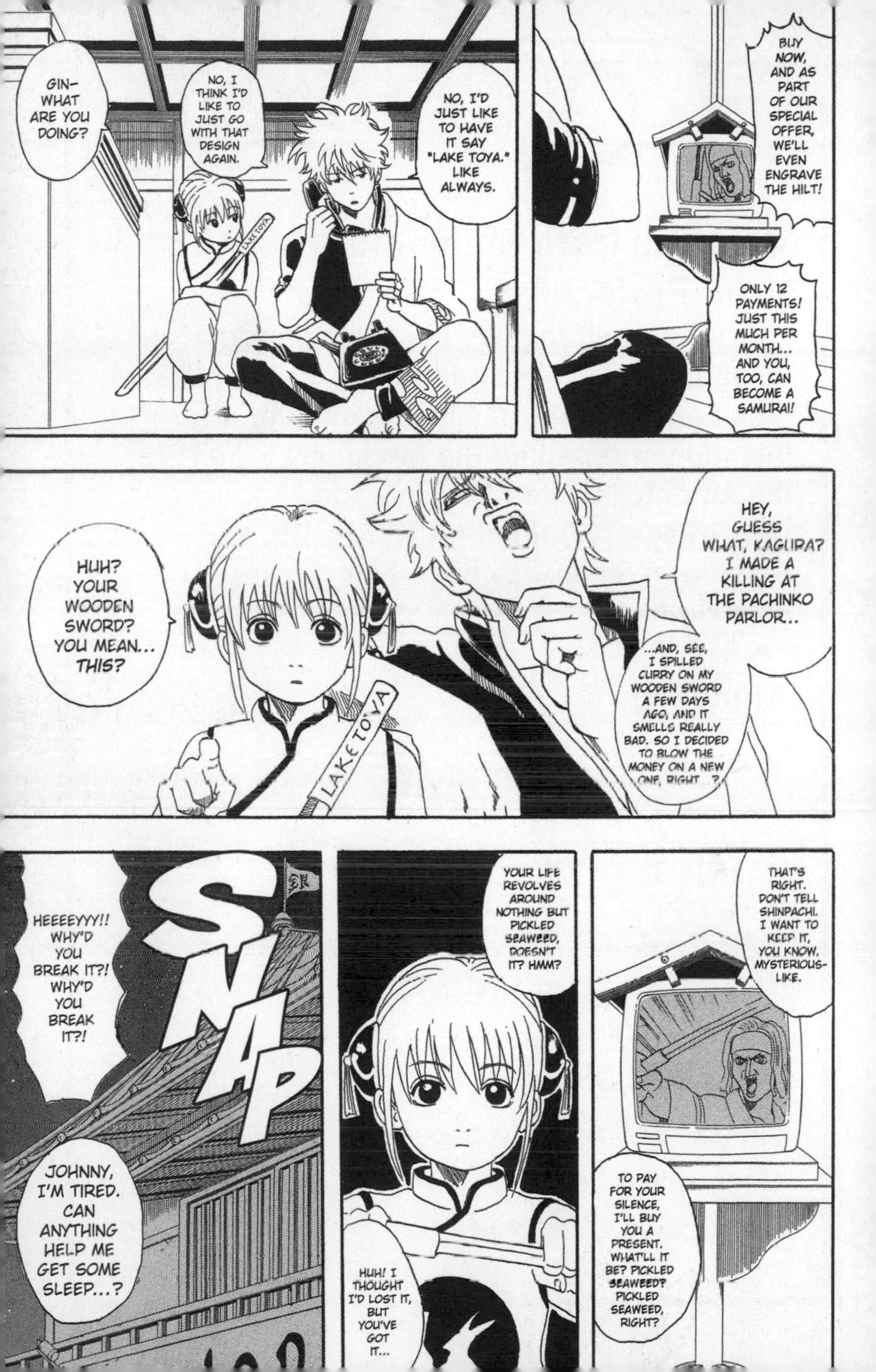
BUY NOW, AND AS PART OF OUR SPECIAL OFFER, WE'LL EVEN ENGRAVE THE HILT!
ONLY 12 PAYMENTS! JUST THIS MUCH PER MONTH... AND YOU, TOO, CAN BECOME A SAMURAI!
NO, I'D JUST LIKE TO HAVE IT SAY "LAKE TOYA." LIKE ALWAYS.
NO, I THINK I'D LIKE TO JUST GO WITH THAT DESIGN AGAIN.
GIN—WHAT ARE YOU DOING?
LAKE TOYA
HEY, GUESS WHAT, KAGURA? I MADE A KILLING AT THE PACHINKO PARLOR..
...AND, SEE, I SPILLED CURRY ON MY WOODEN SWORD A FEW DAYS AGO, AND IT SMELLS REALLY BAD. SO I DECIDED TO BLOW THE MONEY ON A NEW ONE, RIGHT...?
HUH? YOUR WOODEN SWORD? YOU MEAN... THIS?
LAKE TOYA
THAT'S RIGHT. DON'T TELL SHINPACHI. I WANT TO KEEP IT, YOU KNOW, MYSTERIOUS-LIKE.
TO PAY FOR YOUR SILENCE, I'LL BUY YOU A PRESENT. WHAT'LL IT BE? PICKLED SEAWEED? PICKLED SEAWEED, RIGHT?
YOUR LIFE REVOLVES AROUND NOTHING BUT PICKLED SEAWEED, DOESN'T IT? HMM?
HUH! I THOUGHT I'D LOST IT, BUT YOU'VE GOT IT...
SNAP
HEEEEYYY!! WHY'D YOU BREAK IT?! WHY'D YOU BREAK IT?!
JOHNNY, I'M TIRED. CAN ANYTHING HELP ME GET SOME SLEEP...?

Sorachi's Q&A
Hanging with the Readers #8

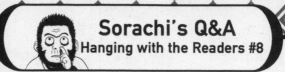

(Question from Shimomura-san from Aichi Prefecture)

There's something I've been wondering about... What, you ask? Well, something Shinpachi said: "The anti-foreigner faction fought with the intention of repelling the foreigners when the Amanto invaded 20 years ago." (Vol. 1 Page 147). In other words, Gin and Katsura must be way past their thirties now, right?

(Answer:)

No problem. Look, um, this will be on the test, so listen up... What's called the anti-foreigner war, you see, wasn't something that ended in just a year or so. It was more complex and chaotic than that. Er... I summarized this point so it would be easy to understand. So, Shimomura, you go ahead and flip to the next omake page.

(Q&A #9 is on page 106)

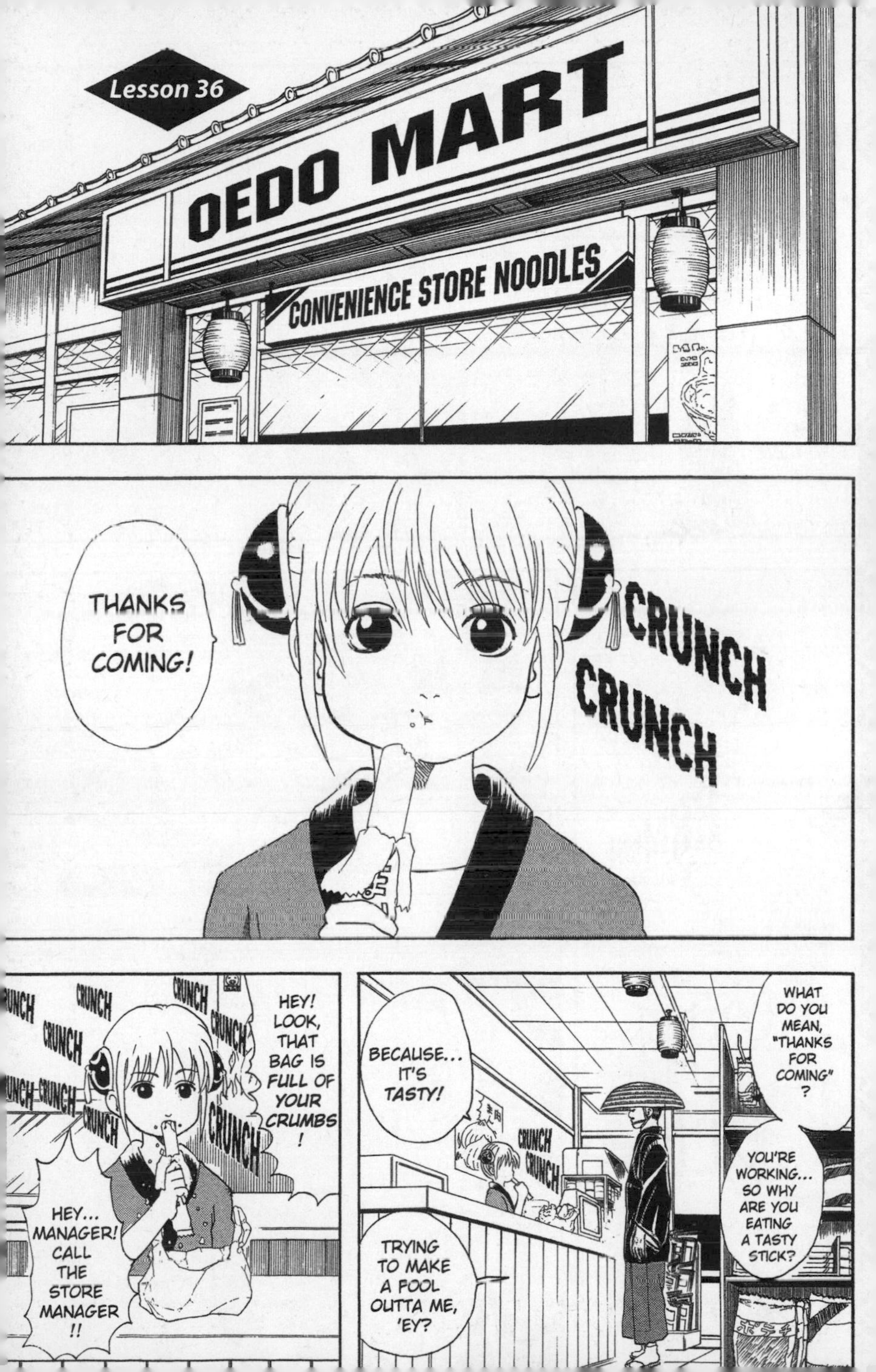
Lesson 36
OEDO MART
CONVENIENCE STORE NOODLES
CRUNCH
CRUNCH
THANKS FOR COMING!
WHAT DO YOU MEAN, "THANKS FOR COMING"?
BECAUSE... IT'S TASTY!
YOU'RE WORKING... SO WHY ARE YOU EATING A TASTY STICK?
CRUNCH CRUNCH
TRYING TO MAKE A FOOL OUTTA ME, 'EY?
HEY! LOOK, THAT BAG IS FULL OF YOUR CRUMBS!
CRUNCH
CRUNCH
CRUNCH
CRUNCH
CRUNCH
CRUNCH
HEY... MANAGER! CALL THE STORE MANAGER!!

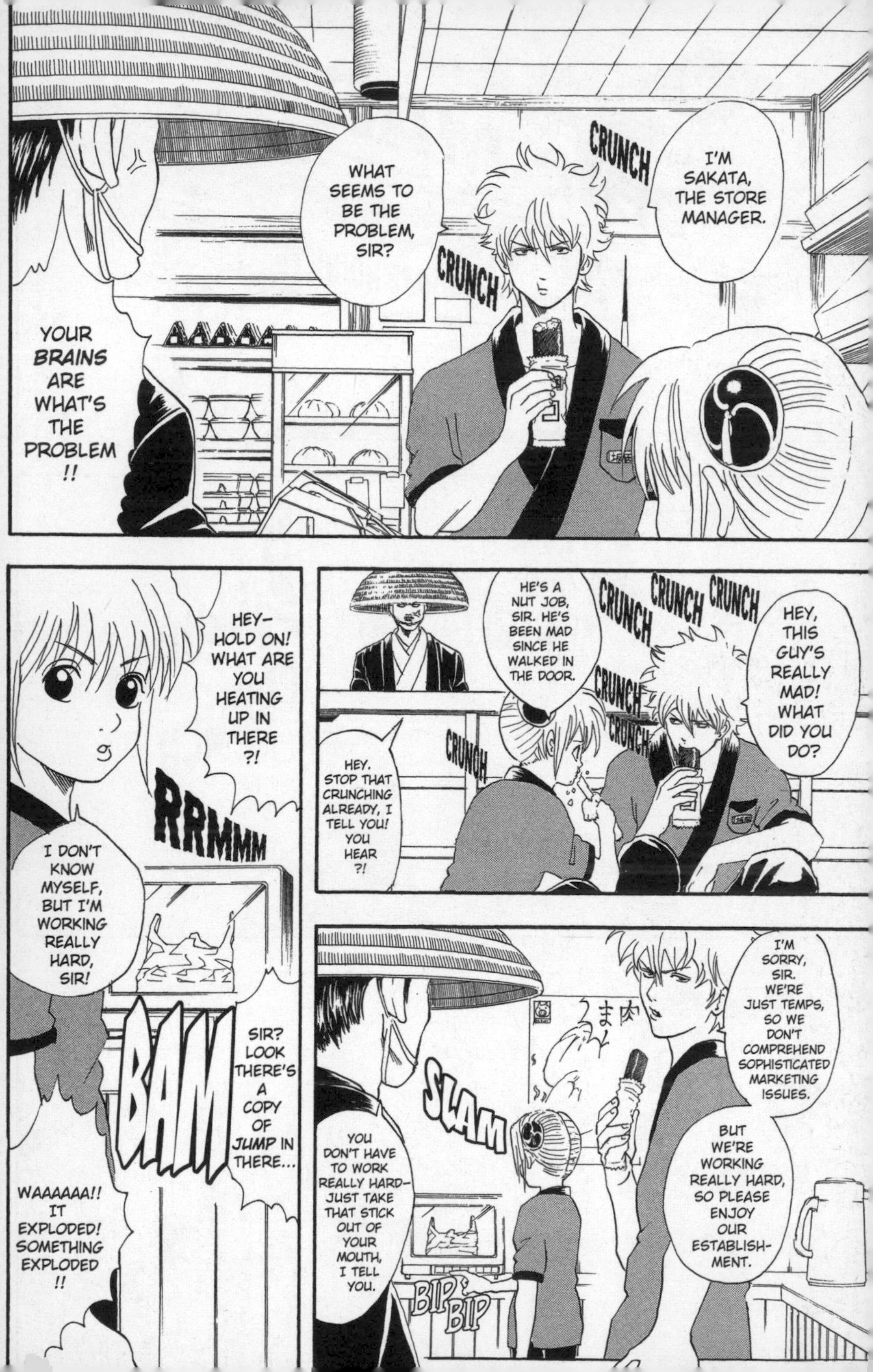
I'M SAKATA, THE STORE MANAGER.
CRUNCH
WHAT SEEMS TO BE THE PROBLEM, SIR?
CRUNCH
YOUR BRAINS ARE WHAT'S THE PROBLEM!!
HEY, THIS GUY'S REALLY MAD! WHAT DID YOU DO?
CRUNCH CRUNCH CRUNCH
HE'S A NUT JOB, SIR. HE'S BEEN MAD SINCE HE WALKED IN THE DOOR.
CRUNCH CRUNCH
CRUNCH
HEY. STOP THAT CRUNCHING ALREADY, I TELL YOU! YOU HEAR?!
I'M SORRY, SIR. WE'RE JUST TEMPS, SO WE DON'T COMPREHEND SOPHISTICATED MARKETING ISSUES.
BUT WE'RE WORKING REALLY HARD, SO PLEASE ENJOY OUR ESTABLISHMENT.
うま肉
SLAM
YOU DON'T HAVE TO WORK REALLY HARD—JUST TAKE THAT STICK OUT OF YOUR MOUTH, I TELL YOU.
BIP BIP
HEY—HOLD ON! WHAT ARE YOU HEATING UP IN THERE?!
RRMMM
I DON'T KNOW MYSELF, BUT I'M WORKING REALLY HARD, SIR!
BAM
SIR? LOOK THERE'S A COPY OF JUMP IN THERE...
WAAAAAA!! IT EXPLODED! SOMETHING EXPLODED!!

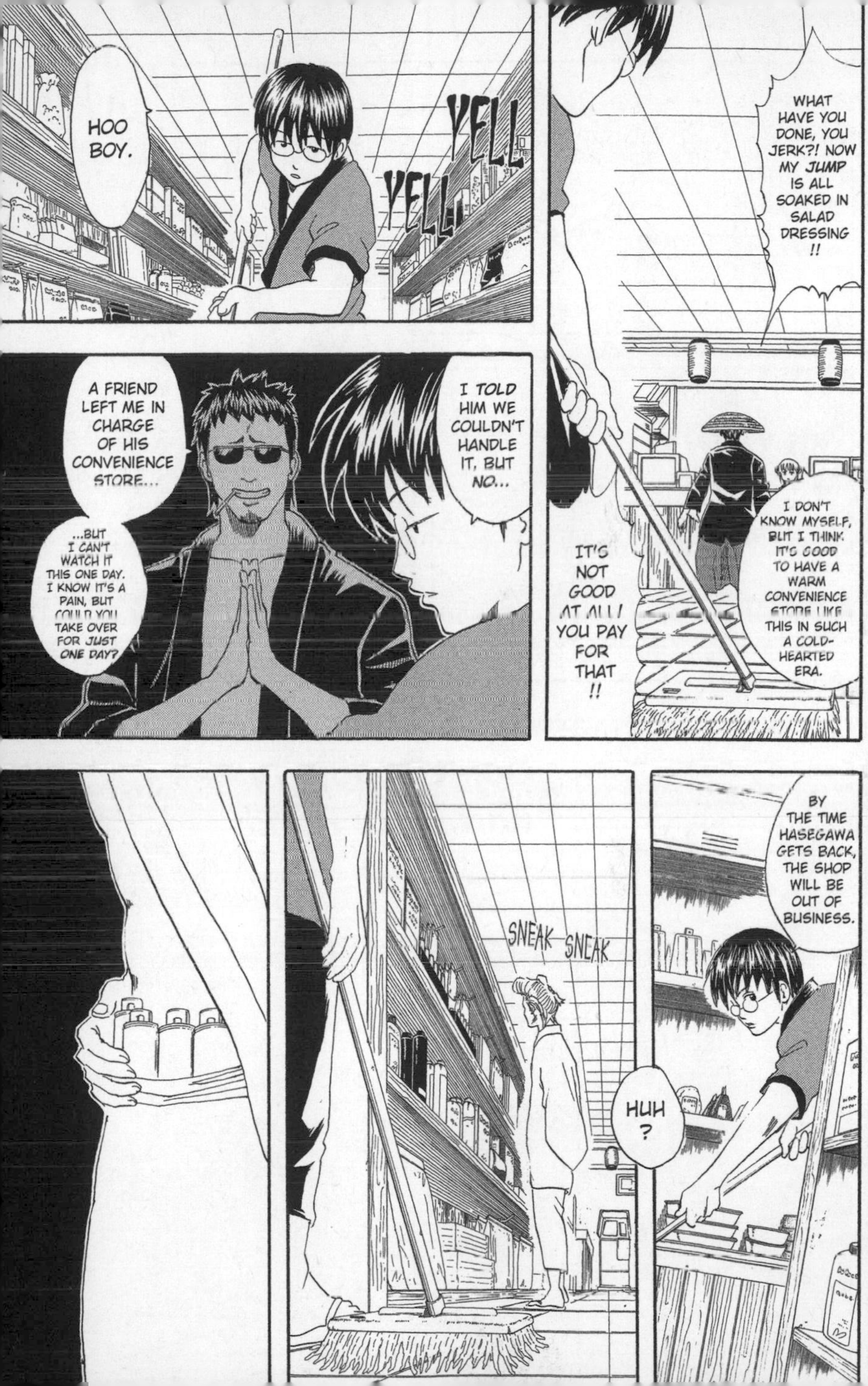
WHAT HAVE YOU DONE, YOU JERK?! NOW MY JUMP IS ALL SOAKED IN SALAD DRESSING !!
I DON'T KNOW MYSELF, BUT I THINK IT'S GOOD TO HAVE A WARM CONVENIENCE STORE LIKE THIS IN SUCH A COLD-HEARTED ERA.
IT'S NOT GOOD AT ALL! YOU PAY FOR THAT !!
YELL YELL
HOO BOY.
I TOLD HIM WE COULDN'T HANDLE IT, BUT NO...
A FRIEND LEFT ME IN CHARGE OF HIS CONVENIENCE STORE...
...BUT I CAN'T WATCH IT THIS ONE DAY. I KNOW IT'S A PAIN, BUT COULD YOU TAKE OVER FOR JUST ONE DAY?
BY THE TIME HASEGAWA GETS BACK, THE SHOP WILL BE OUT OF BUSINESS.
HUH ?
SNEAK SNEAK

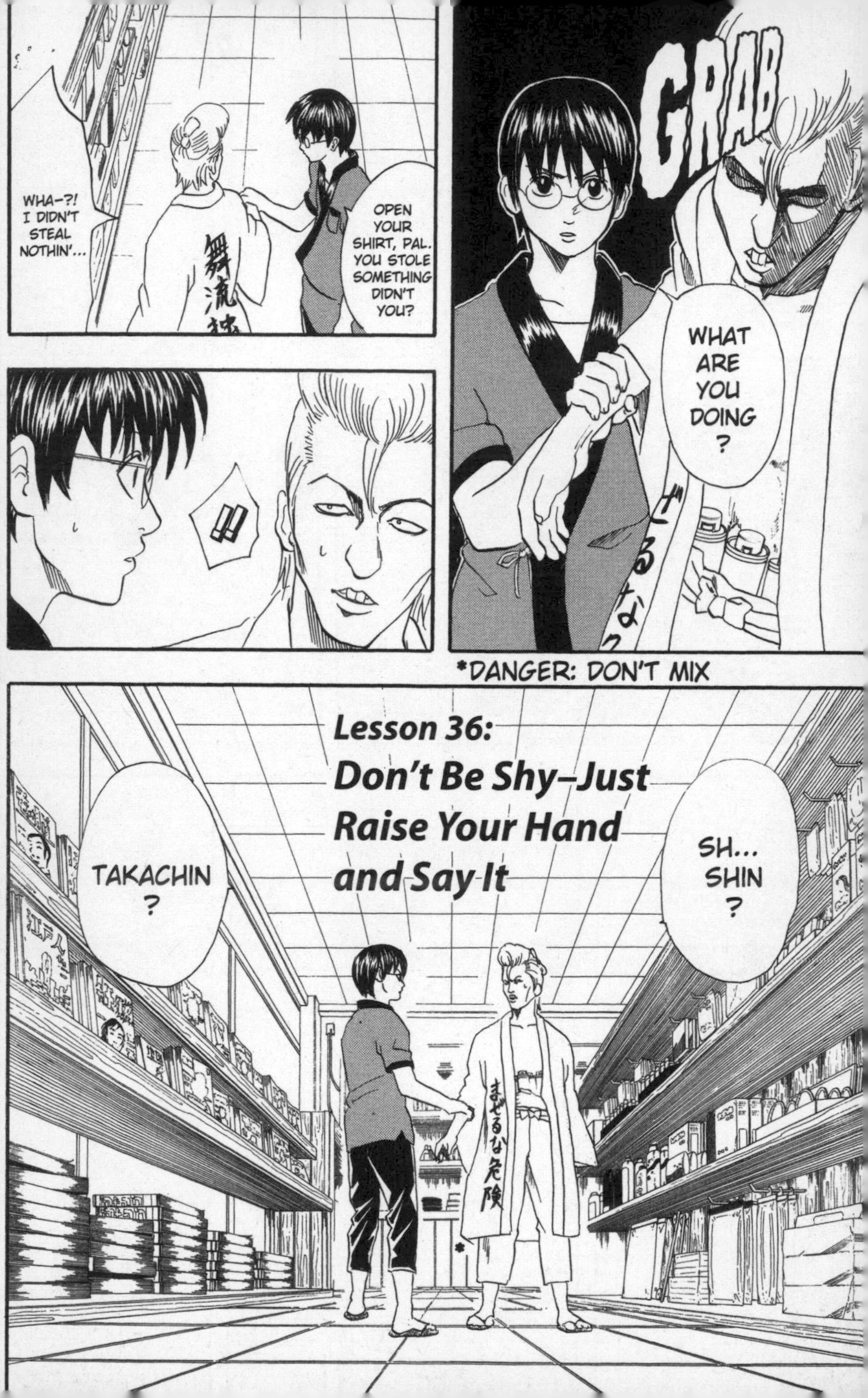
GRAB
WHAT ARE YOU DOING?
OPEN YOUR SHIRT, PAL. YOU STOLE SOMETHING DIDN'T YOU?
WHA-?! I DIDN'T STEAL NOTHIN'...
!!
*DANGER: DON'T MIX
Lesson 36:
Don't Be Shy–Just Raise Your Hand and Say It
SH... SHIN?
TAKACHIN?

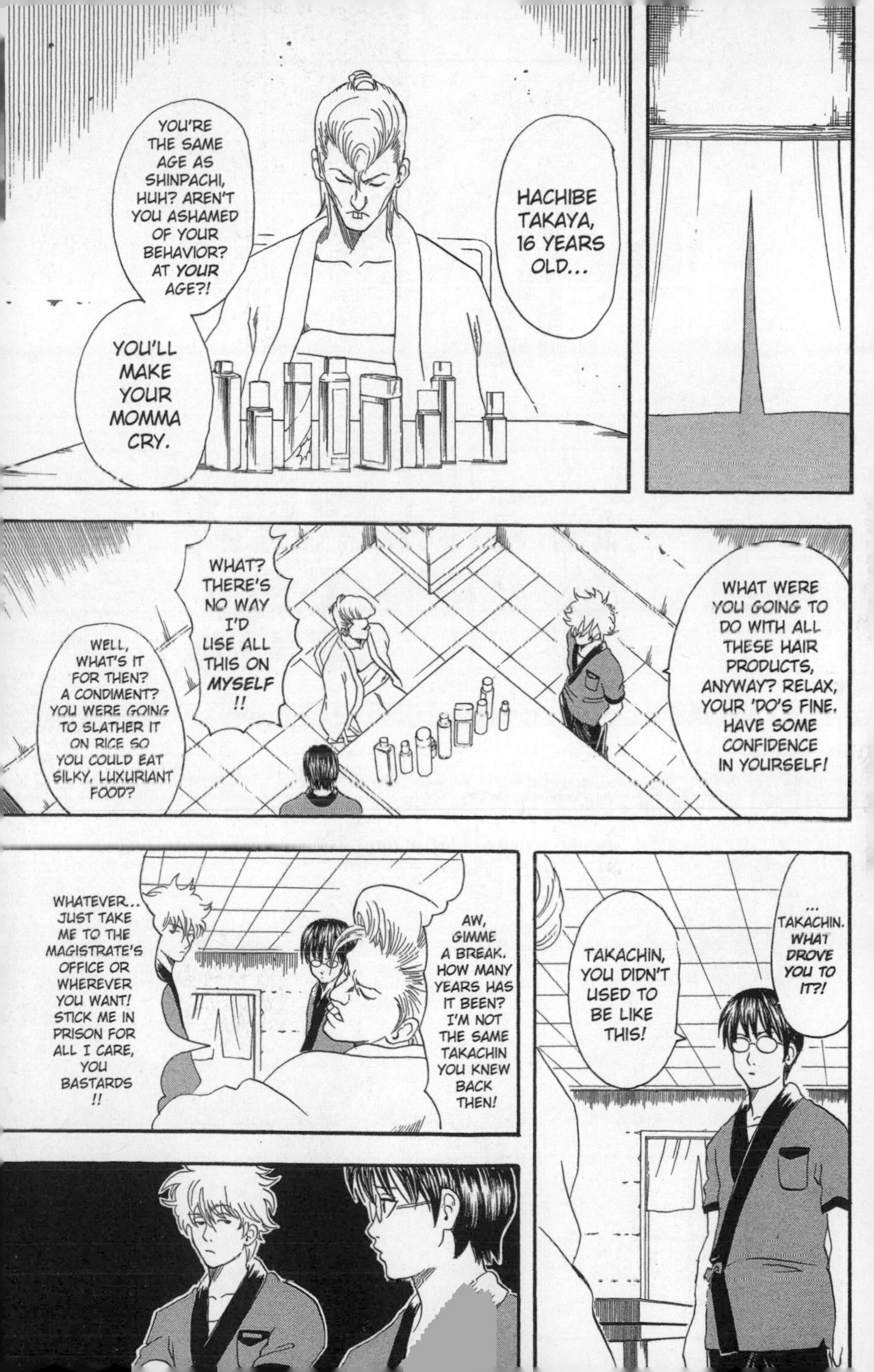
HACHIBE TAKAYA, 16 YEARS OLD...
YOU'RE THE SAME AGE AS SHINPACHI, HUH? AREN'T YOU ASHAMED OF YOUR BEHAVIOR? AT *YOUR* AGE?!
YOU'LL MAKE YOUR MOMMA CRY.
WHAT WERE YOU GOING TO DO WITH ALL THESE HAIR PRODUCTS, ANYWAY? RELAX, YOUR 'DO'S FINE. HAVE SOME CONFIDENCE IN YOURSELF!
WHAT? THERE'S NO WAY I'D USE ALL THIS ON *MYSELF* !!
WELL, WHAT'S IT FOR THEN? A CONDIMENT? YOU WERE GOING TO SLATHER IT ON RICE SO YOU COULD EAT SILKY, LUXURIANT FOOD?
... TAKACHIN. WHAT DROVE YOU TO IT?!
TAKACHIN, YOU DIDN'T USED TO BE LIKE THIS!
AW, GIMME A BREAK. HOW MANY YEARS HAS IT BEEN? I'M NOT THE SAME TAKACHIN YOU KNEW BACK THEN!
WHATEVER... JUST TAKE ME TO THE MAGISTRATE'S OFFICE OR WHEREVER YOU WANT! STICK ME IN PRISON FOR ALL I CARE, YOU BASTARDS !!

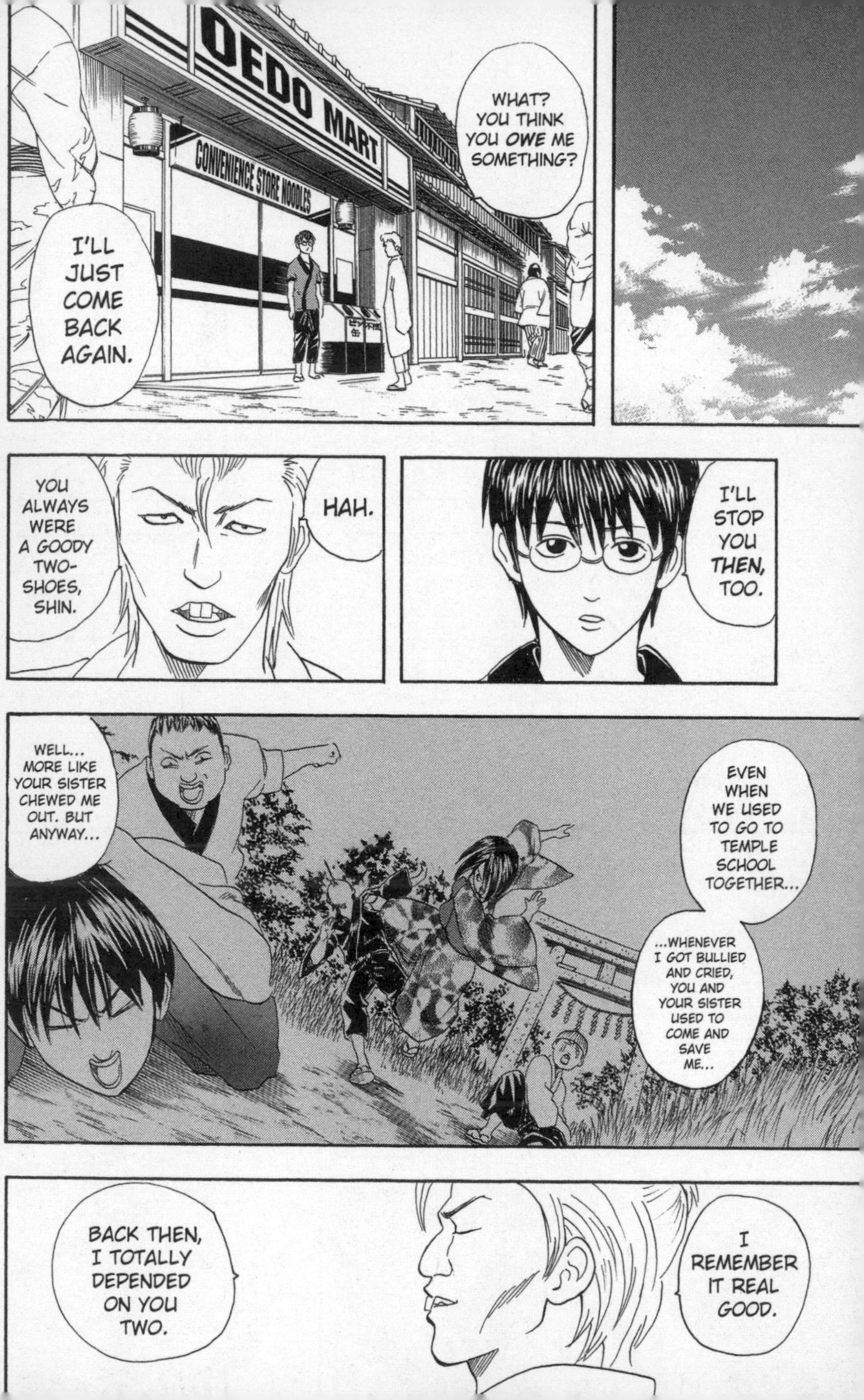
OEDO MART
CONVENIENCE STORE NOODLES
WHAT? YOU THINK YOU *OWE* ME SOMETHING?
I'LL JUST COME BACK AGAIN.
I'LL STOP YOU *THEN*, TOO.
HAH.
YOU ALWAYS WERE A GOODY TWO-SHOES, SHIN.
EVEN WHEN WE USED TO GO TO TEMPLE SCHOOL TOGETHER...
...WHENEVER I GOT BULLIED AND CRIED, YOU AND YOUR SISTER USED TO COME AND SAVE ME...
WELL... MORE LIKE YOUR SISTER CHEWED ME OUT. BUT ANYWAY...
I REMEMBER IT REAL GOOD.
BACK THEN, I TOTALLY DEPENDED ON YOU TWO.

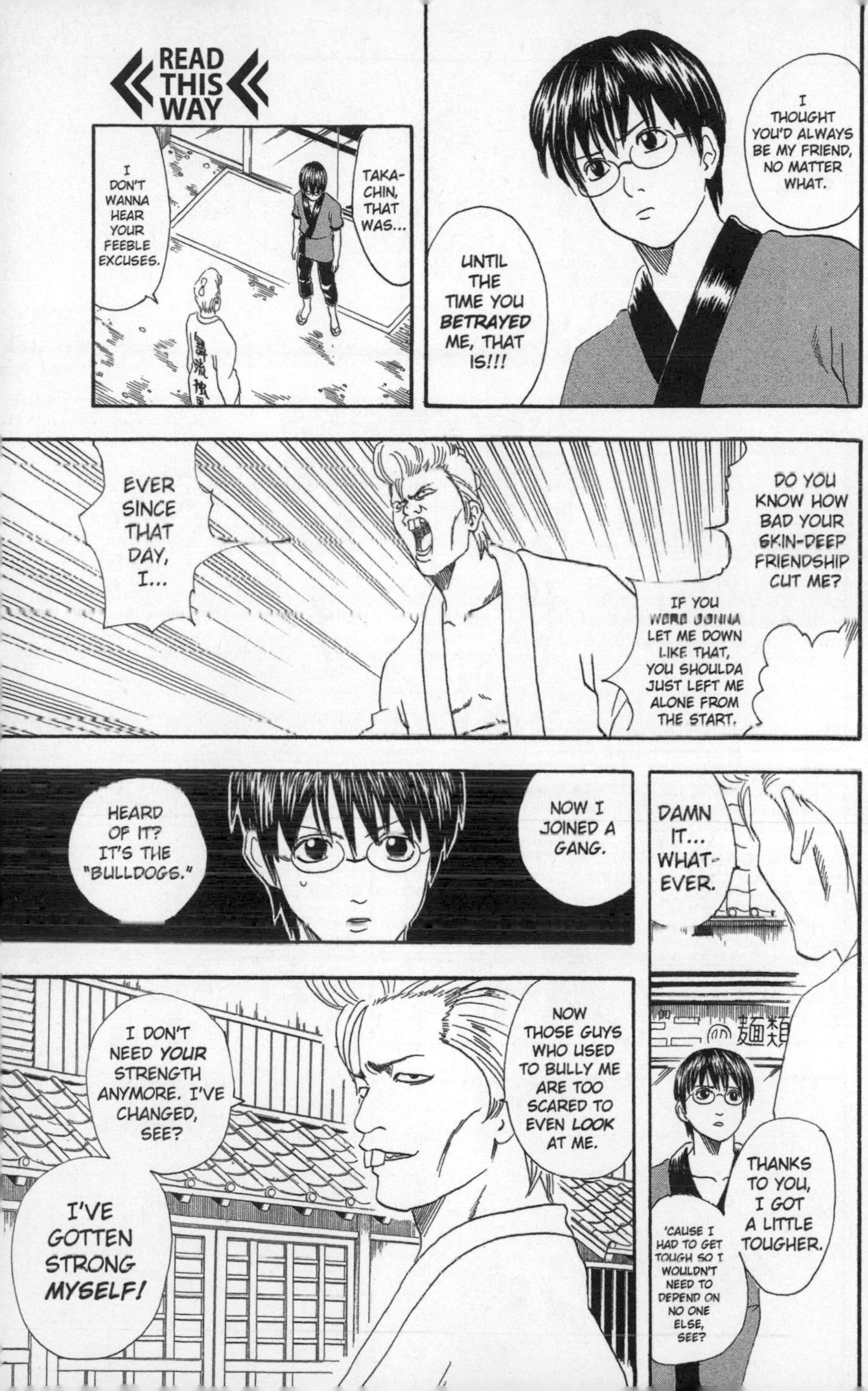
READ THIS WAY
I THOUGHT YOU'D ALWAYS BE MY FRIEND, NO MATTER WHAT.
UNTIL THE TIME YOU BETRAYED ME, THAT IS!!!
TAKA-CHIN, THAT WAS...
I DON'T WANNA HEAR YOUR FEEBLE EXCUSES.
DO YOU KNOW HOW BAD YOUR SKIN-DEEP FRIENDSHIP CUT ME?
IF YOU WERE GONNA LET ME DOWN LIKE THAT, YOU SHOULDA JUST LEFT ME ALONE FROM THE START.
EVER SINCE THAT DAY, I...
DAMN IT... WHATEVER.
THANKS TO YOU, I GOT A LITTLE TOUGHER.
'CAUSE I HAD TO GET TOUGH SO I WOULDN'T NEED TO DEPEND ON NO ONE ELSE, SEE?
NOW I JOINED A GANG.
HEARD OF IT? IT'S THE "BULLDOGS."
NOW THOSE GUYS WHO USED TO BULLY ME ARE TOO SCARED TO EVEN LOOK AT ME.
I DON'T NEED YOUR STRENGTH ANYMORE. I'VE CHANGED, SEE?
I'VE GOTTEN STRONG MYSELF!

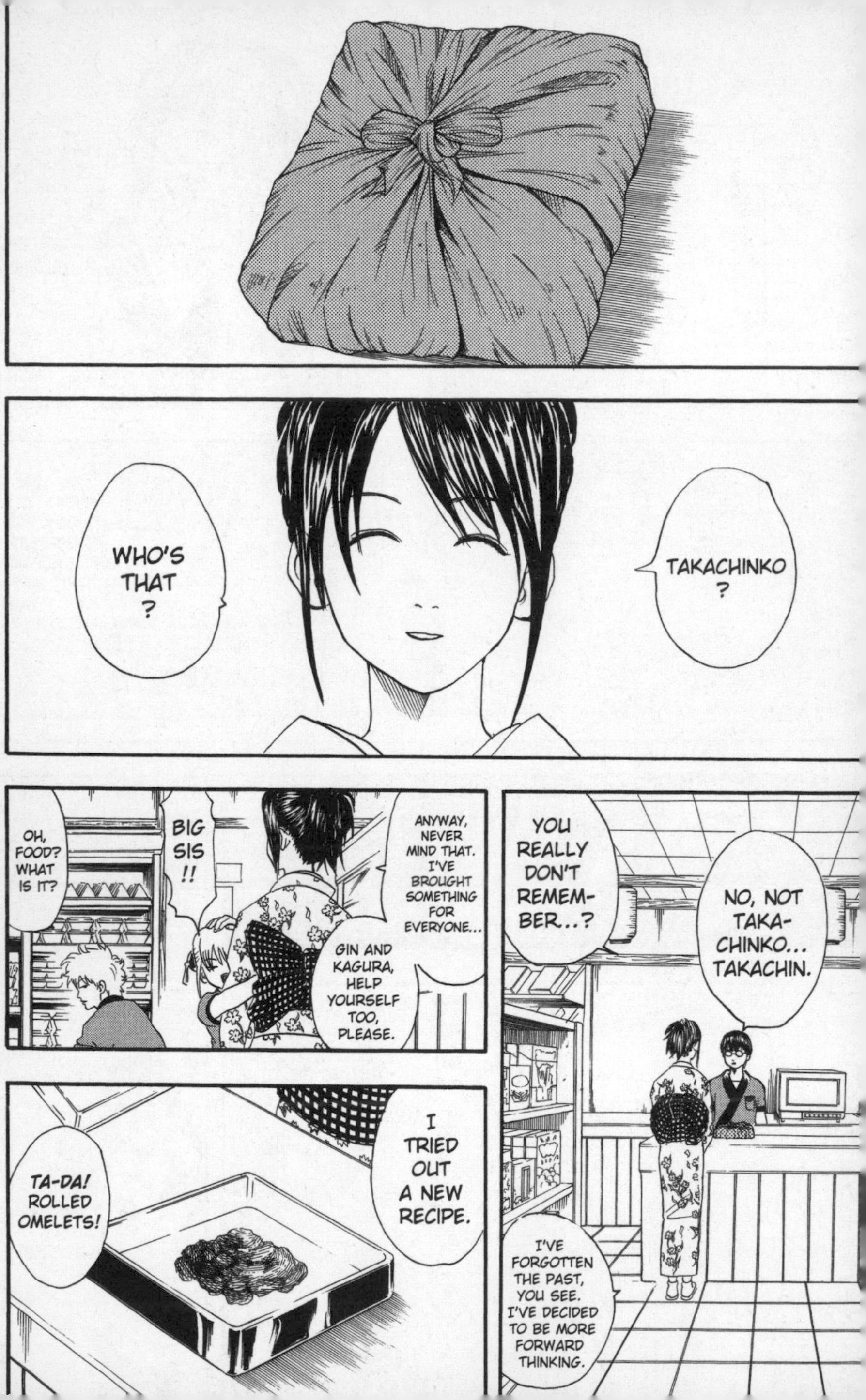
TAKACHINKO ?
WHO'S THAT ?
NO, NOT TAKA-CHINKO... TAKACHIN.
YOU REALLY DON'T REMEM-BER...?
I'VE FORGOTTEN THE PAST, YOU SEE. I'VE DECIDED TO BE MORE FORWARD THINKING.
ANYWAY, NEVER MIND THAT. I'VE BROUGHT SOMETHING FOR EVERYONE...
GIN AND KAGURA, HELP YOURSELF TOO, PLEASE.
BIG SIS !!
OH, FOOD? WHAT IS IT?
I TRIED OUT A NEW RECIPE.
TA-DA! ROLLED OMELETS!

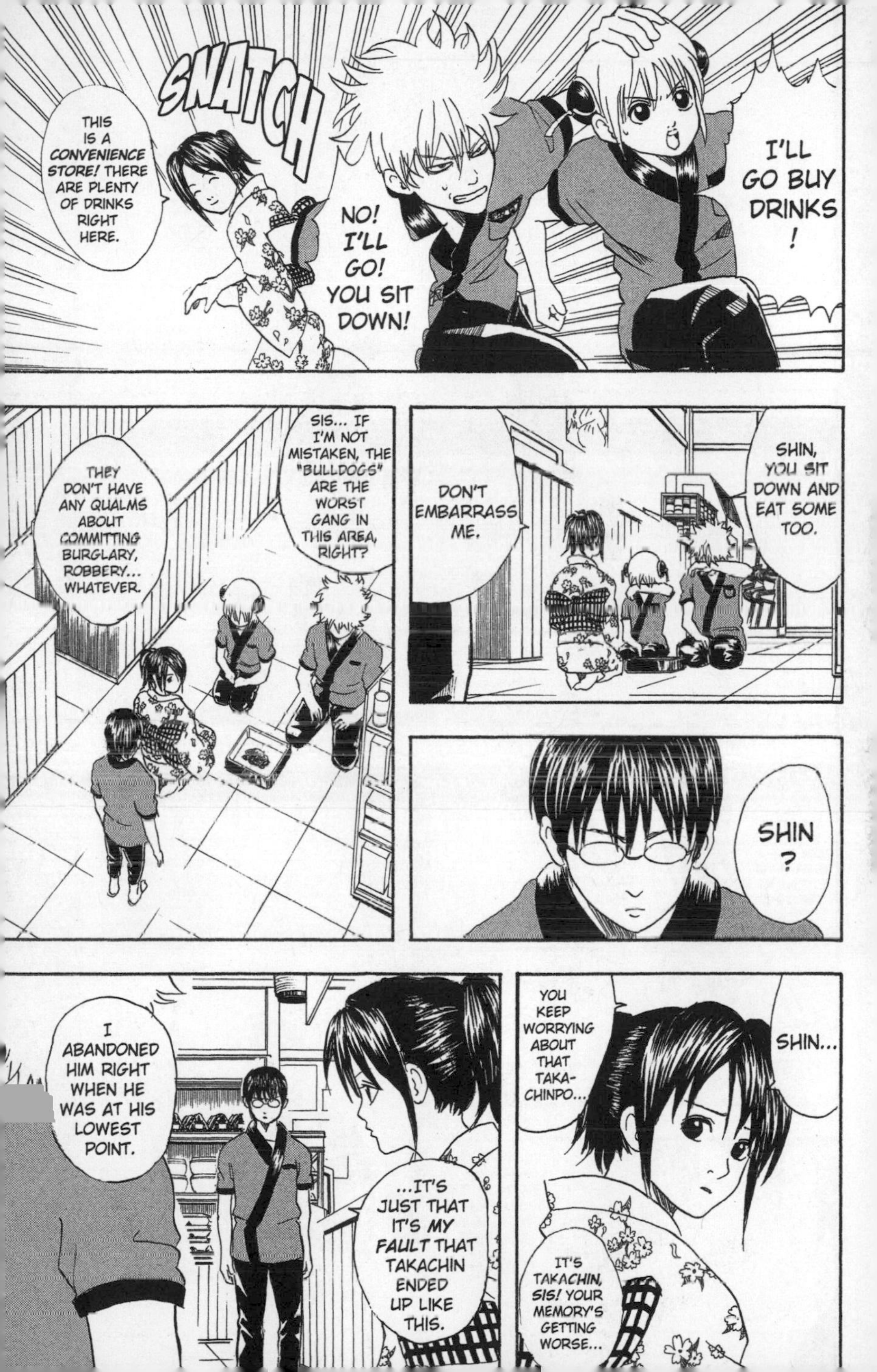

I'LL GO BUY DRINKS!
NO! I'LL GO! YOU SIT DOWN!
SNATCH
THIS IS A CONVENIENCE STORE! THERE ARE PLENTY OF DRINKS RIGHT HERE.
SHIN, YOU SIT DOWN AND EAT SOME TOO.
DON'T EMBARRASS ME.
SHIN?
SIS... IF I'M NOT MISTAKEN, THE "BULLDOGS" ARE THE WORST GANG IN THIS AREA, RIGHT?
THEY DON'T HAVE ANY QUALMS ABOUT COMMITTING BURGLARY, ROBBERY... WHATEVER.
SHIN...
YOU KEEP WORRYING ABOUT THAT TAKA-CHINPO...
IT'S TAKACHIN, SIS! YOUR MEMORY'S GETTING WORSE...
...IT'S JUST THAT IT'S MY FAULT THAT TAKACHIN ENDED UP LIKE THIS.
I ABANDONED HIM RIGHT WHEN HE WAS AT HIS LOWEST POINT.

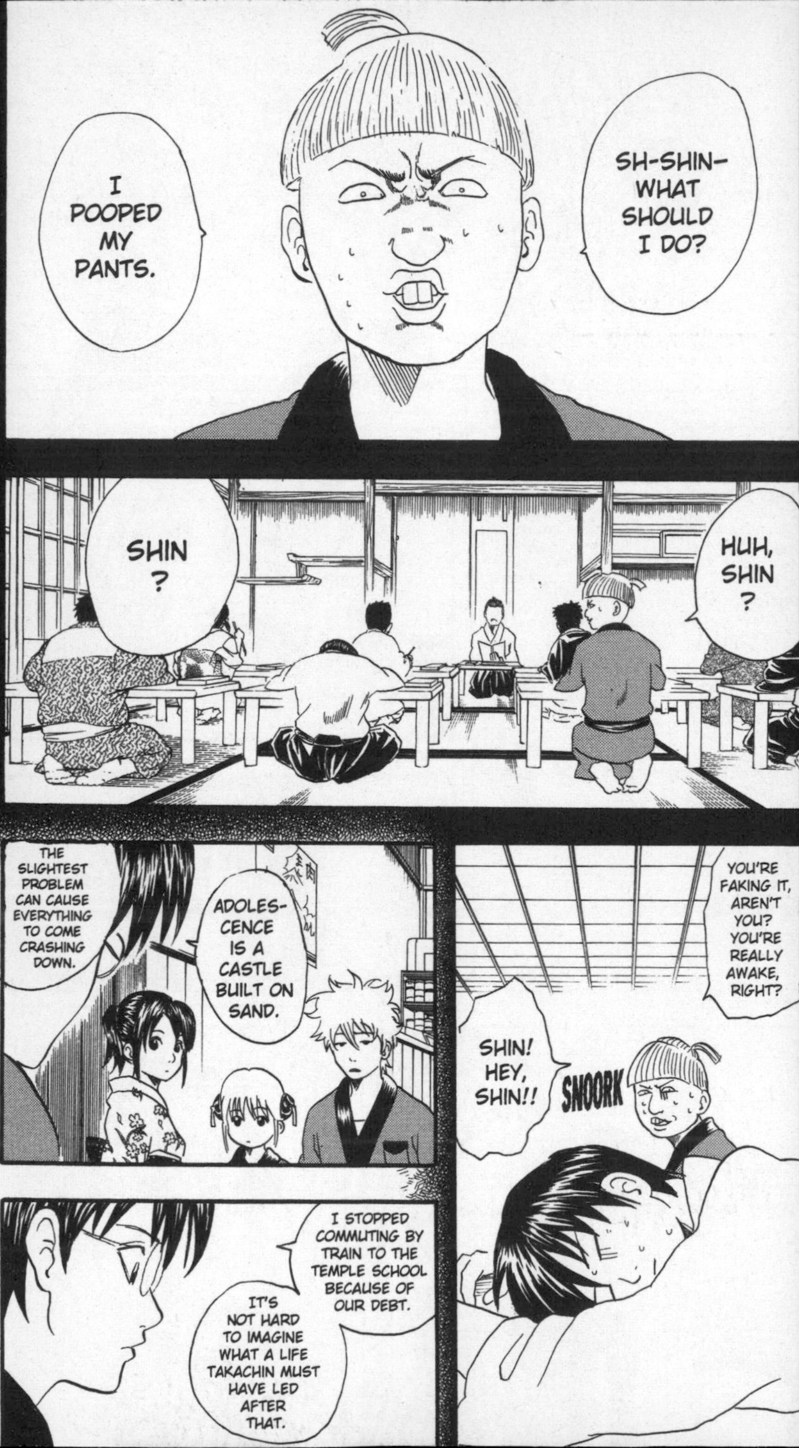
SH-SHIN- WHAT SHOULD I DO?
I POOPED MY PANTS.
HUH, SHIN?
SHIN?
YOU'RE FAKING IT, AREN'T YOU? YOU'RE REALLY AWAKE, RIGHT?
SHIN! HEY, SHIN!!
SNOORK
ADOLES-CENCE IS A CASTLE BUILT ON SAND.
THE SLIGHTEST PROBLEM CAN CAUSE EVERYTHING TO COME CRASHING DOWN.
I STOPPED COMMUTING BY TRAIN TO THE TEMPLE SCHOOL BECAUSE OF OUR DEBT.
IT'S NOT HARD TO IMAGINE WHAT A LIFE TAKACHIN MUST HAVE LED AFTER THAT.

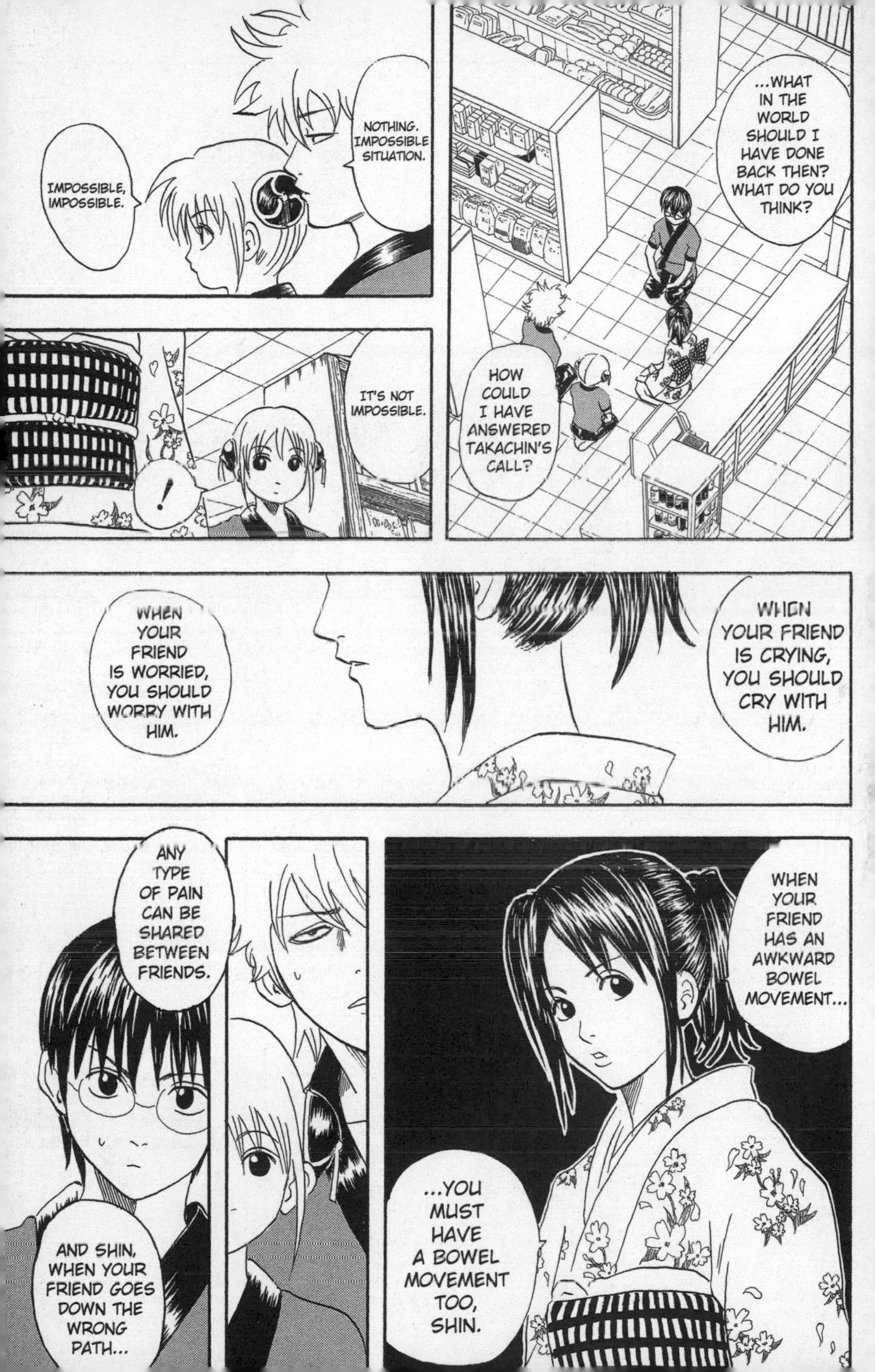
...WHAT IN THE WORLD SHOULD I HAVE DONE BACK THEN? WHAT DO YOU THINK?
HOW COULD I HAVE ANSWERED TAKACHIN'S CALL?
NOTHING. IMPOSSIBLE SITUATION.
IMPOSSIBLE, IMPOSSIBLE.
IT'S NOT IMPOSSIBLE.
!
WHEN YOUR FRIEND IS CRYING, YOU SHOULD CRY WITH HIM.
WHEN YOUR FRIEND IS WORRIED, YOU SHOULD WORRY WITH HIM.
WHEN YOUR FRIEND HAS AN AWKWARD BOWEL MOVEMENT...
...YOU MUST HAVE A BOWEL MOVEMENT TOO, SHIN.
ANY TYPE OF PAIN CAN BE SHARED BETWEEN FRIENDS.
AND SHIN, WHEN YOUR FRIEND GOES DOWN THE WRONG PATH...

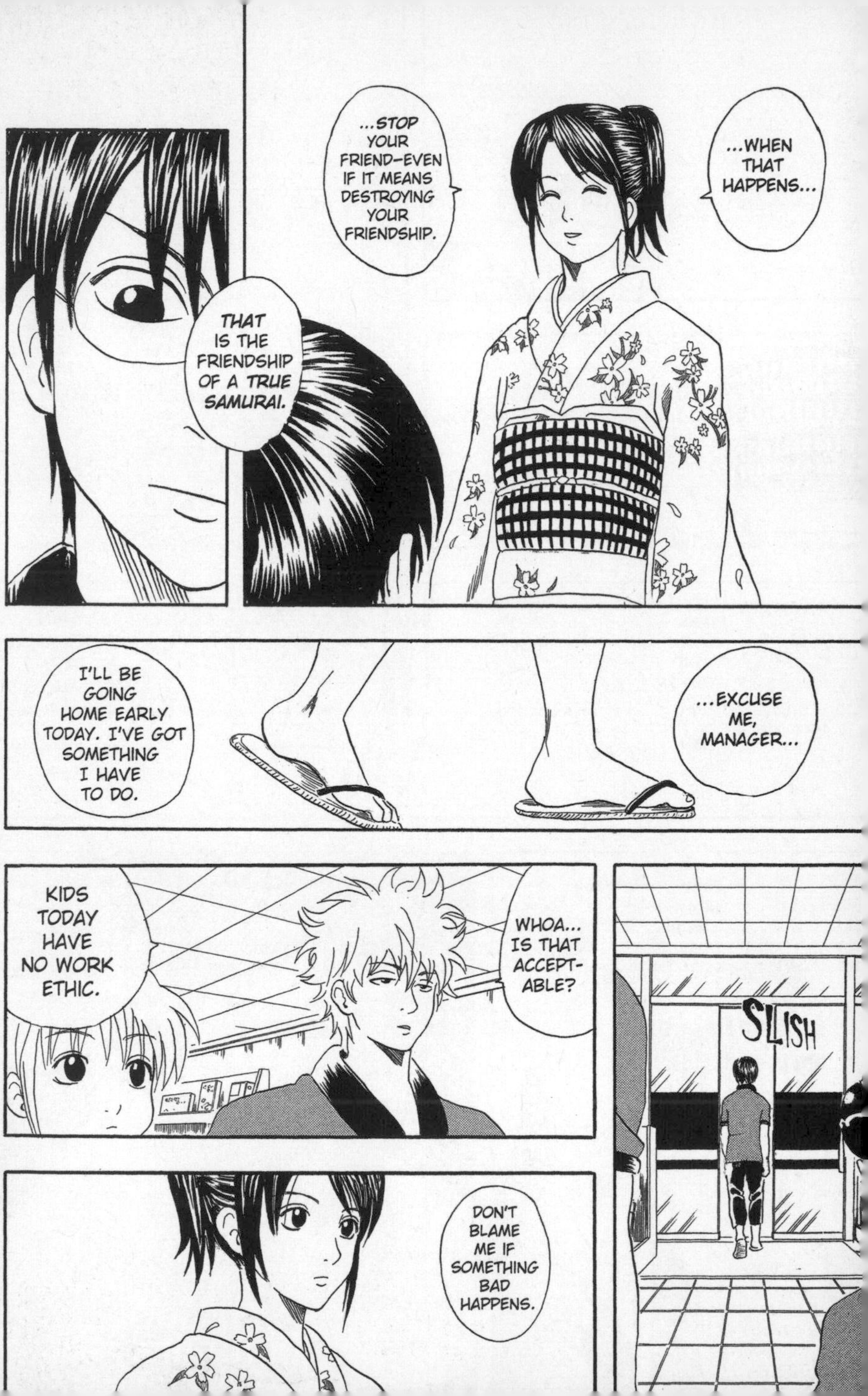
...WHEN THAT HAPPENS...
...STOP YOUR FRIEND—EVEN IF IT MEANS DESTROYING YOUR FRIENDSHIP.
THAT IS THE FRIENDSHIP OF A TRUE SAMURAI.
...EXCUSE ME, MANAGER...
I'LL BE GOING HOME EARLY TODAY. I'VE GOT SOMETHING I HAVE TO DO.
SLISH
WHOA... IS THAT ACCEPTABLE?
KIDS TODAY HAVE NO WORK ETHIC.
DON'T BLAME ME IF SOMETHING BAD HAPPENS.

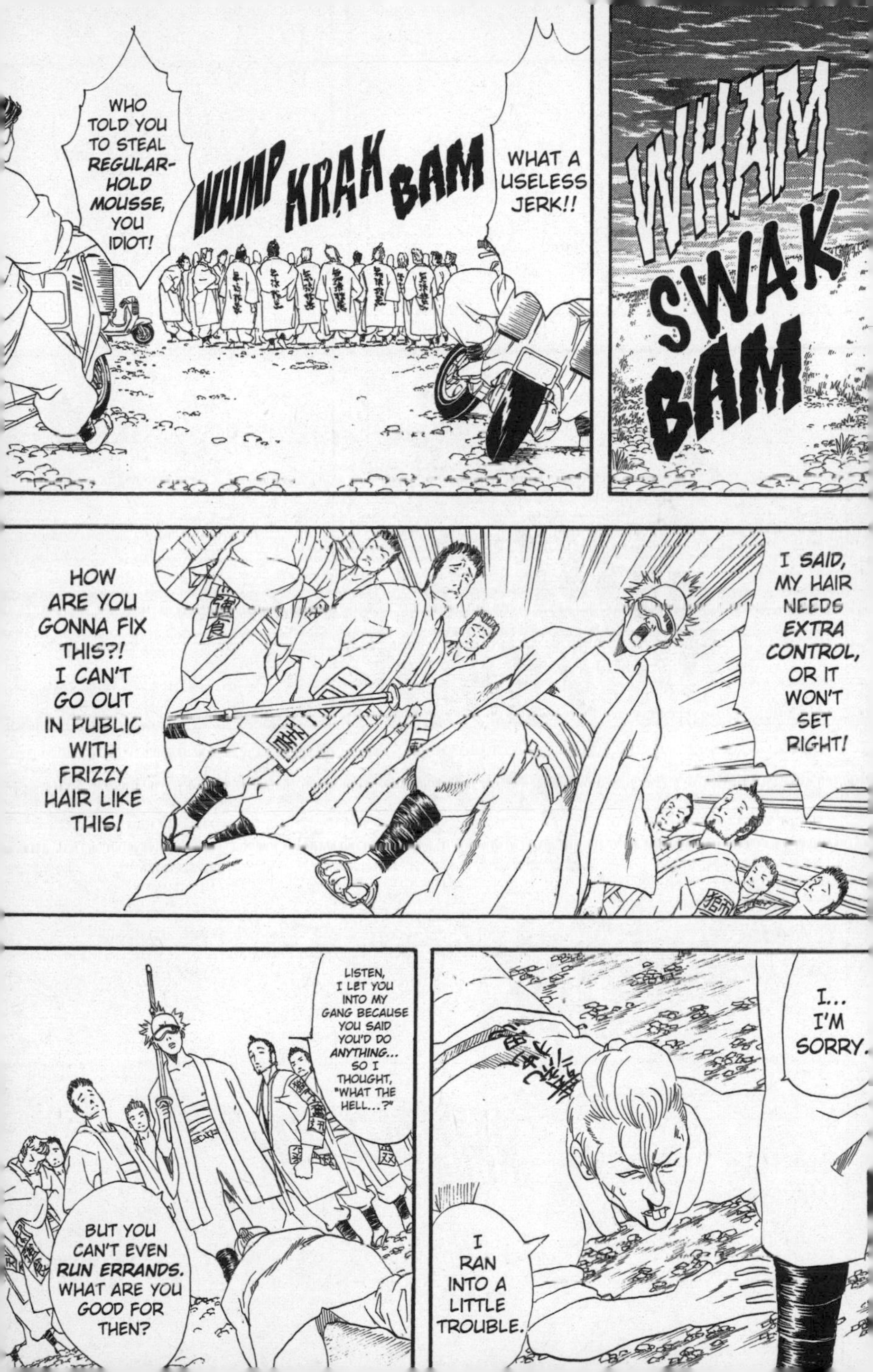
WHAM
SWAK
BAM
WHAT A USELESS JERK!!
WUMP KRAK BAM
WHO TOLD YOU TO STEAL REGULAR-HOLD MOUSSE, YOU IDIOT!
I SAID, MY HAIR NEEDS EXTRA CONTROL, OR IT WON'T SET RIGHT!
HOW ARE YOU GONNA FIX THIS?! I CAN'T GO OUT IN PUBLIC WITH FRIZZY HAIR LIKE THIS!
I... I'M SORRY.
I RAN INTO A LITTLE TROUBLE.
LISTEN, I LET YOU INTO MY GANG BECAUSE YOU SAID YOU'D DO ANYTHING... SO I THOUGHT, "WHAT THE HELL...?"
BUT YOU CAN'T EVEN RUN ERRANDS. WHAT ARE YOU GOOD FOR THEN?

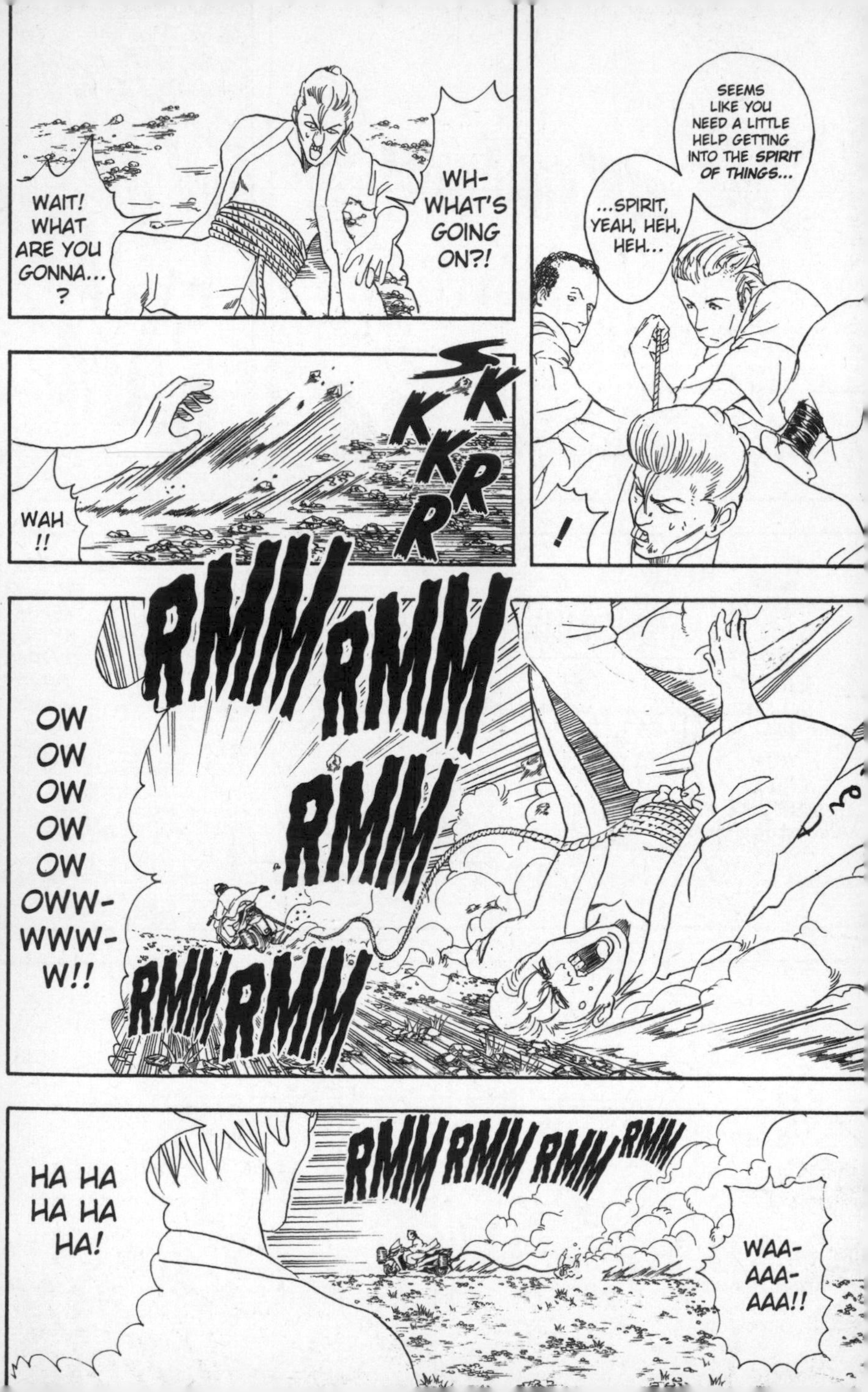
SEEMS LIKE YOU NEED A LITTLE HELP GETTING INTO THE SPIRIT OF THINGS...
...SPIRIT, YEAH, HEH, HEH...
!
WH- WHAT'S GOING ON?!
WAIT! WHAT ARE YOU GONNA... ?
SKKKRRR
WAH !!
RMMRMM RMM RMMRMM
OW OW OW OW OW OWW-WWW-W!!
RMM RMM RMM RMM
WAA-AAA-AAA!!
HA HA HA HA HA!

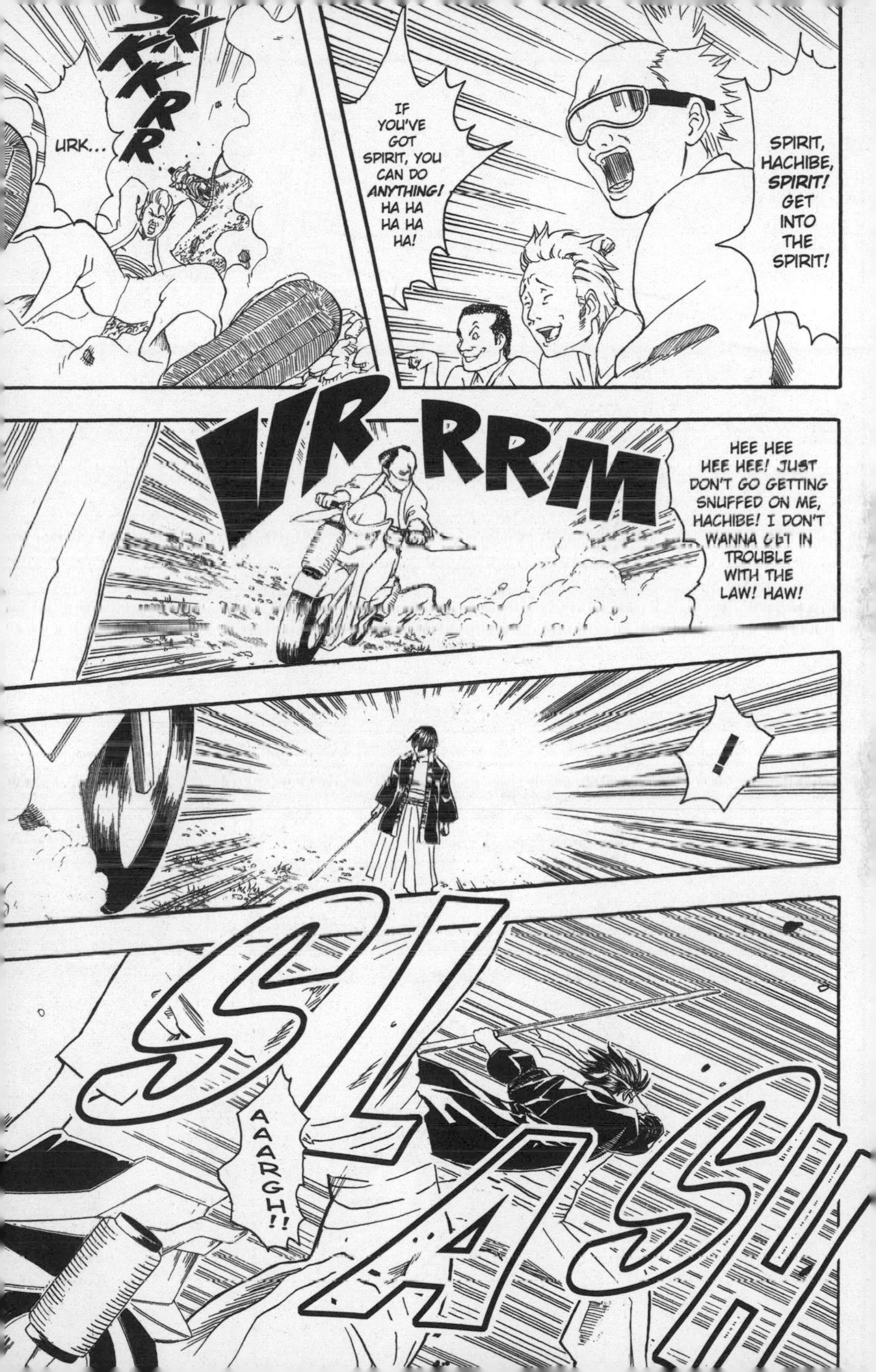
SPIRIT, HACHIBE, SPIRIT! GET INTO THE SPIRIT!
IF YOU'VE GOT SPIRIT, YOU CAN DO ANYTHING! HA HA HA HA HA!
SKKRR
URK...
VRRRM
HEE HEE HEE HEE! JUST DON'T GO GETTING SNUFFED ON ME, HACHIBE! I DON'T WANNA GET IN TROUBLE WITH THE LAW! HAW!
!
SLASH
AAARGH!!

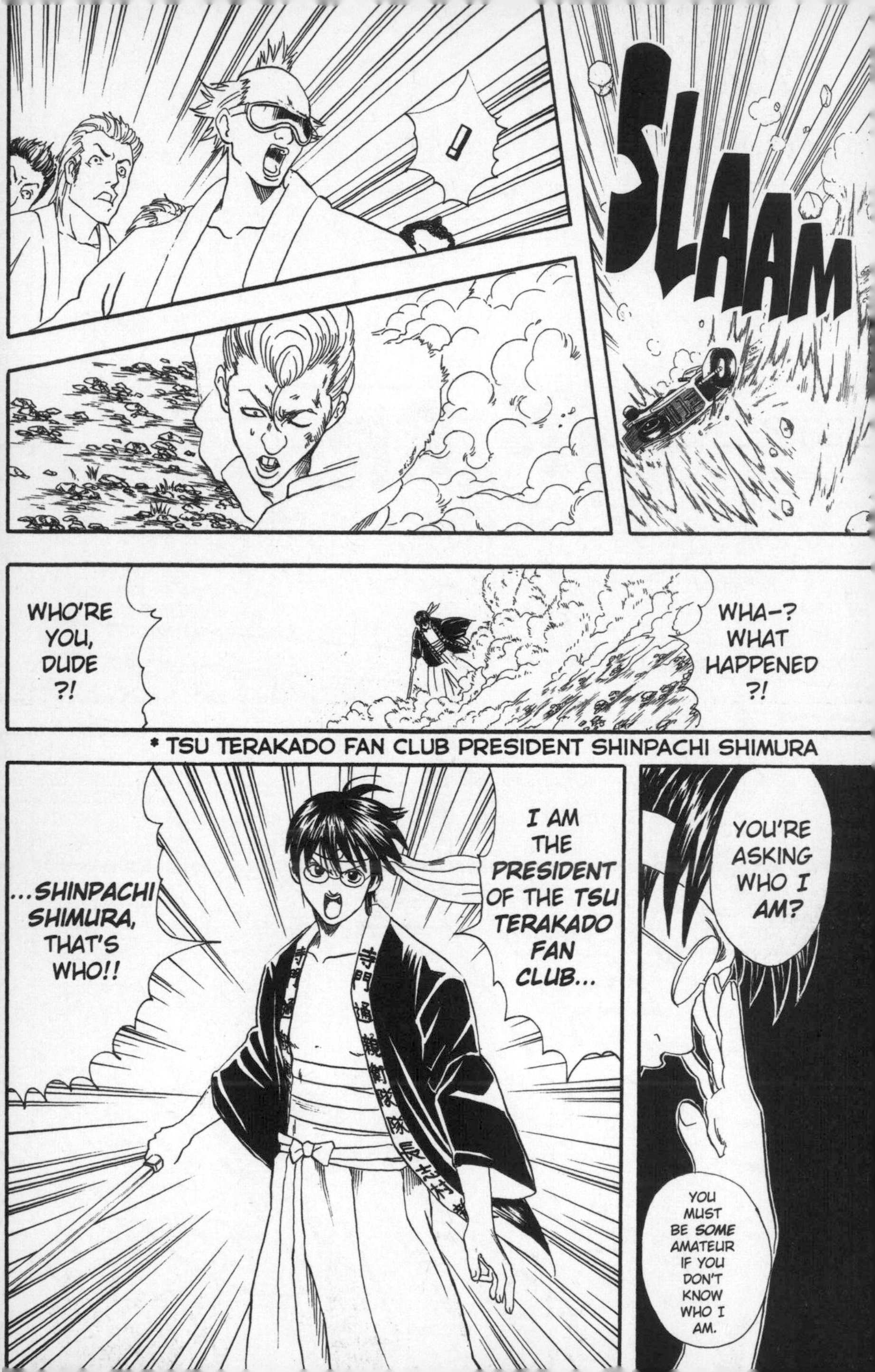
SLAAM
!
WHA-? WHAT HAPPENED ?!
WHO'RE YOU, DUDE ?!
* TSU TERAKADO FAN CLUB PRESIDENT SHINPACHI SHIMURA
YOU'RE ASKING WHO I AM?
YOU MUST BE SOME AMATEUR IF YOU DON'T KNOW WHO I AM.
I AM THE PRESIDENT OF THE TSU TERAKADO FAN CLUB...
...SHINPACHI SHIMURA, THAT'S WHO!!

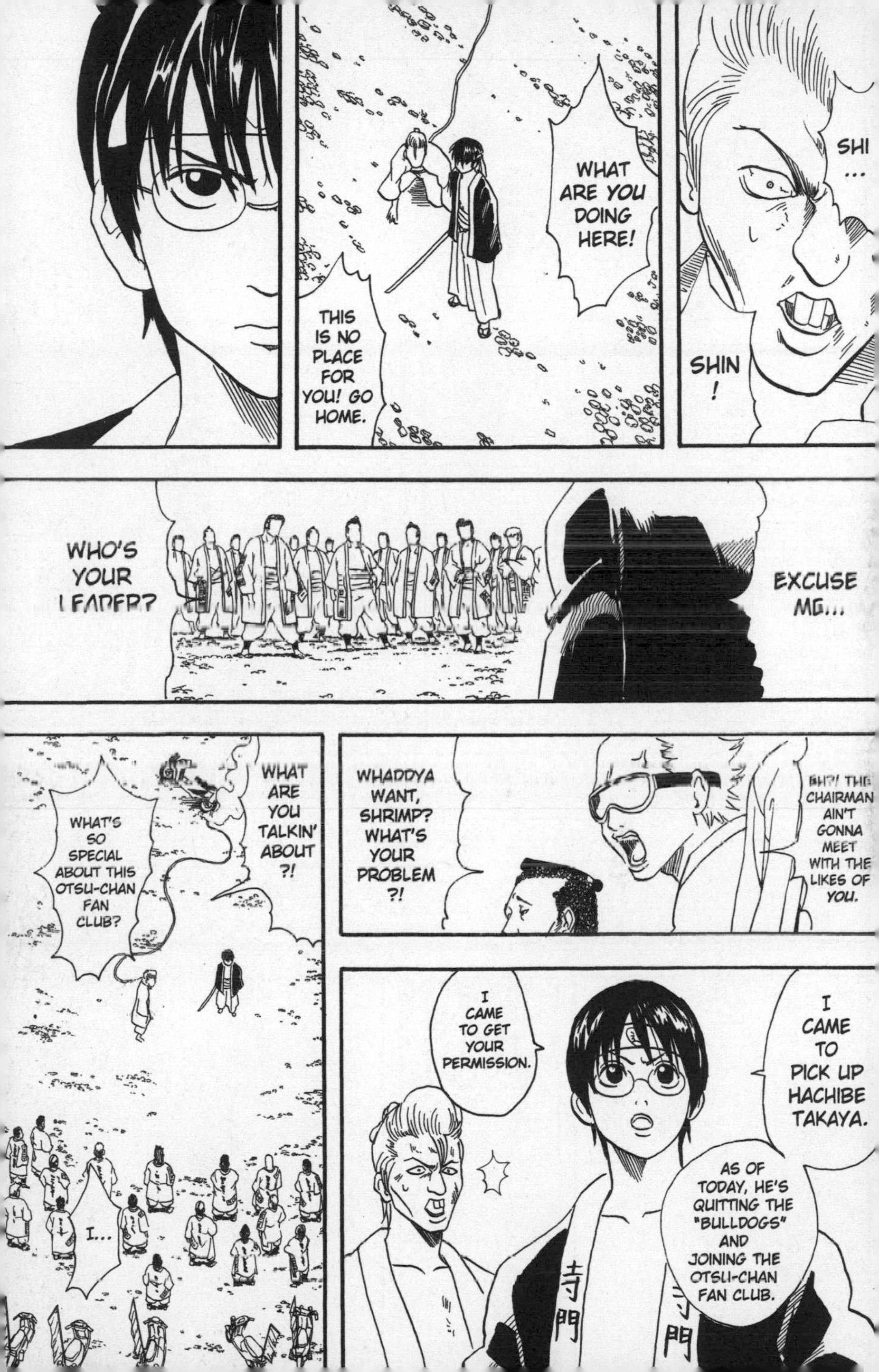
SHI ...
SHIN !
WHAT ARE YOU DOING HERE!
THIS IS NO PLACE FOR YOU! GO HOME.
EXCUSE ME...
WHO'S YOUR LEADER?
EH?! THE CHAIRMAN AIN'T GONNA MEET WITH THE LIKES OF YOU.
WHADDYA WANT, SHRIMP? WHAT'S YOUR PROBLEM ?!
I CAME TO PICK UP HACHIBE TAKAYA.
AS OF TODAY, HE'S QUITTING THE "BULLDOGS" AND JOINING THE OTSU-CHAN FAN CLUB.
I CAME TO GET YOUR PERMISSION.
WHAT ARE YOU TALKIN' ABOUT ?!
WHAT'S SO SPECIAL ABOUT THIS OTSU-CHAN FAN CLUB?
I...

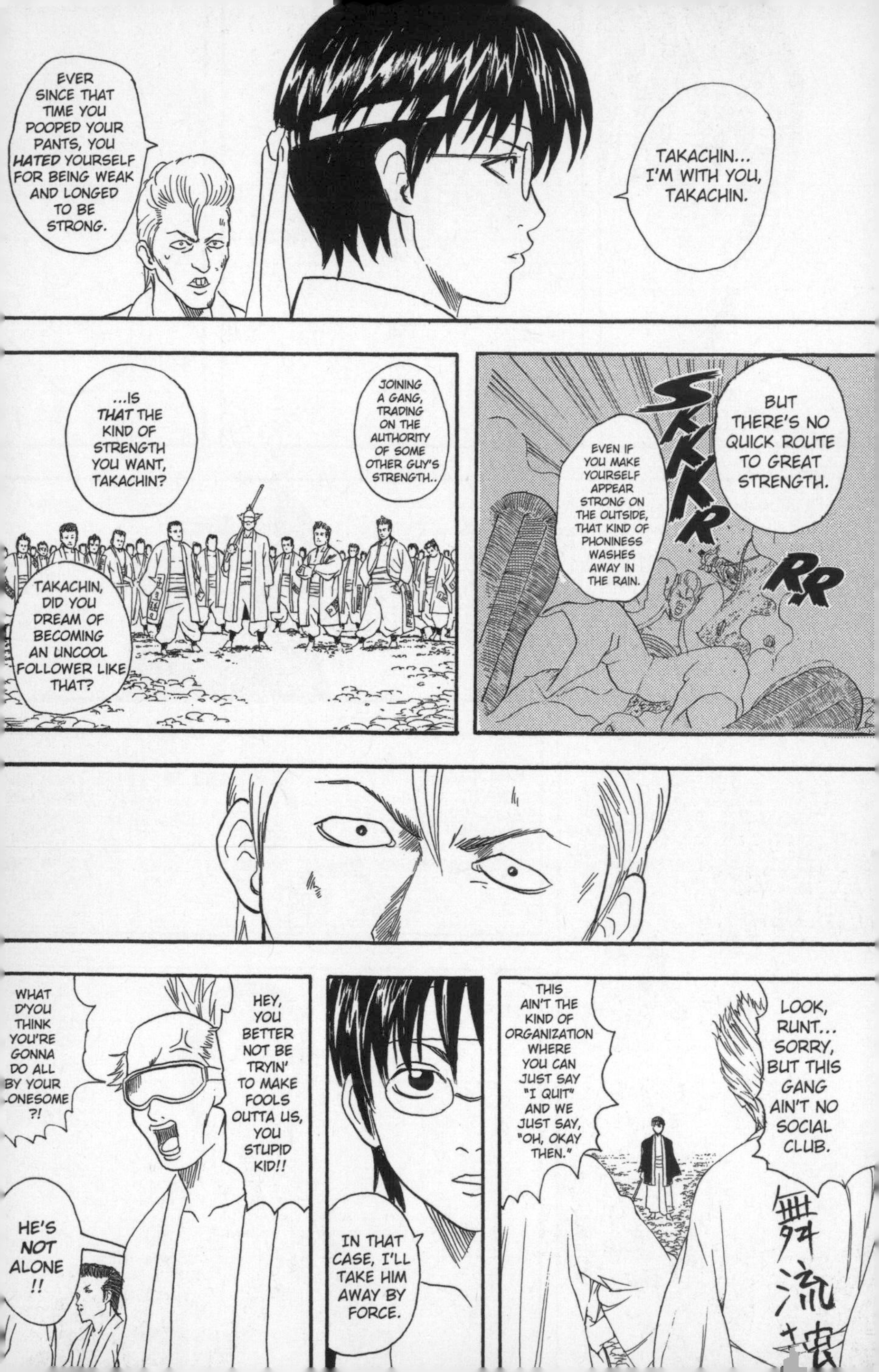
TAKACHIN... I'M WITH YOU, TAKACHIN.
EVER SINCE THAT TIME YOU POOPED YOUR PANTS, YOU *HATED* YOURSELF FOR BEING WEAK AND LONGED TO BE STRONG.
BUT THERE'S NO QUICK ROUTE TO GREAT STRENGTH.
SKKRRRR
EVEN IF YOU MAKE YOURSELF APPEAR STRONG ON THE OUTSIDE, THAT KIND OF PHONINESS WASHES AWAY IN THE RAIN.
JOINING A GANG, TRADING ON THE AUTHORITY OF SOME OTHER GUY'S STRENGTH..
...IS *THAT* THE KIND OF STRENGTH YOU WANT, TAKACHIN?
TAKACHIN, DID YOU DREAM OF BECOMING AN UNCOOL FOLLOWER LIKE THAT?
LOOK, RUNT... SORRY, BUT THIS GANG AIN'T NO SOCIAL CLUB.
THIS AIN'T THE KIND OF ORGANIZATION WHERE YOU CAN JUST SAY "I QUIT" AND WE JUST SAY, "OH, OKAY THEN."
舞流
IN THAT CASE, I'LL TAKE HIM AWAY BY FORCE.
HEY, YOU BETTER NOT BE TRYIN' TO MAKE FOOLS OUTTA US, YOU STUPID KID!!
WHAT D'YOU THINK YOU'RE GONNA DO ALL BY YOUR ONESOME?!
HE'S *NOT* ALONE!!

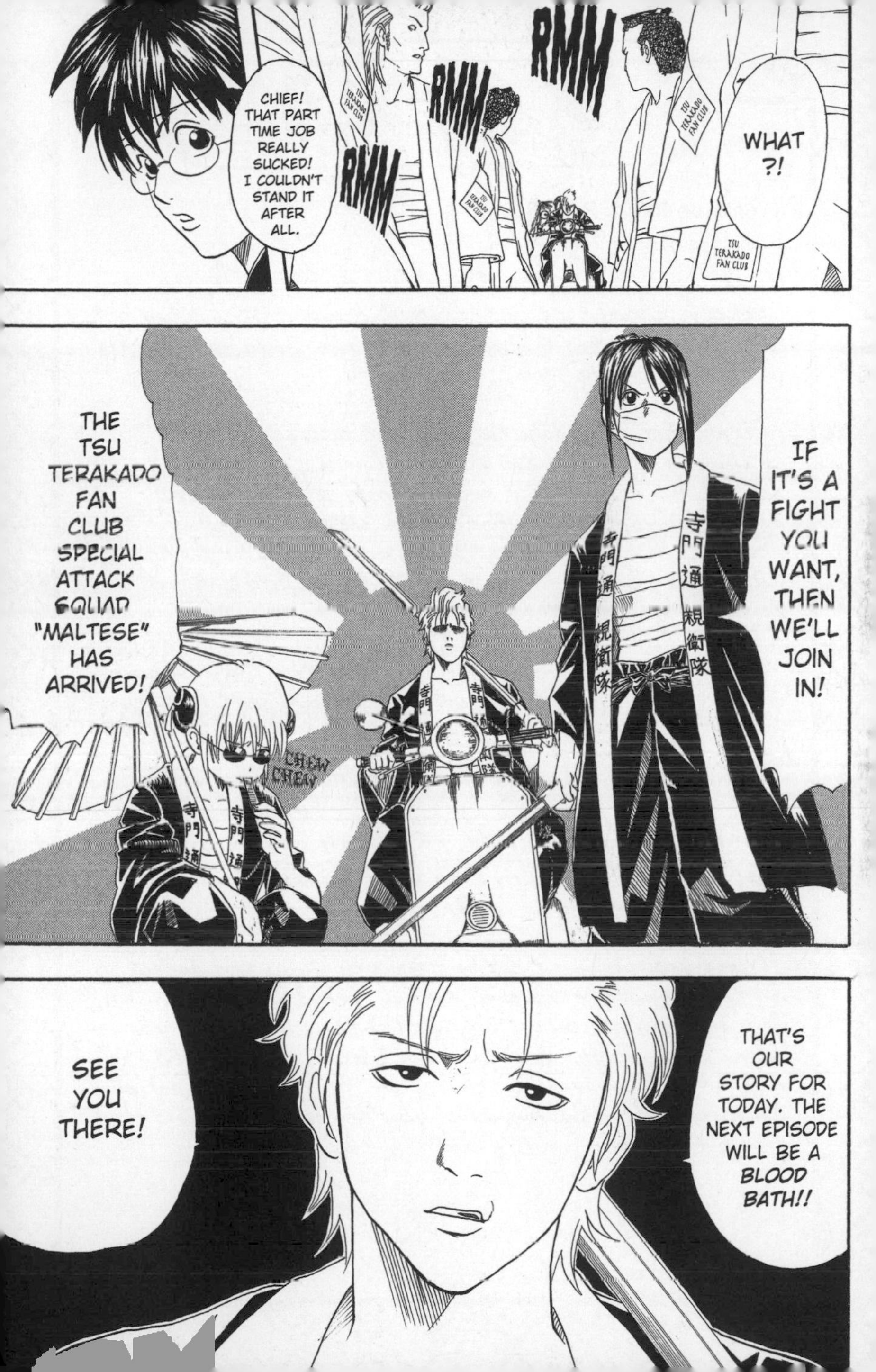
WHAT?!
TSU TERAKADO FAN CLUB
TSU TERAKADO FAN CLUB
RMM
RMM
RMM
TSU TERAKADO FAN CLUB
TSU TERAKADO FAN CLUB
CHIEF! THAT PART TIME JOB REALLY SUCKED! I COULDN'T STAND IT AFTER ALL.
IF IT'S A FIGHT YOU WANT, THEN WE'LL JOIN IN!
寺門通親衛隊
寺門通親衛隊
THE TSU TERAKADO FAN CLUB SPECIAL ATTACK SQUAD "MALTESE" HAS ARRIVED!
CHEW CHEW
THAT'S OUR STORY FOR TODAY. THE NEXT EPISODE WILL BE A BLOOD BATH!!
SEE YOU THERE!

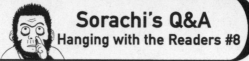

Sorachi's Q&A
Hanging with the Readers #8

(Continued from Page 86)

Twenty years ago, the Amanto came to the Earth. The samurai, though scared, fought bravely—still, they got totally creamed. At the time, Gin was just a little kid without a single pubic hair.

↓

After that, the Bakufu also got scared, so they opened up the country to the Amanto. The Amanto built the Terminal and began immigrating to planet Earth in a huge wave. A few pockets of samurai fought on in a vain attempt to drive out the Amanto, but fared poorly. At that point, Gin's pubic hairs began to grow.

↓

The Amanto wormed their way into the Bakufu government itself, so they ended up always getting their way. A few samurai struggled on. Gin started getting rowdy at about that time...

↓

The Amanto became sick and tired of the samurai and issued the Sword Abolishment Edict. The samurai lost all their strength. Even the samurai who continued to fight are now exhausted.

There you go. That's the story of how the defeat of the samurai occurred over a period of some decades and is collectively called the Anti-Foreigner War. It basically was a losing battle. Gin and his friends got involved in the second half of this period. In conclusion, Shimomura, you go out and stand in the hallway for a while and think about that.

(#9 is on Page 150)

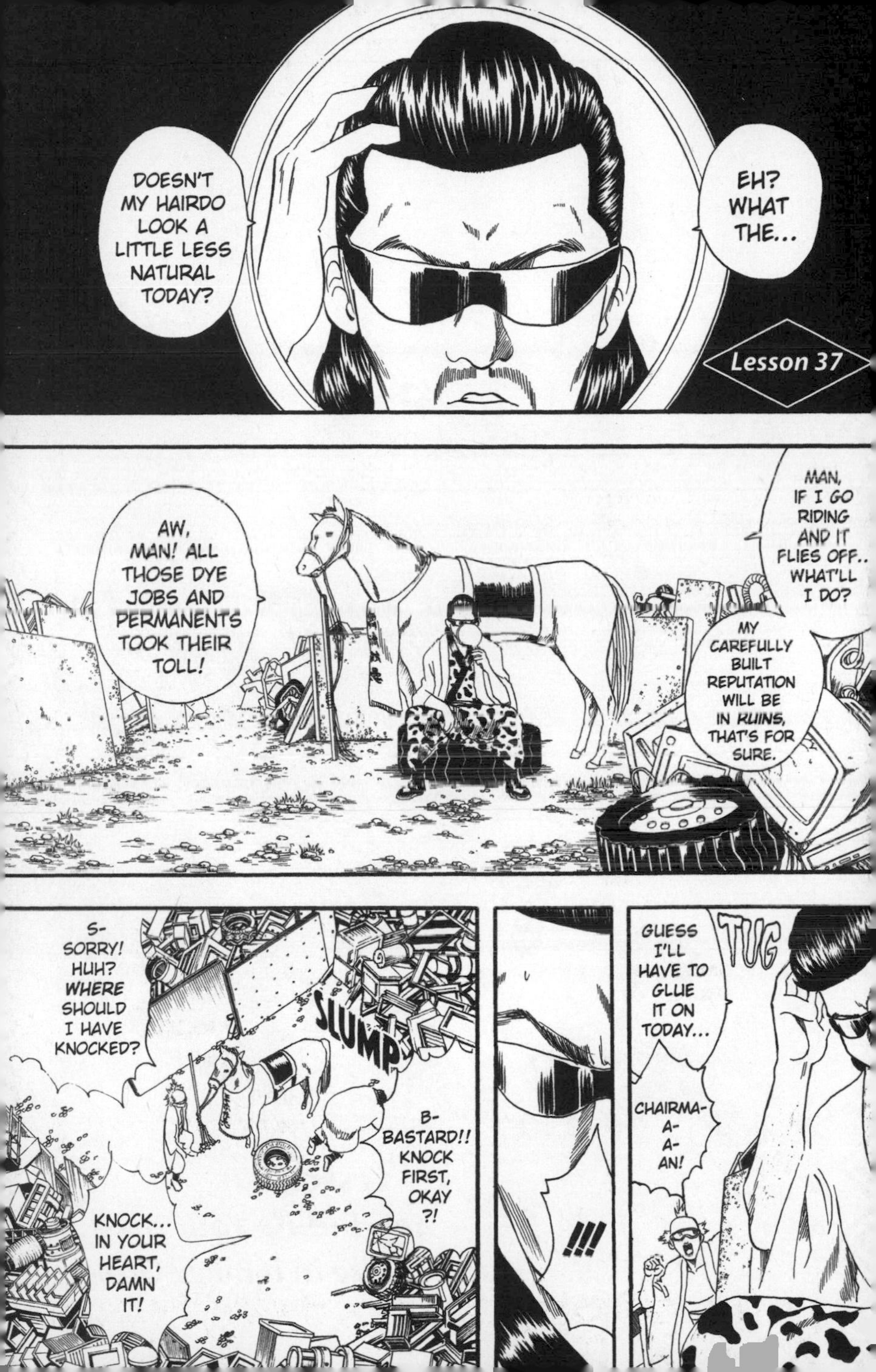
EH? WHAT THE...
DOESN'T MY HAIRDO LOOK A LITTLE LESS NATURAL TODAY?
Lesson 37
MAN, IF I GO RIDING AND IT FLIES OFF... WHAT'LL I DO?
MY CAREFULLY BUILT REPUTATION WILL BE IN RUINS, THAT'S FOR SURE.
AW, MAN! ALL THOSE DYE JOBS AND PERMANENTS TOOK THEIR TOLL!
TUG
GUESS I'LL HAVE TO GLUE IT ON TODAY...
CHAIRMA-A-A-AN!
!!!
SLUMP
B-BASTARD!! KNOCK FIRST, OKAY?!
S-SORRY! HUH? WHERE SHOULD I HAVE KNOCKED?
KNOCK... IN YOUR HEART, DAMN IT!

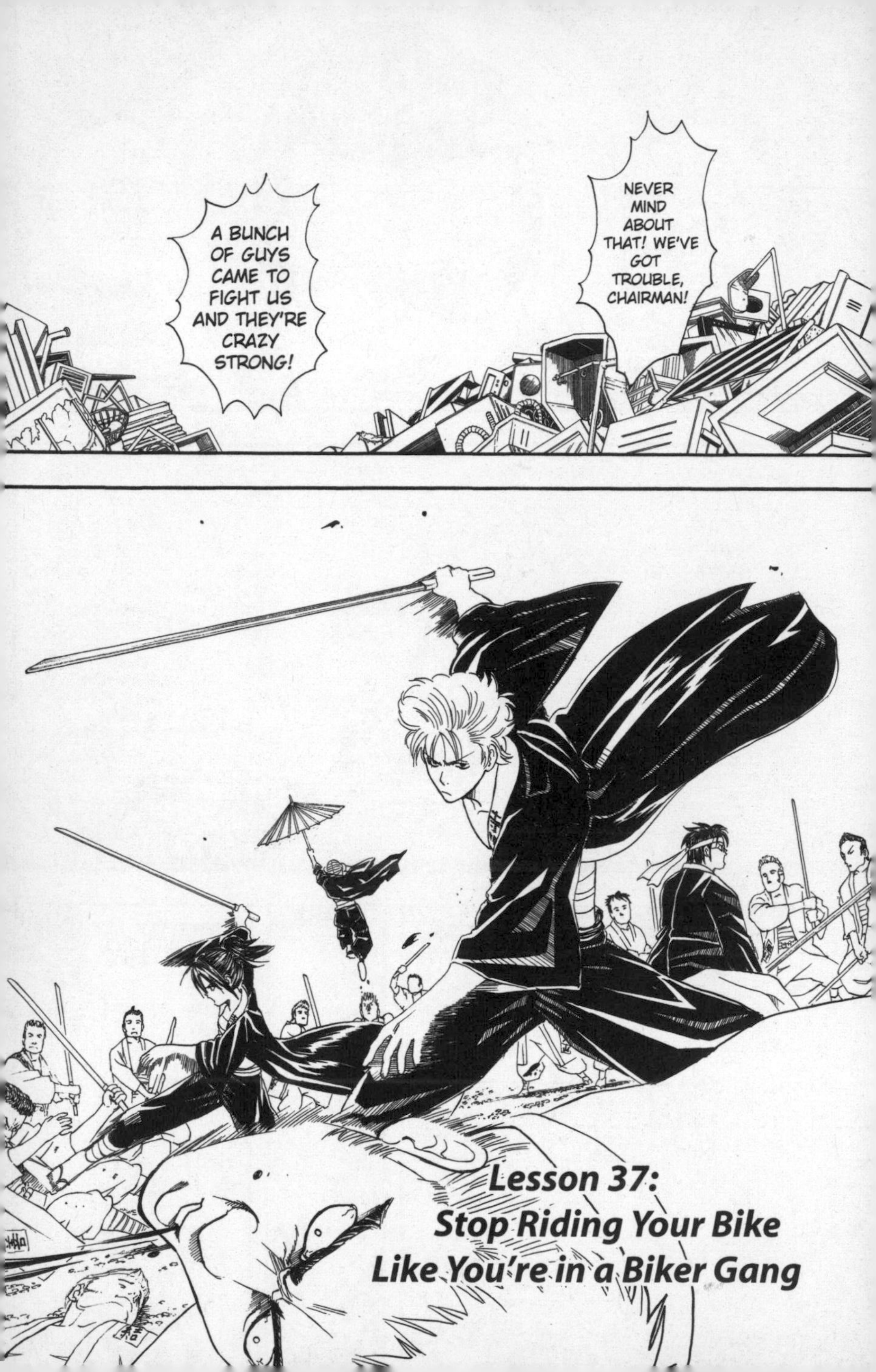
NEVER MIND ABOUT THAT! WE'VE GOT TROUBLE, CHAIRMAN!
A BUNCH OF GUYS CAME TO FIGHT US AND THEY'RE CRAZY STRONG!

Lesson 37: Stop Riding Your Bike Like You're in a Biker Gang

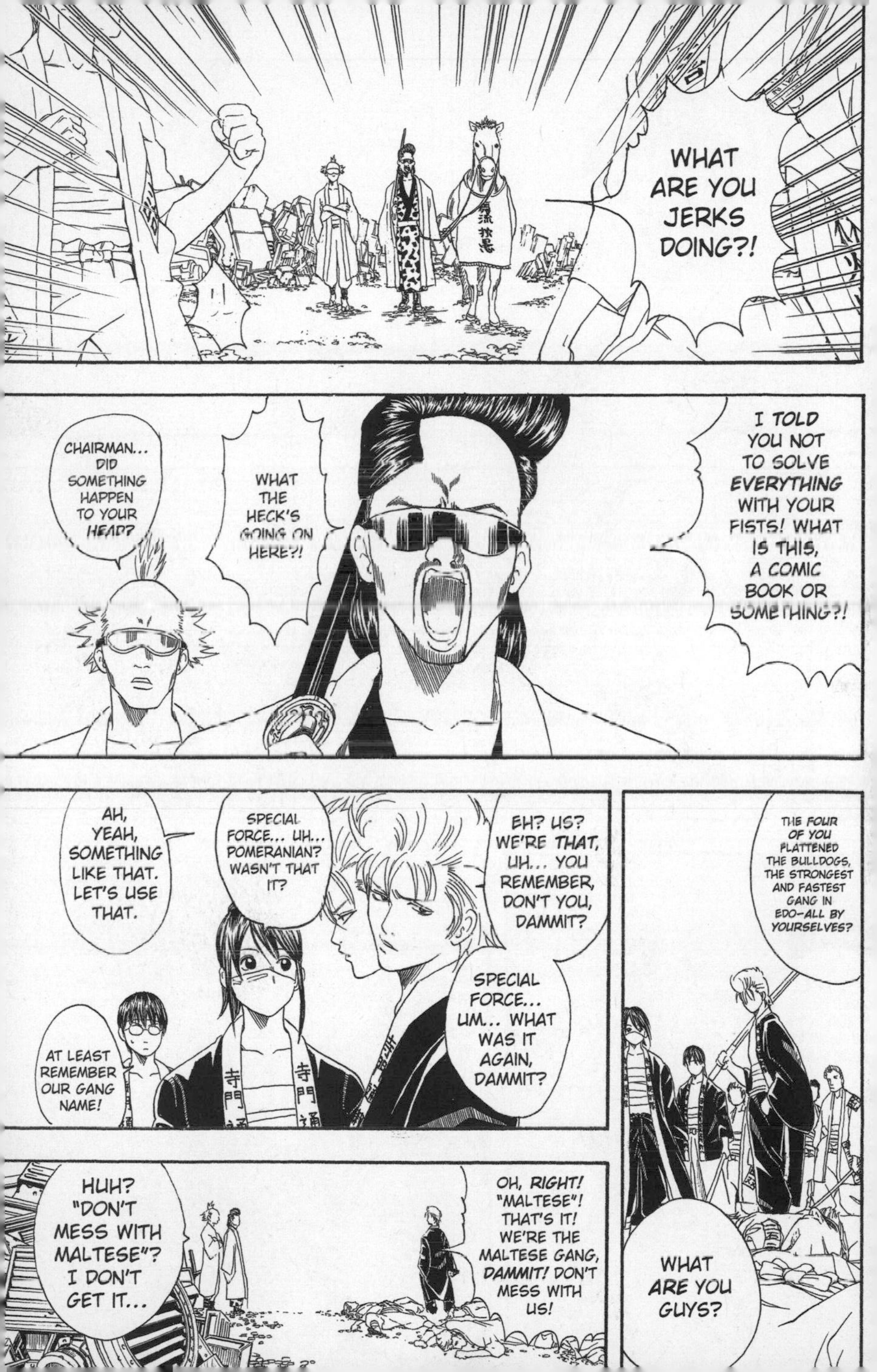
WHAT ARE YOU JERKS DOING?!
I TOLD YOU NOT TO SOLVE EVERYTHING WITH YOUR FISTS! WHAT IS THIS, A COMIC BOOK OR SOMETHING?!
WHAT THE HECK'S GOING ON HERE?!
CHAIRMAN... DID SOMETHING HAPPEN TO YOUR HEAD?
THE FOUR OF YOU FLATTENED THE BULLDOGS, THE STRONGEST AND FASTEST GANG IN EDO—ALL BY YOURSELVES?
WHAT ARE YOU GUYS?
EH? US? WE'RE THAT, UH... YOU REMEMBER, DON'T YOU, DAMMIT?
SPECIAL FORCE... UM... WHAT WAS IT AGAIN, DAMMIT?
SPECIAL FORCE... UH... POMERANIAN? WASN'T THAT IT?
AH, YEAH, SOMETHING LIKE THAT. LET'S USE THAT.
AT LEAST REMEMBER OUR GANG NAME!
OH, RIGHT! "MALTESE"! THAT'S IT! WE'RE THE MALTESE GANG, DAMMIT! DON'T MESS WITH US!
HUH? "DON'T MESS WITH MALTESE"? I DON'T GET IT...

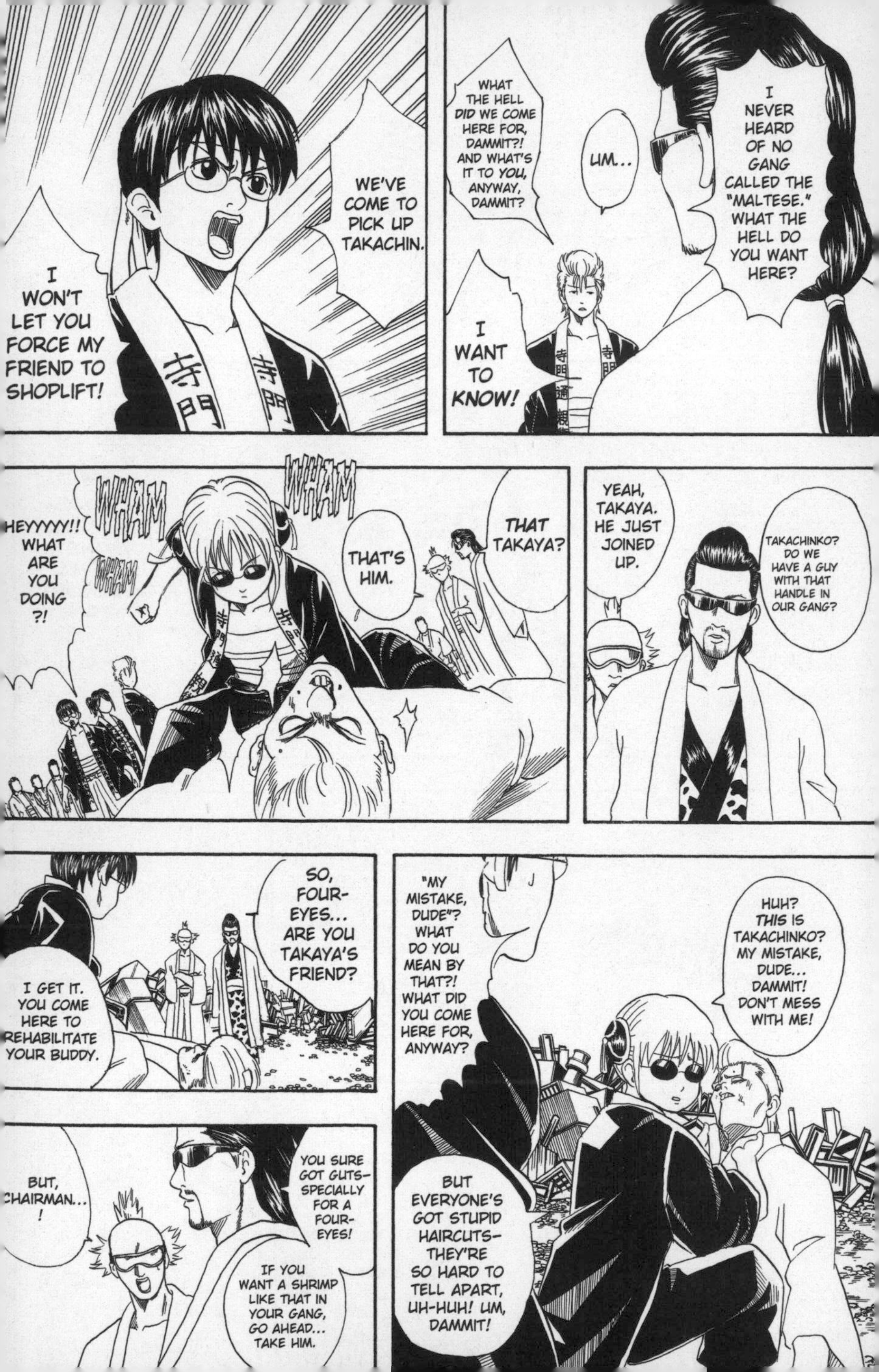
I NEVER HEARD OF NO GANG CALLED THE "MALTESE." WHAT THE HELL DO YOU WANT HERE?
UM...
WHAT THE HELL DID WE COME HERE FOR, DAMMIT?! AND WHAT'S IT TO YOU, ANYWAY, DAMMIT?
I WANT TO KNOW!
WE'VE COME TO PICK UP TAKACHIN.
I WON'T LET YOU FORCE MY FRIEND TO SHOPLIFT!
TAKACHINKO? DO WE HAVE A GUY WITH THAT HANDLE IN OUR GANG?
YEAH, TAKAYA. HE JUST JOINED UP.
THAT TAKAYA?
THAT'S HIM.
WHAM
WHAM
WHAM
HEYYYYY!! WHAT ARE YOU DOING ?!
HUH? THIS IS TAKACHINKO? MY MISTAKE, DUDE... DAMMIT! DON'T MESS WITH ME!
"MY MISTAKE, DUDE"? WHAT DO YOU MEAN BY THAT?! WHAT DID YOU COME HERE FOR, ANYWAY?
BUT EVERYONE'S GOT STUPID HAIRCUTS- THEY'RE SO HARD TO TELL APART, UH-HUH! UM, DAMMIT!
SO, FOUR-EYES... ARE YOU TAKAYA'S FRIEND?
I GET IT. YOU COME HERE TO REHABILITATE YOUR BUDDY.
YOU SURE GOT GUTS-SPECIALLY FOR A FOUR-EYES!
IF YOU WANT A SHRIMP LIKE THAT IN YOUR GANG, GO AHEAD... TAKE HIM.
BUT, CHAIRMAN... !

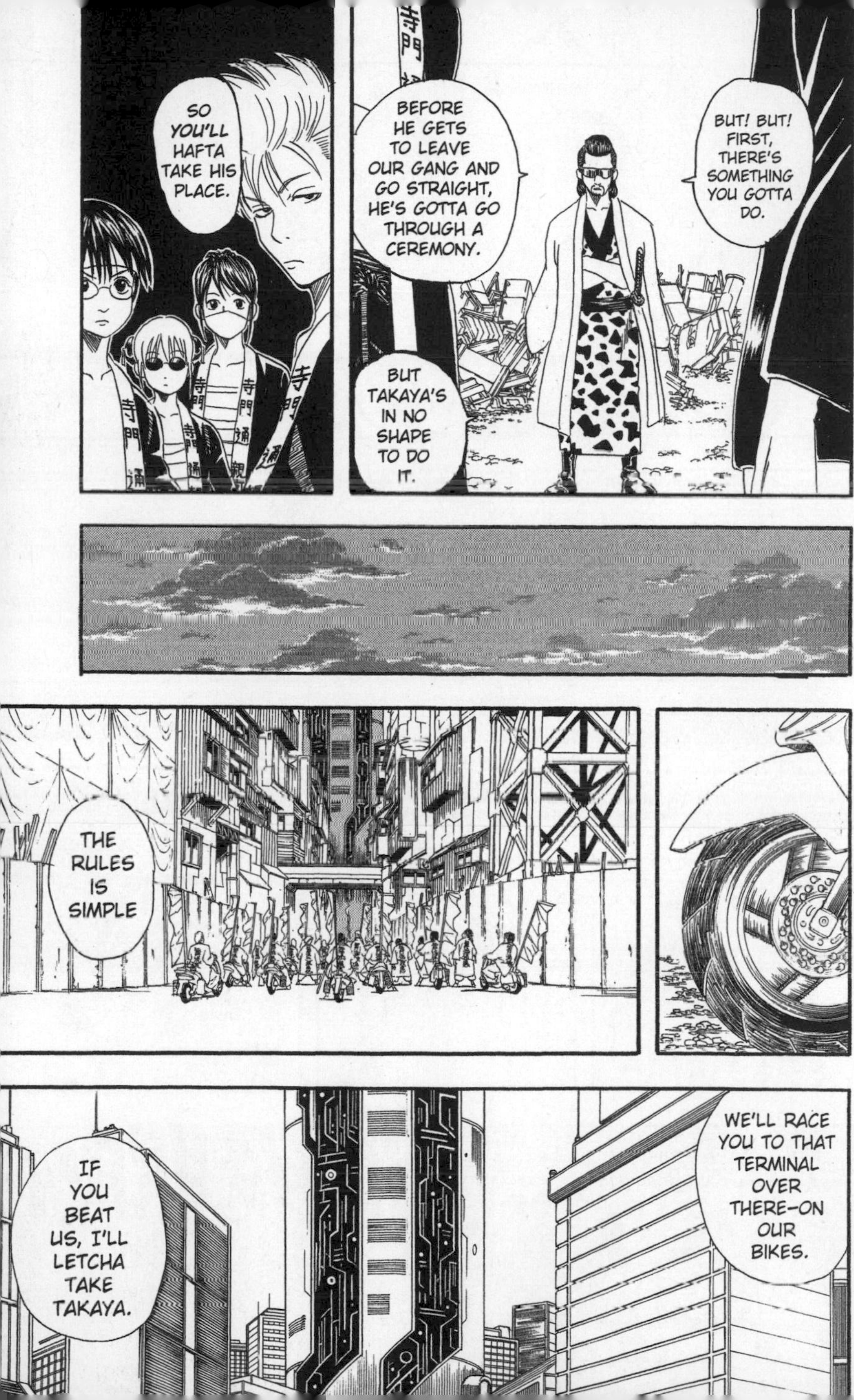
BUT! BUT! FIRST, THERE'S SOMETHING YOU GOTTA DO.
BEFORE HE GETS TO LEAVE OUR GANG AND GO STRAIGHT, HE'S GOTTA GO THROUGH A CEREMONY.
BUT TAKAYA'S IN NO SHAPE TO DO IT.
SO YOU'LL HAFTA TAKE HIS PLACE.
THE RULES IS SIMPLE
WE'LL RACE YOU TO THAT TERMINAL OVER THERE—ON OUR BIKES.
IF YOU BEAT US, I'LL LETCHA TAKE TAKAYA.

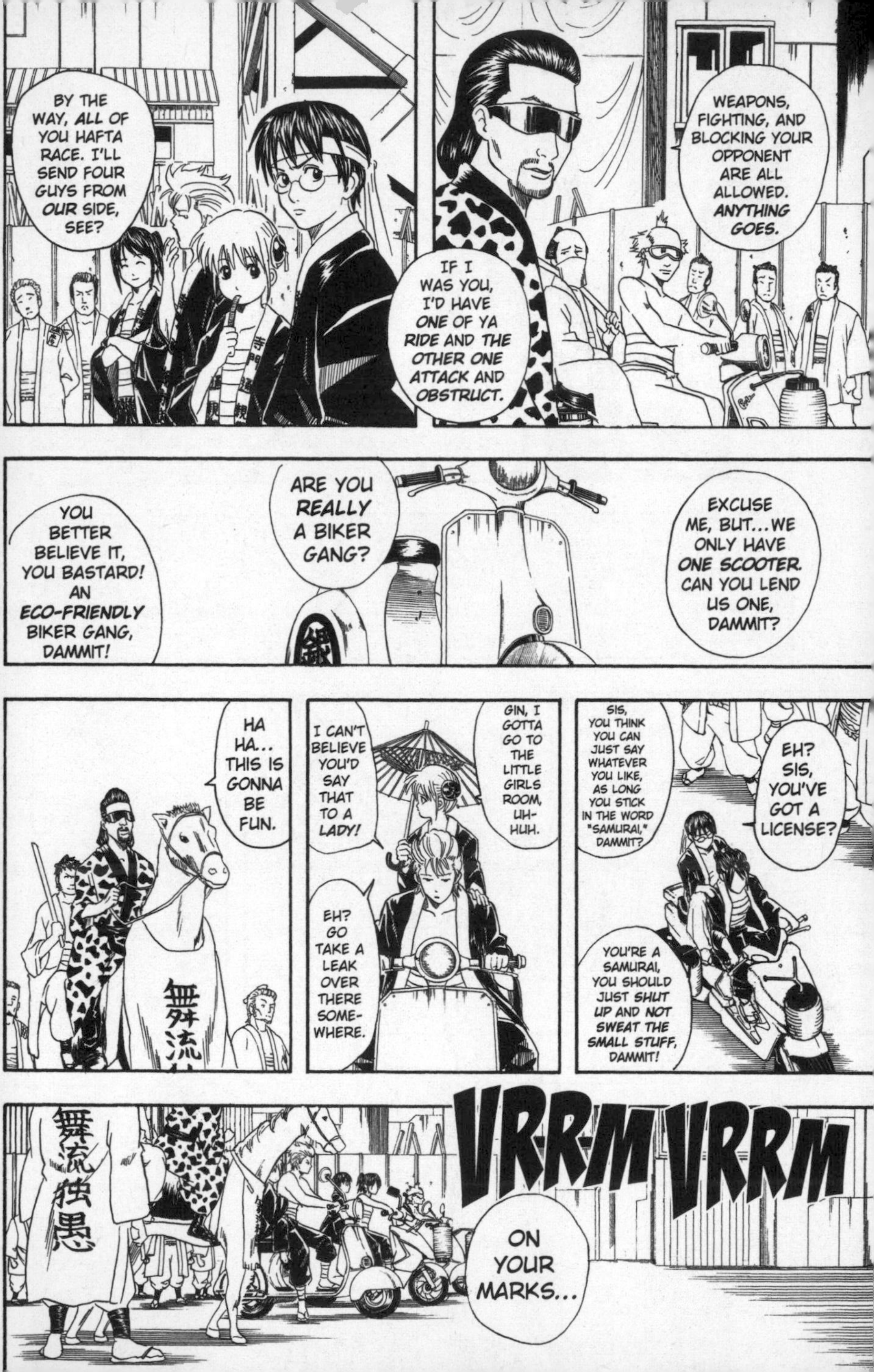
WEAPONS, FIGHTING, AND BLOCKING YOUR OPPONENT ARE ALL ALLOWED. ANYTHING GOES.
IF I WAS YOU, I'D HAVE ONE OF YA RIDE AND THE OTHER ONE ATTACK AND OBSTRUCT.
BY THE WAY, ALL OF YOU HAFTA RACE. I'LL SEND FOUR GUYS FROM OUR SIDE, SEE?
EXCUSE ME, BUT...WE ONLY HAVE ONE SCOOTER. CAN YOU LEND US ONE, DAMMIT?
ARE YOU REALLY A BIKER GANG?
YOU BETTER BELIEVE IT, YOU BASTARD! AN ECO-FRIENDLY BIKER GANG, DAMMIT!
EH? SIS, YOU'VE GOT A LICENSE?
SIS, YOU THINK YOU CAN JUST SAY WHATEVER YOU LIKE, AS LONG YOU STICK IN THE WORD "SAMURAI," DAMMIT?
YOU'RE A SAMURAI, YOU SHOULD JUST SHUT UP AND NOT SWEAT THE SMALL STUFF, DAMMIT!
GIN, I GOTTA GO TO THE LITTLE GIRLS ROOM, UH-HUH.
I CAN'T BELIEVE YOU'D SAY THAT TO A LADY!
EH? GO TAKE A LEAK OVER THERE SOME-WHERE.
HA HA... THIS IS GONNA BE FUN.
VR-RM VRRM
ON YOUR MARKS...
舞流独愚

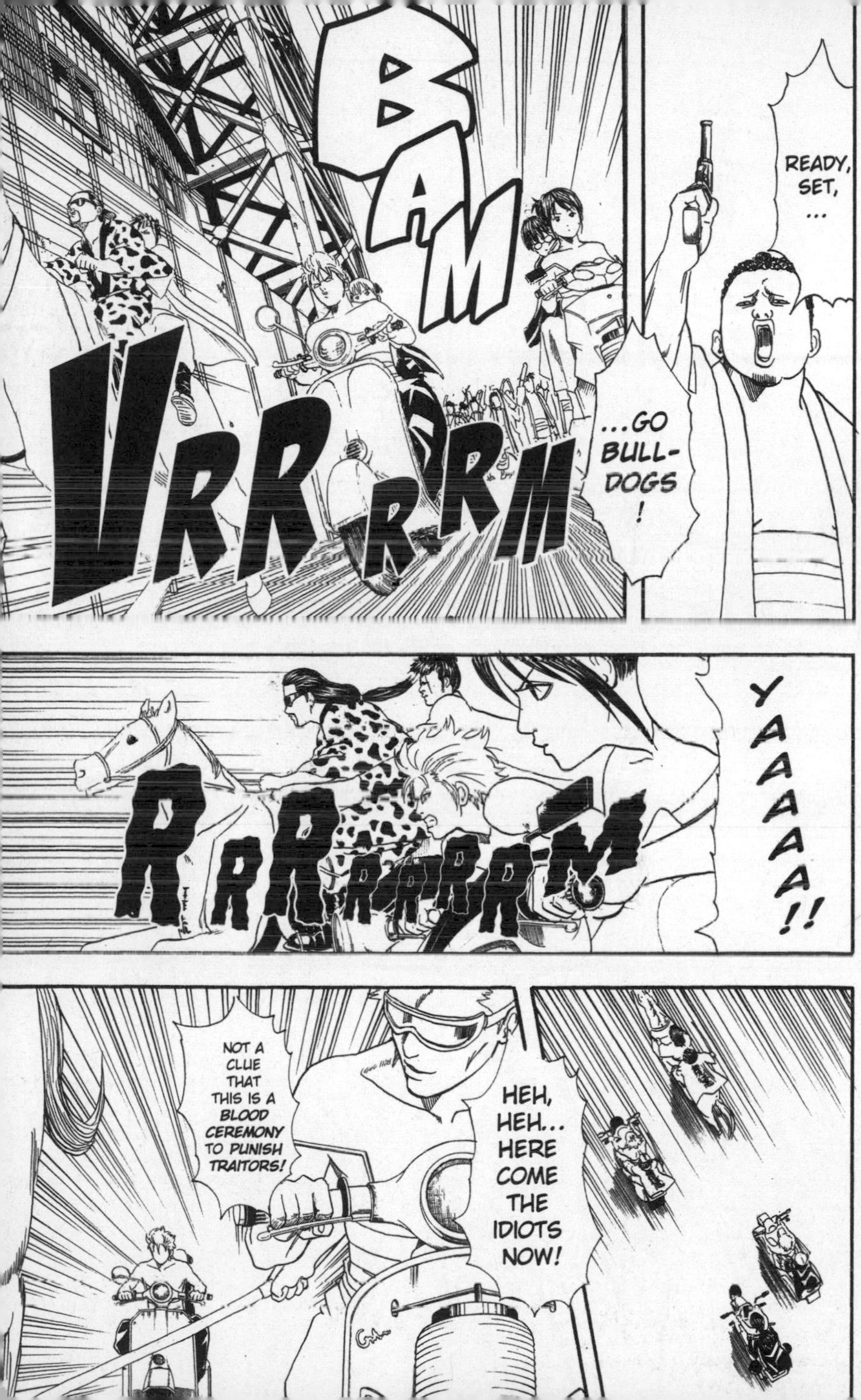
READY, SET, ...
...GO BULL-DOGS!
BAM
VRRRRM
YAAAAA!!
RRRRRRRM
HEH, HEH... HERE COME THE IDIOTS NOW!
NOT A CLUE THAT THIS IS A BLOOD CEREMONY TO PUNISH TRAITORS!

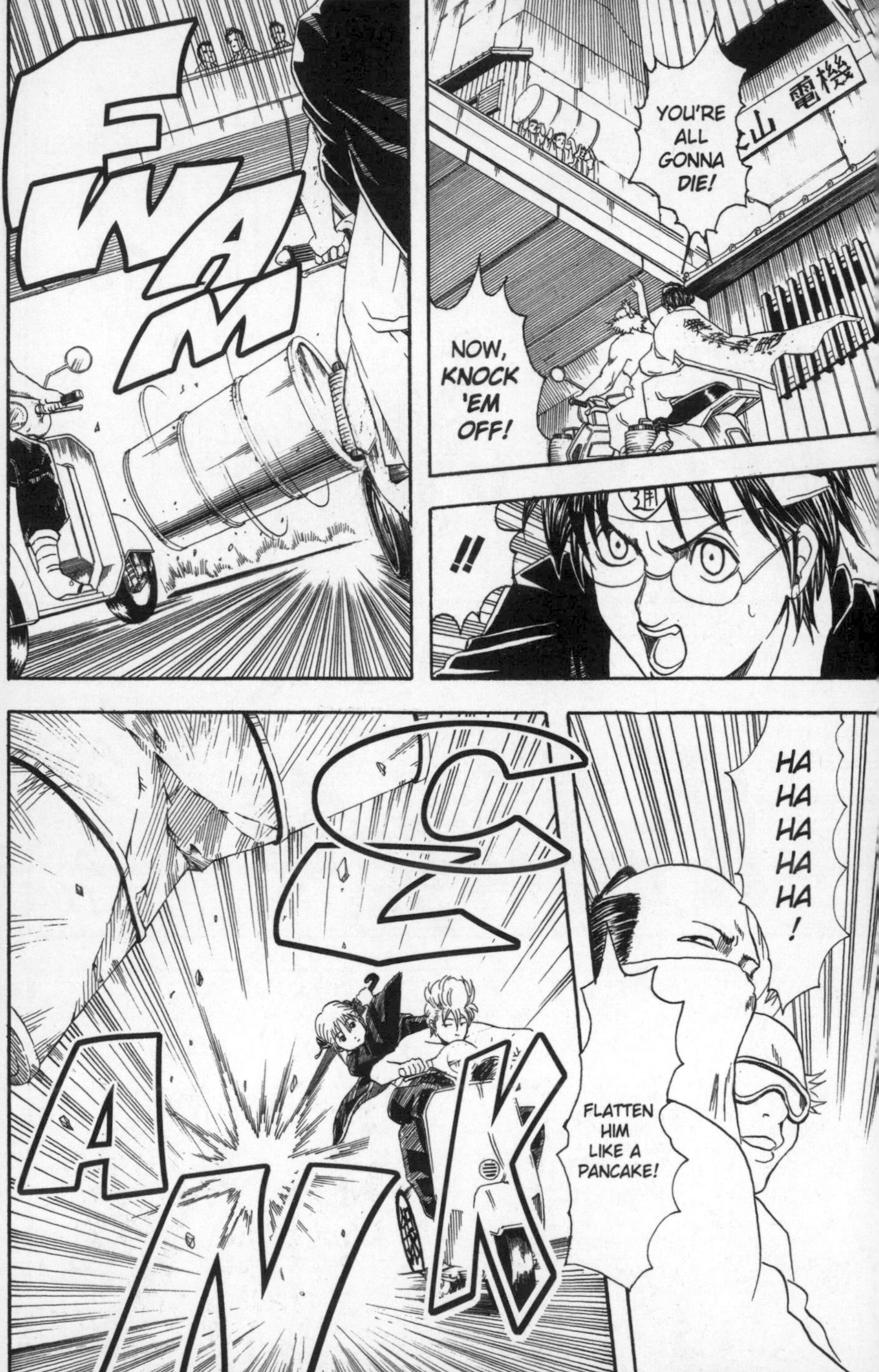
YOU'RE ALL GONNA DIE!
NOW, KNOCK 'EM OFF!
!!
HA HA HA HA HA!
FLATTEN HIM LIKE A PANCAKE!

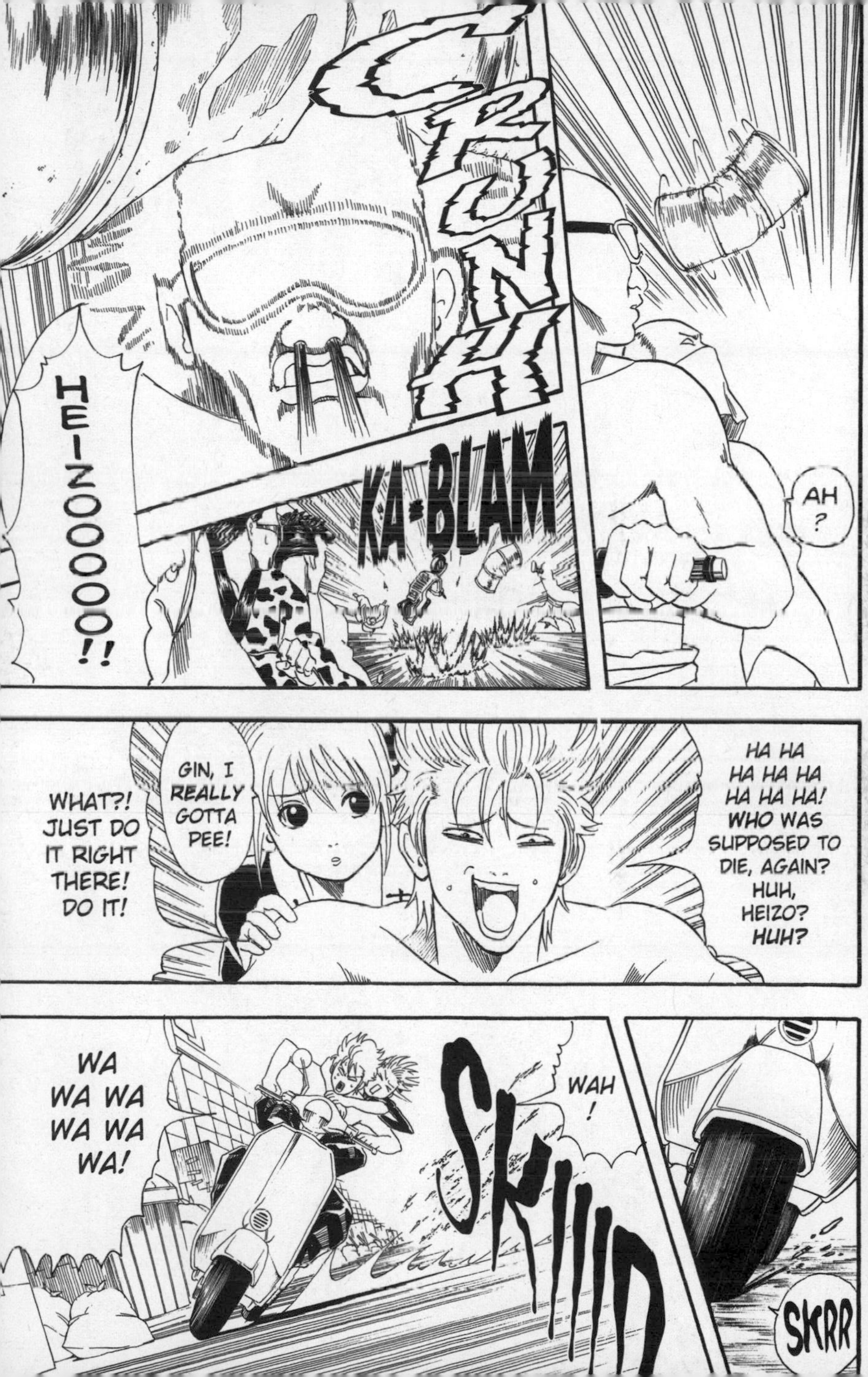
AH?
CRUNCH
KA-BLAM
HEIZOOOOO!!
HA HA HA HA HA HA HA HA! WHO WAS SUPPOSED TO DIE, AGAIN? HUH, HEIZO? HUH?
GIN, I REALLY GOTTA PEE!
WHAT?! JUST DO IT RIGHT THERE! DO IT!
SKRR
SKIIID
WAH!
WA WA WA WA WA WA!

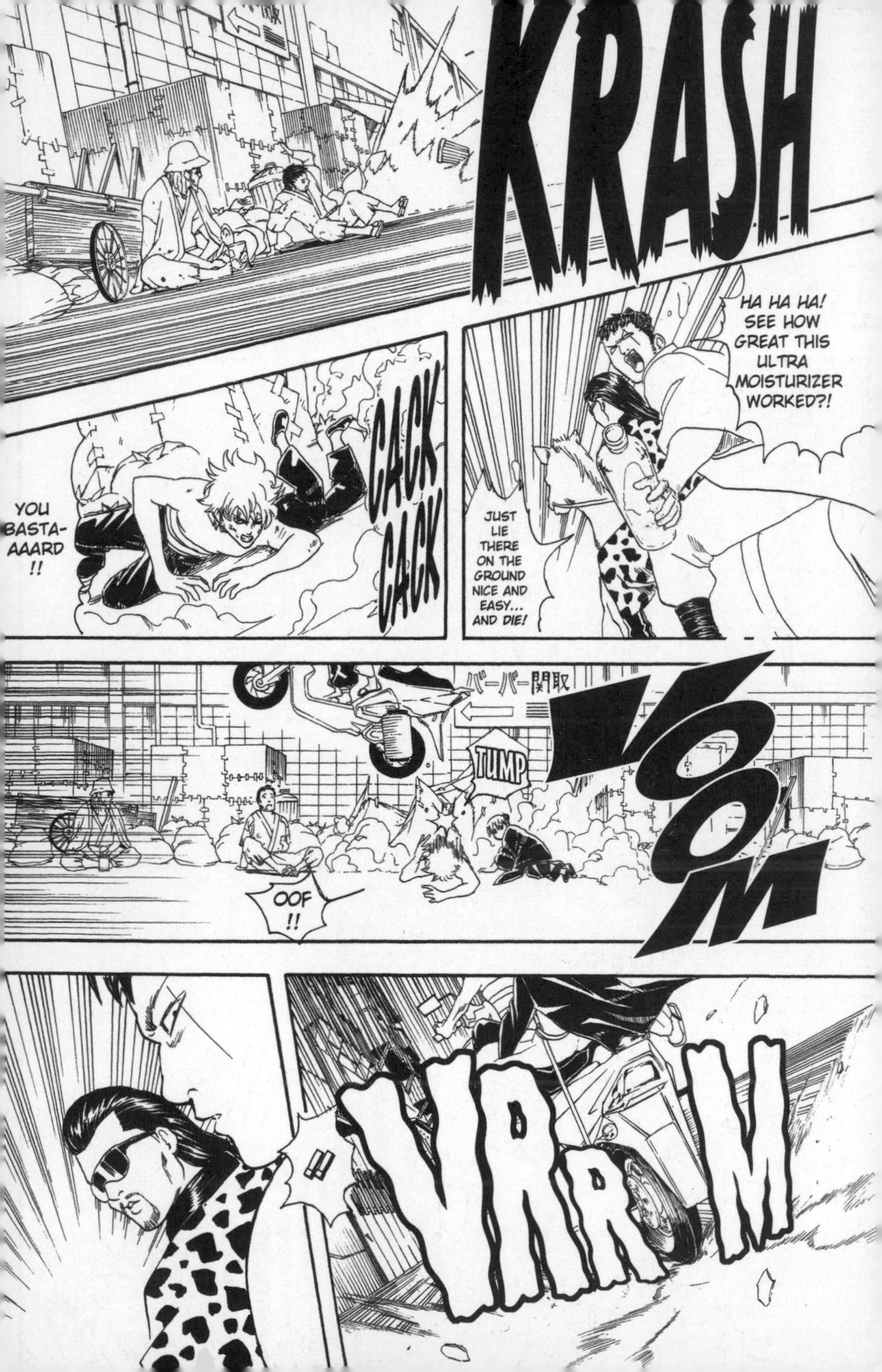
KRASH
HA HA HA! SEE HOW GREAT THIS ULTRA MOISTURIZER WORKED?!
JUST LIE THERE ON THE GROUND NICE AND EASY... AND DIE!
CACK CACK
YOU BASTA-AAARD !!
バーバー関取
VOOM
TUMP
OOF !!
VRRM
!!

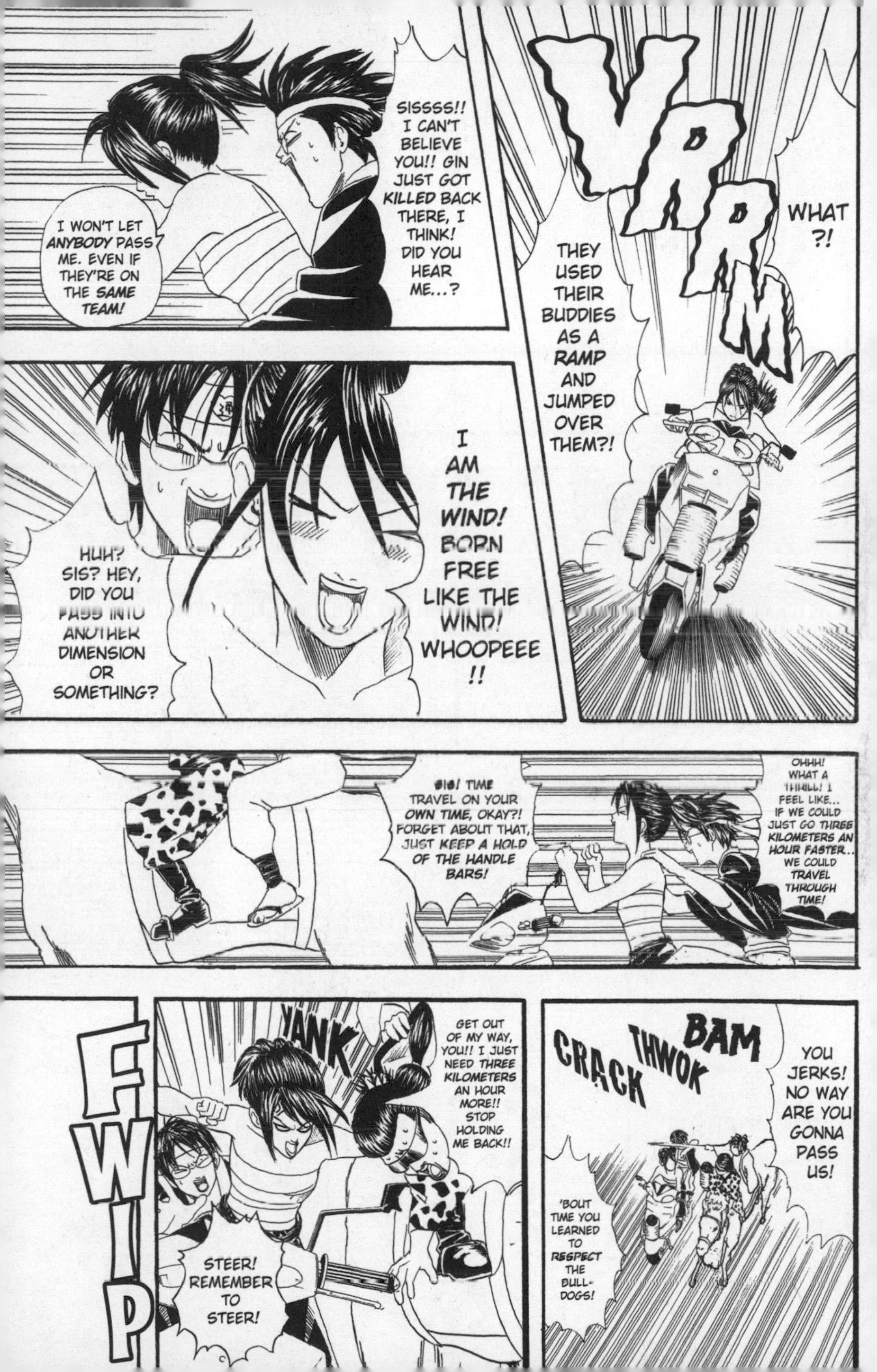
VRRM
WHAT?!
THEY USED THEIR BUDDIES AS A RAMP AND JUMPED OVER THEM?!
SISSSS!! I CAN'T BELIEVE YOU!! GIN JUST GOT KILLED BACK THERE, I THINK! DID YOU HEAR ME...?
I WON'T LET ANYBODY PASS ME. EVEN IF THEY'RE ON THE SAME TEAM!
I AM THE WIND! BORN FREE LIKE THE WIND! WHOOPEEE!!
HUH? SIS? HEY, DID YOU PASS INTO ANOTHER DIMENSION OR SOMETHING?
OHHH! WHAT A THRILL! I FEEL LIKE... IF WE COULD JUST GO THREE KILOMETERS AN HOUR FASTER... WE COULD TRAVEL THROUGH TIME!
SIS! TIME TRAVEL ON YOUR OWN TIME, OKAY?! FORGET ABOUT THAT, JUST KEEP A HOLD OF THE HANDLE BARS!
BAM
THWOK
CRACK
YOU JERKS! NO WAY ARE YOU GONNA PASS US!
'BOUT TIME YOU LEARNED TO RESPECT THE BULL-DOGS!
YANK
GET OUT OF MY WAY, YOU!! I JUST NEED THREE KILOMETERS AN HOUR MORE!! STOP HOLDING ME BACK!!
STEER! REMEMBER TO STEER!
FWIP

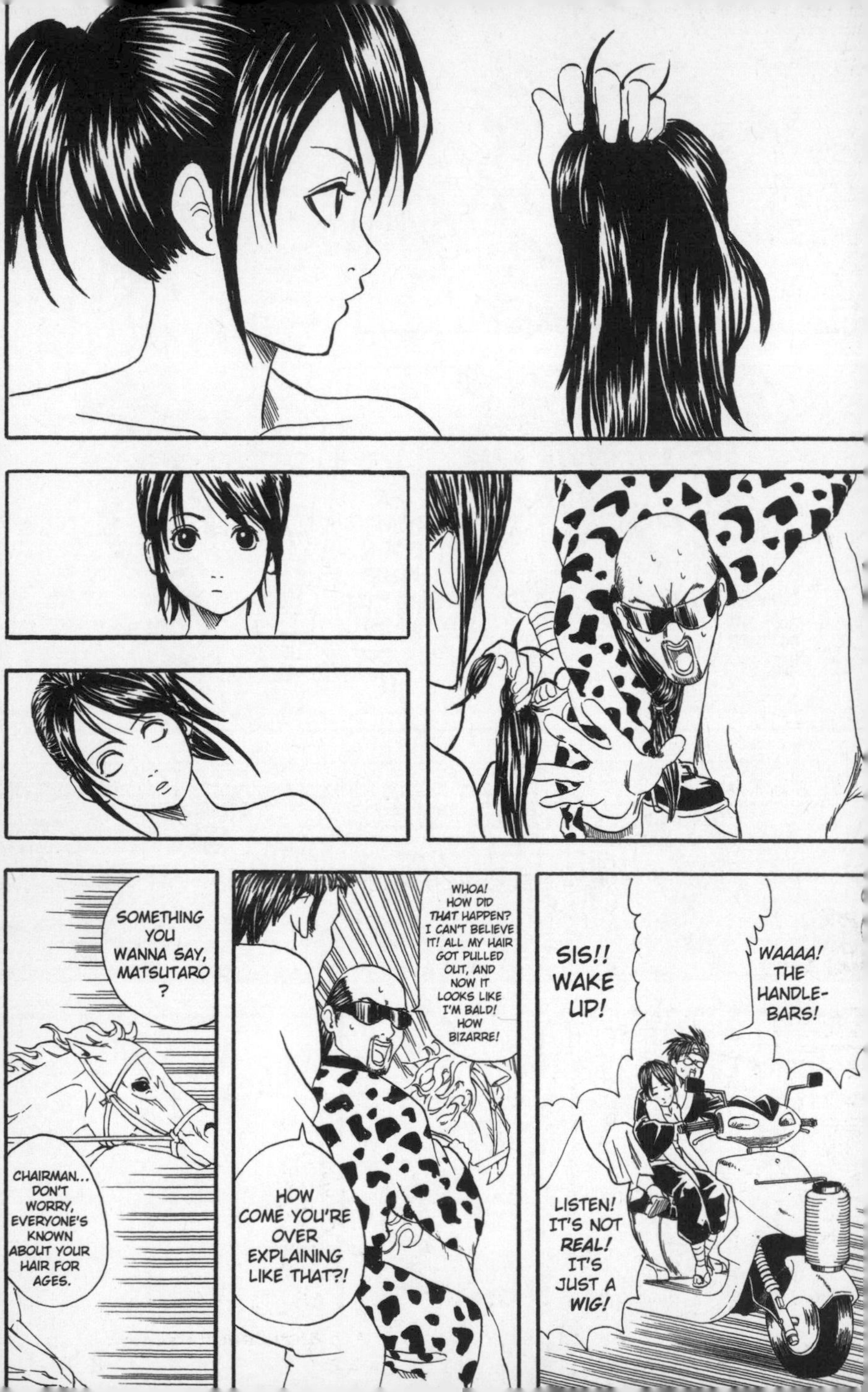
WAAAA! THE HANDLE-BARS!
SIS!! WAKE UP!
LISTEN! IT'S NOT REAL! IT'S JUST A WIG!
WHOA! HOW DID THAT HAPPEN? I CAN'T BELIEVE IT! ALL MY HAIR GOT PULLED OUT, AND NOW IT LOOKS LIKE I'M BALD! HOW BIZARRE!
HOW COME YOU'RE OVER EXPLAINING LIKE THAT?!
SOMETHING YOU WANNA SAY, MATSUTARO ?
CHAIRMAN... DON'T WORRY, EVERYONE'S KNOWN ABOUT YOUR HAIR FOR AGES.

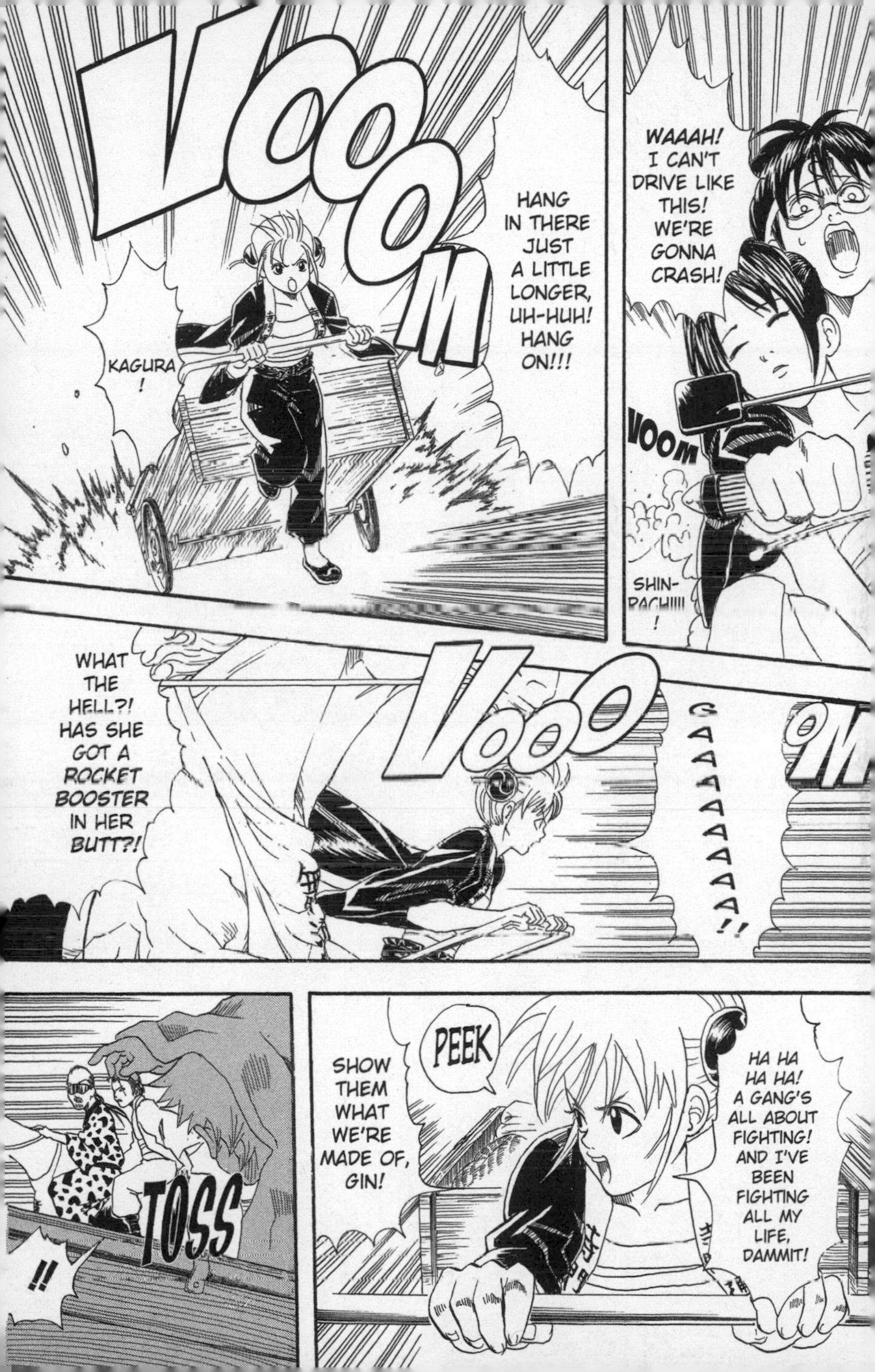
WAAAH! I CAN'T DRIVE LIKE THIS! WE'RE GONNA CRASH!
VOOM
SHIN-PACHIIII!
VOOOOM
HANG IN THERE JUST A LITTLE LONGER, UH-HUH! HANG ON!!!
KAGURA!
VOOOOM
GAAAAAAAAAAA!!
WHAT THE HELL?! HAS SHE GOT A ROCKET BOOSTER IN HER BUTT?!
HA HA HA HA! A GANG'S ALL ABOUT FIGHTING! AND I'VE BEEN FIGHTING ALL MY LIFE, DAMMIT!
PEEK
SHOW THEM WHAT WE'RE MADE OF, GIN!
TOSS
!!

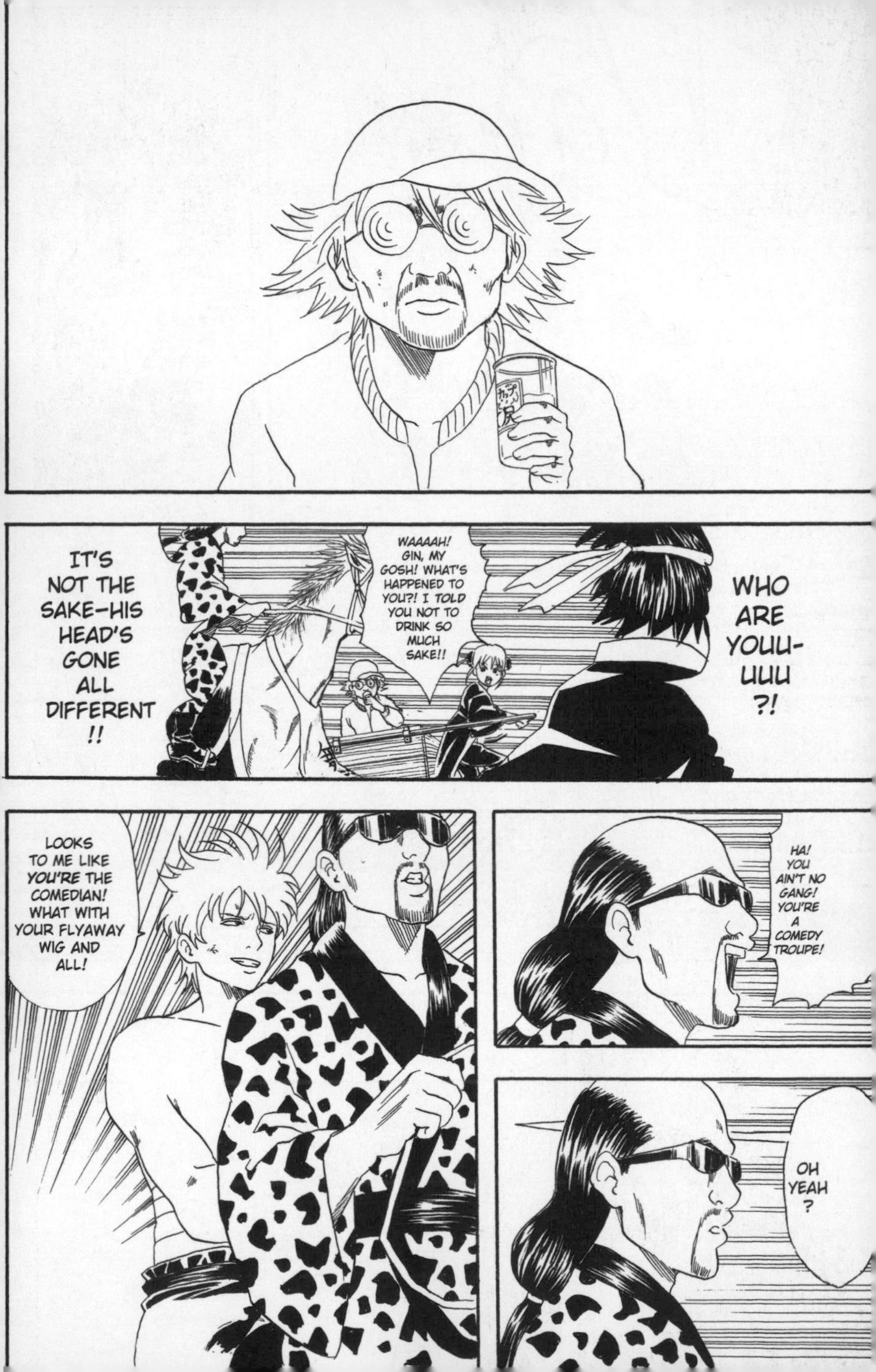
WHO ARE YOUUU-UUU?!
WAAAAH! GIN, MY GOSH! WHAT'S HAPPENED TO YOU?! I TOLD YOU NOT TO DRINK SO MUCH SAKE!!
IT'S NOT THE SAKE—HIS HEAD'S GONE ALL DIFFERENT!!
HA! YOU AIN'T NO GANG! YOU'RE A COMEDY TROUPE!
OH YEAH?
LOOKS TO ME LIKE *YOU'RE* THE COMEDIAN! WHAT WITH YOUR FLYAWAY WIG AND ALL!

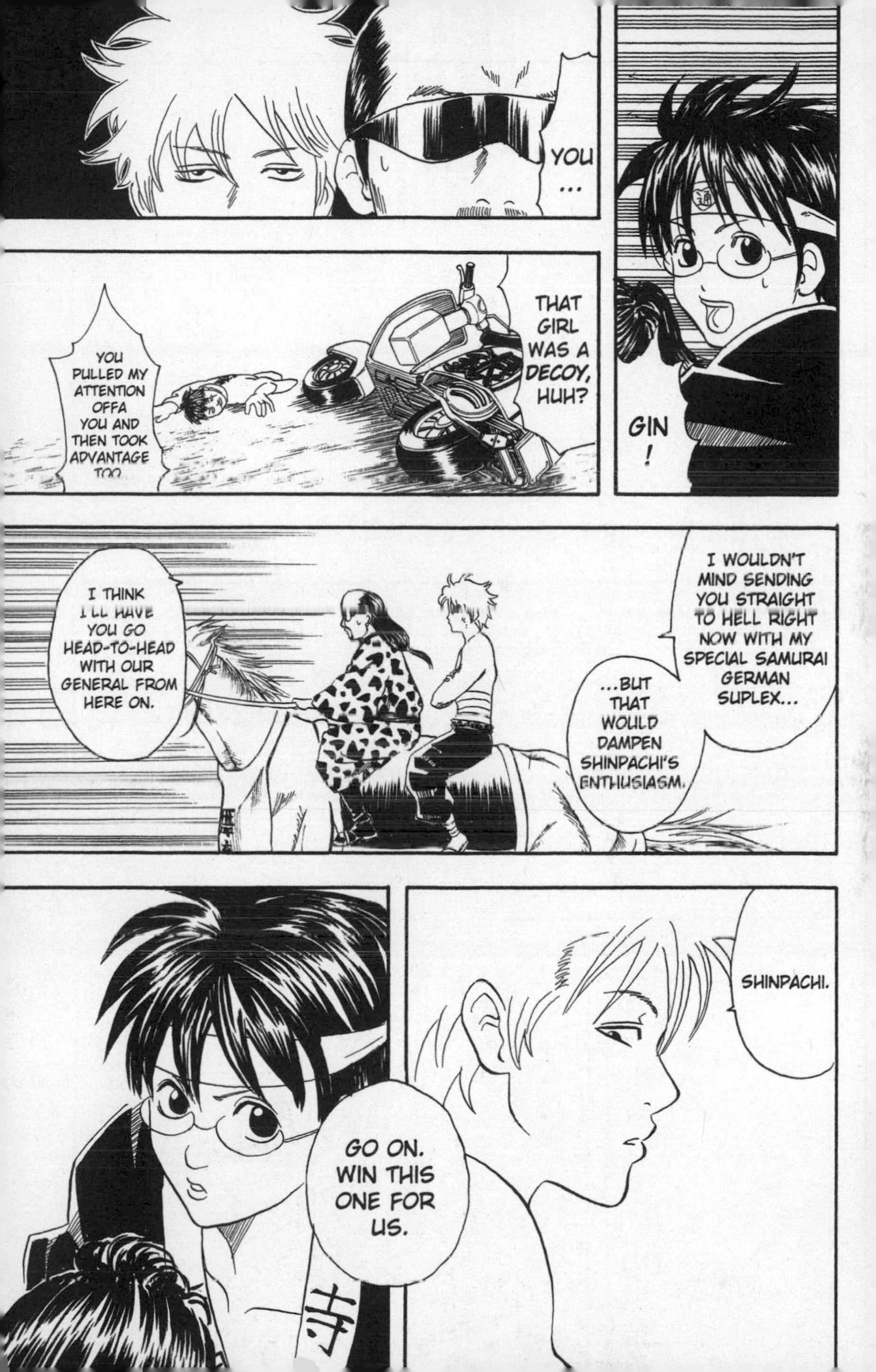
GIN!
YOU ...
THAT GIRL WAS A DECOY, HUH?
YOU PULLED MY ATTENTION OFFA YOU AND THEN TOOK ADVANTAGE TOO.
I WOULDN'T MIND SENDING YOU STRAIGHT TO HELL RIGHT NOW WITH MY SPECIAL SAMURAI GERMAN SUPLEX...
...BUT THAT WOULD DAMPEN SHINPACHI'S ENTHUSIASM.
I THINK I'LL HAVE YOU GO HEAD-TO-HEAD WITH OUR GENERAL FROM HERE ON.
SHINPACHI.
GO ON. WIN THIS ONE FOR US.

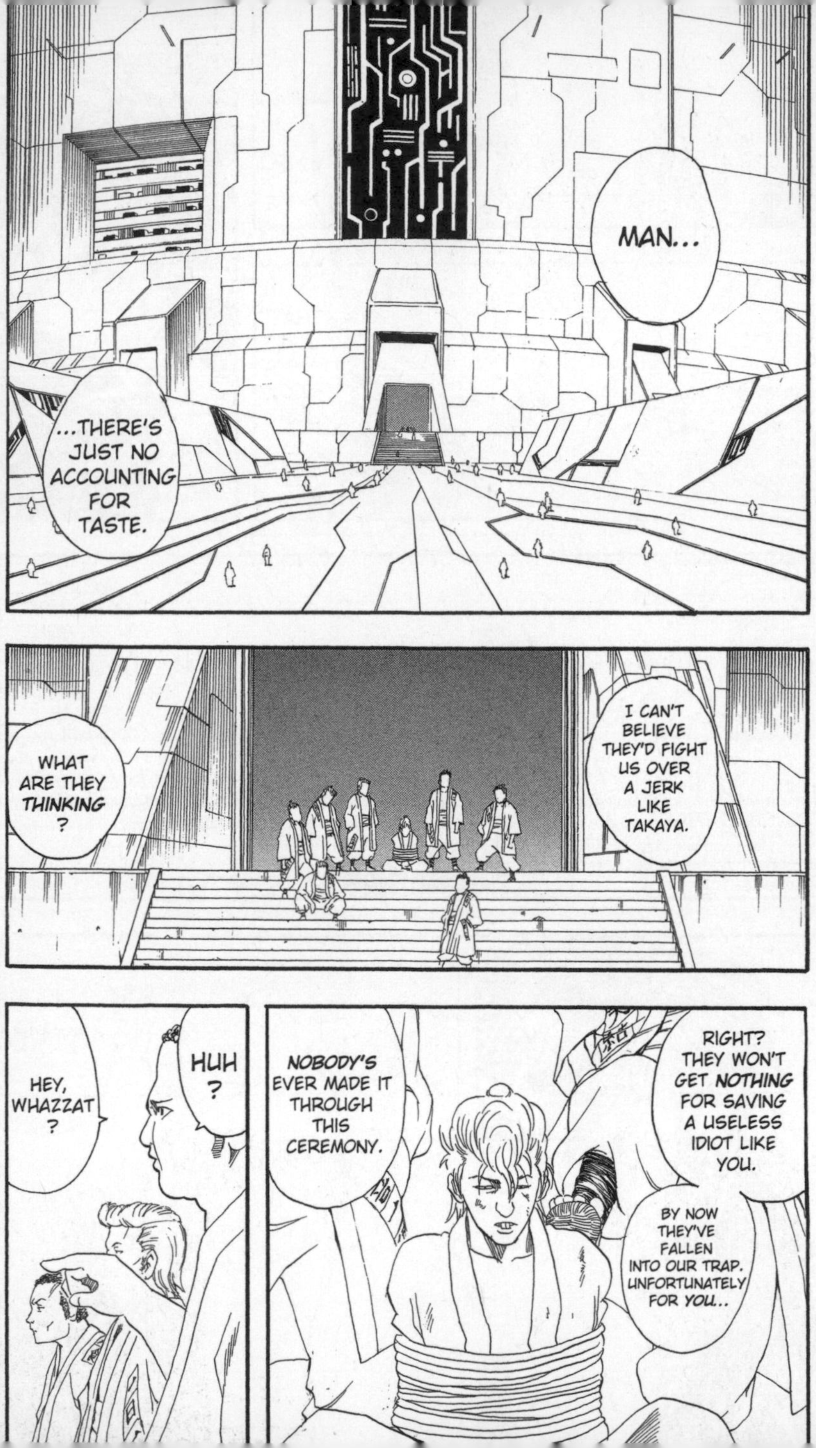
MAN...
...THERE'S JUST NO ACCOUNTING FOR TASTE.
I CAN'T BELIEVE THEY'D FIGHT US OVER A JERK LIKE TAKAYA.
WHAT ARE THEY *THINKING* ?
RIGHT? THEY WON'T GET *NOTHING* FOR SAVING A USELESS IDIOT LIKE YOU.
BY NOW THEY'VE FALLEN INTO OUR TRAP. UNFORTUNATELY FOR *YOU*...
NOBODY'S EVER MADE IT THROUGH THIS CEREMONY.
HUH ?
HEY, WHAZZAT ?

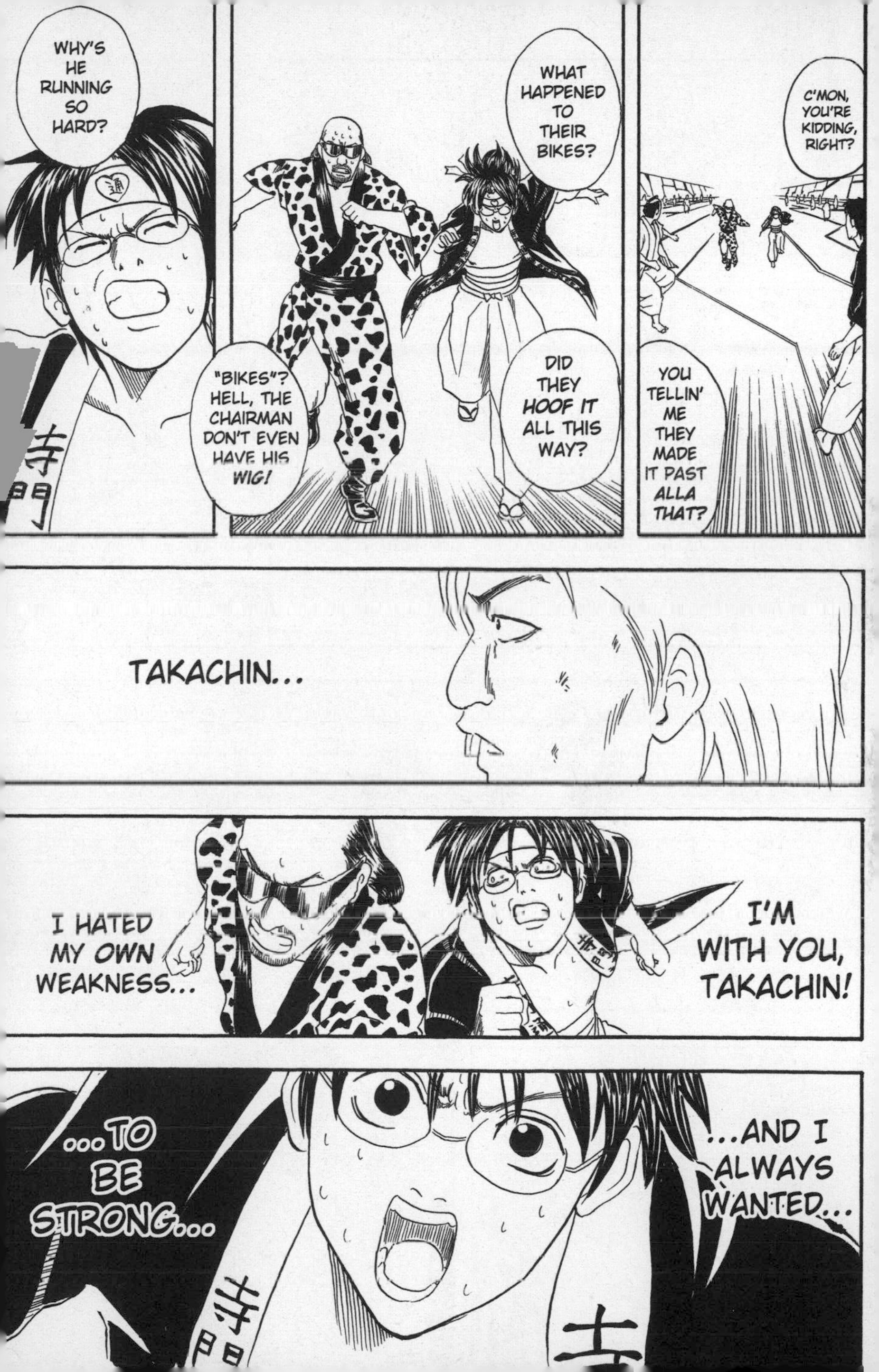
C'MON, YOU'RE KIDDING, RIGHT?
YOU TELLIN' ME THEY MADE IT PAST ALLA THAT?
WHAT HAPPENED TO THEIR BIKES?
DID THEY *HOOF IT* ALL THIS WAY?
"BIKES"? HELL, THE CHAIRMAN DON'T EVEN HAVE HIS *WIG!*
WHY'S HE RUNNING SO HARD?
TAKACHIN...
I'M WITH YOU, TAKACHIN!
I HATED MY *OWN* WEAKNESS...
...AND I ALWAYS WANTED...
...TO BE STRONG...

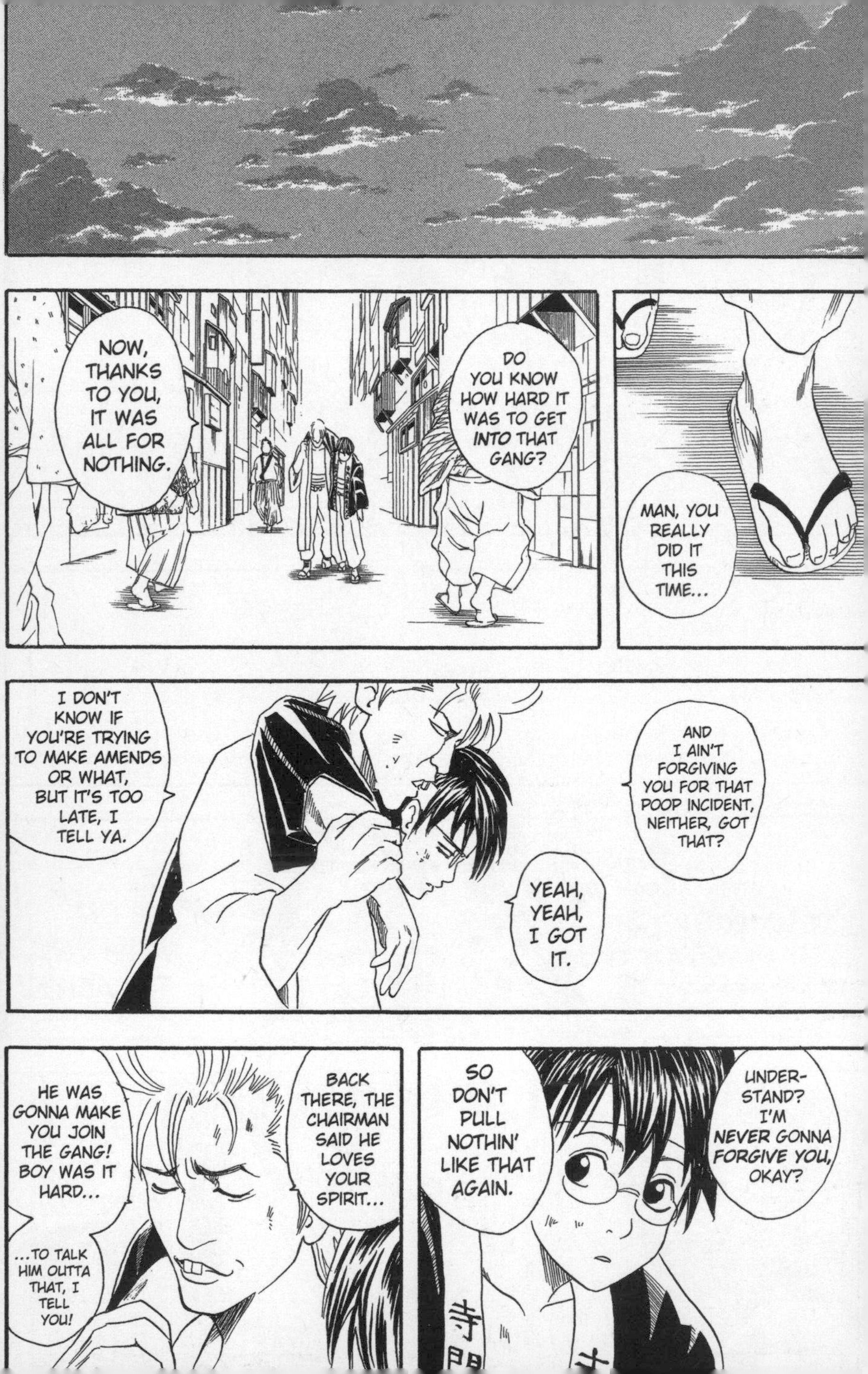
MAN, YOU REALLY DID IT THIS TIME...
DO YOU KNOW HOW HARD IT WAS TO GET INTO THAT GANG?
NOW, THANKS TO YOU, IT WAS ALL FOR NOTHING.
I DON'T KNOW IF YOU'RE TRYING TO MAKE AMENDS OR WHAT, BUT IT'S TOO LATE, I TELL YA.
AND I AIN'T FORGIVING YOU FOR THAT POOP INCIDENT, NEITHER, GOT THAT?
YEAH, YEAH, I GOT IT.
UNDER-STAND? I'M NEVER GONNA FORGIVE YOU, OKAY?
SO DON'T PULL NOTHIN' LIKE THAT AGAIN.
BACK THERE, THE CHAIRMAN SAID HE LOVES YOUR SPIRIT...
HE WAS GONNA MAKE YOU JOIN THE GANG! BOY WAS IT HARD...
...TO TALK HIM OUTTA THAT, I TELL YOU!

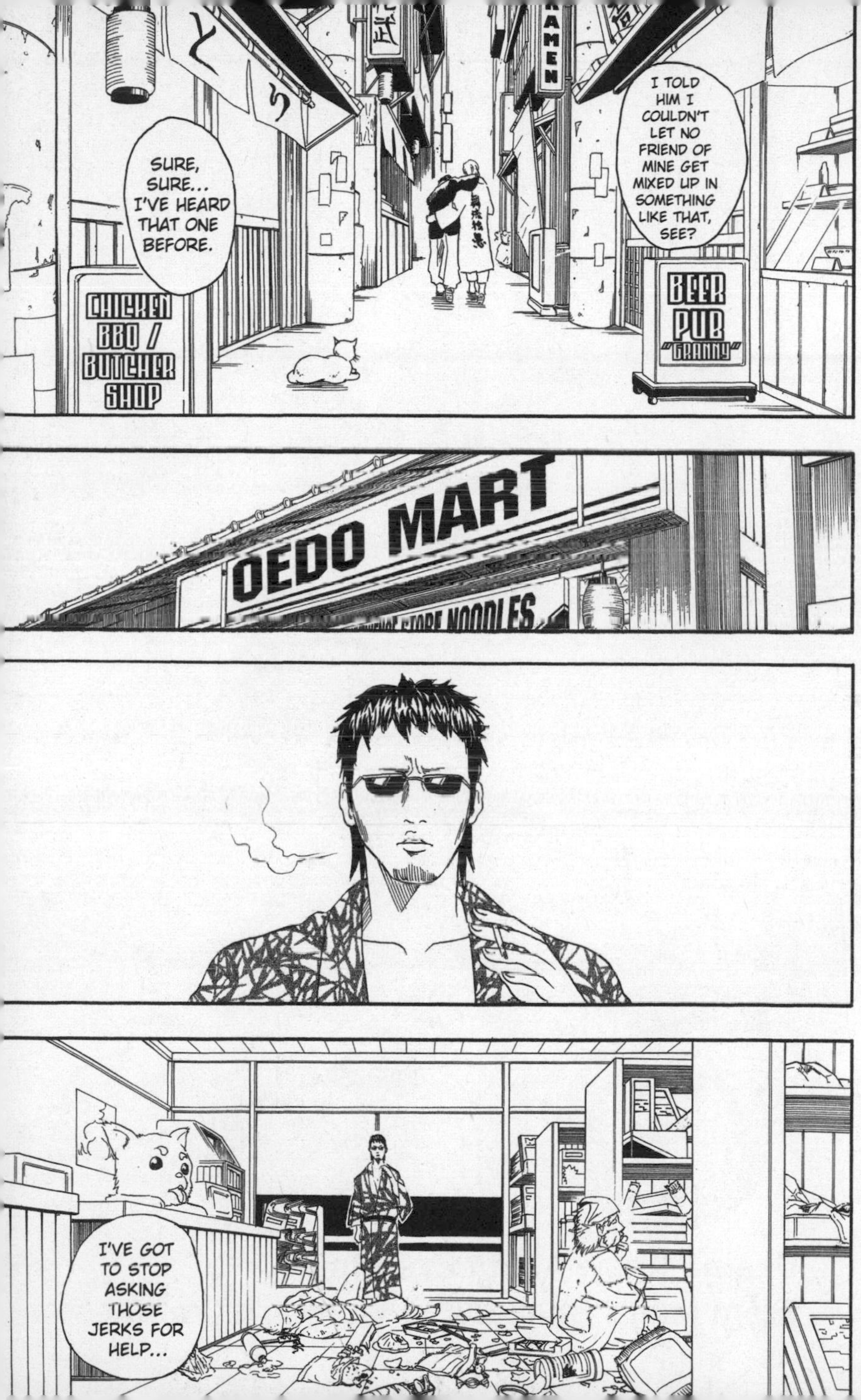
RAMEN
I TOLD HIM I COULDN'T LET NO FRIEND OF MINE GET MIXED UP IN SOMETHING LIKE THAT, SEE?
SURE, SURE... I'VE HEARD THAT ONE BEFORE.
BEER PUB "GRANNY"
CHICKEN BBQ / BUTCHER SHOP
OEDO MART
NOODLES
I'VE GOT TO STOP ASKING THOSE JERKS FOR HELP...

AMA

SORACHI HIDEAKI

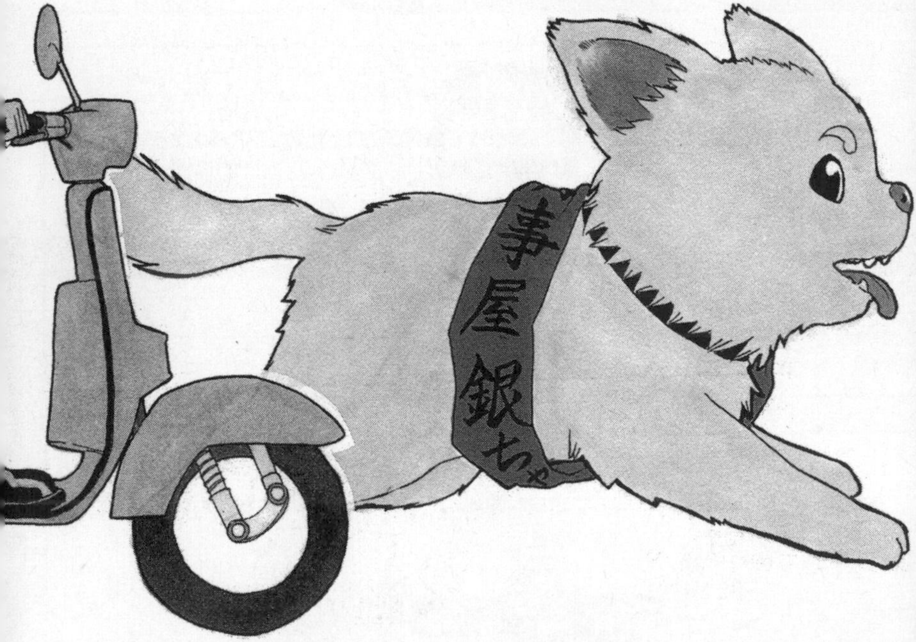
事屋銀ちゃ

Okama Know About Everything, From Men's Stupidity to Women's Craftiness

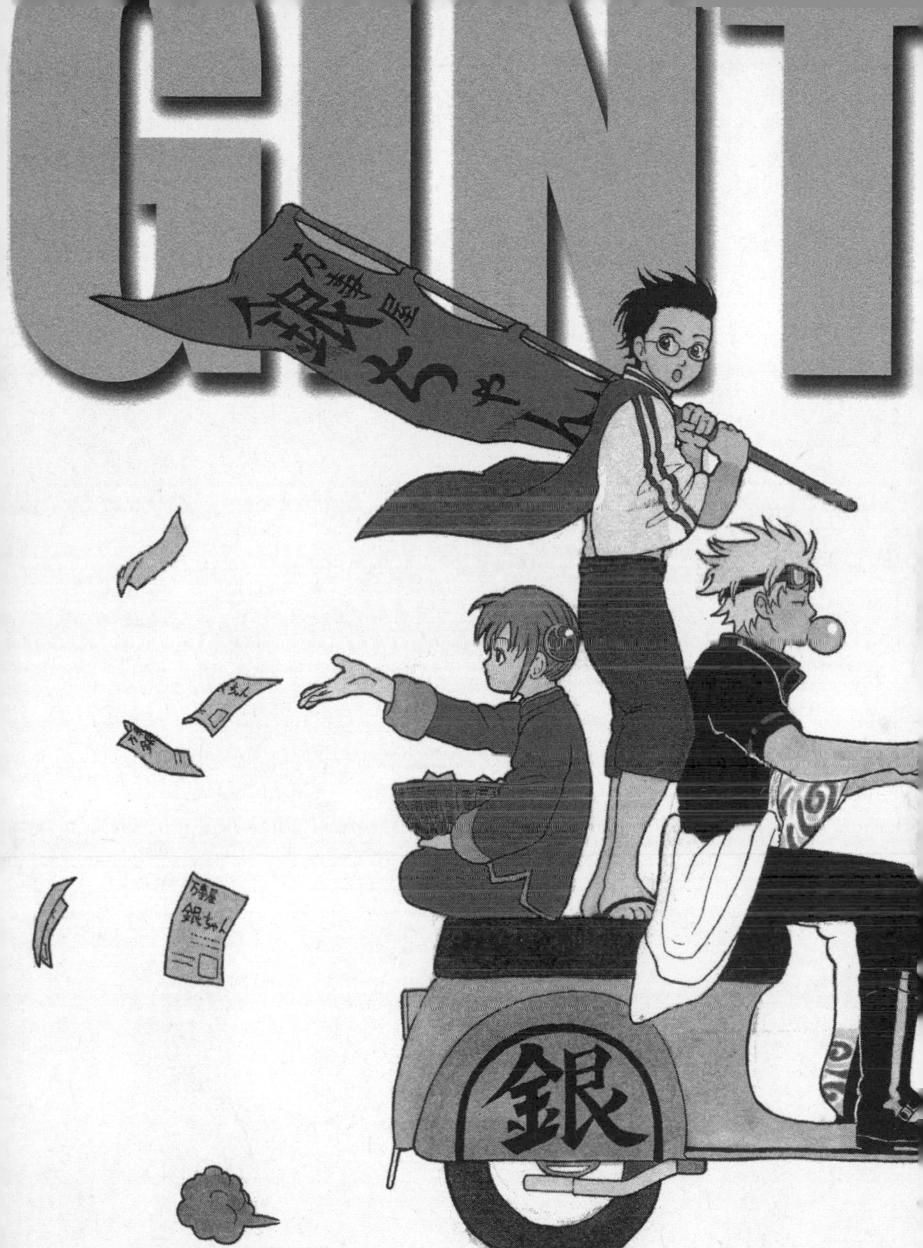
GINT
万事屋
銀ちゃん
銀

ODD JOBS GIN

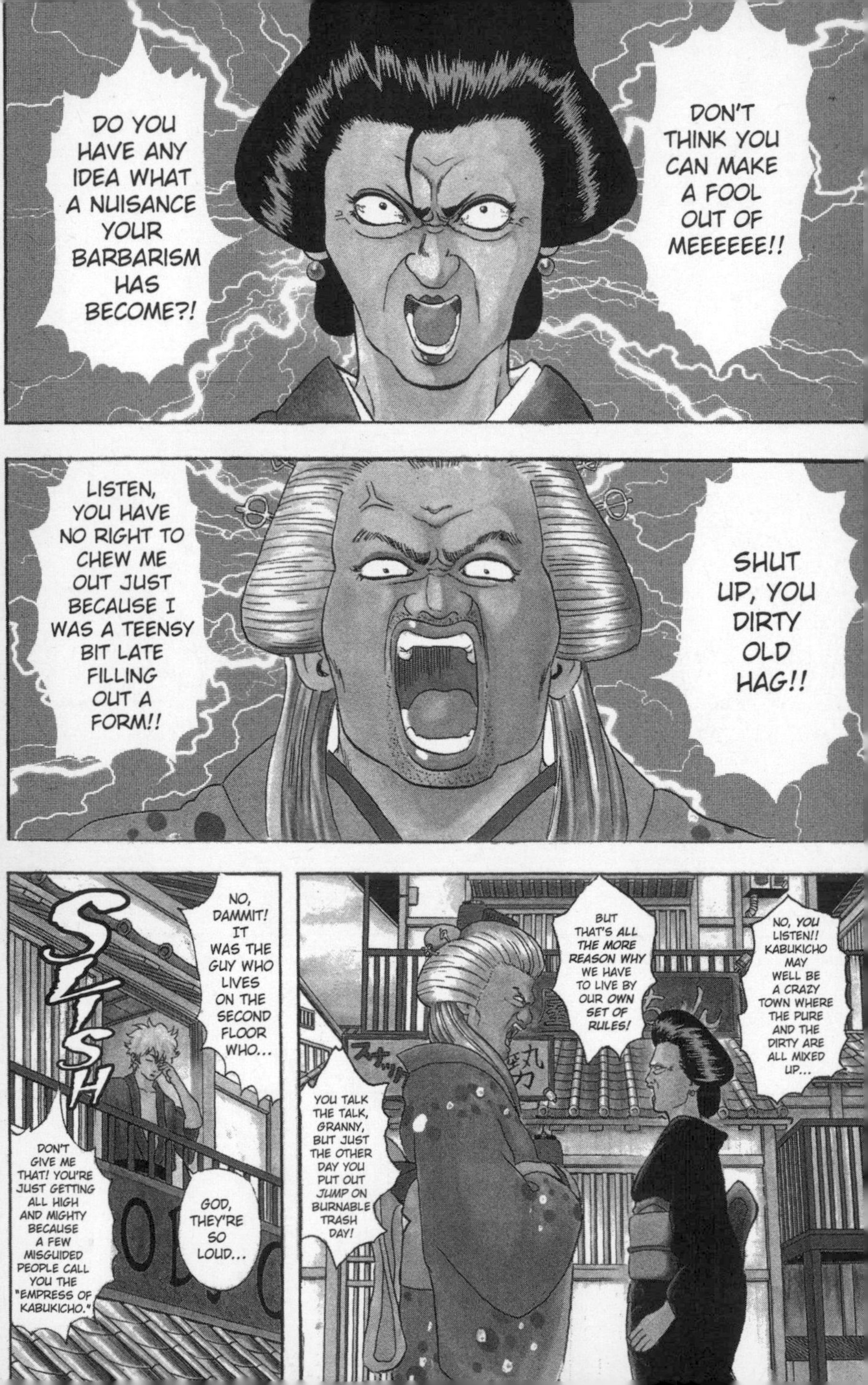
DON'T THINK YOU CAN MAKE A FOOL OUT OF MEEEEEE!!
DO YOU HAVE ANY IDEA WHAT A NUISANCE YOUR BARBARISM HAS BECOME?!
SHUT UP, YOU DIRTY OLD HAG!!
LISTEN, YOU HAVE NO RIGHT TO CHEW ME OUT JUST BECAUSE I WAS A TEENSY BIT LATE FILLING OUT A FORM!!
NO, *YOU* LISTEN!! KABUKICHO MAY WELL BE A CRAZY TOWN WHERE THE PURE AND THE DIRTY ARE ALL MIXED UP...
BUT THAT'S ALL THE MORE REASON WHY WE HAVE TO LIVE BY OUR OWN SET OF RULES!
YOU TALK THE TALK, GRANNY, BUT JUST THE OTHER DAY YOU PUT OUT *JUMP* ON BURNABLE TRASH DAY!
NO, DAMMIT! IT WAS THE GUY WHO LIVES ON THE SECOND FLOOR WHO...
SLISH
DON'T GIVE ME THAT! YOU'RE JUST GETTING ALL HIGH AND MIGHTY BECAUSE A FEW MISGUIDED PEOPLE CALL YOU THE "EMPRESS OF KABUKICHO."
GOD, THEY'RE SO LOUD...

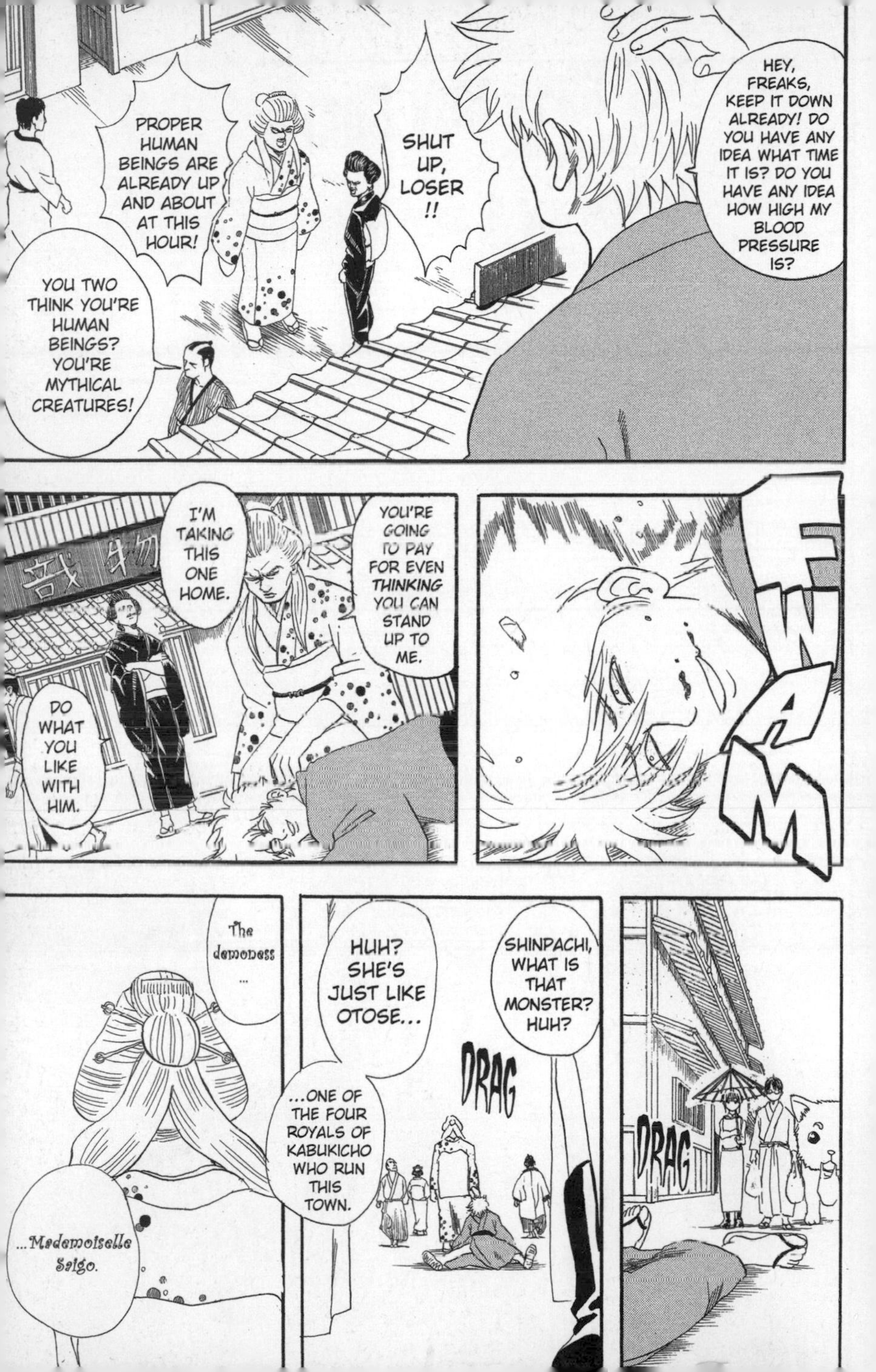
HEY, FREAKS, KEEP IT DOWN ALREADY! DO YOU HAVE ANY IDEA WHAT TIME IT IS? DO YOU HAVE ANY IDEA HOW HIGH MY BLOOD PRESSURE IS?
SHUT UP, LOSER!!
PROPER HUMAN BEINGS ARE ALREADY UP AND ABOUT AT THIS HOUR!
YOU TWO THINK YOU'RE HUMAN BEINGS? YOU'RE MYTHICAL CREATURES!
FWAM
YOU'RE GOING TO PAY FOR EVEN THINKING YOU CAN STAND UP TO ME.
I'M TAKING THIS ONE HOME.
DO WHAT YOU LIKE WITH HIM.
SHINPACHI, WHAT IS THAT MONSTER? HUH?
DRAG
HUH? SHE'S JUST LIKE OTOSE...
DRAG
...ONE OF THE FOUR ROYALS OF KABUKICHO WHO RUN THIS TOWN.
The demoness ...
...Mademoiselle Saigo.

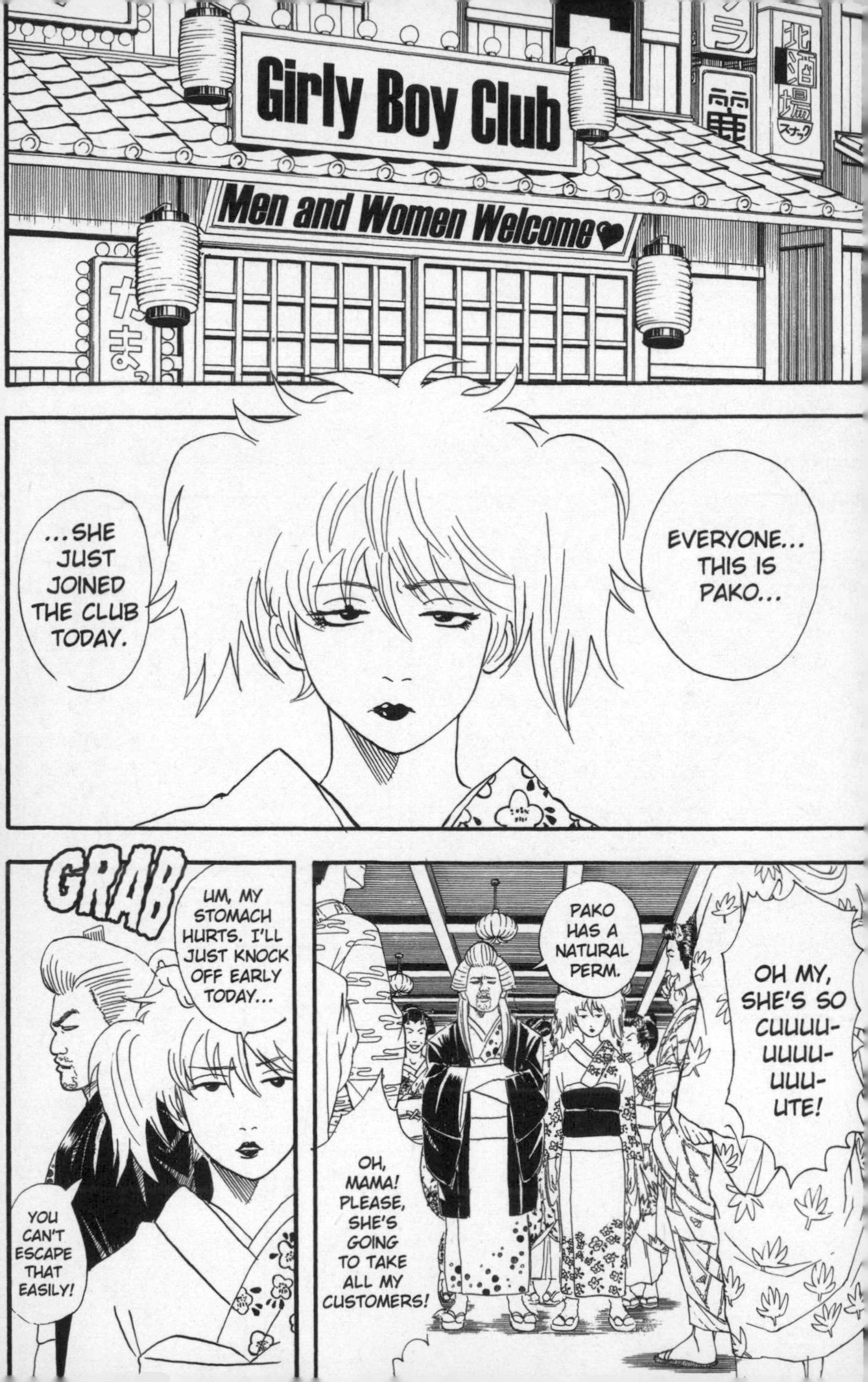
Girly Boy Club
Men and Women Welcome♥
EVERYONE... THIS IS PAKO...
...SHE JUST JOINED THE CLUB TODAY.
PAKO HAS A NATURAL PERM.
OH MY, SHE'S SO CUUUU-UUUU-UUU-UTE!
OH, MAMA! PLEASE, SHE'S GOING TO TAKE ALL MY CUSTOMERS!
GRAB
UM, MY STOMACH HURTS. I'LL JUST KNOCK OFF EARLY TODAY...
YOU CAN'T ESCAPE THAT EASILY!

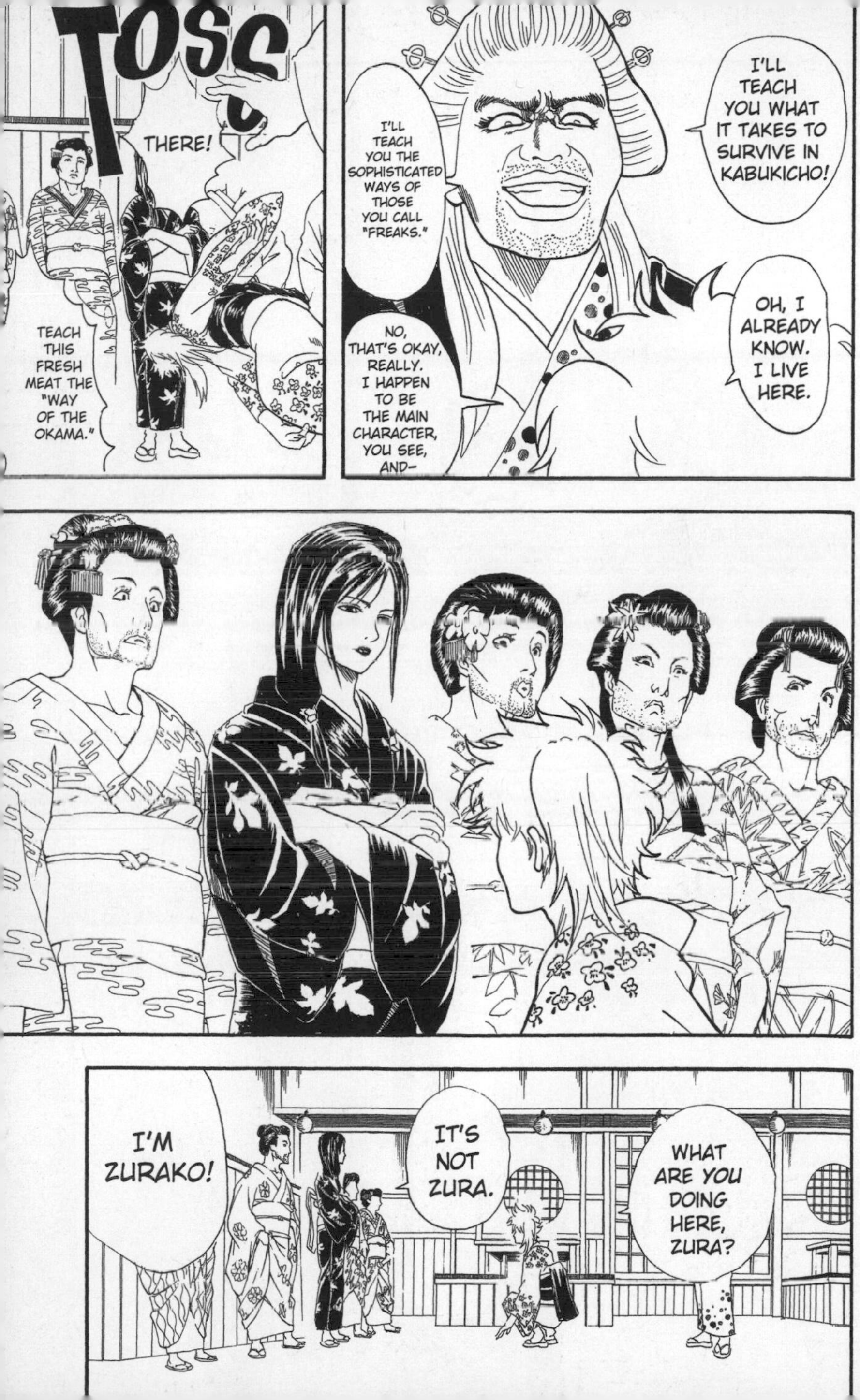
I'LL TEACH YOU WHAT IT TAKES TO SURVIVE IN KABUKICHO!
I'LL TEACH YOU THE SOPHISTICATED WAYS OF THOSE YOU CALL "FREAKS."
OH, I ALREADY KNOW. I LIVE HERE.
NO, THAT'S OKAY, REALLY. I HAPPEN TO BE THE MAIN CHARACTER, YOU SEE, AND–
TOSS
THERE!
TEACH THIS FRESH MEAT THE "WAY OF THE OKAMA."
WHAT ARE YOU DOING HERE, ZURA?
IT'S NOT ZURA.
I'M ZURAKO!

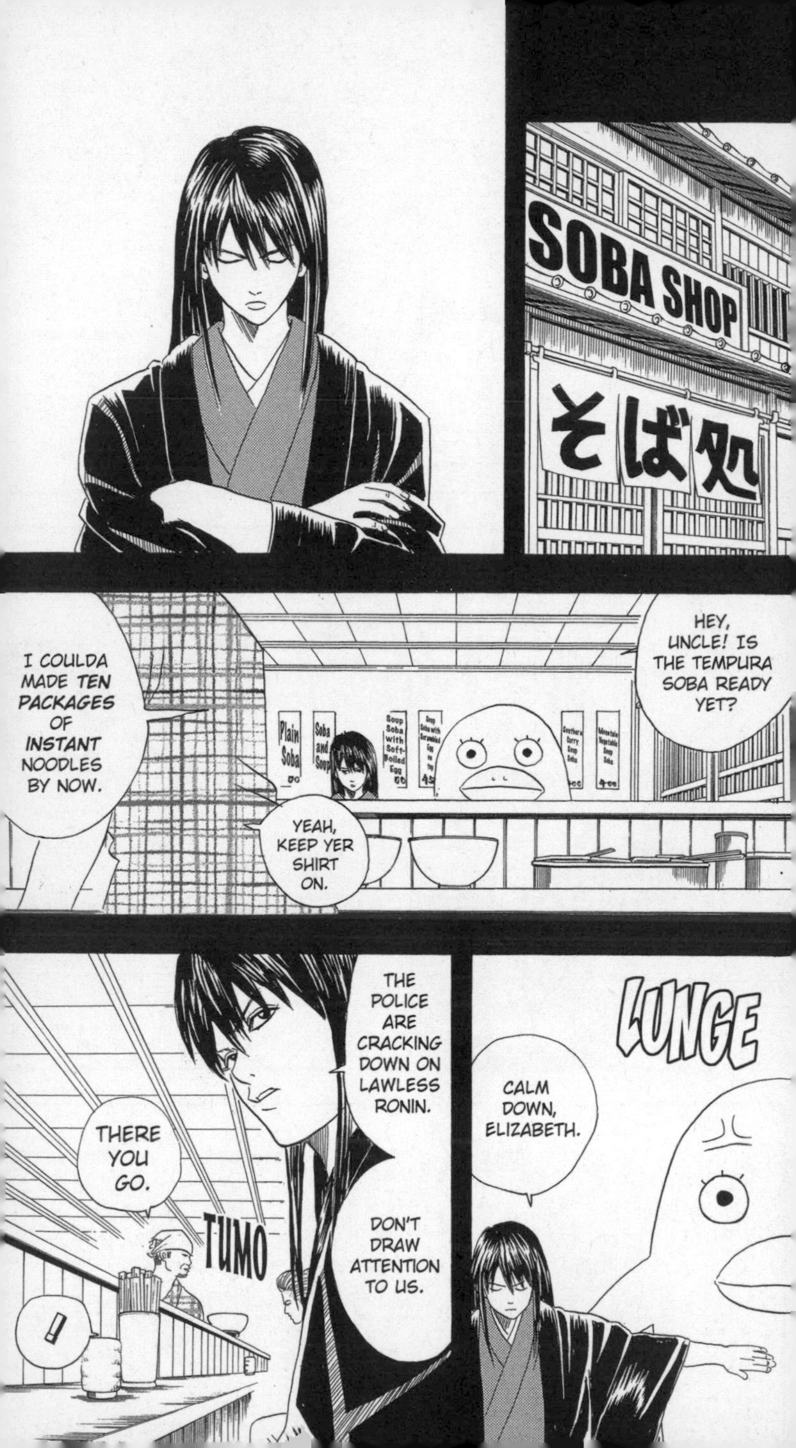

SOBA SHOP
そば処
HEY, UNCLE! IS THE TEMPURA SOBA READY YET?
I COULDA MADE TEN PACKAGES OF INSTANT NOODLES BY NOW.
Plain Soba
Soba and Soup
Soup Soba with Soft-Boiled Egg
YEAH, KEEP YER SHIRT ON.
LUNGE
CALM DOWN, ELIZABETH.
THE POLICE ARE CRACKING DOWN ON LAWLESS RONIN.
DON'T DRAW ATTENTION TO US.
THERE YOU GO.
TUMO
!

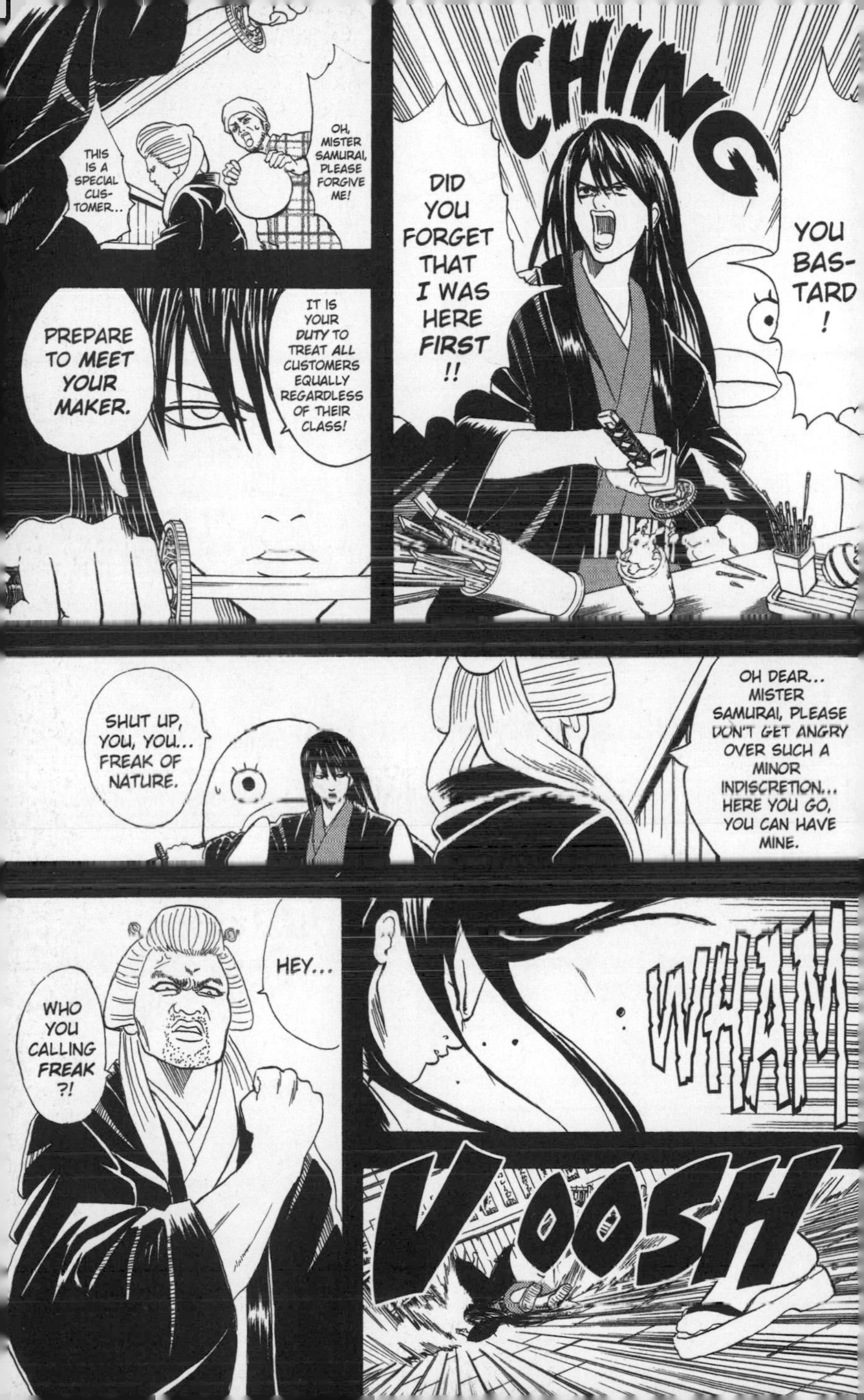
CHING
YOU BASTARD!
DID YOU FORGET THAT I WAS HERE FIRST!!
OH, MISTER SAMURAI, PLEASE FORGIVE ME!
THIS IS A SPECIAL CUSTOMER...
IT IS YOUR DUTY TO TREAT ALL CUSTOMERS EQUALLY REGARDLESS OF THEIR CLASS!
PREPARE TO MEET YOUR MAKER.
OH DEAR... MISTER SAMURAI, PLEASE DON'T GET ANGRY OVER SUCH A MINOR INDISCRETION... HERE YOU GO, YOU CAN HAVE MINE.
SHUT UP, YOU, YOU... FREAK OF NATURE.
WHAM
VOOSH
HEY...
WHO YOU CALLING FREAK?!

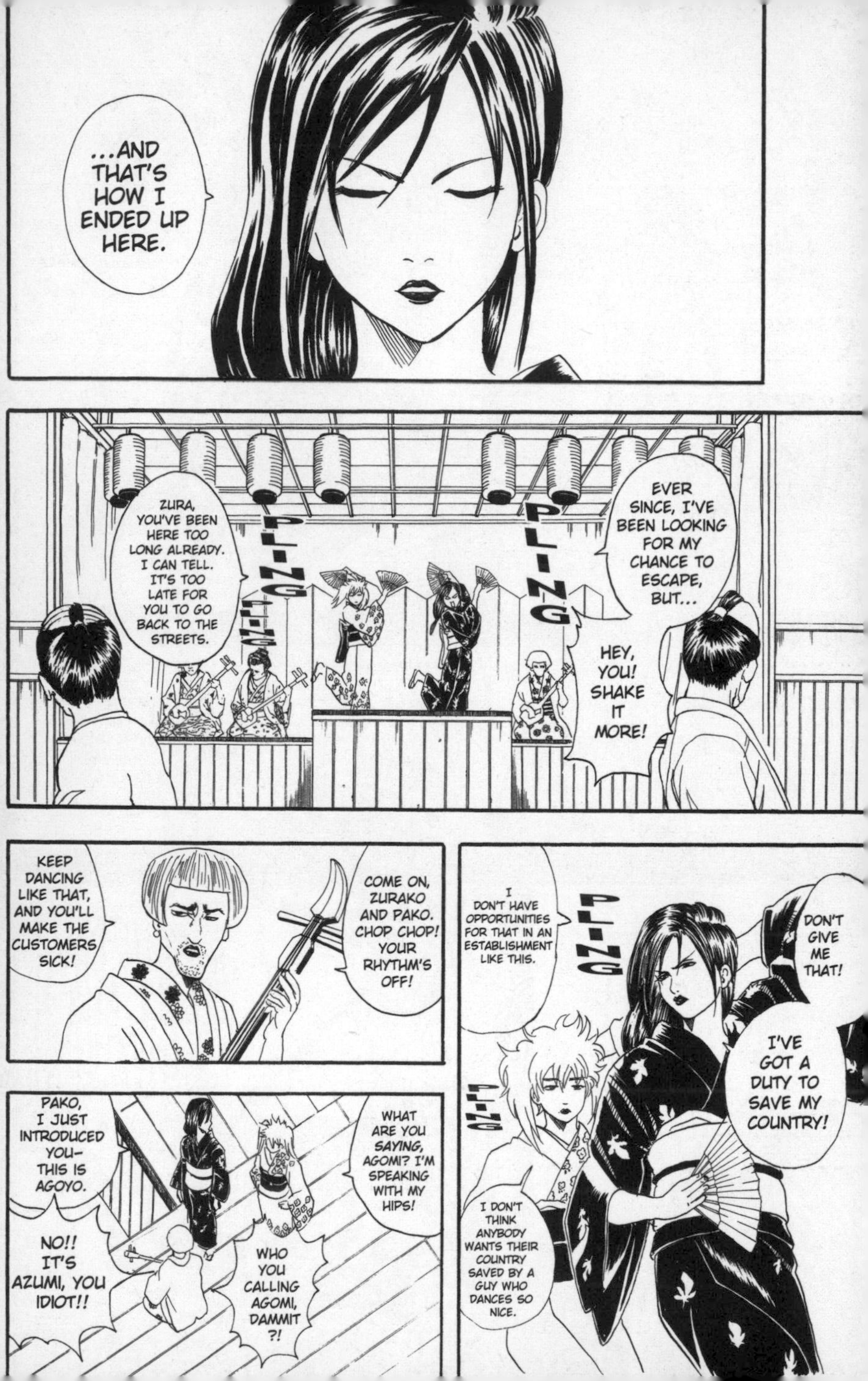

...AND THAT'S HOW I ENDED UP HERE.
EVER SINCE, I'VE BEEN LOOKING FOR MY CHANCE TO ESCAPE, BUT...
PLING
HEY, YOU! SHAKE IT MORE!
PLING
ZURA, YOU'VE BEEN HERE TOO LONG ALREADY. I CAN TELL. IT'S TOO LATE FOR YOU TO GO BACK TO THE STREETS.
PLING
DON'T GIVE ME THAT!
PLING
I DON'T HAVE OPPORTUNITIES FOR THAT IN AN ESTABLISHMENT LIKE THIS.
I'VE GOT A DUTY TO SAVE MY COUNTRY!
PLING
I DON'T THINK ANYBODY WANTS THEIR COUNTRY SAVED BY A GUY WHO DANCES SO NICE.
COME ON, ZURAKO AND PAKO. CHOP CHOP! YOUR RHYTHM'S OFF!
KEEP DANCING LIKE THAT, AND YOU'LL MAKE THE CUSTOMERS SICK!
WHAT ARE YOU SAYING, AGOMI? I'M SPEAKING WITH MY HIPS!
PAKO, I JUST INTRODUCED YOU— THIS IS AGOYO.
WHO YOU CALLING AGOMI, DAMMIT?!
NO!! IT'S AZUMI, YOU IDIOT!!

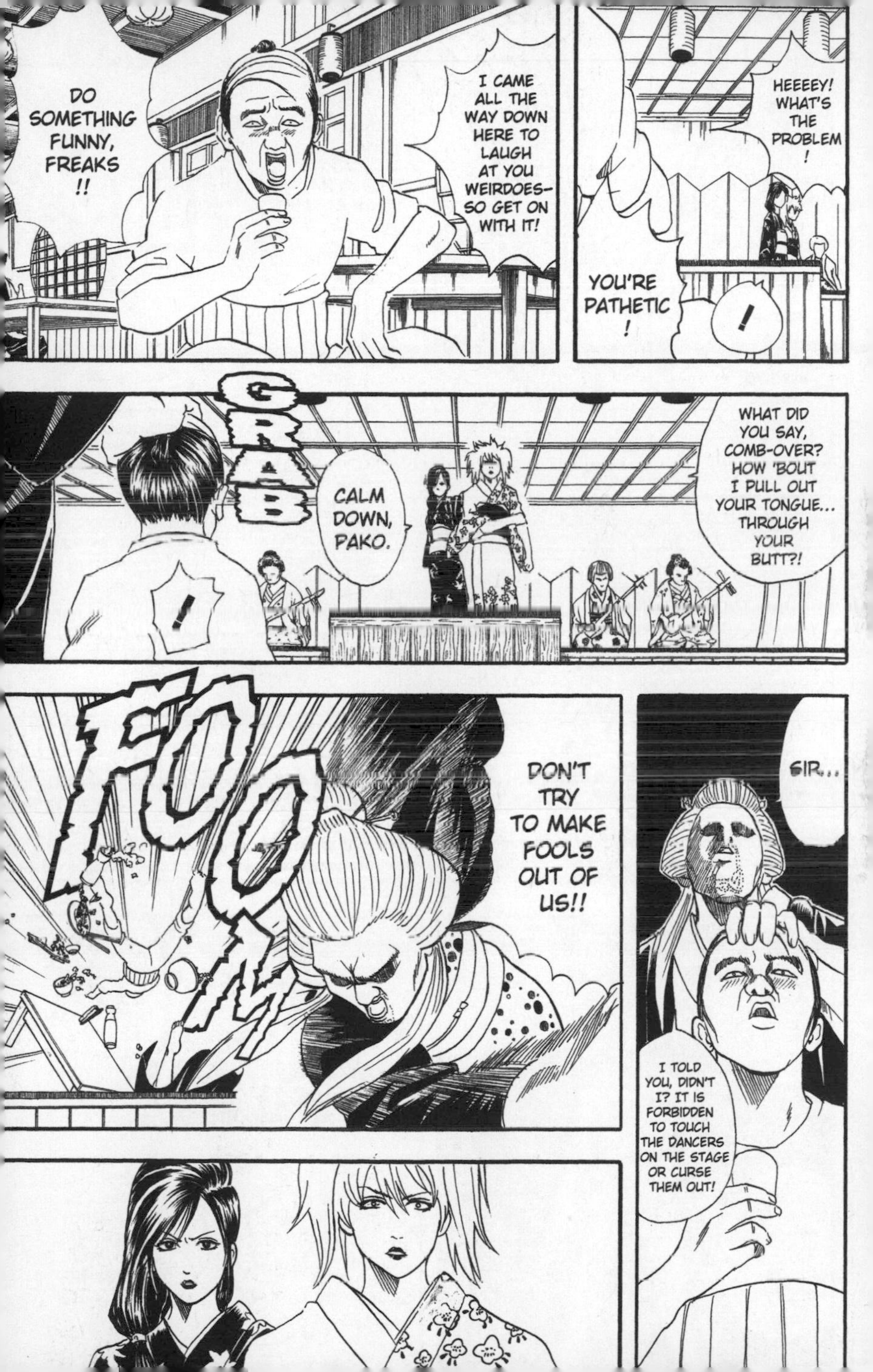
HEEEEY! WHAT'S THE PROBLEM!
YOU'RE PATHETIC!
!
I CAME ALL THE WAY DOWN HERE TO LAUGH AT YOU WEIRDOES-SO GET ON WITH IT!
DO SOMETHING FUNNY, FREAKS!!
WHAT DID YOU SAY, COMB-OVER? HOW 'BOUT I PULL OUT YOUR TONGUE... THROUGH YOUR BUTT?!
CALM DOWN, PAKO.
GRAB
!
SIR...
I TOLD YOU, DIDN'T I? IT IS FORBIDDEN TO TOUCH THE DANCERS ON THE STAGE OR CURSE THEM OUT!
DON'T TRY TO MAKE FOOLS OUT OF US!!
FOOM

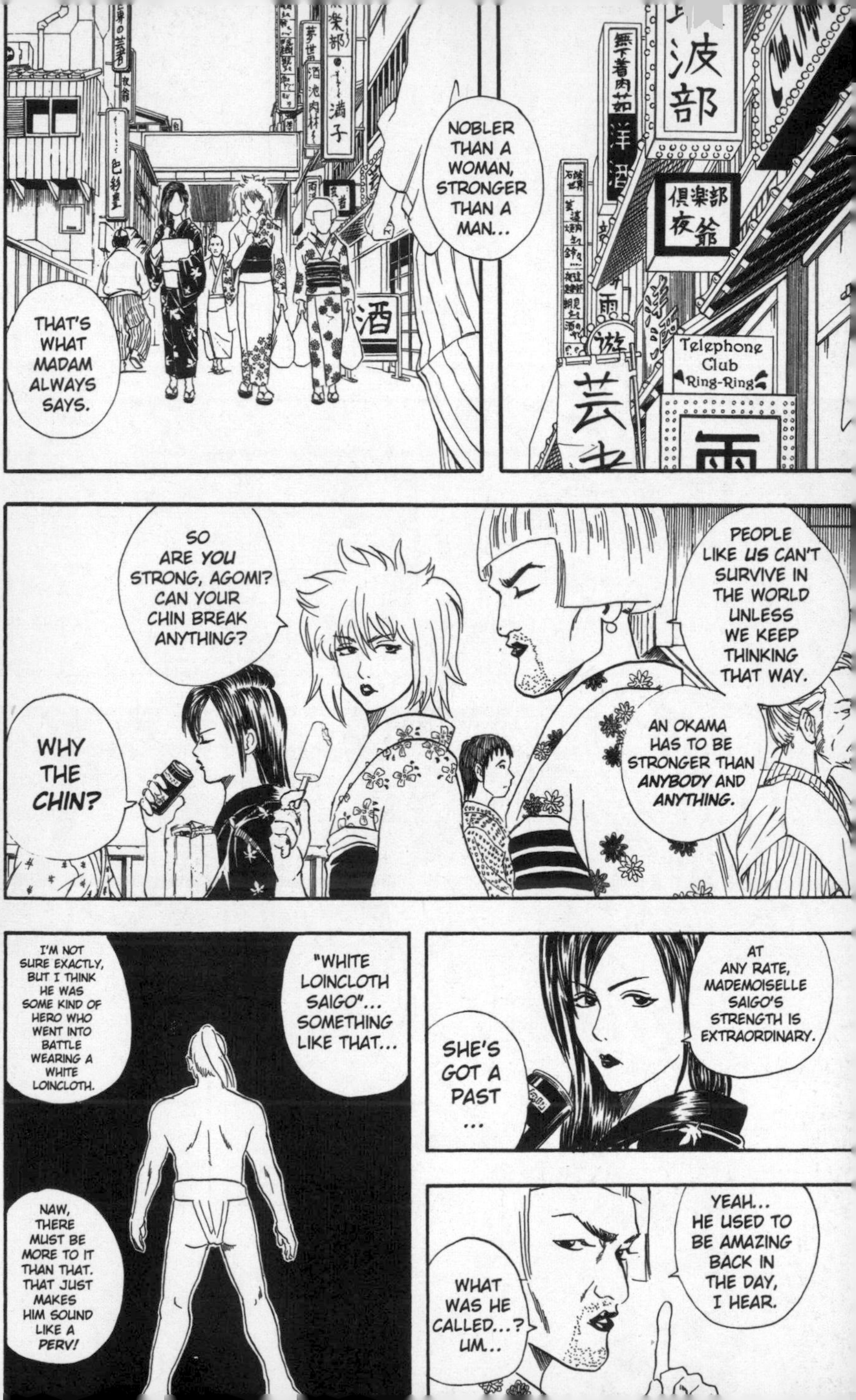
Telephone Club Ring-Ring
NOBLER THAN A WOMAN, STRONGER THAN A MAN...
THAT'S WHAT MADAM ALWAYS SAYS.
PEOPLE LIKE *US* CAN'T SURVIVE IN THE WORLD UNLESS WE KEEP THINKING THAT WAY.
AN OKAMA HAS TO BE STRONGER THAN *ANYBODY* AND *ANYTHING*.
SO ARE *YOU* STRONG, AGOMI? CAN YOUR CHIN BREAK ANYTHING?
WHY THE *CHIN*?
AT ANY RATE, MADEMOISELLE SAIGO'S STRENGTH IS EXTRAORDINARY.
SHE'S GOT A PAST...
YEAH... HE USED TO BE AMAZING BACK IN THE DAY, I HEAR.
WHAT WAS HE CALLED...? UM...
"WHITE LOINCLOTH SAIGO"... SOMETHING LIKE THAT...
I'M NOT SURE EXACTLY, BUT I THINK HE WAS SOME KIND OF HERO WHO WENT INTO BATTLE WEARING A WHITE LOINCLOTH.
NAW, THERE MUST BE MORE TO IT THAN THAT. THAT JUST MAKES HIM SOUND LIKE A *PERV!*

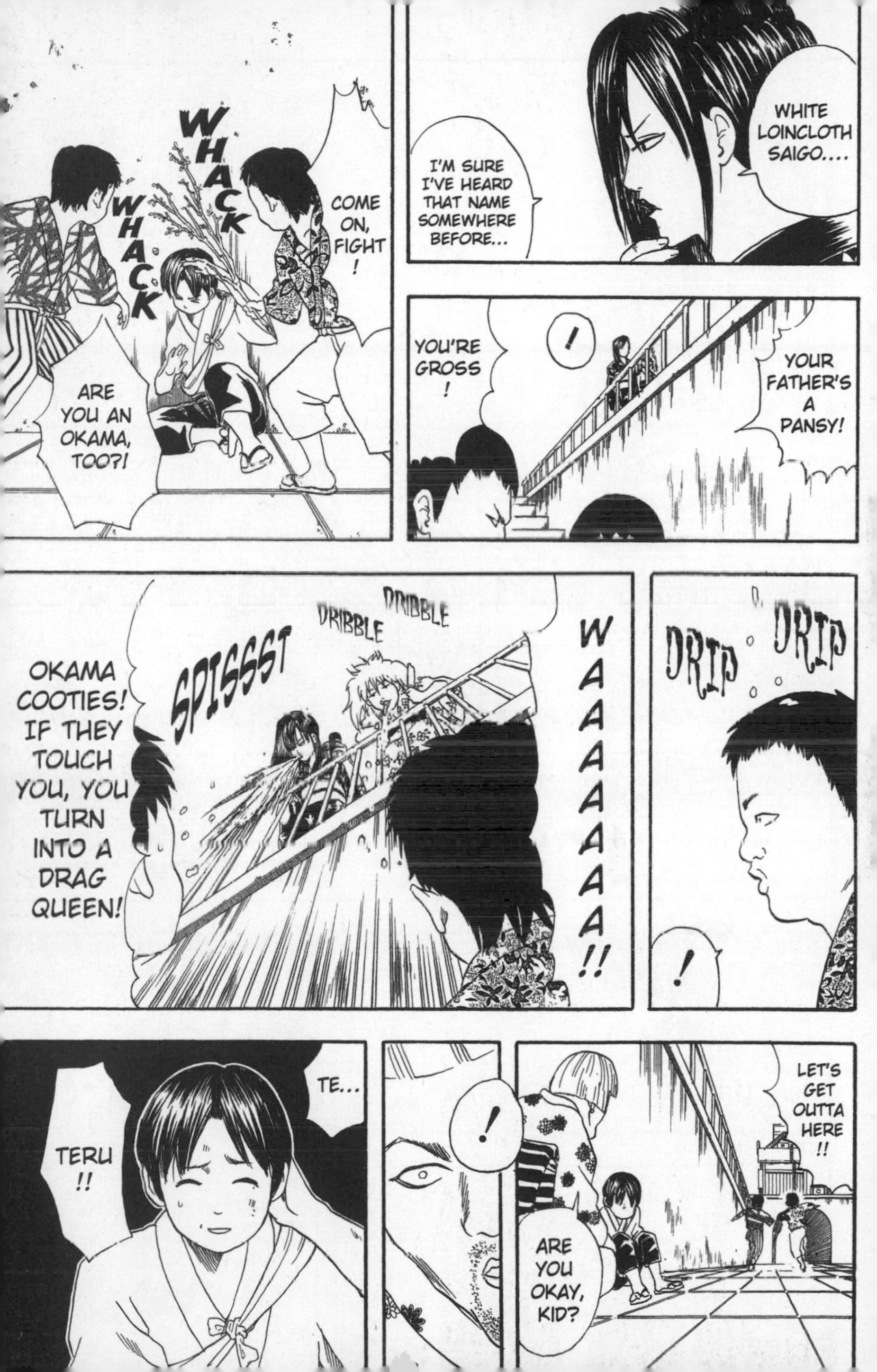
WHITE LOINCLOTH SAIGO....
I'M SURE I'VE HEARD THAT NAME SOMEWHERE BEFORE...
YOUR FATHER'S A PANSY!
!
YOU'RE GROSS!
WHACK
WHACK
COME ON, FIGHT!
ARE YOU AN OKAMA, TOO?!
DRIP
DRIP
!
WAAAAAAAAA!!
DRIBBLE
DRIBBLE
SPISSST
OKAMA COOTIES! IF THEY TOUCH YOU, YOU TURN INTO A DRAG QUEEN!
LET'S GET OUTTA HERE!!
ARE YOU OKAY, KID?
!
TE...
TERU!!

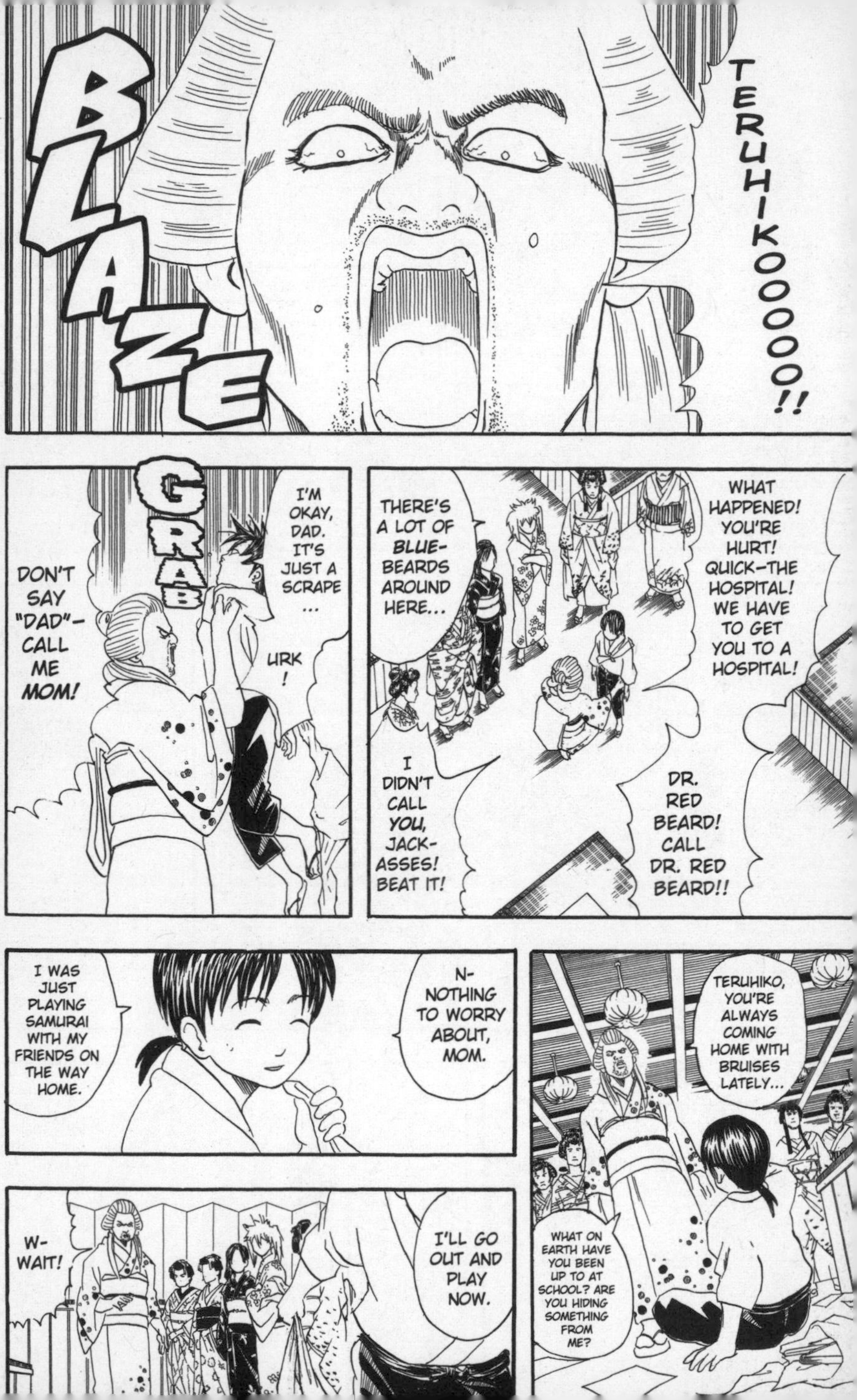
TERUHIKOOOOOO!!
BLAZE
WHAT HAPPENED! YOU'RE HURT! QUICK—THE HOSPITAL! WE HAVE TO GET YOU TO A HOSPITAL!
THERE'S A LOT OF BLUE-BEARDS AROUND HERE...
DR. RED BEARD! CALL DR. RED BEARD!!
I DIDN'T CALL YOU, JACK-ASSES! BEAT IT!
I'M OKAY, DAD. IT'S JUST A SCRAPE...
GRAB
DON'T SAY "DAD"—CALL ME MOM!
URK!
TERUHIKO, YOU'RE ALWAYS COMING HOME WITH BRUISES LATELY...
WHAT ON EARTH HAVE YOU BEEN UP TO AT SCHOOL? ARE YOU HIDING SOMETHING FROM ME?
N-NOTHING TO WORRY ABOUT, MOM.
I WAS JUST PLAYING SAMURAI WITH MY FRIENDS ON THE WAY HOME.
I'LL GO OUT AND PLAY NOW.
W-WAIT!

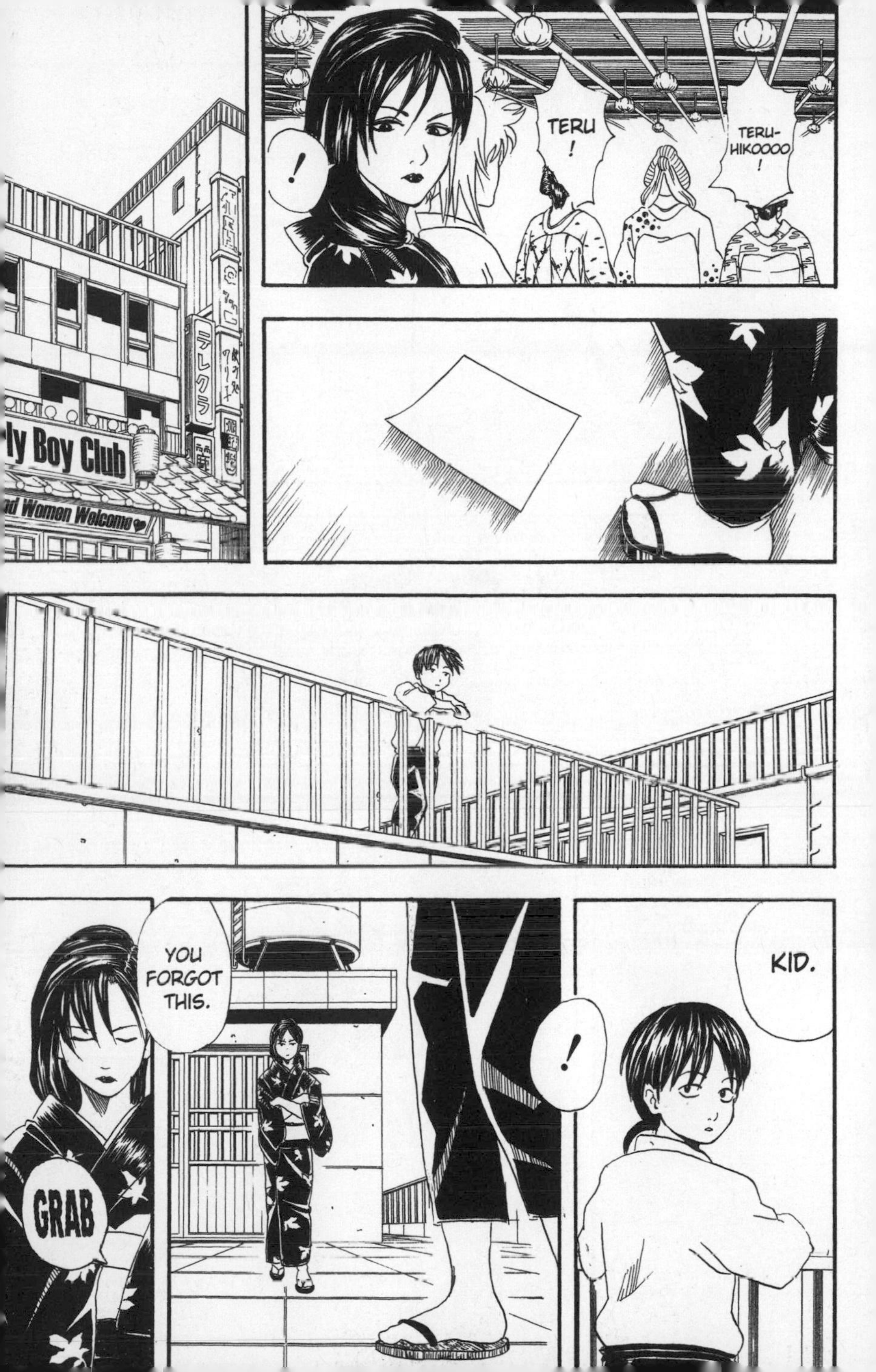
TERU-HIKOOOO!
TERU!
!
テレクラ
ly Boy Club
ad Women Welcome
KID.
!
YOU FORGOT THIS.
GRAB

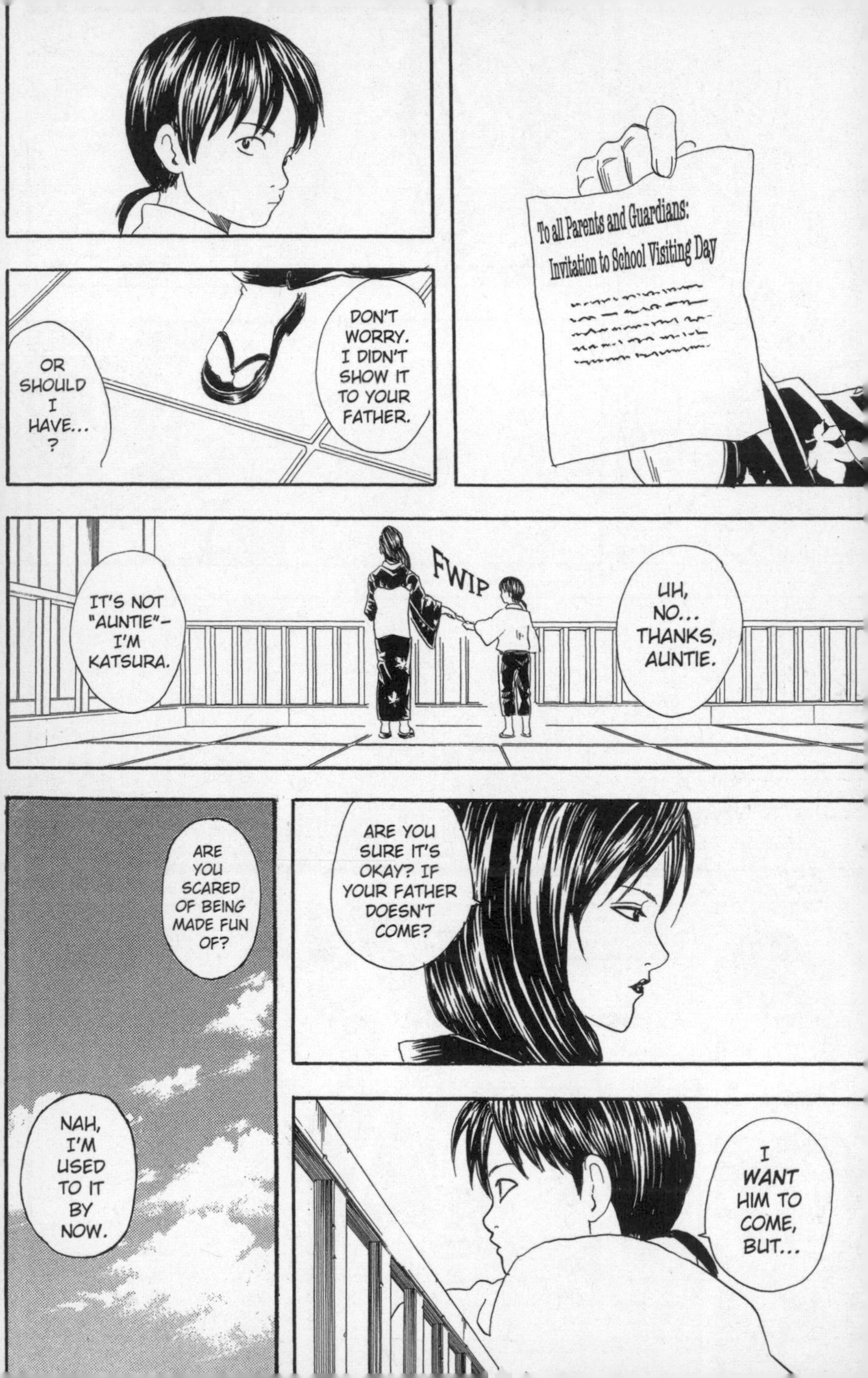
To all Parents and Guardians:
Invitation to School Visiting Day
DON'T WORRY. I DIDN'T SHOW IT TO YOUR FATHER.
OR SHOULD I HAVE...?
UH, NO... THANKS, AUNTIE.
FWIP
IT'S NOT "AUNTIE"— I'M KATSURA.
ARE YOU SURE IT'S OKAY? IF YOUR FATHER DOESN'T COME?
I WANT HIM TO COME, BUT...
ARE YOU SCARED OF BEING MADE FUN OF?
NAH, I'M USED TO IT BY NOW.

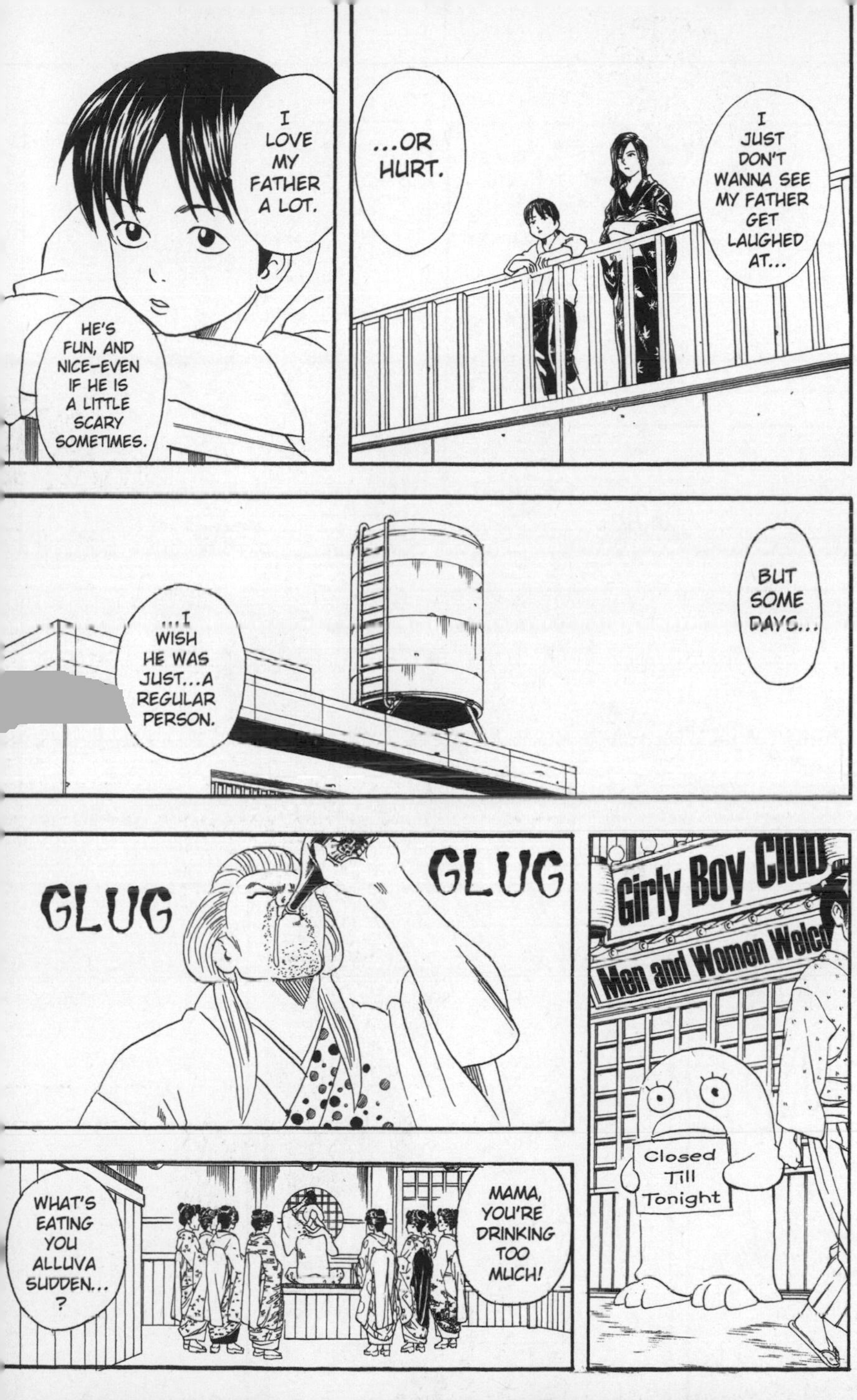
I JUST DON'T WANNA SEE MY FATHER GET LAUGHED AT...
...OR HURT.
I LOVE MY FATHER A LOT.
HE'S FUN, AND NICE-EVEN IF HE IS A LITTLE SCARY SOMETIMES.
BUT SOME DAYS...
...I WISH HE WAS JUST...A REGULAR PERSON.
Girly Boy Club
Men and Women Welco
Closed Till Tonight
GLUG
GLUG
MAMA, YOU'RE DRINKING TOO MUCH!
WHAT'S EATING YOU ALLUVA SUDDEN...?

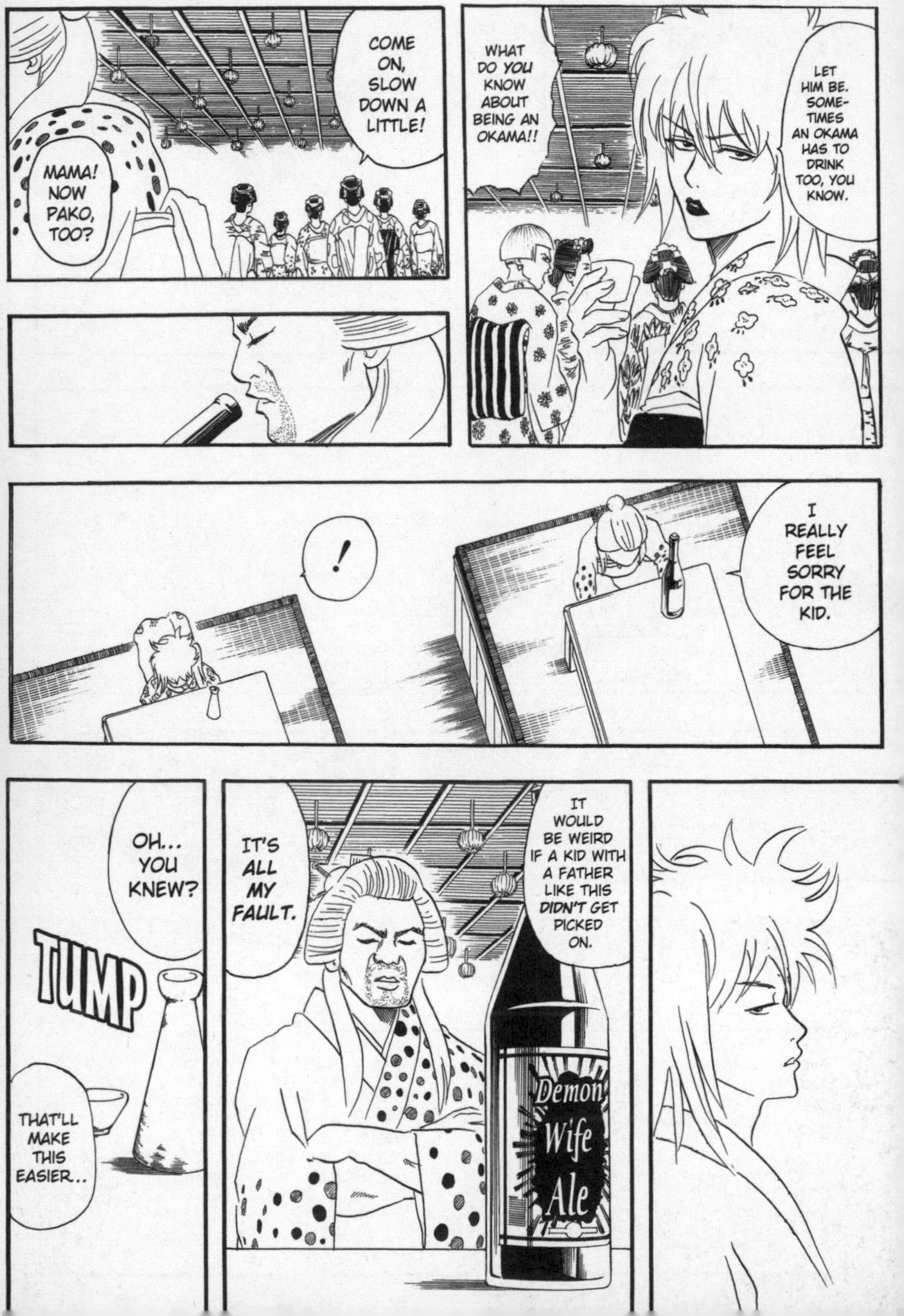
LET HIM BE. SOME-TIMES AN OKAMA HAS TO DRINK TOO, YOU KNOW.
WHAT DO *YOU* KNOW ABOUT BEING AN OKAMA!!
COME ON, SLOW DOWN A LITTLE!
MAMA! NOW PAKO, TOO?
I REALLY FEEL SORRY FOR THE KID.
!
IT WOULD BE WEIRD IF A KID WITH A FATHER LIKE THIS *DIDN'T* GET PICKED ON.
IT'S ALL MY FAULT.
Demon Wife Ale
OH... YOU KNEW?
TUMP
THAT'LL MAKE THIS EASIER...

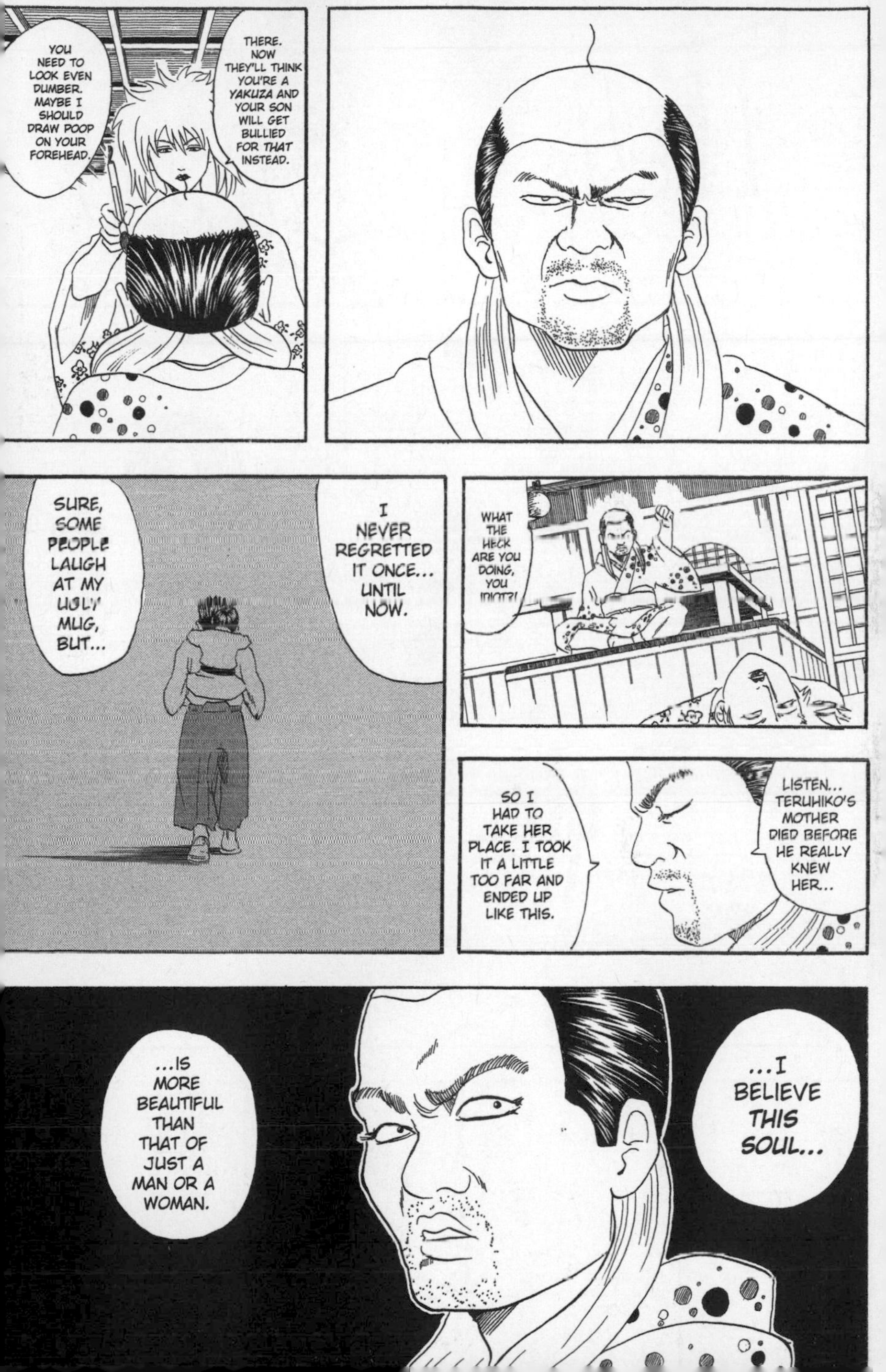
THERE. NOW THEY'LL THINK YOU'RE A *YAKUZA* AND YOUR SON WILL GET BULLIED FOR *THAT* INSTEAD.
YOU NEED TO LOOK EVEN DUMBER. MAYBE I SHOULD DRAW POOP ON YOUR FOREHEAD.
WHAT THE HECK ARE YOU DOING, YOU IDIOT?!
LISTEN... TERUHIKO'S MOTHER DIED BEFORE HE REALLY KNEW HER...
SO I HAD TO TAKE HER PLACE. I TOOK IT A LITTLE TOO FAR AND ENDED UP LIKE THIS.
I NEVER REGRETTED IT ONCE... UNTIL NOW.
SURE, SOME PEOPLE LAUGH AT MY UGLY MUG, BUT...
...I BELIEVE THIS SOUL...
...IS MORE BEAUTIFUL THAN THAT OF JUST A MAN OR A WOMAN.

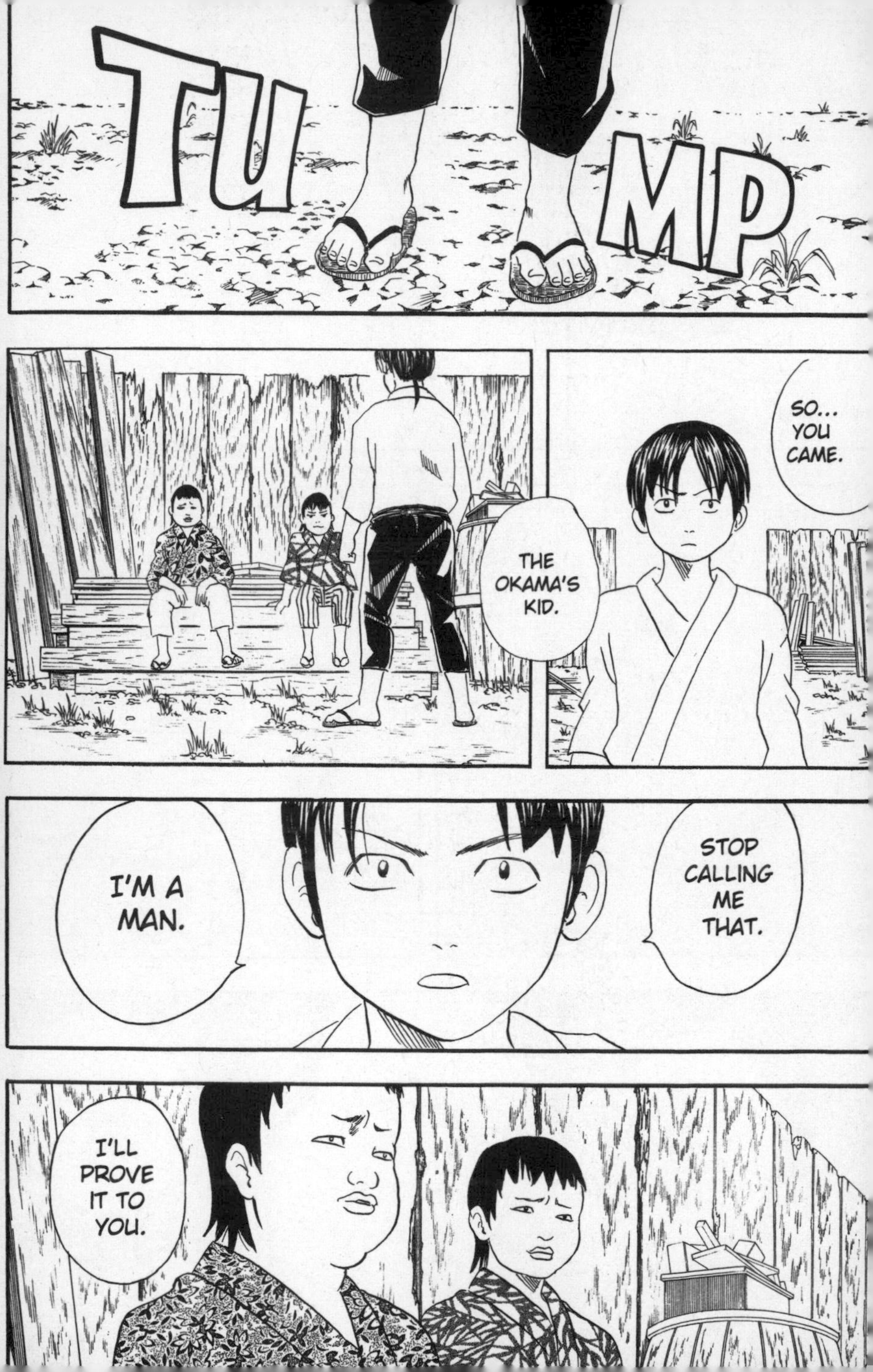
TUMP
SO... YOU CAME.
THE OKAMA'S KID.
STOP CALLING ME THAT.
I'M A MAN.
I'LL PROVE IT TO YOU.

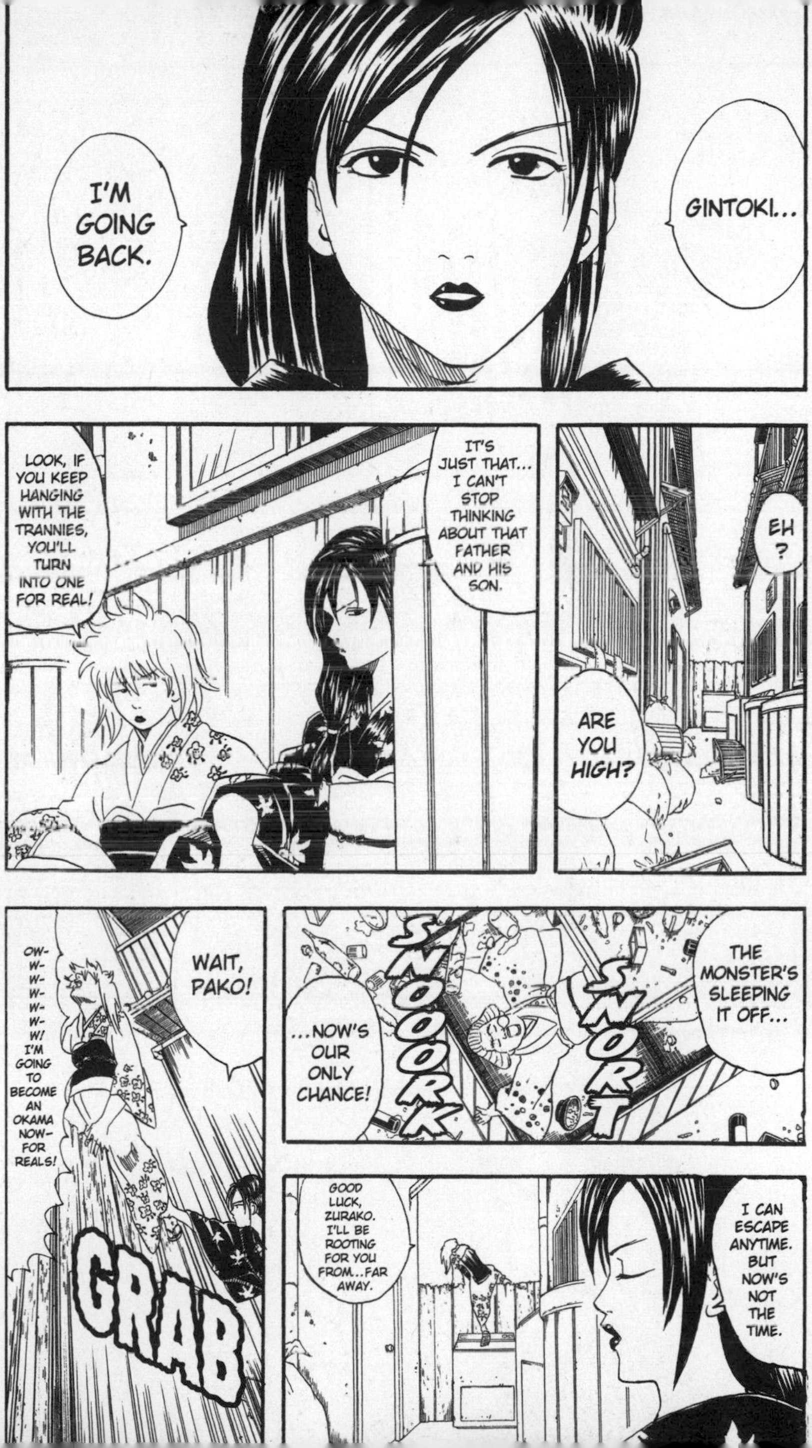
GINTOKI...
I'M GOING BACK.
EH?
ARE YOU HIGH?
IT'S JUST THAT... I CAN'T STOP THINKING ABOUT THAT FATHER AND HIS SON.
LOOK, IF YOU KEEP HANGING WITH THE TRANNIES, YOU'LL TURN INTO ONE FOR REAL!
THE MONSTER'S SLEEPING IT OFF...
SNORT
SNOOORK
...NOW'S OUR ONLY CHANCE!
I CAN ESCAPE ANYTIME. BUT NOW'S NOT THE TIME.
GOOD LUCK, ZURAKO. I'LL BE ROOTING FOR YOU FROM...FAR AWAY.
WAIT, PAKO!
OW-W-W-W-W-W-W! I'M GOING TO BECOME AN OKAMA NOW-FOR REALS!
GRAB

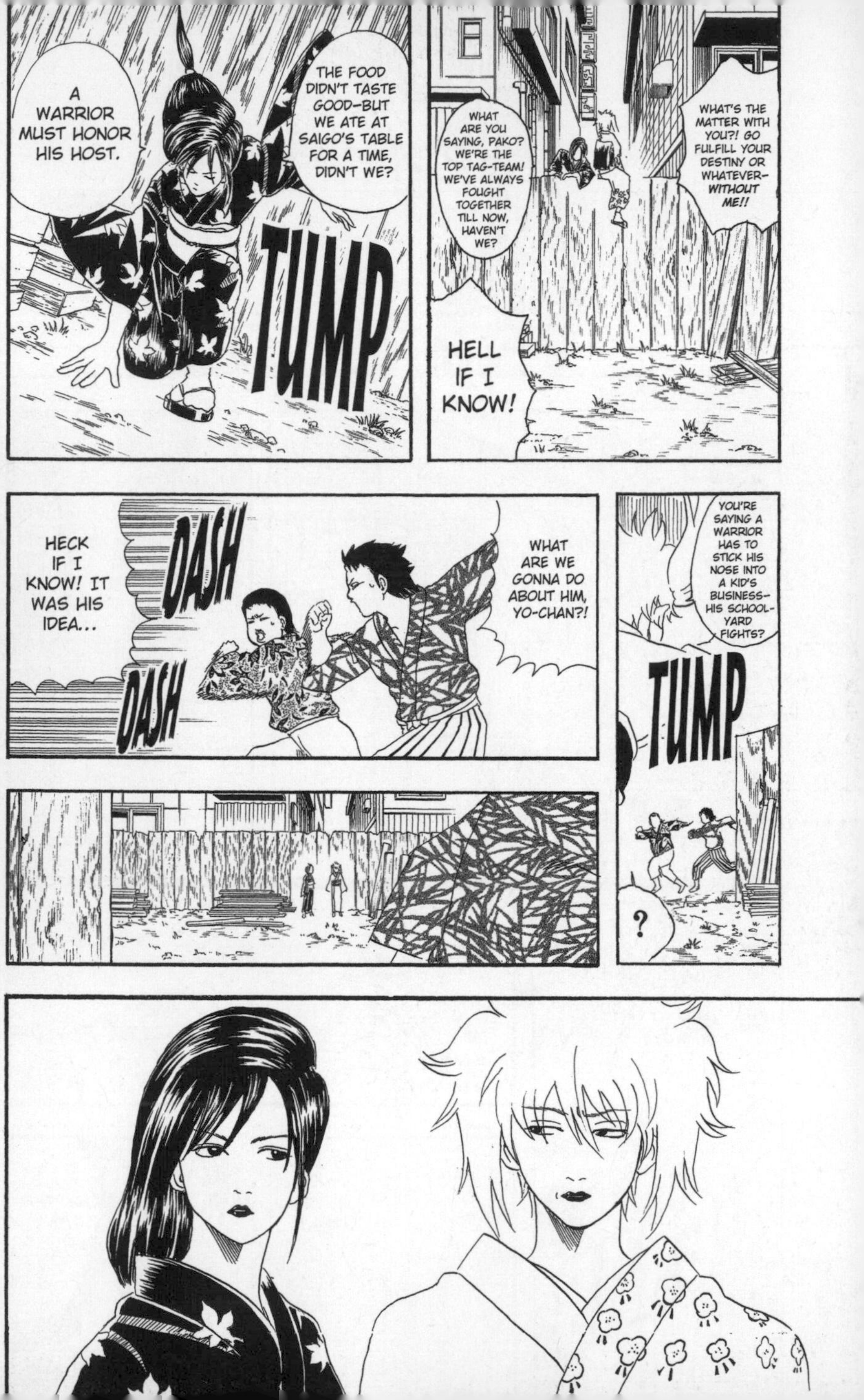
WHAT'S THE MATTER WITH YOU?! GO FULFILL YOUR DESTINY OR WHATEVER— *WITHOUT ME!!*
WHAT ARE YOU SAYING, PAKO? WE'RE THE TOP TAG-TEAM! WE'VE ALWAYS FOUGHT TOGETHER TILL NOW, HAVEN'T WE?
HELL IF I KNOW!
THE FOOD DIDN'T TASTE GOOD—BUT WE ATE AT SAIGO'S TABLE FOR A TIME, DIDN'T WE?
A WARRIOR MUST HONOR HIS HOST.
TUMP
YOU'RE SAYING A WARRIOR HAS TO STICK HIS NOSE INTO A KID'S BUSINESS— HIS SCHOOL-YARD FIGHTS?
TUMP
?
WHAT ARE WE GONNA DO ABOUT HIM, YO-CHAN?!
HECK IF I KNOW! IT WAS HIS IDEA...
DASH
DASH

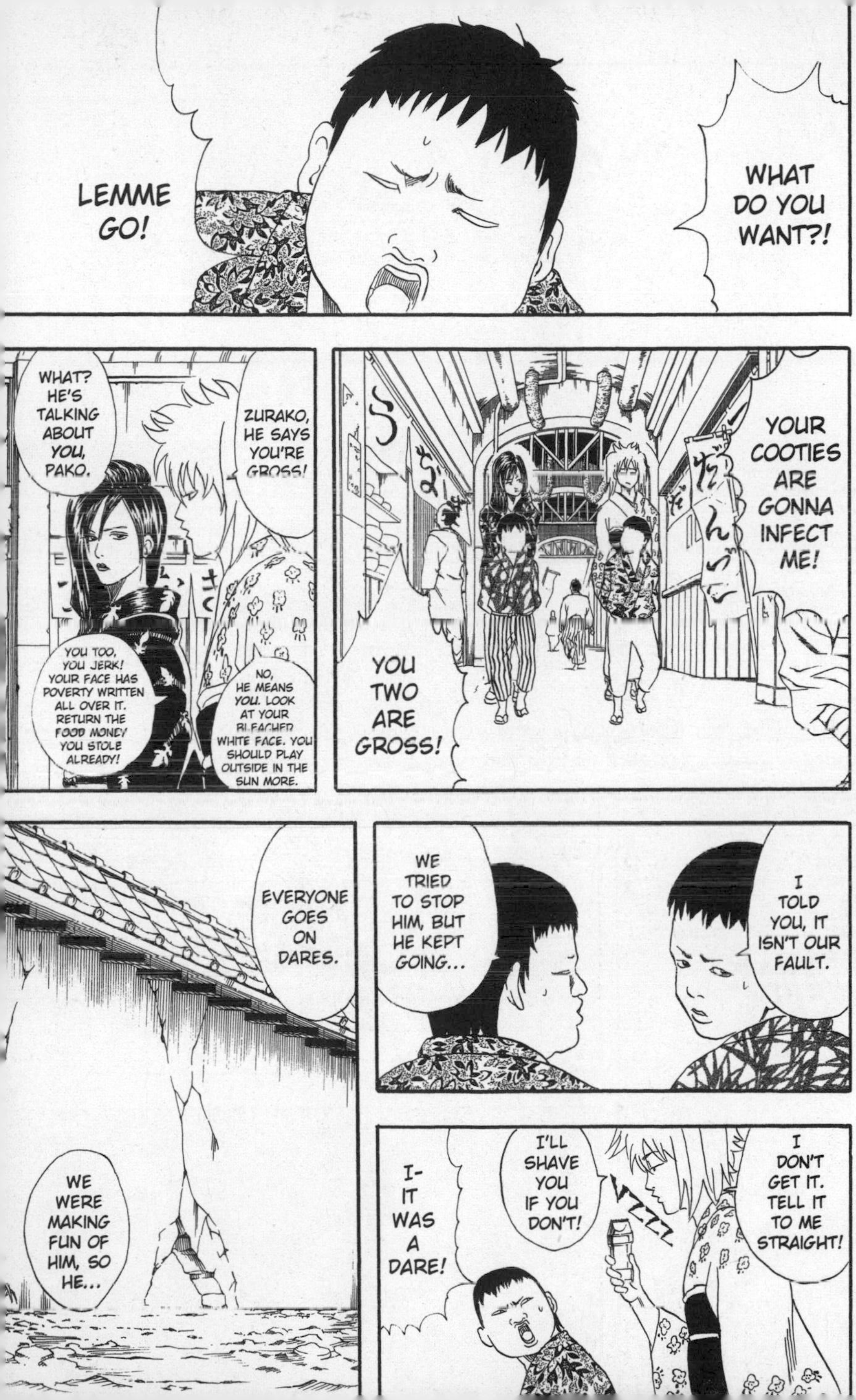
WHAT DO YOU WANT?!
LEMME GO!
YOUR COOTIES ARE GONNA INFECT ME!
YOU TWO ARE GROSS!
ZURAKO, HE SAYS YOU'RE GROSS!
WHAT? HE'S TALKING ABOUT YOU, PAKO.
NO, HE MEANS YOU. LOOK AT YOUR BLEACHED WHITE FACE. YOU SHOULD PLAY OUTSIDE IN THE SUN MORE.
YOU TOO, YOU JERK! YOUR FACE HAS POVERTY WRITTEN ALL OVER IT. RETURN THE FOOD MONEY YOU STOLE ALREADY!
I TOLD YOU, IT ISN'T OUR FAULT.
WE TRIED TO STOP HIM, BUT HE KEPT GOING...
I DON'T GET IT. TELL IT TO ME STRAIGHT!
VZZZ
I'LL SHAVE YOU IF YOU DON'T!
I- IT WAS A DARE!
EVERYONE GOES ON DARES.
WE WERE MAKING FUN OF HIM, SO HE...

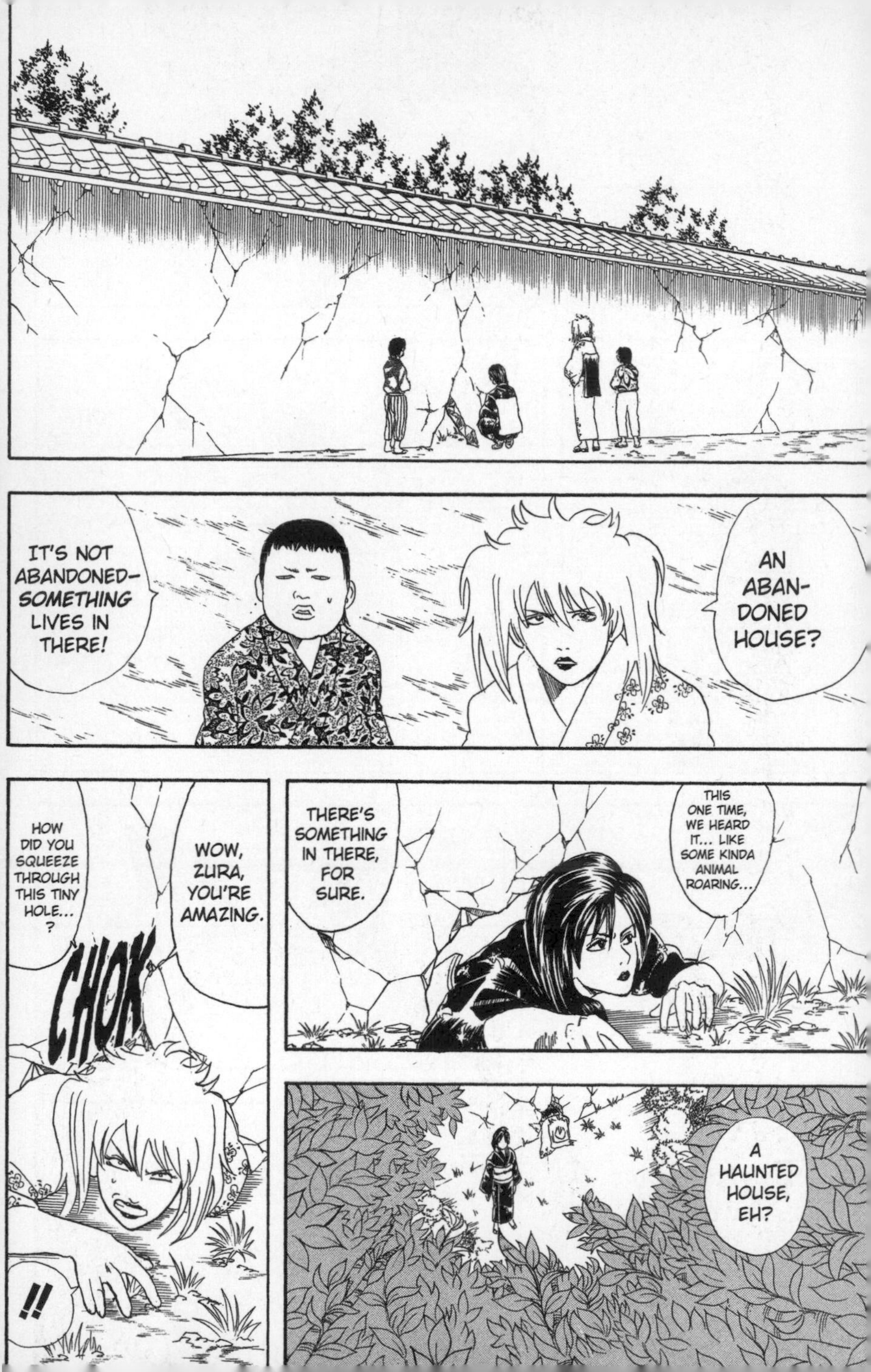
AN ABAN-DONED HOUSE?
IT'S NOT ABANDONED-SOMETHING LIVES IN THERE!
THIS ONE TIME, WE HEARD IT... LIKE SOME KINDA ANIMAL ROARING...
THERE'S SOMETHING IN THERE, FOR SURE.
A HAUNTED HOUSE, EH?
WOW, ZURA, YOU'RE AMAZING.
HOW DID YOU SQUEEZE THROUGH THIS TINY HOLE...?
CHOK
!!

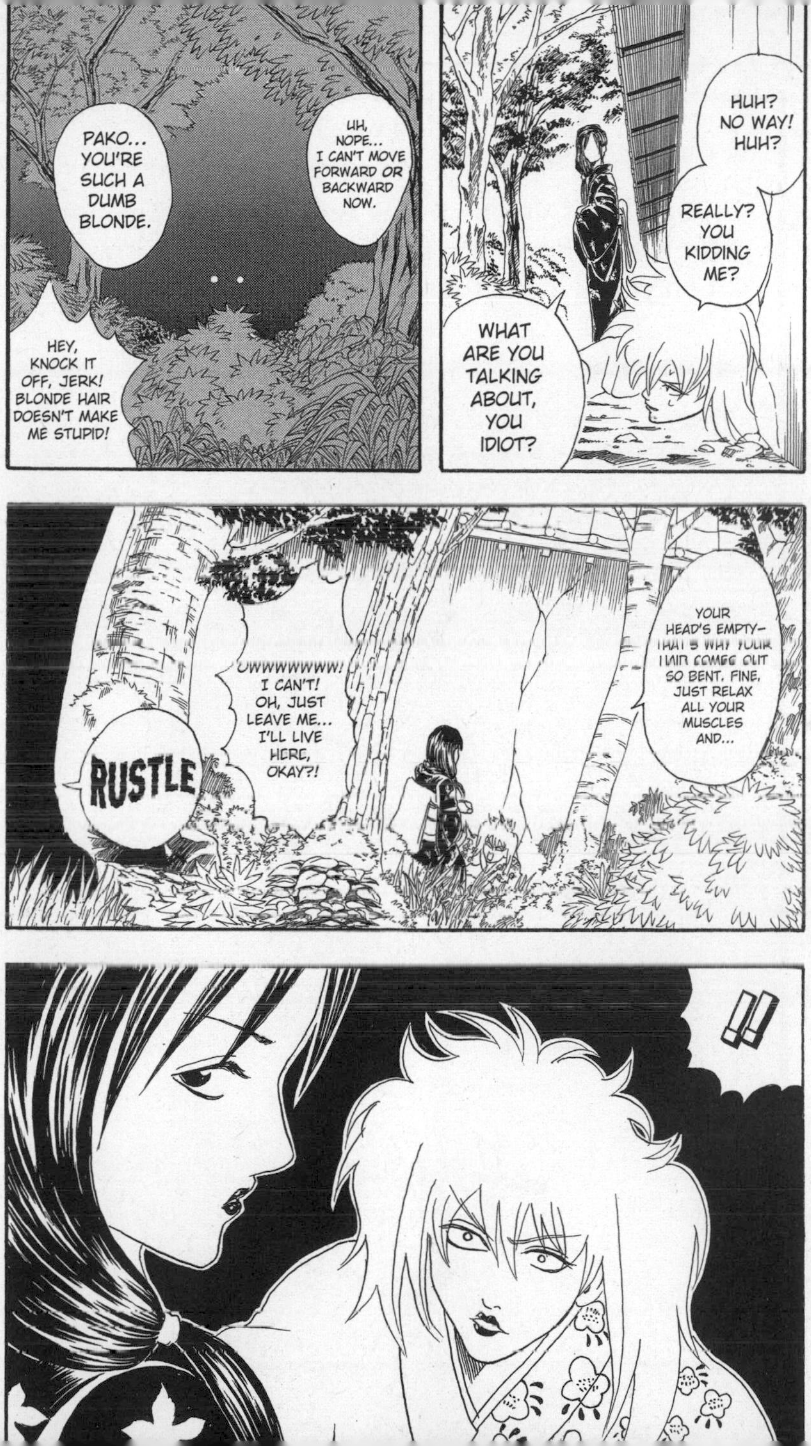
HUH? NO WAY! HUH?
REALLY? YOU KIDDING ME?
WHAT ARE YOU TALKING ABOUT, YOU IDIOT?
UH, NOPE... I CAN'T MOVE FORWARD OR BACKWARD NOW.
PAKO... YOU'RE SUCH A DUMB BLONDE.
HEY, KNOCK IT OFF, JERK! BLONDE HAIR DOESN'T MAKE ME STUPID!
YOUR HEAD'S EMPTY—THAT'S WHY YOUR HAIR COMES OUT SO BENT. FINE, JUST RELAX ALL YOUR MUSCLES AND...
UWWWWWWW! I CAN'T! OH, JUST LEAVE ME... I'LL LIVE HERE, OKAY?!
RUSTLE
!!

Sorachi's Q&A
Hanging with the Readers #9

<Question from pen name Ami Mizuki of Osaka>
No matter how I try, I can't draw Gin's hair well.
Can you give me just a hint, please?

<Answer>

The guy's head looks like a mess but there's actually a system to achieving that effect. The key is having the hair go backwards in four places. First, let's draw a normal head.

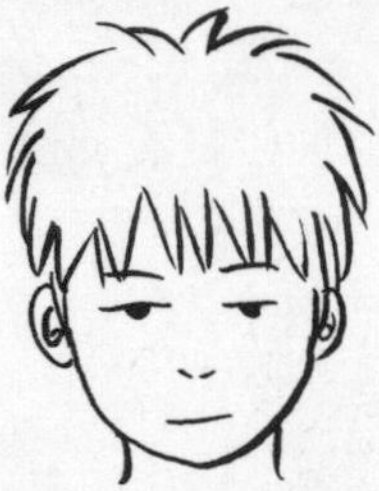

Um, next, we make some reversed hair on the top of his head—a little on the left and right sides.

And then, about where the eyes are, make some reversed hair, and then elongate the hair in front.

And there you go!

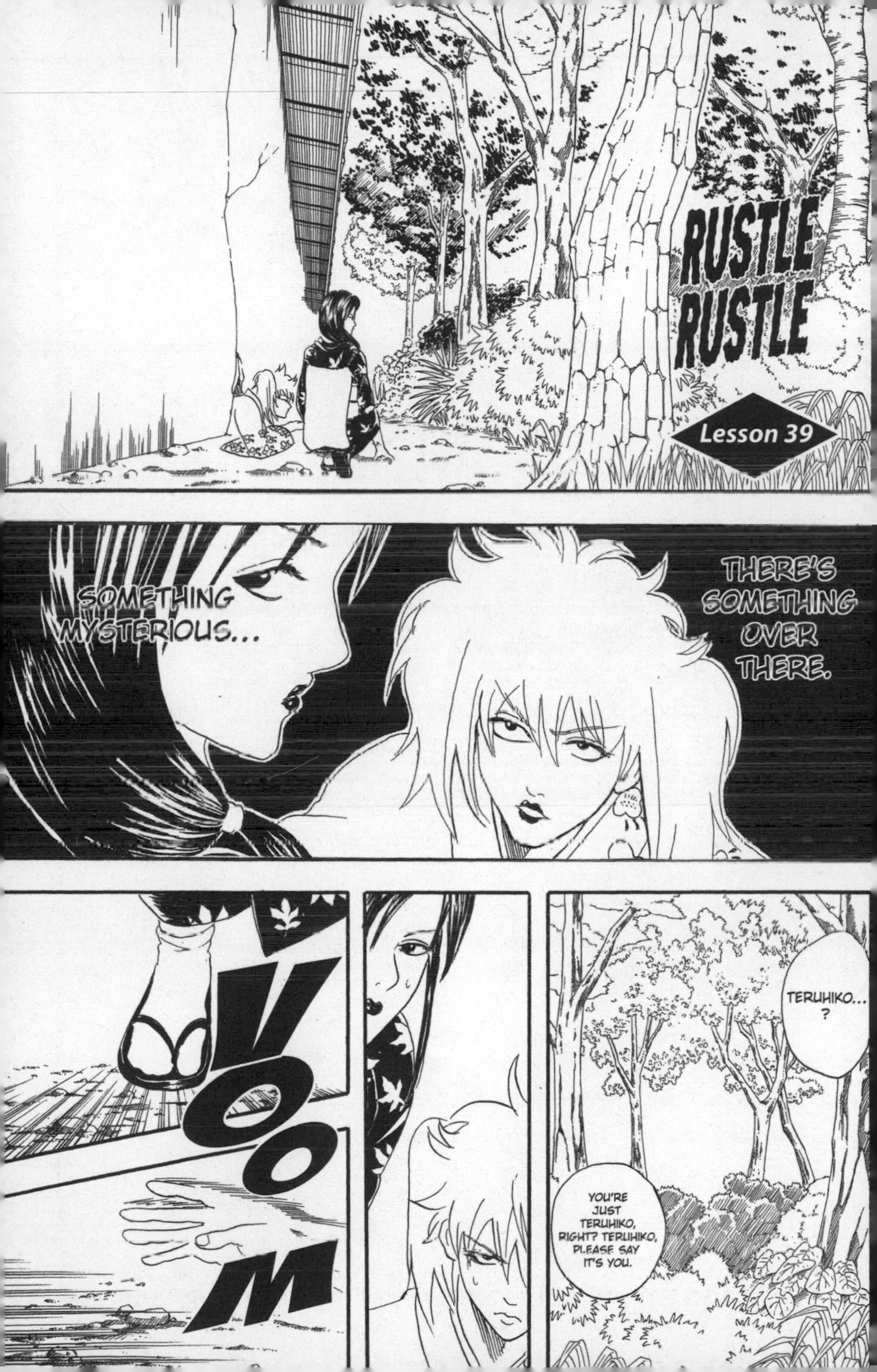
RUSTLE RUSTLE
Lesson 39
THERE'S SOMETHING OVER THERE.
SOMETHING MYSTERIOUS...
TERUHIKO... ?
YOU'RE JUST TERUHIKO, RIGHT? TERUHIKO, PLEASE SAY IT'S YOU.
VOOM

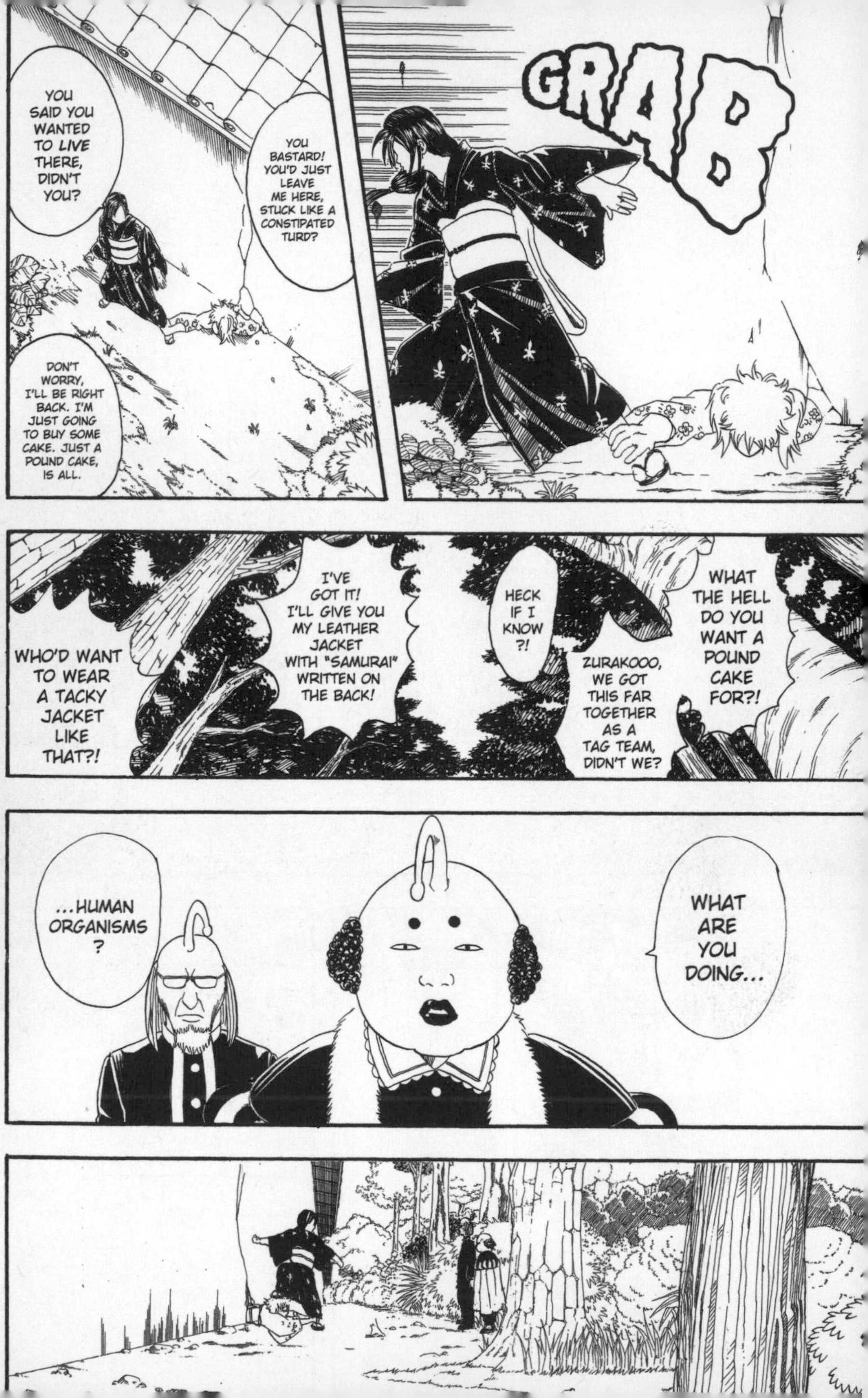
GRAB
YOU BASTARD! YOU'D JUST LEAVE ME HERE, STUCK LIKE A CONSTIPATED TURD?
YOU SAID YOU WANTED TO *LIVE* THERE, DIDN'T YOU?
DON'T WORRY, I'LL BE RIGHT BACK. I'M JUST GOING TO BUY SOME CAKE. JUST A POUND CAKE, IS ALL.
WHAT THE HELL DO YOU WANT A POUND CAKE FOR?!
ZURAKOOO, WE GOT THIS FAR TOGETHER AS A TAG TEAM, DIDN'T WE?
HECK IF I KNOW?!
I'VE GOT IT! I'LL GIVE YOU MY LEATHER JACKET WITH "SAMURAI" WRITTEN ON THE BACK!
WHO'D WANT TO WEAR A TACKY JACKET LIKE THAT?!
WHAT ARE YOU DOING...
...HUMAN ORGANISMS?

Lesson 39:
Cute Faces Are Always Hiding Something

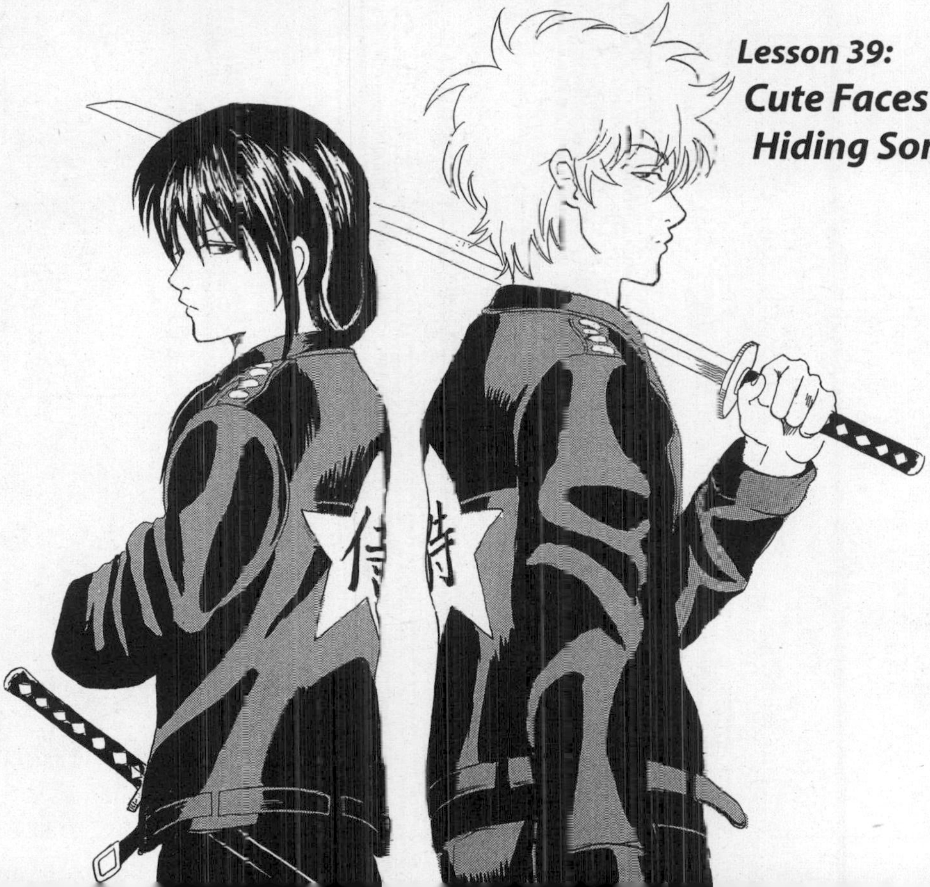
侍
侍

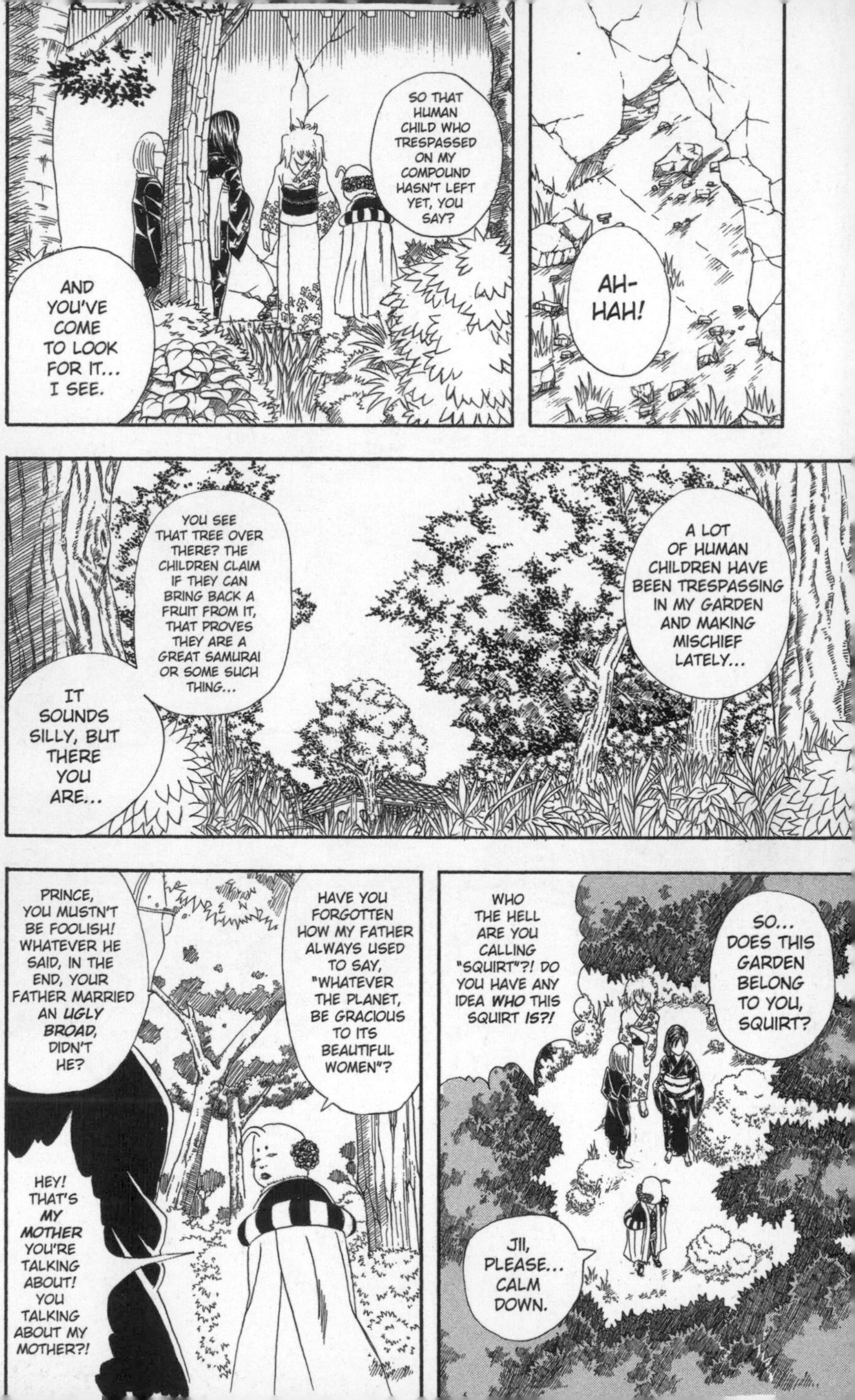
AH-HAH!
SO THAT HUMAN CHILD WHO TRESPASSED ON MY COMPOUND HASN'T LEFT YET, YOU SAY?
AND YOU'VE COME TO LOOK FOR IT... I SEE.
A LOT OF HUMAN CHILDREN HAVE BEEN TRESPASSING IN MY GARDEN AND MAKING MISCHIEF LATELY...
YOU SEE THAT TREE OVER THERE? THE CHILDREN CLAIM IF THEY CAN BRING BACK A FRUIT FROM IT, THAT PROVES THEY ARE A GREAT SAMURAI OR SOME SUCH THING...
IT SOUNDS SILLY, BUT THERE YOU ARE...
SO... DOES THIS GARDEN BELONG TO YOU, SQUIRT?
WHO THE HELL ARE YOU CALLING "SQUIRT"?! DO YOU HAVE ANY IDEA *WHO* THIS SQUIRT *IS*?!
JII, PLEASE... CALM DOWN.
HAVE YOU FORGOTTEN HOW MY FATHER ALWAYS USED TO SAY, "WHATEVER THE PLANET, BE GRACIOUS TO ITS BEAUTIFUL WOMEN"?
PRINCE, YOU MUSTN'T BE FOOLISH! WHATEVER HE SAID, IN THE END, YOUR FATHER MARRIED AN *UGLY BROAD*, DIDN'T HE?
HEY! THAT'S *MY MOTHER* YOU'RE TALKING ABOUT! YOU TALKING ABOUT MY MOTHER?!

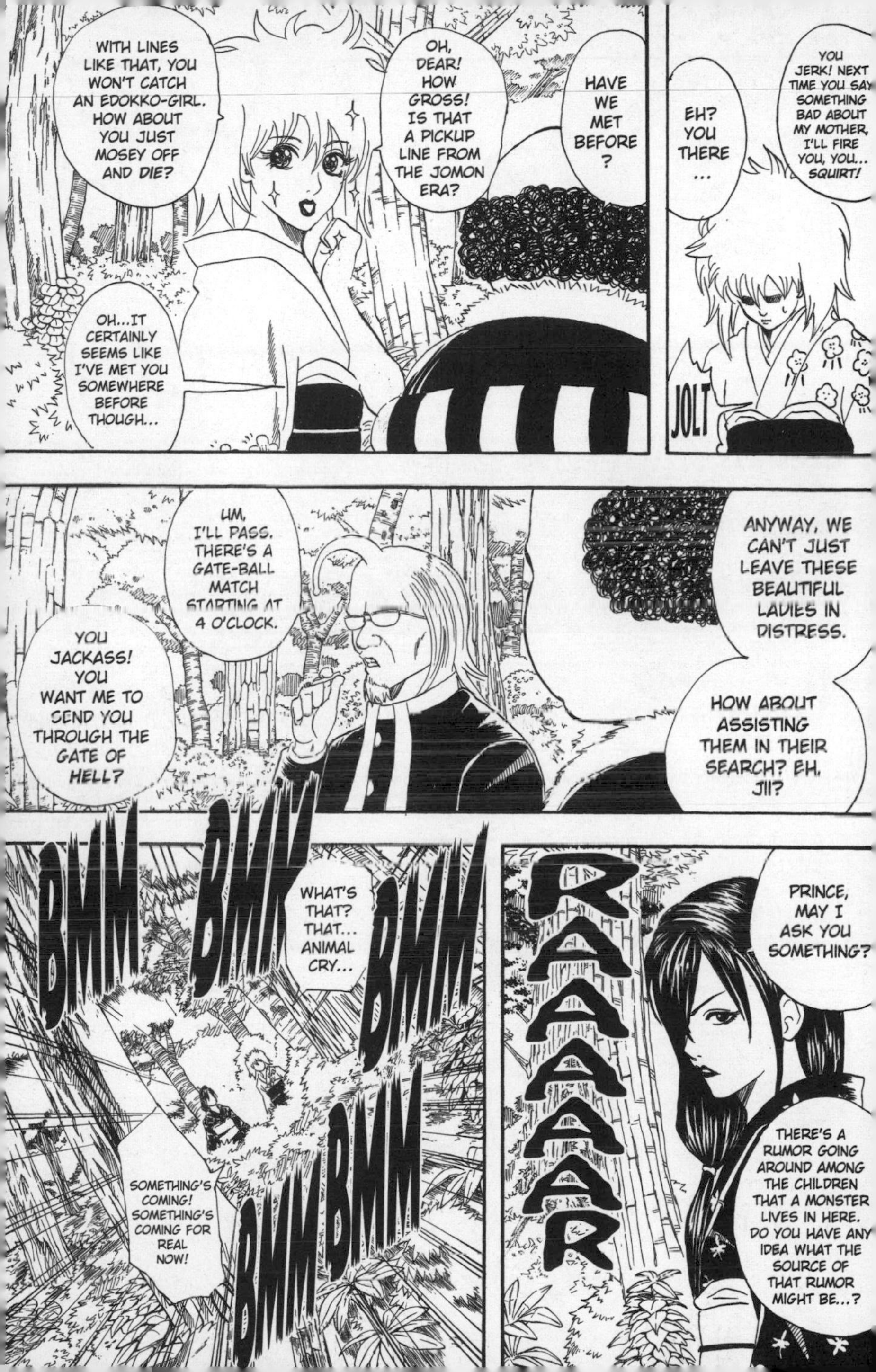
YOU JERK! NEXT TIME YOU SAY SOMETHING BAD ABOUT MY MOTHER, I'LL FIRE YOU, YOU... SQUIRT!
EH? YOU THERE...
JOLT
HAVE WE MET BEFORE?
OH, DEAR! HOW GROSS! IS THAT A PICKUP LINE FROM THE JOMON ERA?
WITH LINES LIKE THAT, YOU WON'T CATCH AN EDOKKO-GIRL. HOW ABOUT YOU JUST MOSEY OFF AND DIE?
OH...IT CERTAINLY SEEMS LIKE I'VE MET YOU SOMEWHERE BEFORE THOUGH...
ANYWAY, WE CAN'T JUST LEAVE THESE BEAUTIFUL LADIES IN DISTRESS.
HOW ABOUT ASSISTING THEM IN THEIR SEARCH? EH, JII?
UM, I'LL PASS. THERE'S A GATE-BALL MATCH STARTING AT 4 O'CLOCK.
YOU JACKASS! YOU WANT ME TO SEND YOU THROUGH THE GATE OF HELL?
RAAAAAAR
PRINCE, MAY I ASK YOU SOMETHING?
THERE'S A RUMOR GOING AROUND AMONG THE CHILDREN THAT A MONSTER LIVES IN HERE. DO YOU HAVE ANY IDEA WHAT THE SOURCE OF THAT RUMOR MIGHT BE...?
BMM
BMM
BMM
WHAT'S THAT? THAT... ANIMAL CRY...
BMK
BMM
SOMETHING'S COMING! SOMETHING'S COMING FOR REAL NOW!

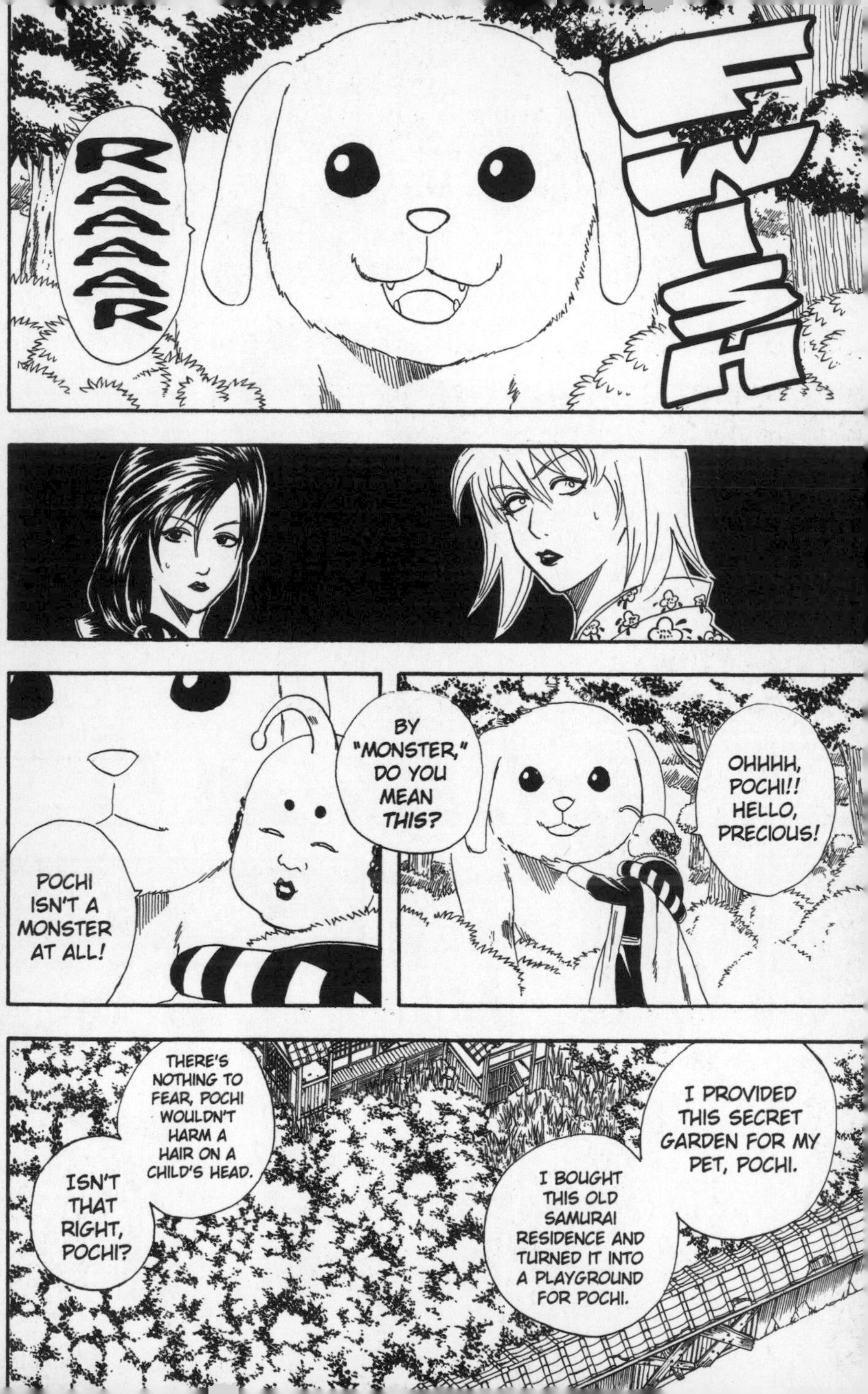
RAAAAR
OHHHH, POCHI!! HELLO, PRECIOUS!
BY "MONSTER," DO YOU MEAN THIS?
POCHI ISN'T A MONSTER AT ALL!
I PROVIDED THIS SECRET GARDEN FOR MY PET, POCHI.
I BOUGHT THIS OLD SAMURAI RESIDENCE AND TURNED IT INTO A PLAYGROUND FOR POCHI.
THERE'S NOTHING TO FEAR, POCHI WOULDN'T HARM A HAIR ON A CHILD'S HEAD.
ISN'T THAT RIGHT, POCHI?

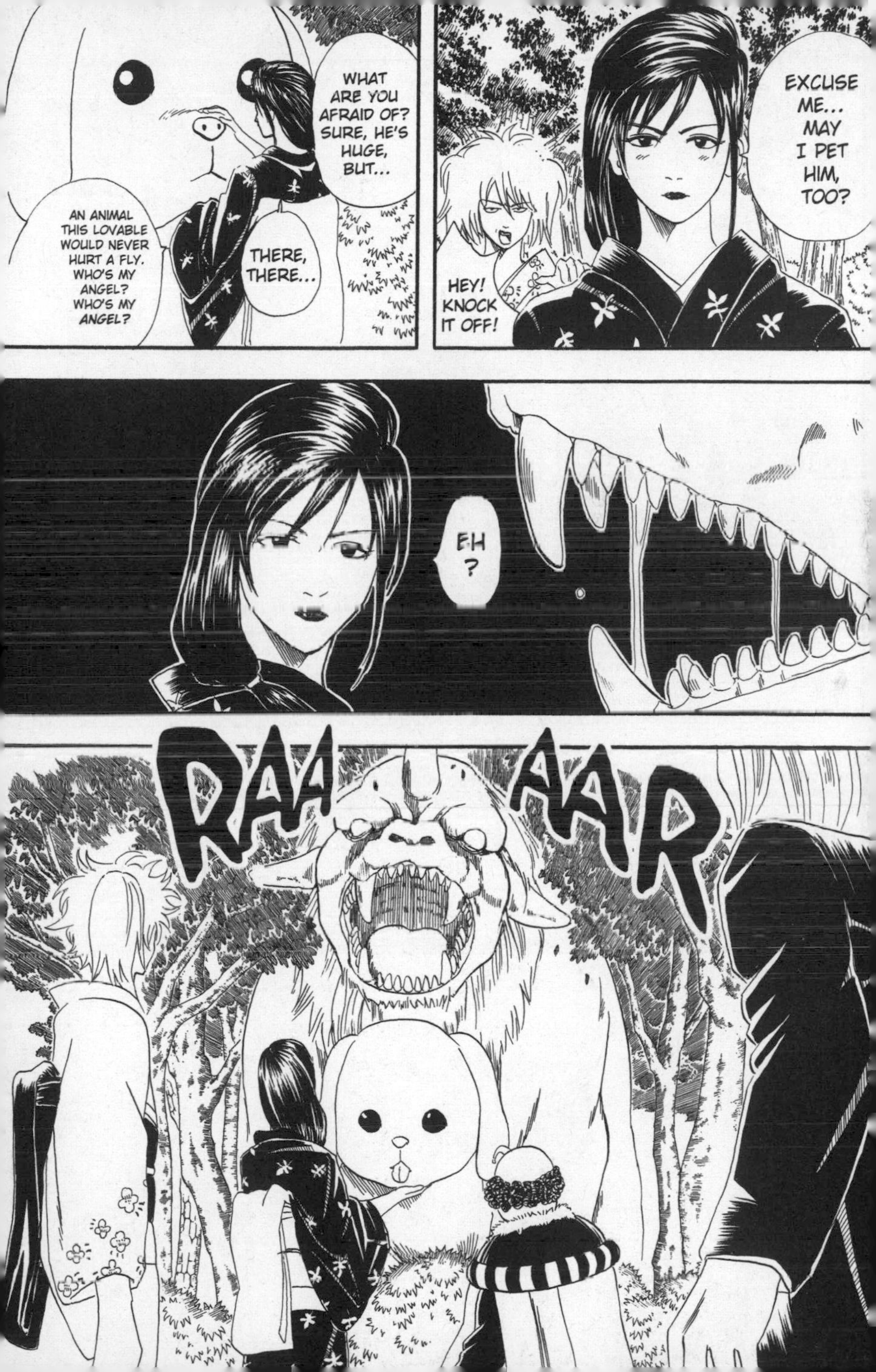
EXCUSE ME... MAY I PET HIM, TOO?
HEY! KNOCK IT OFF!
WHAT ARE YOU AFRAID OF? SURE, HE'S HUGE, BUT...
THERE, THERE...
AN ANIMAL THIS LOVABLE WOULD NEVER HURT A FLY. WHO'S MY ANGEL? WHO'S MY ANGEL?
EH ?
RAAAAR

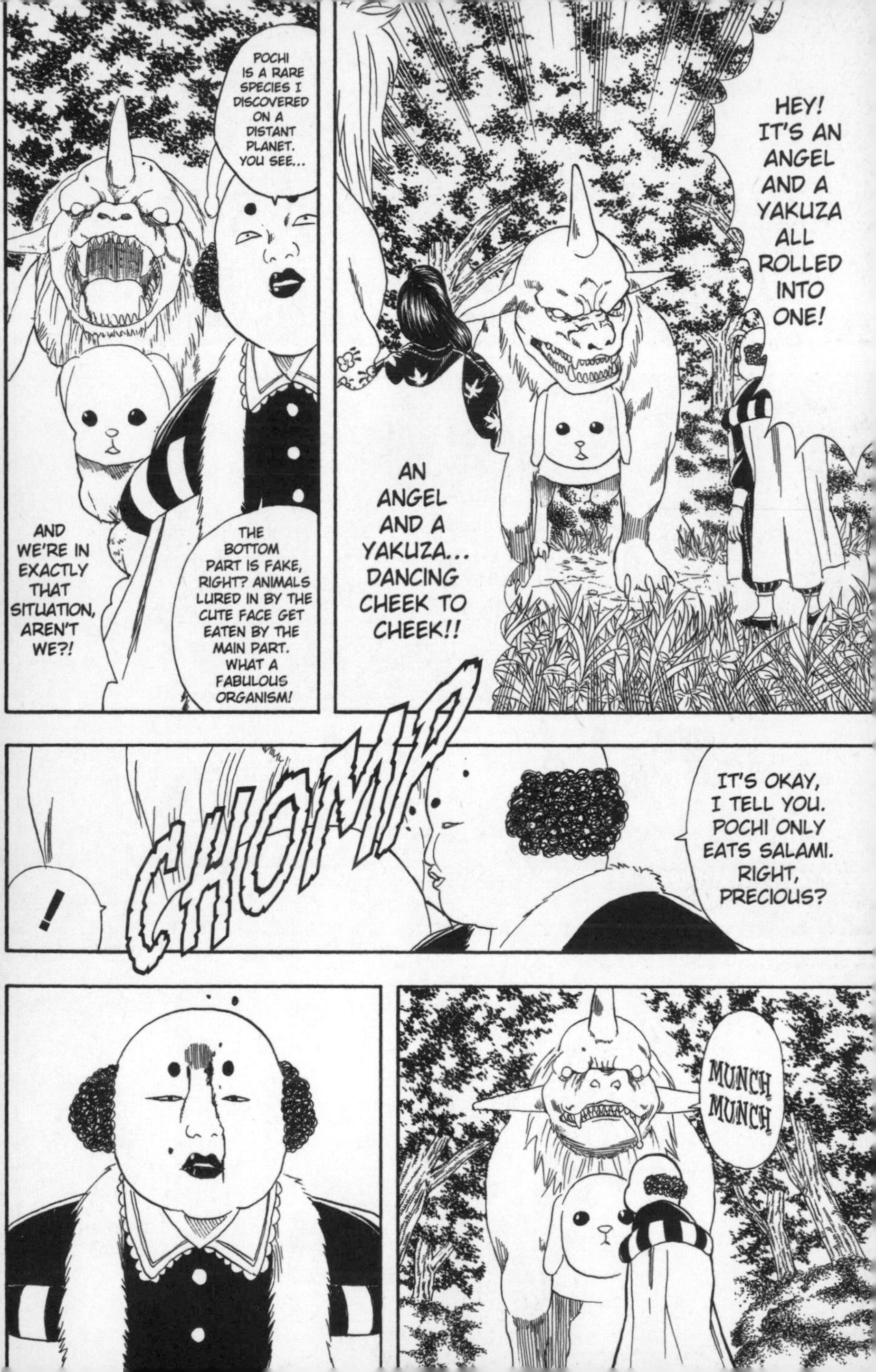
HEY! IT'S AN ANGEL AND A YAKUZA ALL ROLLED INTO ONE!
AN ANGEL AND A YAKUZA... DANCING CHEEK TO CHEEK!!
POCHI IS A RARE SPECIES I DISCOVERED ON A DISTANT PLANET. YOU SEE...
THE BOTTOM PART IS FAKE, RIGHT? ANIMALS LURED IN BY THE CUTE FACE GET EATEN BY THE MAIN PART. WHAT A FABULOUS ORGANISM!
AND WE'RE IN EXACTLY THAT SITUATION, AREN'T WE?!
IT'S OKAY, I TELL YOU. POCHI ONLY EATS SALAMI. RIGHT, PRECIOUS?
CHOMP
!
MUNCH MUNCH

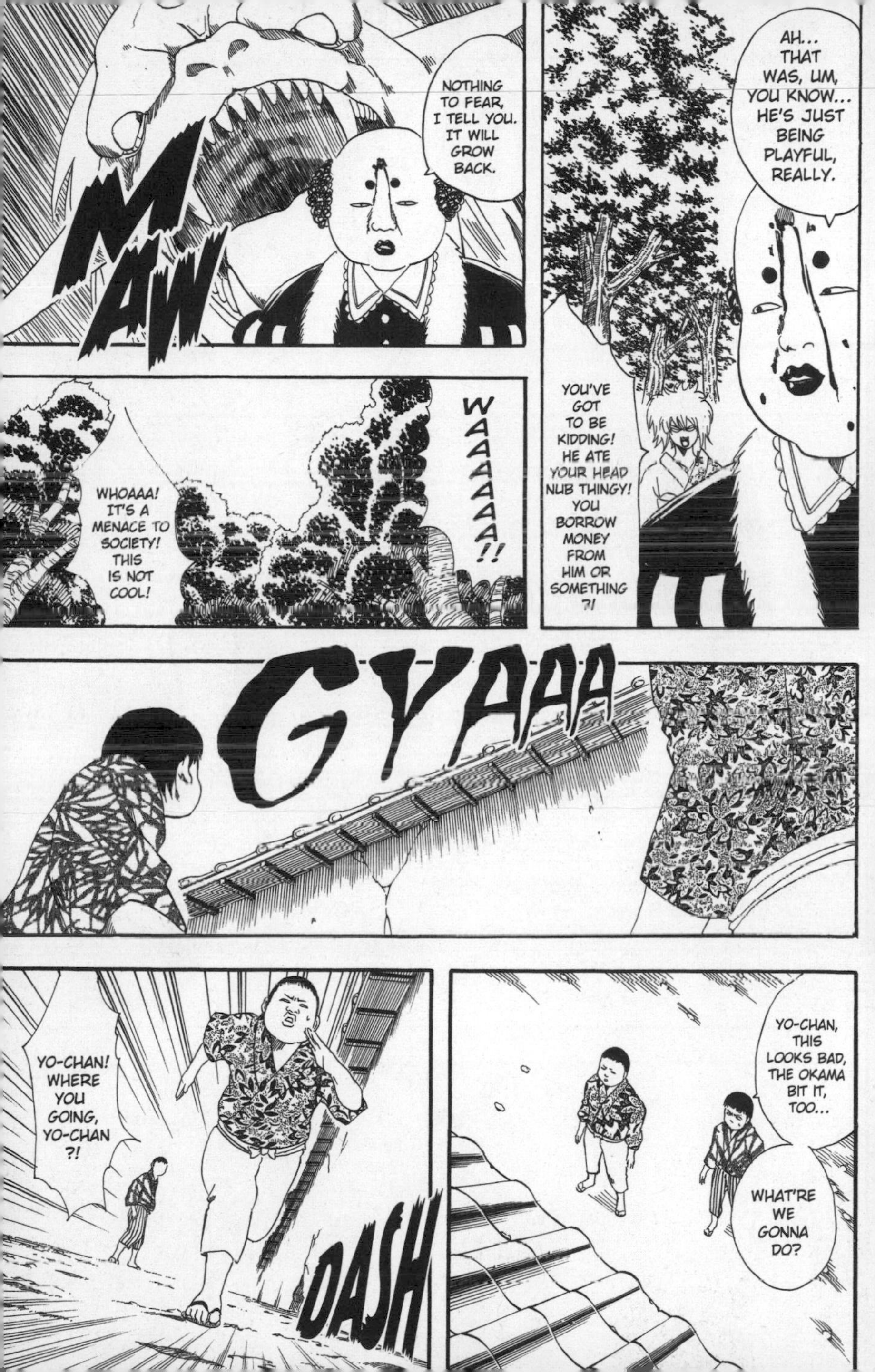
AH... THAT WAS, UM, YOU KNOW... HE'S JUST BEING PLAYFUL, REALLY.
YOU'VE GOT TO BE KIDDING! HE ATE YOUR HEAD NUB THINGY! YOU BORROW MONEY FROM HIM OR SOMETHING?!
MAW
NOTHING TO FEAR, I TELL YOU. IT WILL GROW BACK.
WAAAAAAA!!
WHOAAA! IT'S A MENACE TO SOCIETY! THIS IS NOT COOL!
GYAAA
YO-CHAN, THIS LOOKS BAD, THE OKAMA BIT IT, TOO...
WHAT'RE WE GONNA DO?
YO-CHAN! WHERE YOU GOING, YO-CHAN?!
DASH

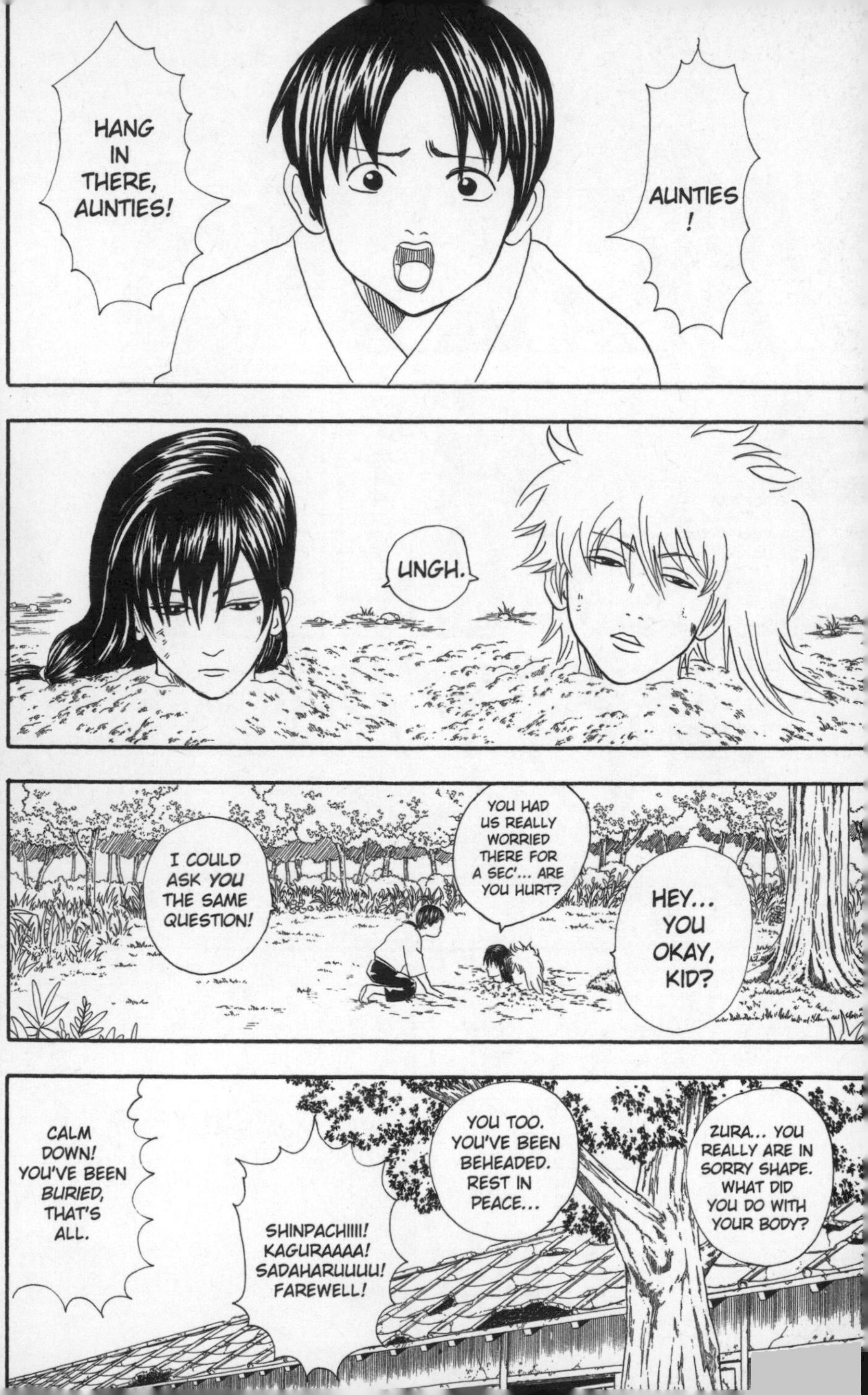
AUNTIES!
HANG IN THERE, AUNTIES!
UNGH.
HEY... YOU OKAY, KID?
YOU HAD US REALLY WORRIED THERE FOR A SEC'... ARE YOU HURT?
I COULD ASK YOU THE SAME QUESTION!
ZURA... YOU REALLY ARE IN SORRY SHAPE. WHAT DID YOU DO WITH YOUR BODY?
YOU TOO. YOU'VE BEEN BEHEADED. REST IN PEACE...
SHINPACHIIII! KAGURAAAA! SADAHARUUUU! FAREWELL!
CALM DOWN! YOU'VE BEEN BURIED, THAT'S ALL.

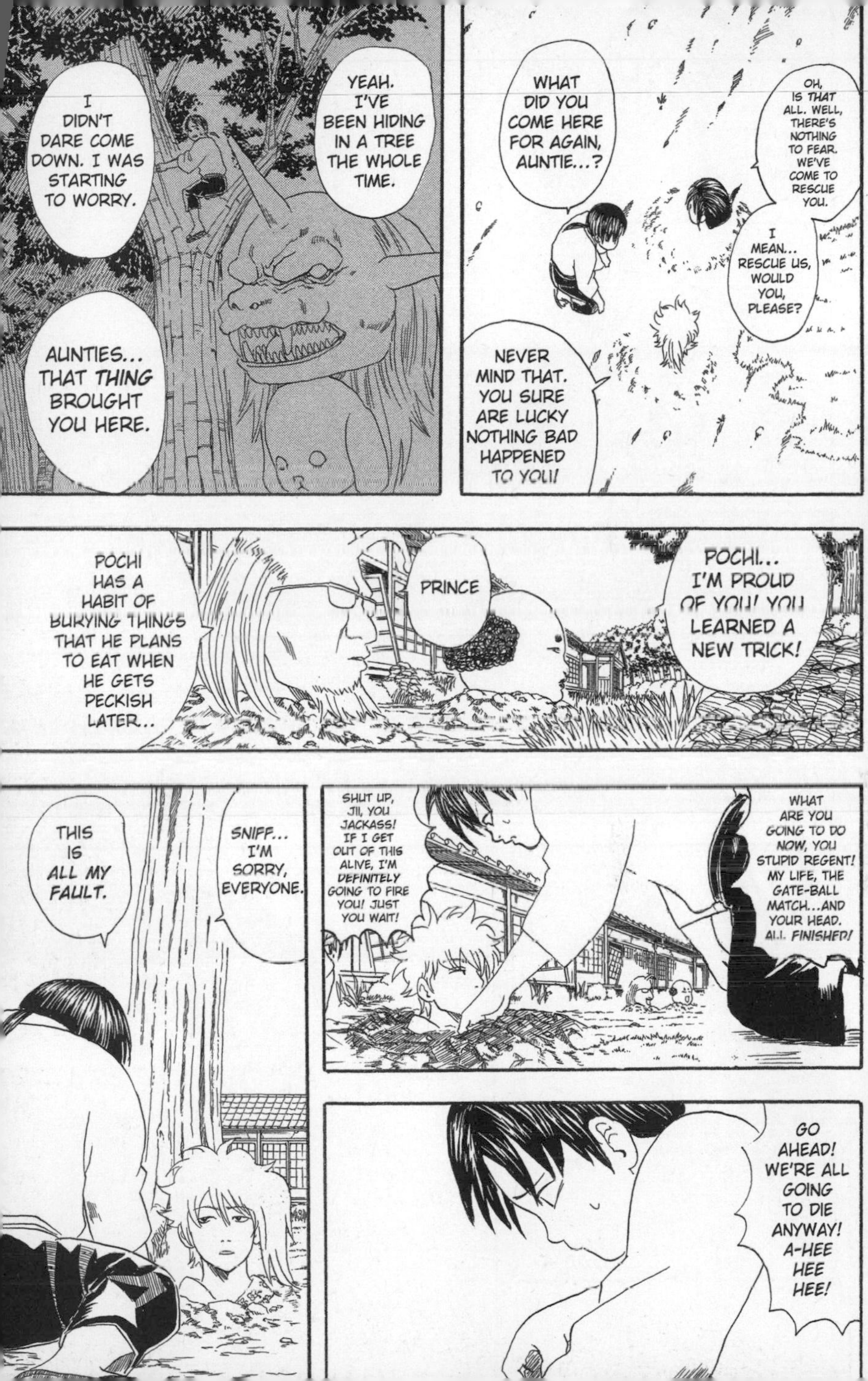
WHAT DID YOU COME HERE FOR AGAIN, AUNTIE...?
OH, IS THAT ALL. WELL, THERE'S NOTHING TO FEAR. WE'VE COME TO RESCUE YOU.
I MEAN... RESCUE US, WOULD YOU, PLEASE?
NEVER MIND THAT. YOU SURE ARE LUCKY NOTHING BAD HAPPENED TO YOU!
YEAH. I'VE BEEN HIDING IN A TREE THE WHOLE TIME.
I DIDN'T DARE COME DOWN. I WAS STARTING TO WORRY.
AUNTIES... THAT THING BROUGHT YOU HERE.
POCHI... I'M PROUD OF YOU! YOU LEARNED A NEW TRICK!
PRINCE
POCHI HAS A HABIT OF BURYING THINGS THAT HE PLANS TO EAT WHEN HE GETS PECKISH LATER...
WHAT ARE YOU GOING TO DO NOW, YOU STUPID REGENT! MY LIFE, THE GATE-BALL MATCH...AND YOUR HEAD. ALL FINISHED!
SHUT UP, JII, YOU JACKASS! IF I GET OUT OF THIS ALIVE, I'M DEFINITELY GOING TO FIRE YOU! JUST YOU WAIT!
GO AHEAD! WE'RE ALL GOING TO DIE ANYWAY! A-HEE HEE HEE!
SNIFF... I'M SORRY, EVERYONE.
THIS IS ALL MY FAULT.

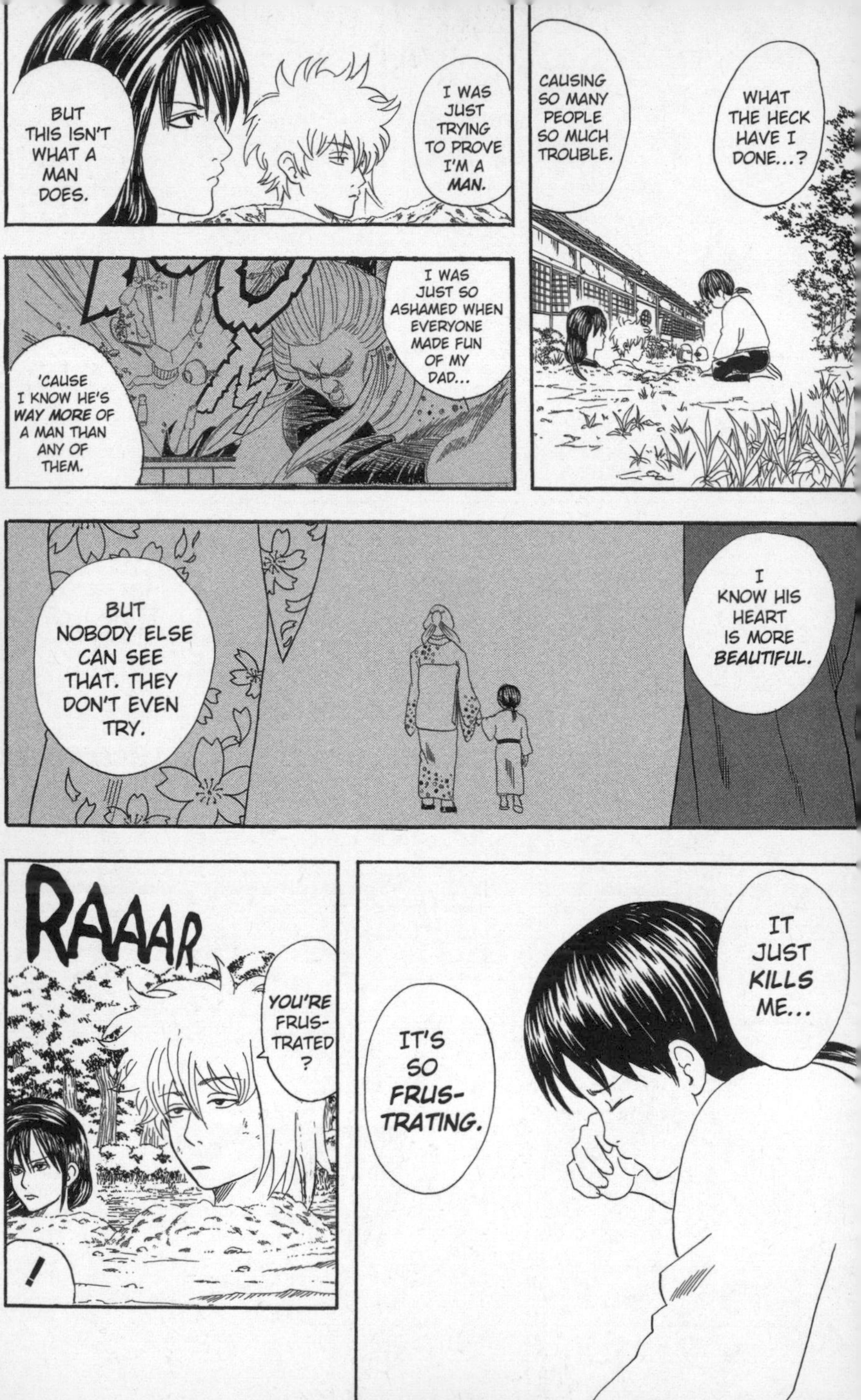
WHAT THE HECK HAVE I DONE...?
CAUSING SO MANY PEOPLE SO MUCH TROUBLE.
I WAS JUST TRYING TO PROVE I'M A *MAN*.
BUT THIS ISN'T WHAT A MAN DOES.
I WAS JUST SO ASHAMED WHEN EVERYONE MADE FUN OF MY DAD...
'CAUSE I KNOW HE'S *WAY MORE* OF A MAN THAN ANY OF THEM.
I KNOW HIS HEART IS MORE *BEAUTIFUL*.
BUT NOBODY ELSE CAN SEE THAT. THEY DON'T EVEN TRY.
IT JUST KILLS ME...
IT'S SO FRUSTRATING.
RAAAR
YOU'RE FRUSTRATED?
!

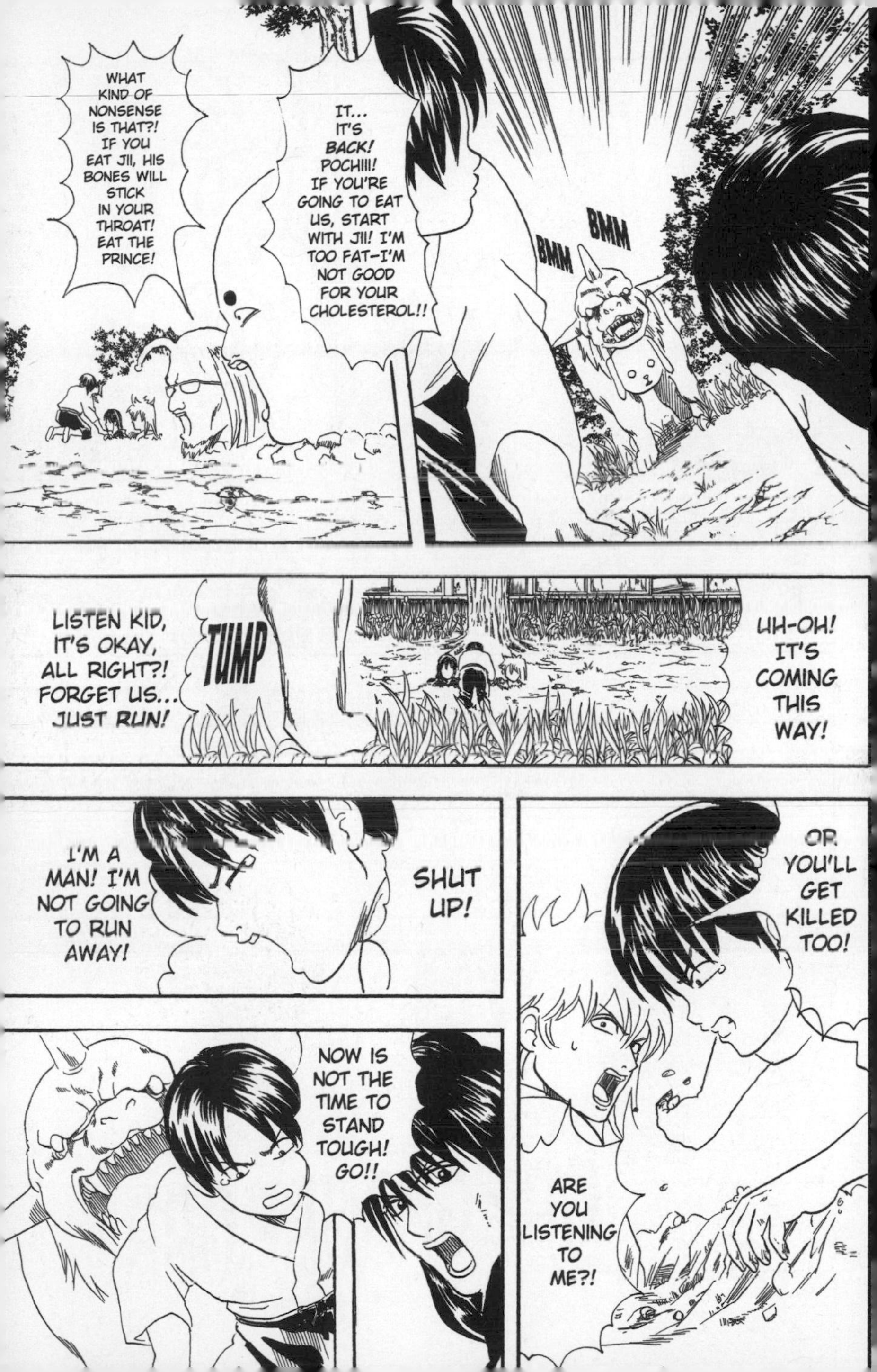
BMM
BMM
IT... IT'S BACK! POCHIIII! IF YOU'RE GOING TO EAT US, START WITH JII! I'M TOO FAT—I'M NOT GOOD FOR YOUR CHOLESTEROL!!
WHAT KIND OF NONSENSE IS THAT?! IF YOU EAT JII, HIS BONES WILL STICK IN YOUR THROAT! EAT THE PRINCE!
UH-OH! IT'S COMING THIS WAY!
TUMP
LISTEN KID, IT'S OKAY, ALL RIGHT?! FORGET US... JUST RUN!
OR YOU'LL GET KILLED TOO!
ARE YOU LISTENING TO ME?!
SHUT UP!
I'M A MAN! I'M NOT GOING TO RUN AWAY!
NOW IS NOT THE TIME TO STAND TOUGH! GO!!

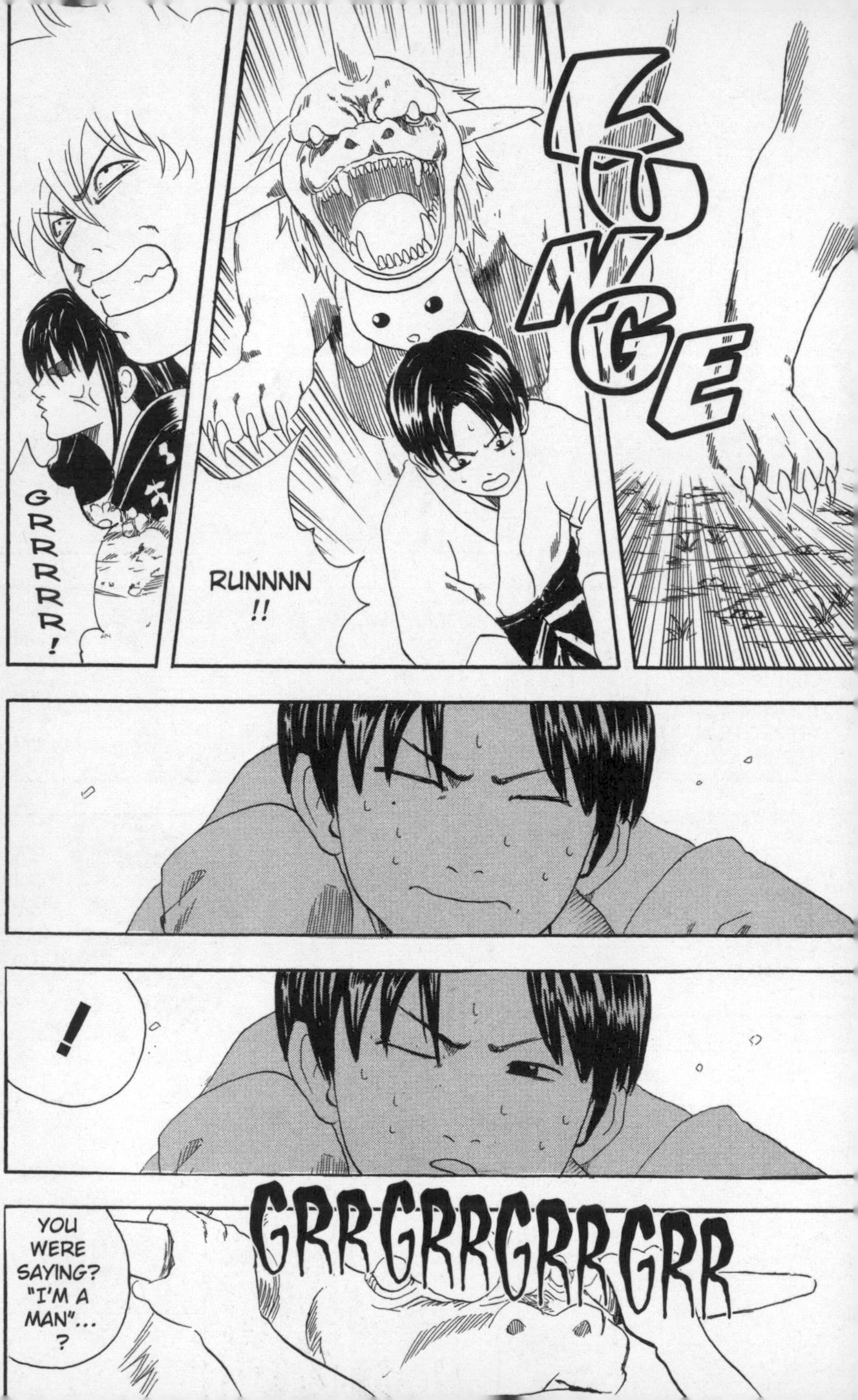
LUNGE
RUNNNN!!
GRRRRR!
!
GRRGRRGRRGRR
YOU WERE SAYING? "I'M A MAN"...?

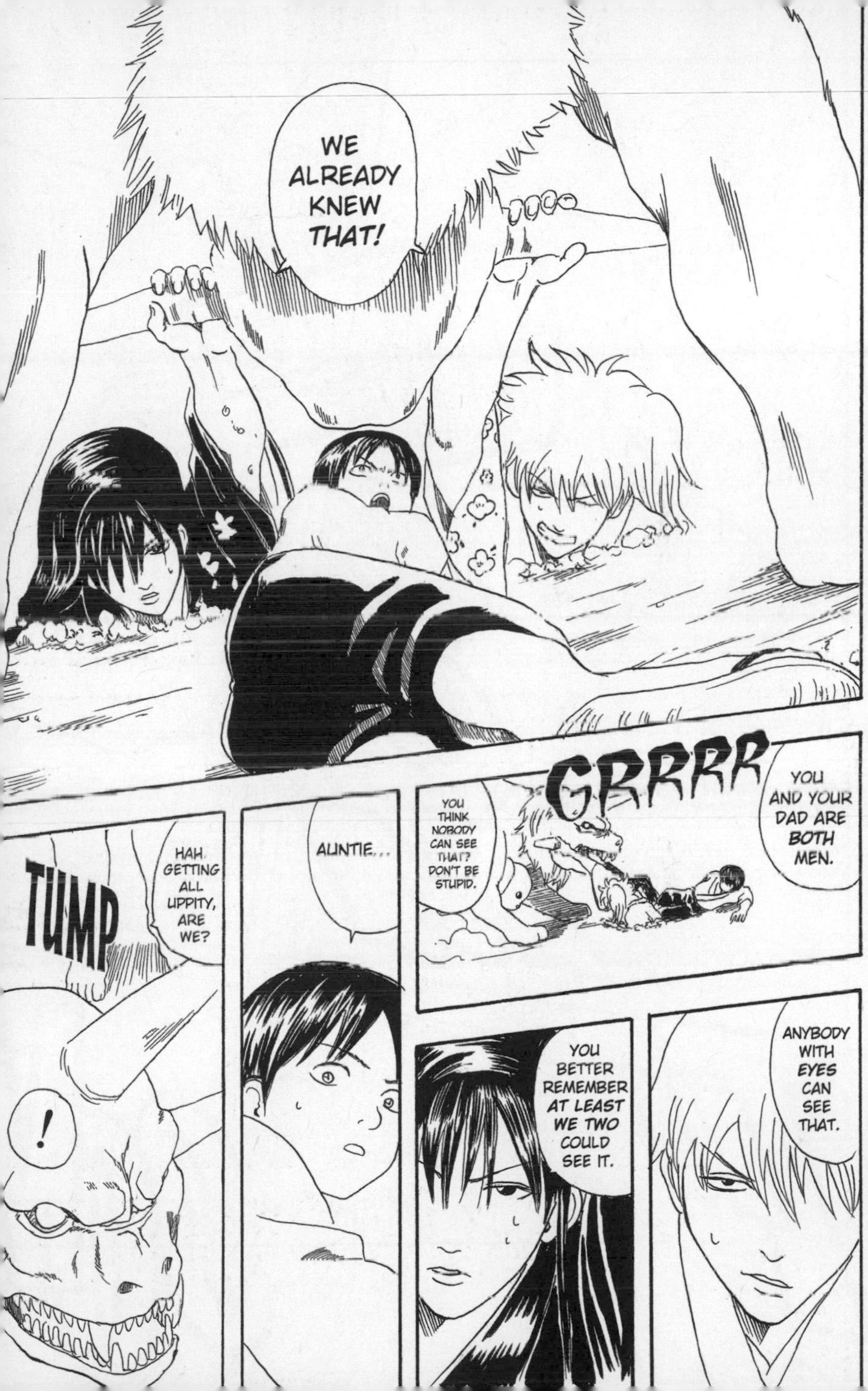
WE ALREADY KNEW THAT!
YOU AND YOUR DAD ARE BOTH MEN.
GRRRR
YOU THINK NOBODY CAN SEE THAT? DON'T BE STUPID.
ANYBODY WITH EYES CAN SEE THAT.
YOU BETTER REMEMBER AT LEAST WE TWO COULD SEE IT.
AUNTIE...
HAH. GETTING ALL UPPITY, ARE WE?
TUMP
!

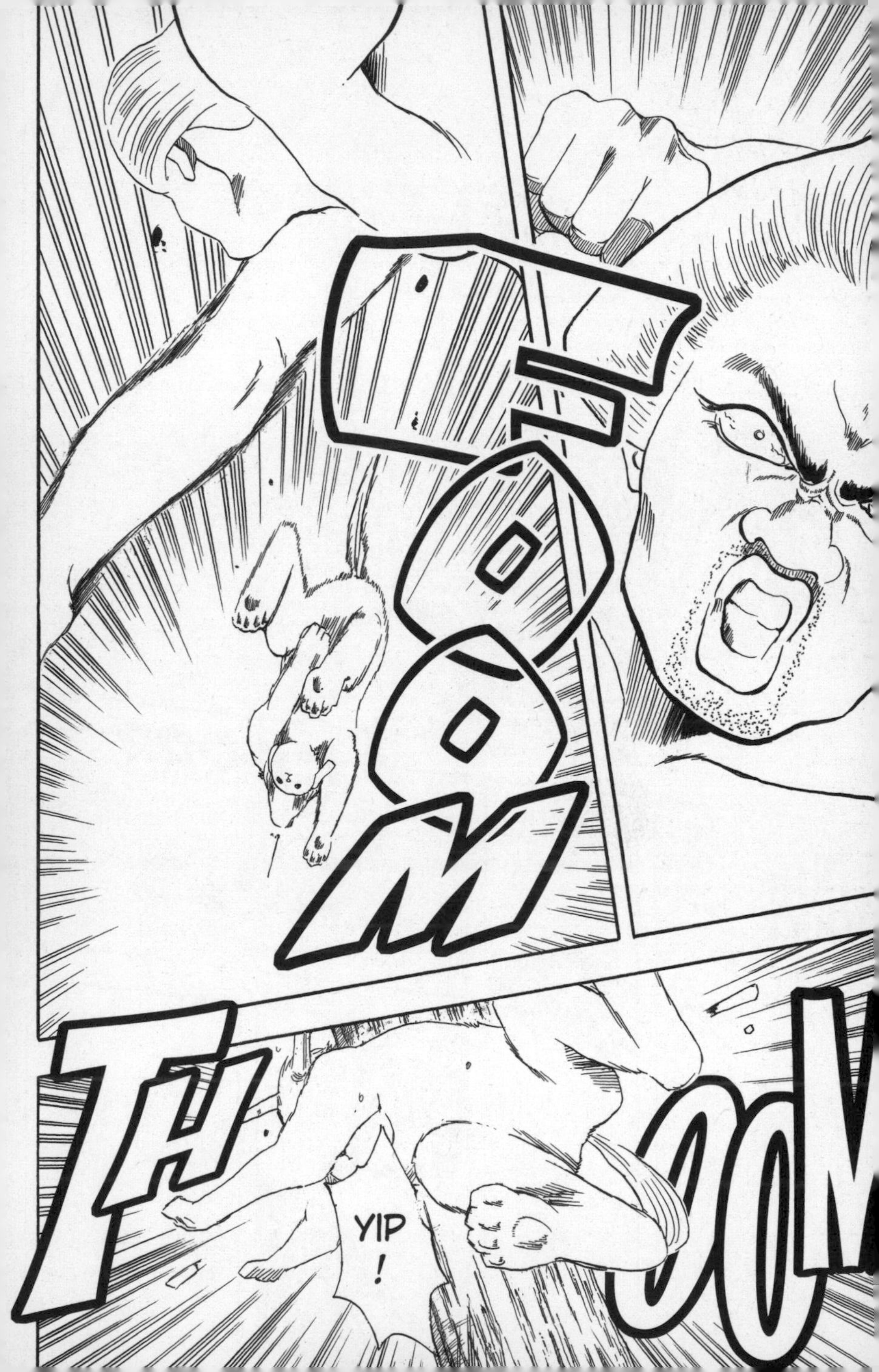
DOOM
THOOM
YIP
!

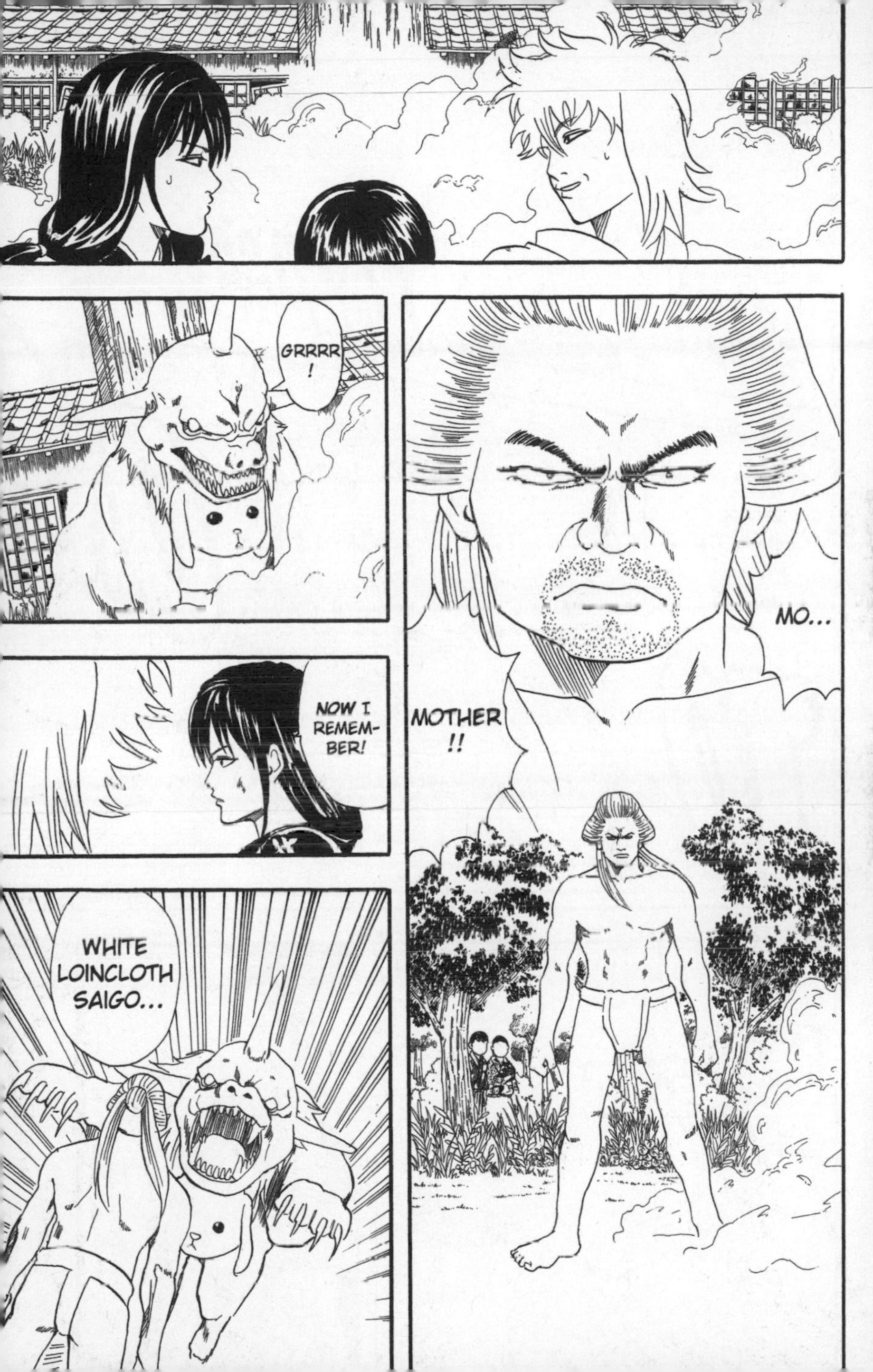
MO...
MOTHER !!
GRRRR !
NOW I REMEMBER!
WHITE LOINCLOTH SAIGO...

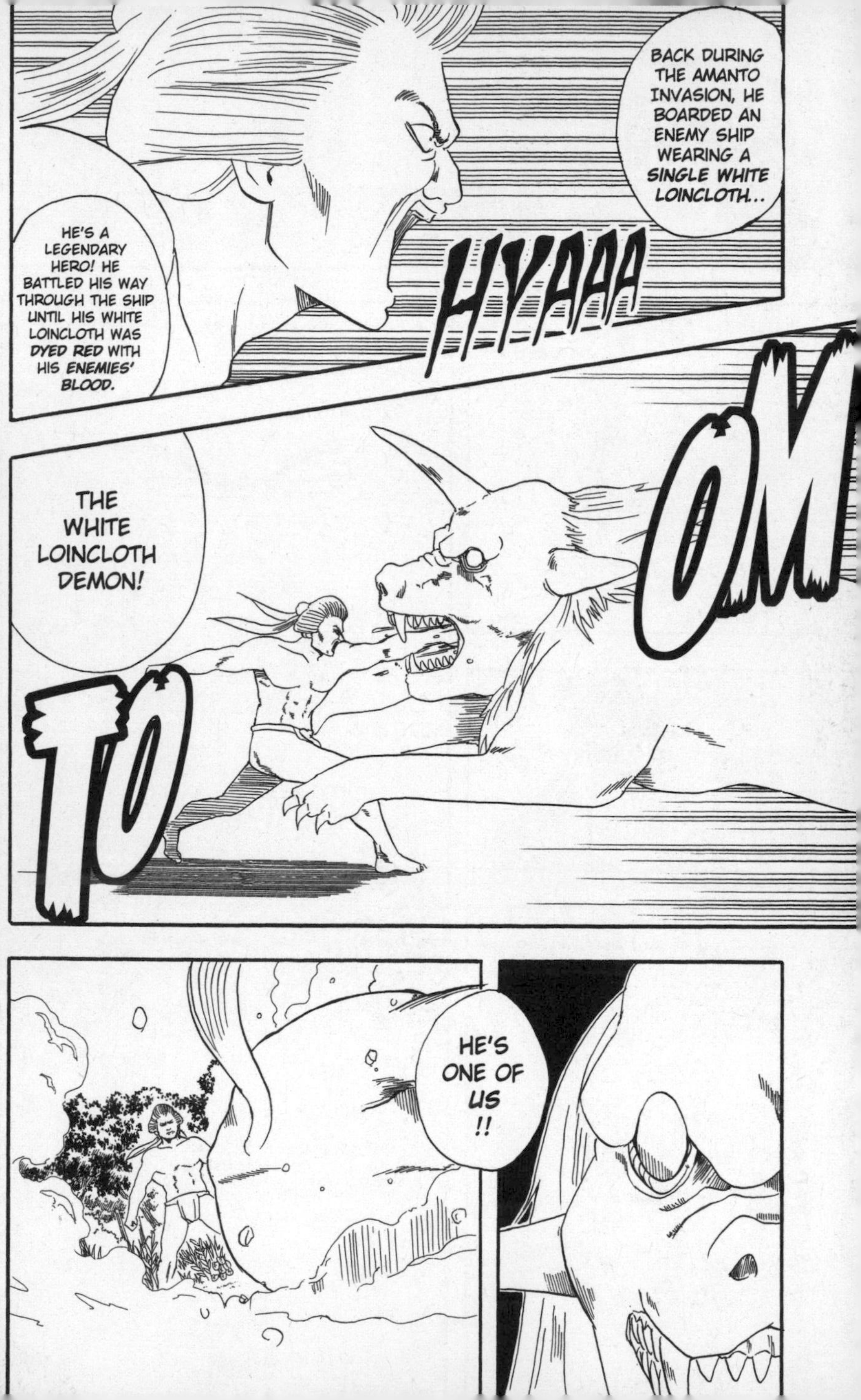
BACK DURING THE AMANTO INVASION, HE BOARDED AN ENEMY SHIP WEARING A SINGLE WHITE LOINCLOTH...
HYAAA
HE'S A LEGENDARY HERO! HE BATTLED HIS WAY THROUGH THE SHIP UNTIL HIS WHITE LOINCLOTH WAS DYED RED WITH HIS ENEMIES' BLOOD.
OM
THE WHITE LOINCLOTH DEMON!
TO
HE'S ONE OF US !!

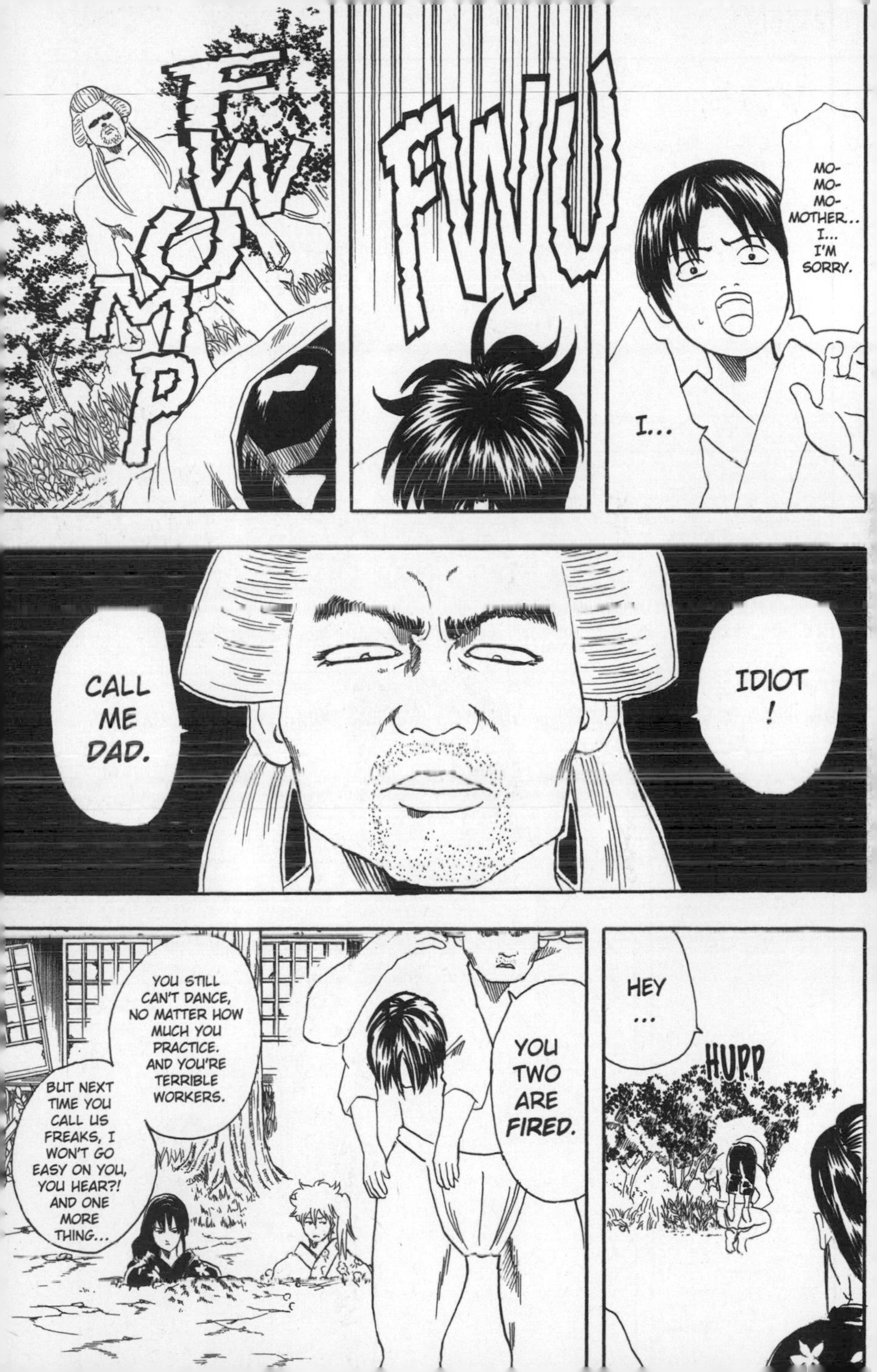
MO-MO-MO-MOTHER... I... I'M SORRY.
I...
FWU
FWUMP
IDIOT!
CALL ME DAD.
HEY...
HUPP
YOU TWO ARE FIRED.
YOU STILL CAN'T DANCE, NO MATTER HOW MUCH YOU PRACTICE. AND YOU'RE TERRIBLE WORKERS.
BUT NEXT TIME YOU CALL US FREAKS, I WON'T GO EASY ON YOU, YOU HEAR?! AND ONE MORE THING...

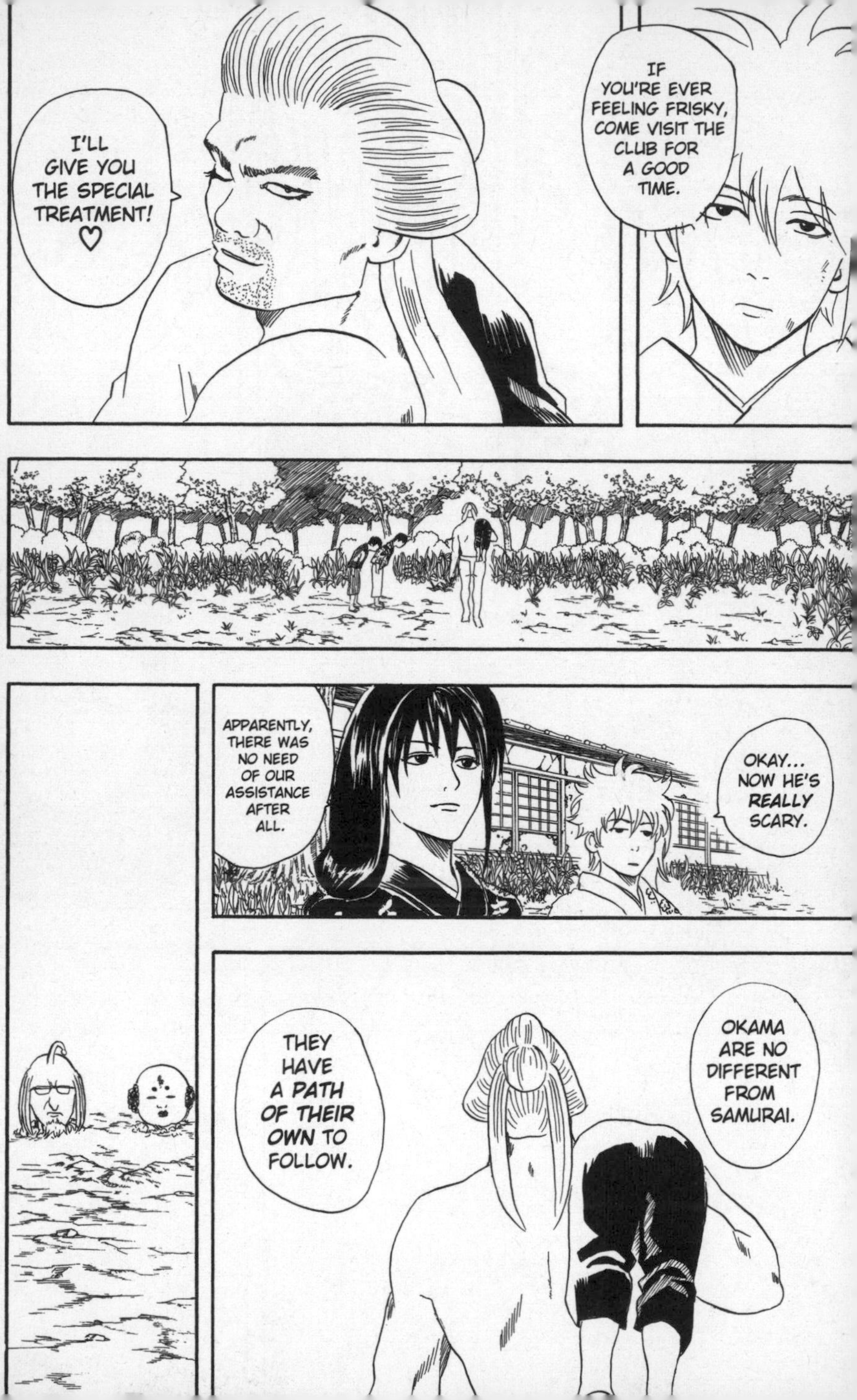
IF YOU'RE EVER FEELING FRISKY, COME VISIT THE CLUB FOR A GOOD TIME.
I'LL GIVE YOU THE SPECIAL TREATMENT! ♡
OKAY... NOW HE'S REALLY SCARY.
APPARENTLY, THERE WAS NO NEED OF OUR ASSISTANCE AFTER ALL.
OKAMA ARE NO DIFFERENT FROM SAMURAI.
THEY HAVE A PATH OF THEIR OWN TO FOLLOW.

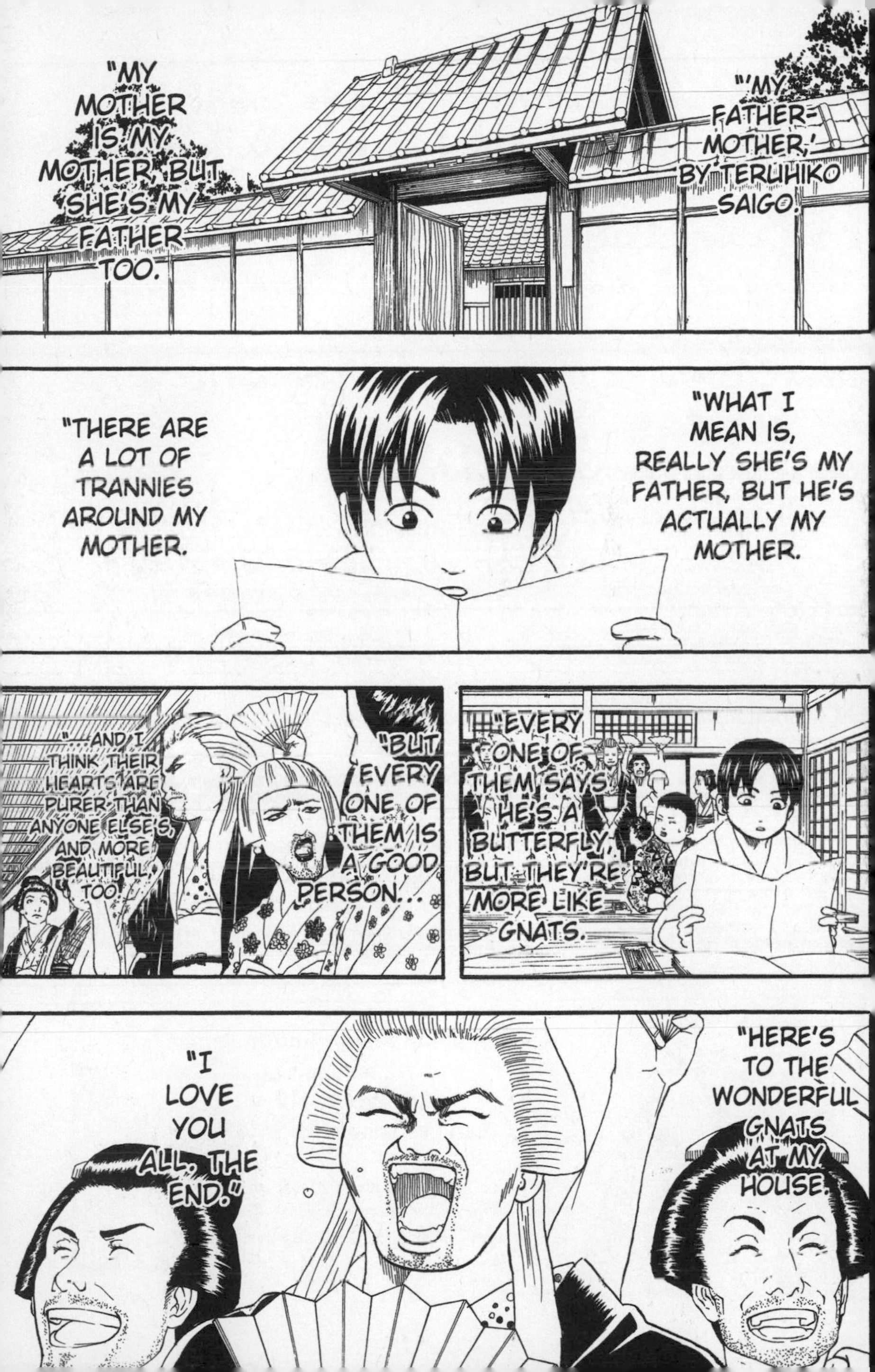
"'MY FATHER-MOTHER,' BY TERUHIKO SAIGO.
"MY MOTHER IS MY MOTHER, BUT SHE'S MY FATHER TOO.
"WHAT I MEAN IS, REALLY SHE'S MY FATHER, BUT HE'S ACTUALLY MY MOTHER.
"THERE ARE A LOT OF TRANNIES AROUND MY MOTHER.
"EVERY ONE OF THEM SAYS HE'S A BUTTERFLY, BUT THEY'RE MORE LIKE GNATS.
"BUT EVERY ONE OF THEM IS A GOOD PERSON...
"...AND I THINK THEIR HEARTS ARE PURER THAN ANYONE ELSE'S, AND MORE BEAUTIFUL, TOO.
"HERE'S TO THE WONDERFUL GNATS AT MY HOUSE.
"I LOVE YOU ALL, THE END."

So, how do you like it? The omake page this time around is pretty good, don't you think? No complaints about this one, I bet. I worked hard on it! I'm glad I did! But now I don't have any time to do a storyboard!

Next time, I'll do something a little different.

Keep your eyes peeled!

I'm still waiting for your questions, so please send then in. Complaints are okay, too!

The address is below. See you next year. Sayoooooonara!

ATTN: Manager in charge of
Shonen Jump Gin Tama Volume 5:
"No, me saying it's a pain in the neck is just a pose because I'm shy, but I really want to reach out and make contact with my readers."

Shonen Jump Advanced/Gin Tama
c/o VIZ Media, LLC
P.O. Box 77010
San Francisco, CA 94107

Post Script: "Nah, that's not what I'm saying, Gin-chan is really who I want to reach out and make contact with"-san

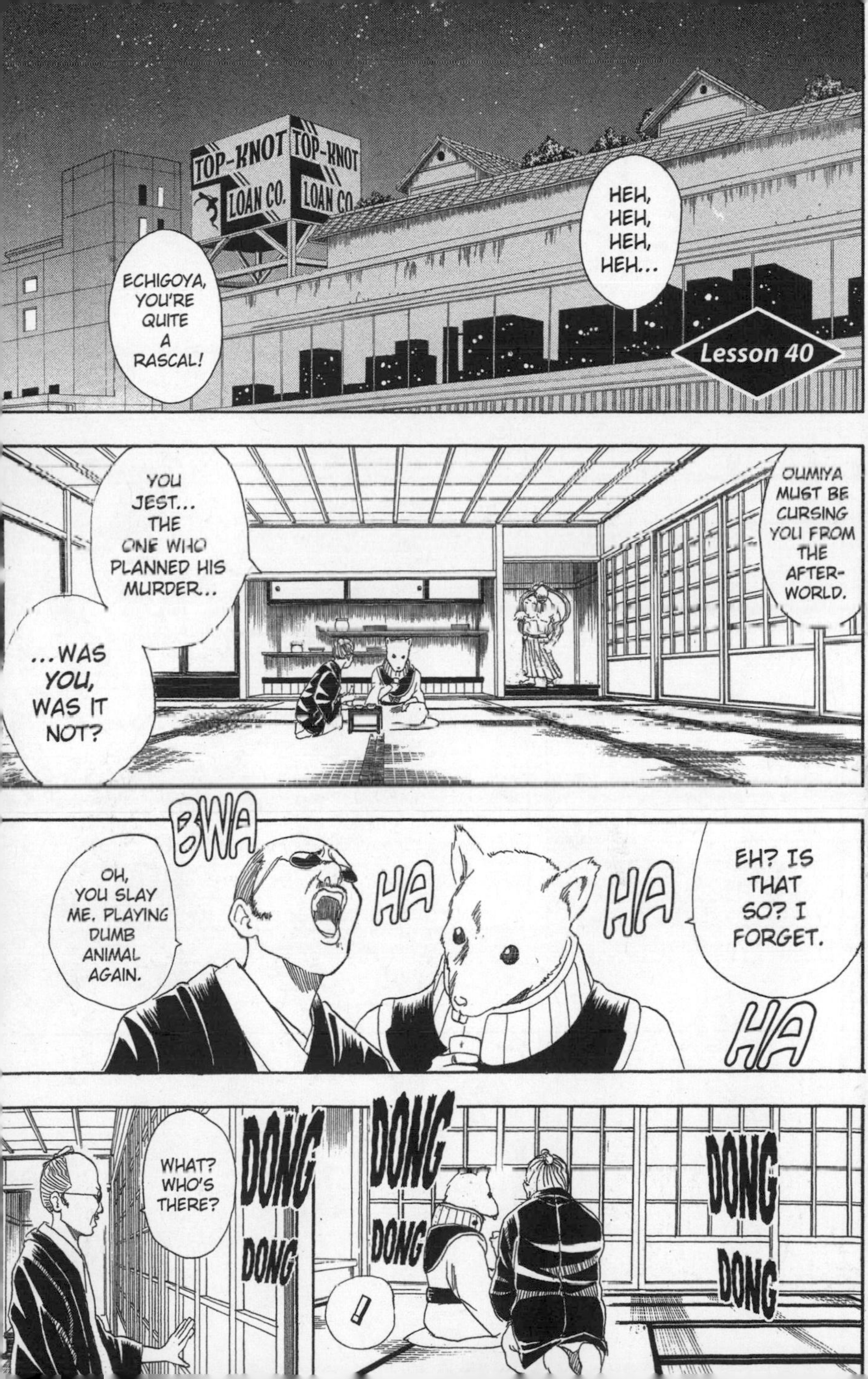
TOP-KNOT LOAN CO.
HEH, HEH, HEH, HEH...
ECHIGOYA, YOU'RE QUITE A RASCAL!
Lesson 40
OUMIYA MUST BE CURSING YOU FROM THE AFTER-WORLD.
YOU JEST... THE ONE WHO PLANNED HIS MURDER...
...WAS *YOU*, WAS IT NOT?
EH? IS THAT SO? I FORGET.
BWA HA HA HA
OH, YOU SLAY ME. PLAYING DUMB ANIMAL AGAIN.
DONG DONG
DONG DONG
DONG DONG
!
DONG DONG
WHAT? WHO'S THERE?

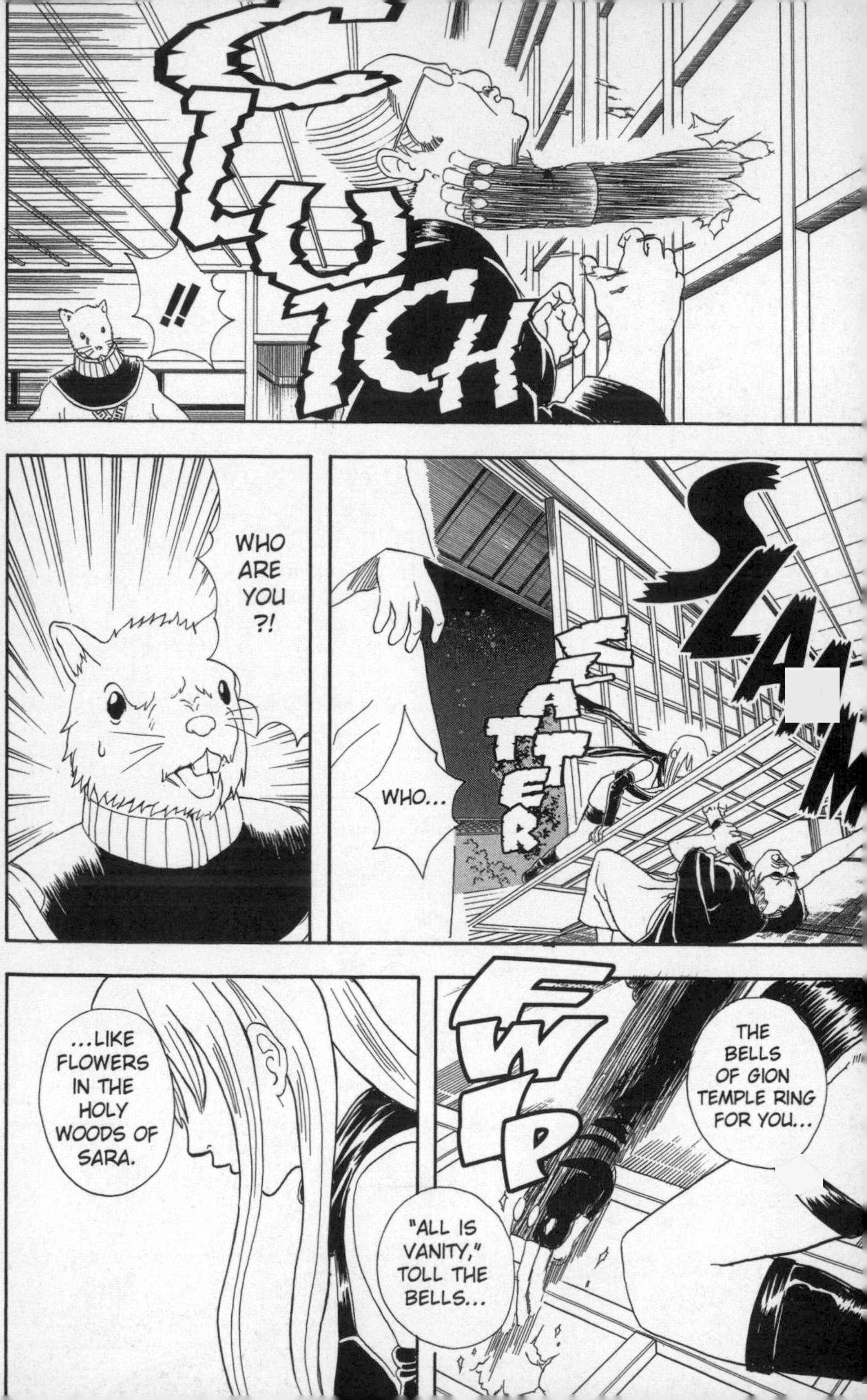
CLUTCH
!!
SLAM
SHATTER
WHO...
WHO ARE YOU ?!
FWIP
THE BELLS OF GION TEMPLE RING FOR YOU...
"ALL IS VANITY," TOLL THE BELLS...
...LIKE FLOWERS IN THE HOLY WOODS OF SARA.

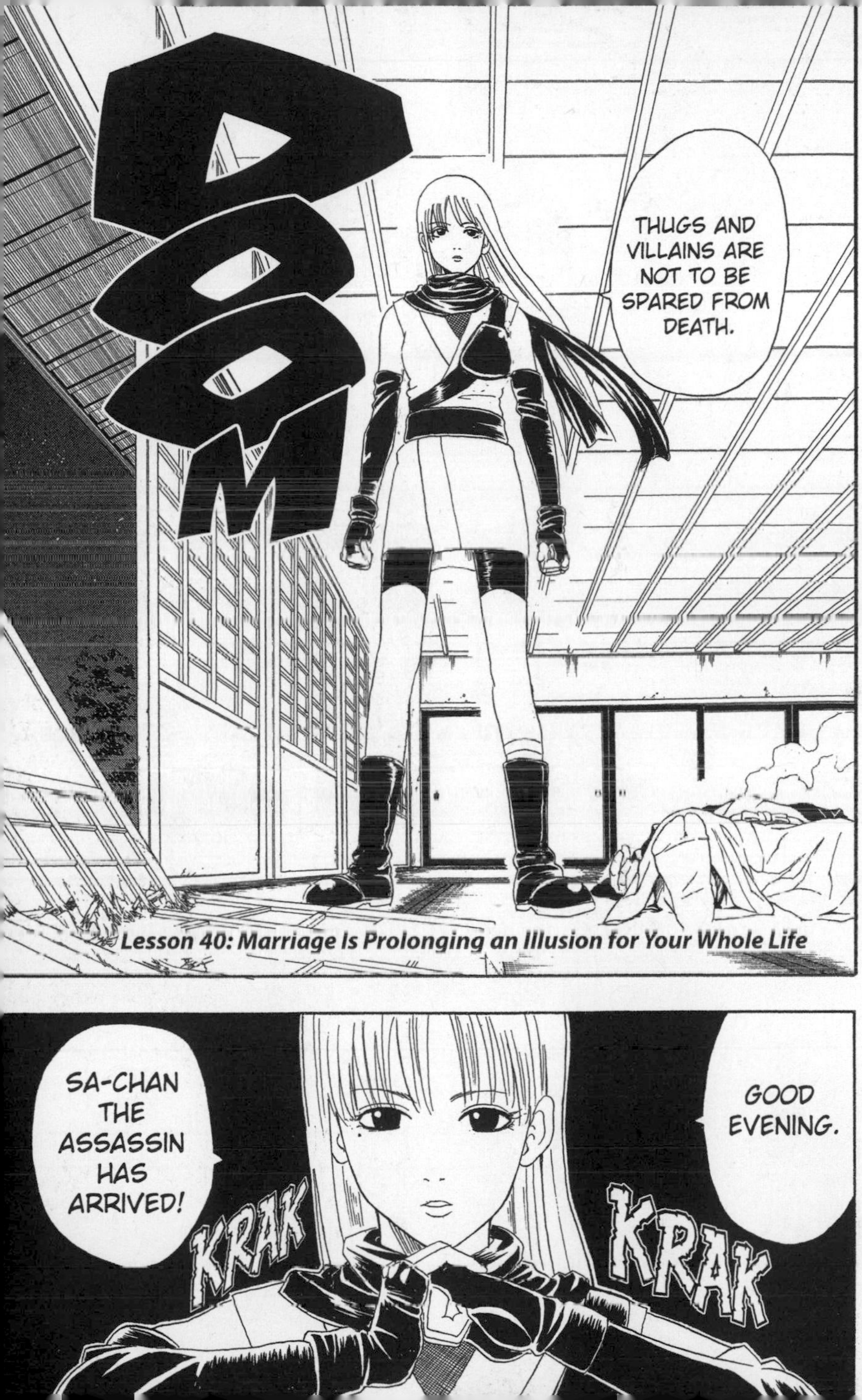
THUGS AND VILLAINS ARE NOT TO BE SPARED FROM DEATH.
DOOM
Lesson 40: Marriage Is Prolonging an Illusion for Your Whole Life
GOOD EVENING.
KRAK
SA-CHAN THE ASSASSIN HAS ARRIVED!
KRAK

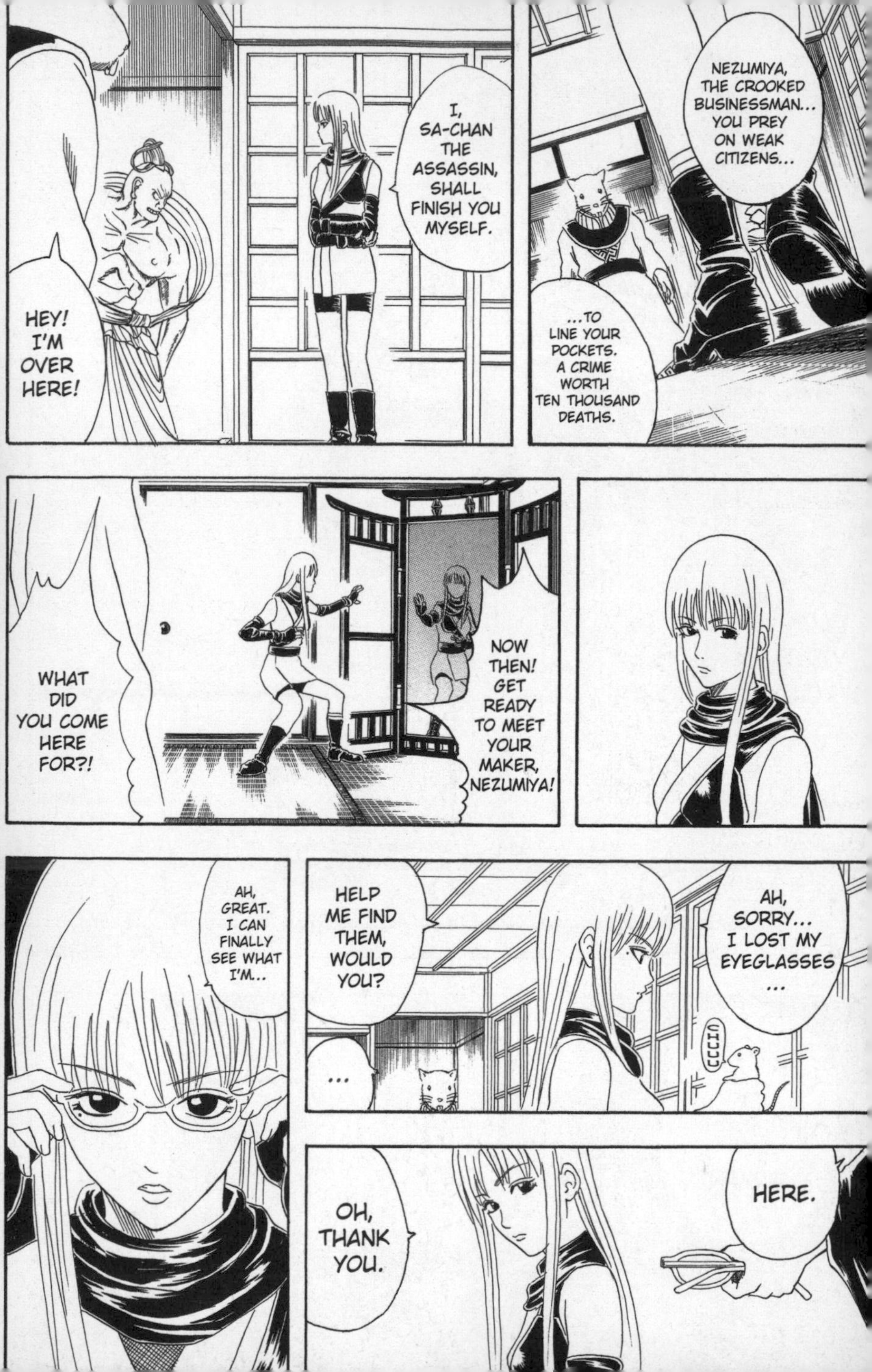
NEZUMIYA, THE CROOKED BUSINESSMAN... YOU PREY ON WEAK CITIZENS...
...TO LINE YOUR POCKETS. A CRIME WORTH TEN THOUSAND DEATHS.
I, SA-CHAN THE ASSASSIN, SHALL FINISH YOU MYSELF.
HEY! I'M OVER HERE!
NOW THEN! GET READY TO MEET YOUR MAKER, NEZUMIYA!
WHAT DID YOU COME HERE FOR?!
AH, SORRY... I LOST MY EYEGLASSES ...
CHUUU
HELP ME FIND THEM, WOULD YOU?
...
HERE.
OH, THANK YOU.
AH, GREAT. I CAN FINALLY SEE WHAT I'M...

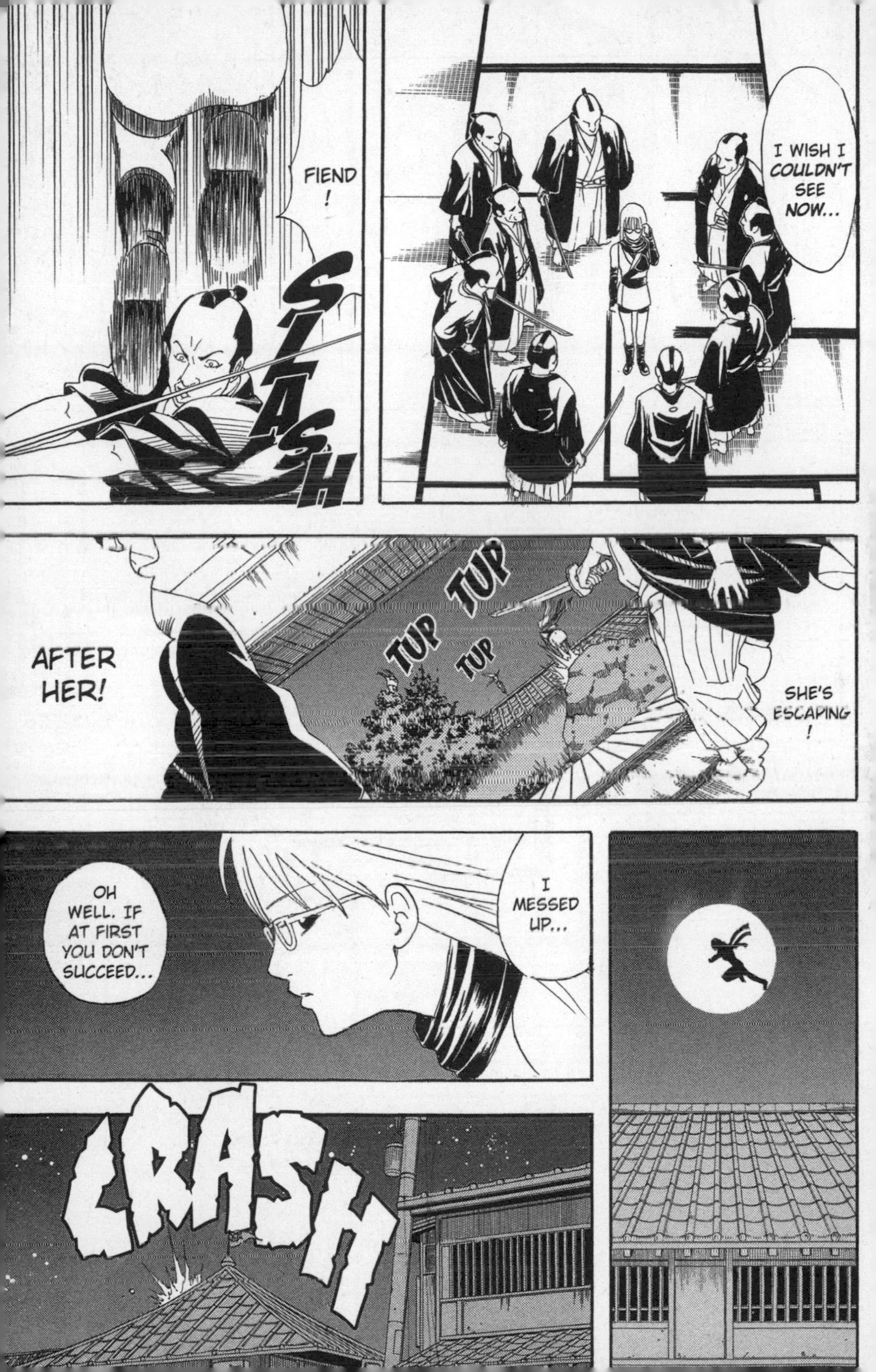
I WISH I COULDN'T SEE NOW...
FIEND!
SLASH
SHE'S ESCAPING!
TUP TUP
TUP TUP
AFTER HER!
I MESSED UP...
OH WELL. IF AT FIRST YOU DON'T SUCCEED...
CRASH

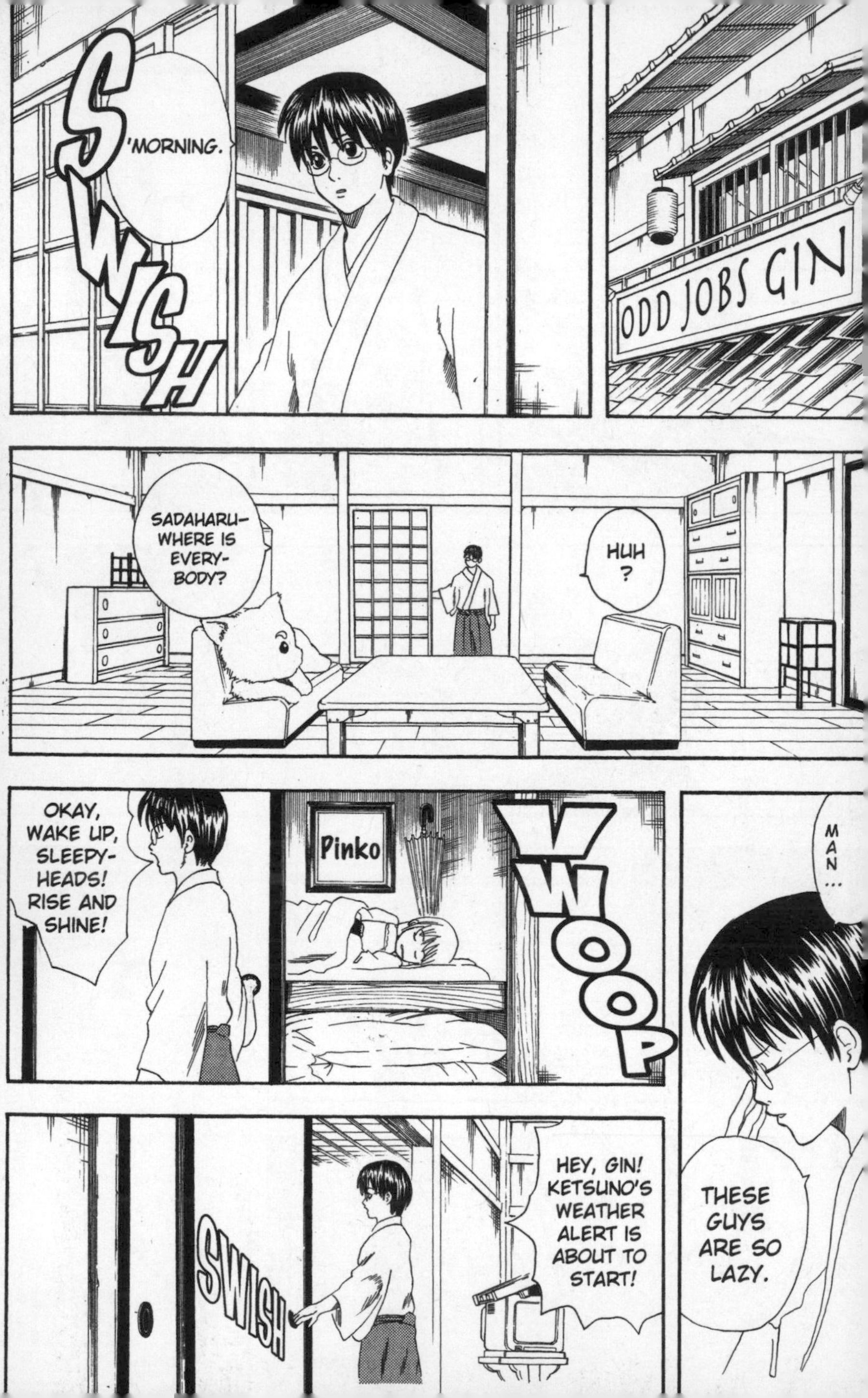
ODD JOBS GIN
SWISH
'MORNING.
SADAHARU- WHERE IS EVERY-BODY?
HUH?
MAN...
THESE GUYS ARE SO LAZY.
VWOOP
Pinko
OKAY, WAKE UP, SLEEPY-HEADS! RISE AND SHINE!
HEY, GIN! KETSUNO'S WEATHER ALERT IS ABOUT TO START!
SWISH

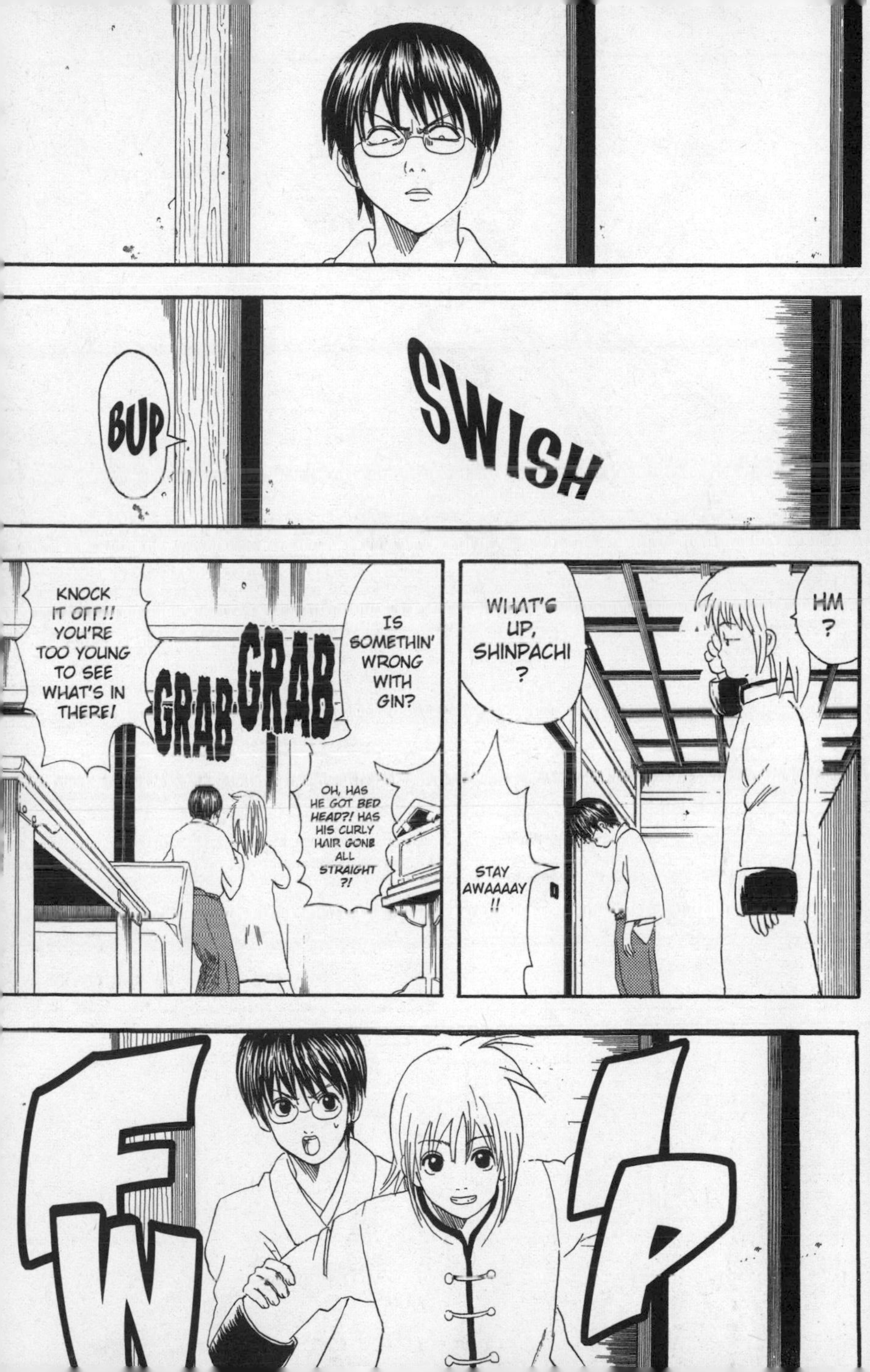
SWISH
BUP
HM?
WHAT'S UP, SHINPACHI?
STAY AWAAAAY!!
IS SOMETHIN' WRONG WITH GIN?
OH, HAS HE GOT BED HEAD?! HAS HIS CURLY HAIR GONE ALL STRAIGHT?!
GRAB GRAB
KNOCK IT OFF!! YOU'RE TOO YOUNG TO SEE WHAT'S IN THERE!
FWIP

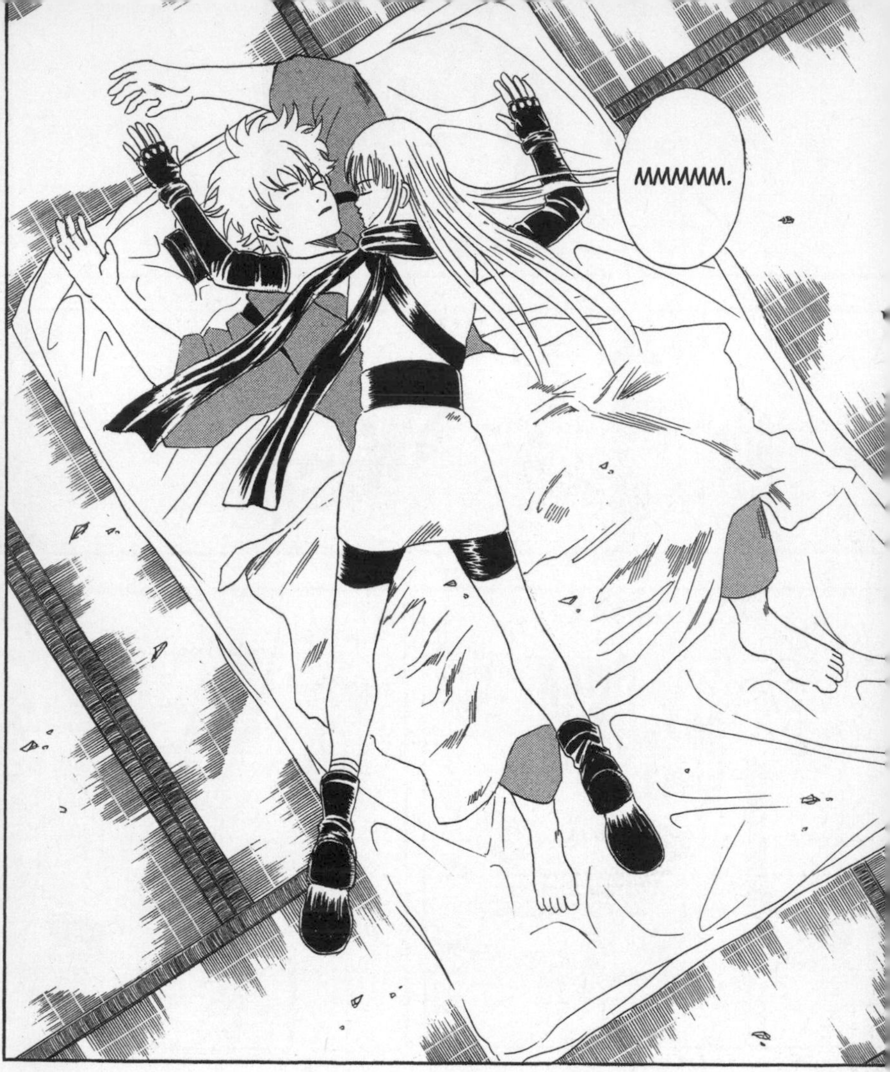
MMMMM.

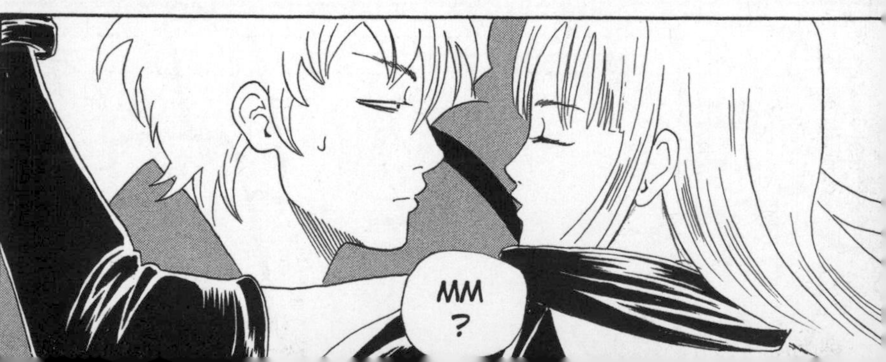
MM
?

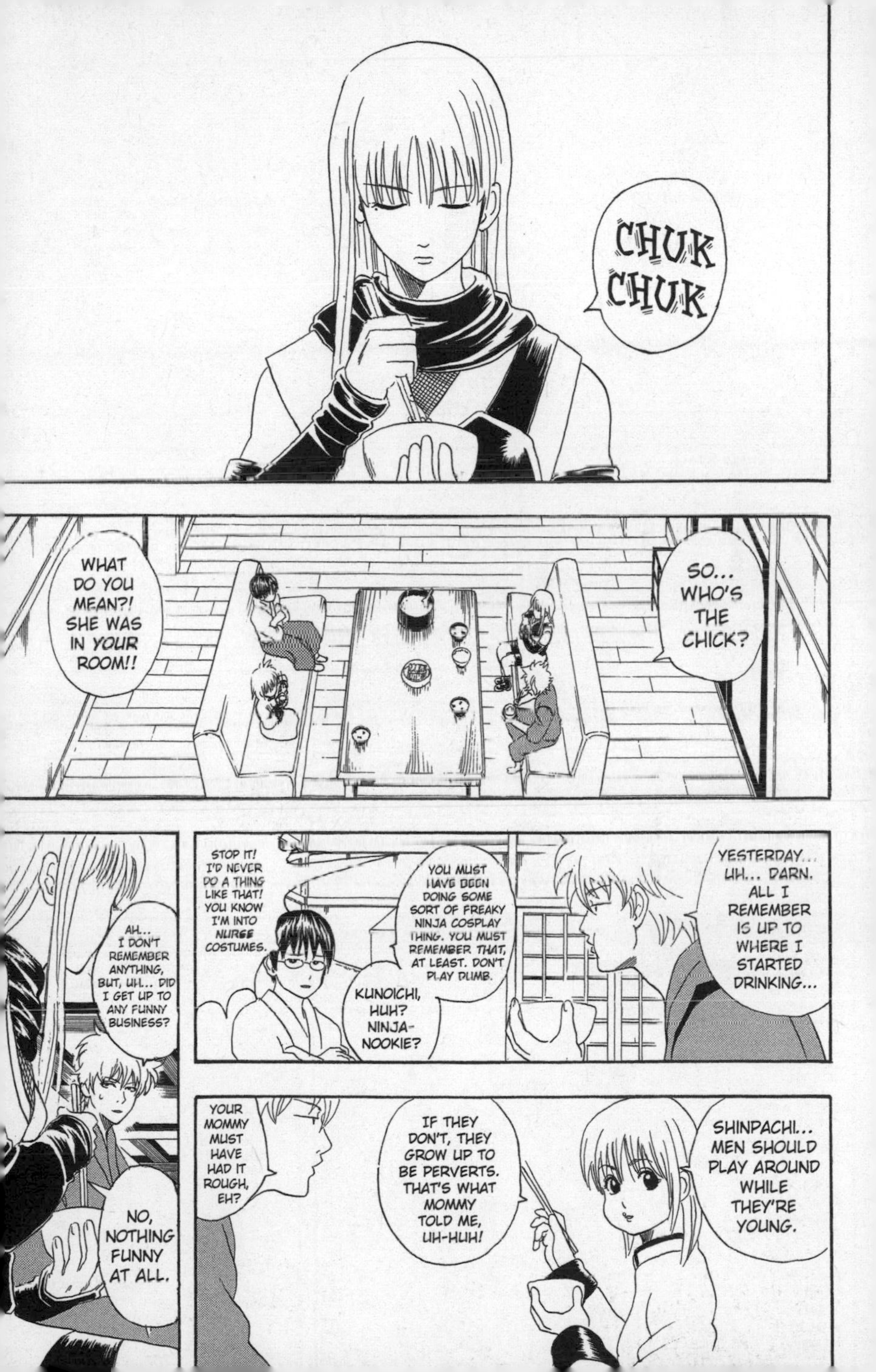
CHUK CHUK
SO... WHO'S THE CHICK?
WHAT DO YOU MEAN?! SHE WAS IN YOUR ROOM!!
YESTERDAY... UH... DARN. ALL I REMEMBER IS UP TO WHERE I STARTED DRINKING...
YOU MUST HAVE BEEN DOING SOME SORT OF FREAKY NINJA COSPLAY THING. YOU MUST REMEMBER THAT, AT LEAST. DON'T PLAY DUMB.
KUNOICHI, HUH? NINJA-NOOKIE?
STOP IT! I'D NEVER DO A THING LIKE THAT! YOU KNOW I'M INTO NURSE COSTUMES.
SHINPACHI... MEN SHOULD PLAY AROUND WHILE THEY'RE YOUNG.
IF THEY DON'T, THEY GROW UP TO BE PERVERTS. THAT'S WHAT MOMMY TOLD ME, UH-HUH!
YOUR MOMMY MUST HAVE HAD IT ROUGH, EH?
AH... I DON'T REMEMBER ANYTHING, BUT, UH... DID I GET UP TO ANY FUNNY BUSINESS?
NO, NOTHING FUNNY AT ALL.

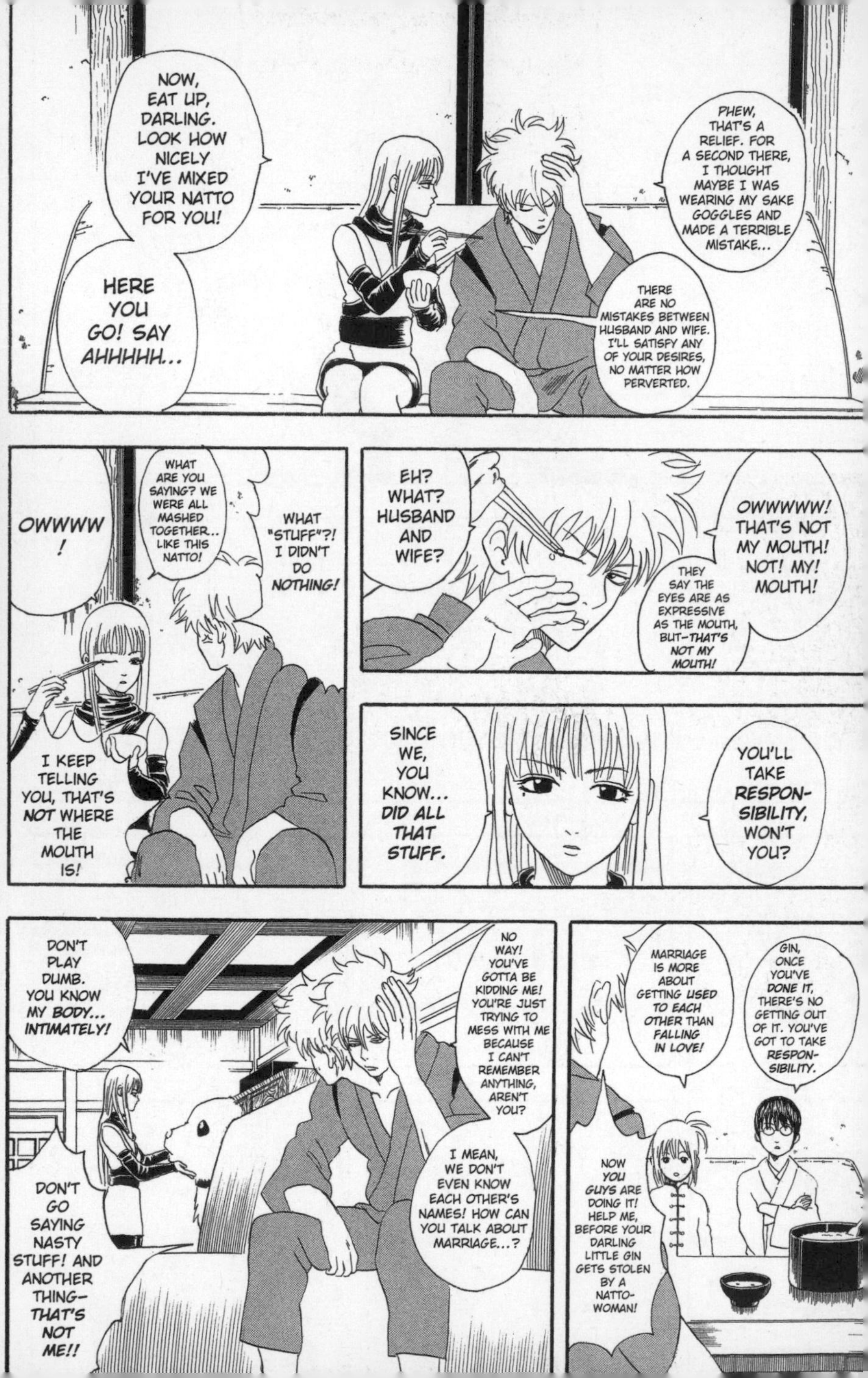
PHEW, THAT'S A RELIEF. FOR A SECOND THERE, I THOUGHT MAYBE I WAS WEARING MY SAKE GOGGLES AND MADE A TERRIBLE MISTAKE...
THERE ARE NO MISTAKES BETWEEN HUSBAND AND WIFE. I'LL SATISFY ANY OF YOUR DESIRES, NO MATTER HOW PERVERTED.
NOW, EAT UP, DARLING. LOOK HOW NICELY I'VE MIXED YOUR NATTO FOR YOU!
HERE YOU GO! SAY AHHHHH...
OWWWWW! THAT'S NOT MY MOUTH! NOT! MY! MOUTH!
THEY SAY THE EYES ARE AS EXPRESSIVE AS THE MOUTH, BUT—THAT'S NOT MY MOUTH!
EH? WHAT? HUSBAND AND WIFE?
YOU'LL TAKE RESPONSIBILITY, WON'T YOU?
SINCE WE, YOU KNOW... DID ALL THAT STUFF.
WHAT "STUFF"?! I DIDN'T DO NOTHING!
WHAT ARE YOU SAYING? WE WERE ALL MASHED TOGETHER... LIKE THIS NATTO!
OWWWW!
I KEEP TELLING YOU, THAT'S NOT WHERE THE MOUTH IS!
GIN, ONCE YOU'VE DONE IT, THERE'S NO GETTING OUT OF IT. YOU'VE GOT TO TAKE RESPONSIBILITY.
MARRIAGE IS MORE ABOUT GETTING USED TO EACH OTHER THAN FALLING IN LOVE!
NOW YOU GUYS ARE DOING IT! HELP ME, BEFORE YOUR DARLING LITTLE GIN GETS STOLEN BY A NATTO-WOMAN!
NO WAY! YOU'VE GOTTA BE KIDDING ME! YOU'RE JUST TRYING TO MESS WITH ME BECAUSE I CAN'T REMEMBER ANYTHING, AREN'T YOU?
I MEAN, WE DON'T EVEN KNOW EACH OTHER'S NAMES! HOW CAN YOU TALK ABOUT MARRIAGE...?
DON'T PLAY DUMB. YOU KNOW MY BODY... INTIMATELY!
DON'T GO SAYING NASTY STUFF! AND ANOTHER THING—THAT'S NOT ME!!

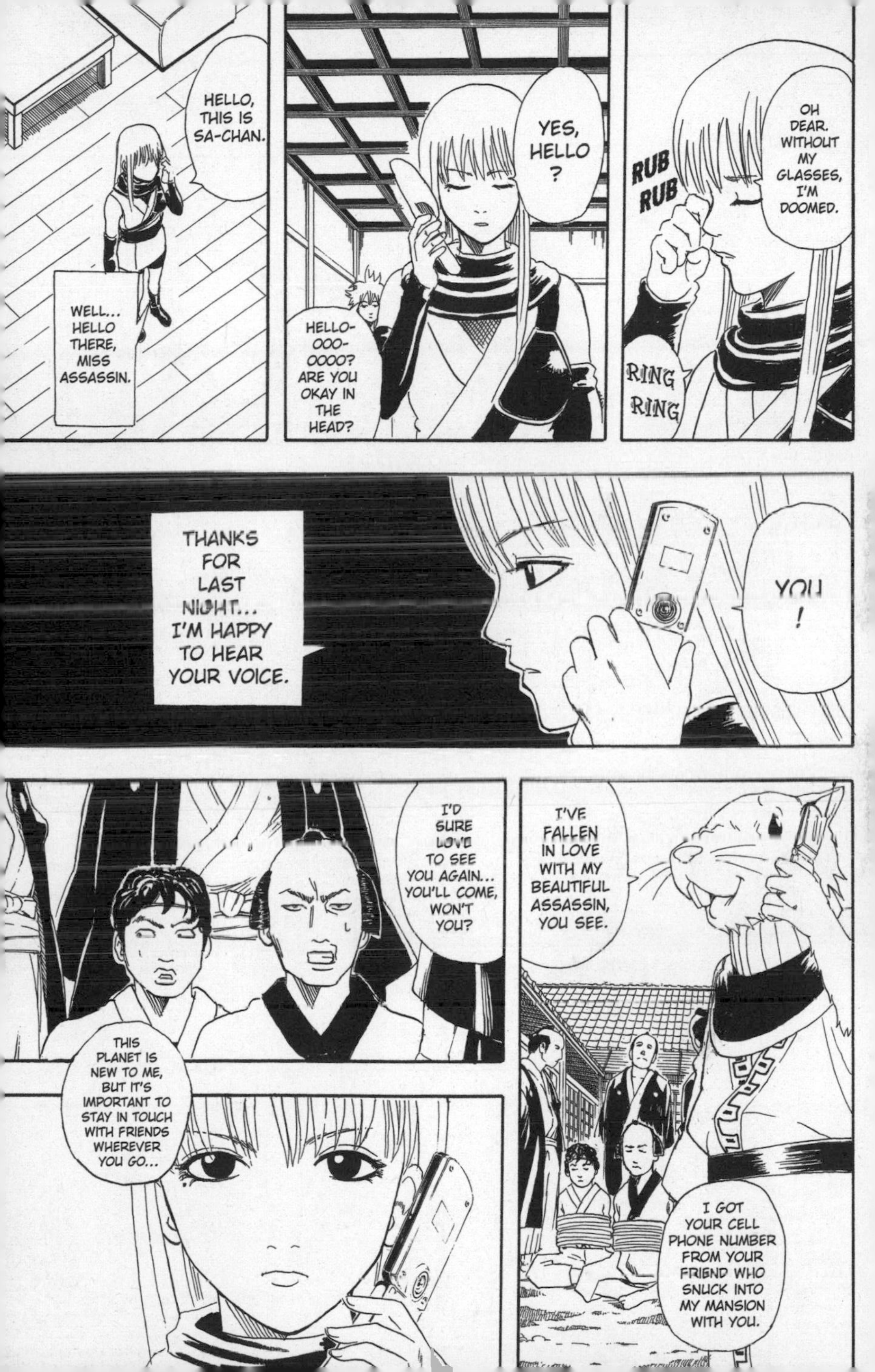
RUB RUB
OH DEAR. WITHOUT MY GLASSES, I'M DOOMED.
RING RING
YES, HELLO?
HELLO-OOO-OOOO? ARE YOU OKAY IN THE HEAD?
HELLO, THIS IS SA-CHAN.
WELL... HELLO THERE, MISS ASSASSIN.
YOU!
THANKS FOR LAST NIGHT... I'M HAPPY TO HEAR YOUR VOICE.
I'VE FALLEN IN LOVE WITH MY BEAUTIFUL ASSASSIN, YOU SEE.
I GOT YOUR CELL PHONE NUMBER FROM YOUR FRIEND WHO SNUCK INTO MY MANSION WITH YOU.
I'D SURE LOVE TO SEE YOU AGAIN... YOU'LL COME, WON'T YOU?
THIS PLANET IS NEW TO ME, BUT IT'S IMPORTANT TO STAY IN TOUCH WITH FRIENDS WHEREVER YOU GO...

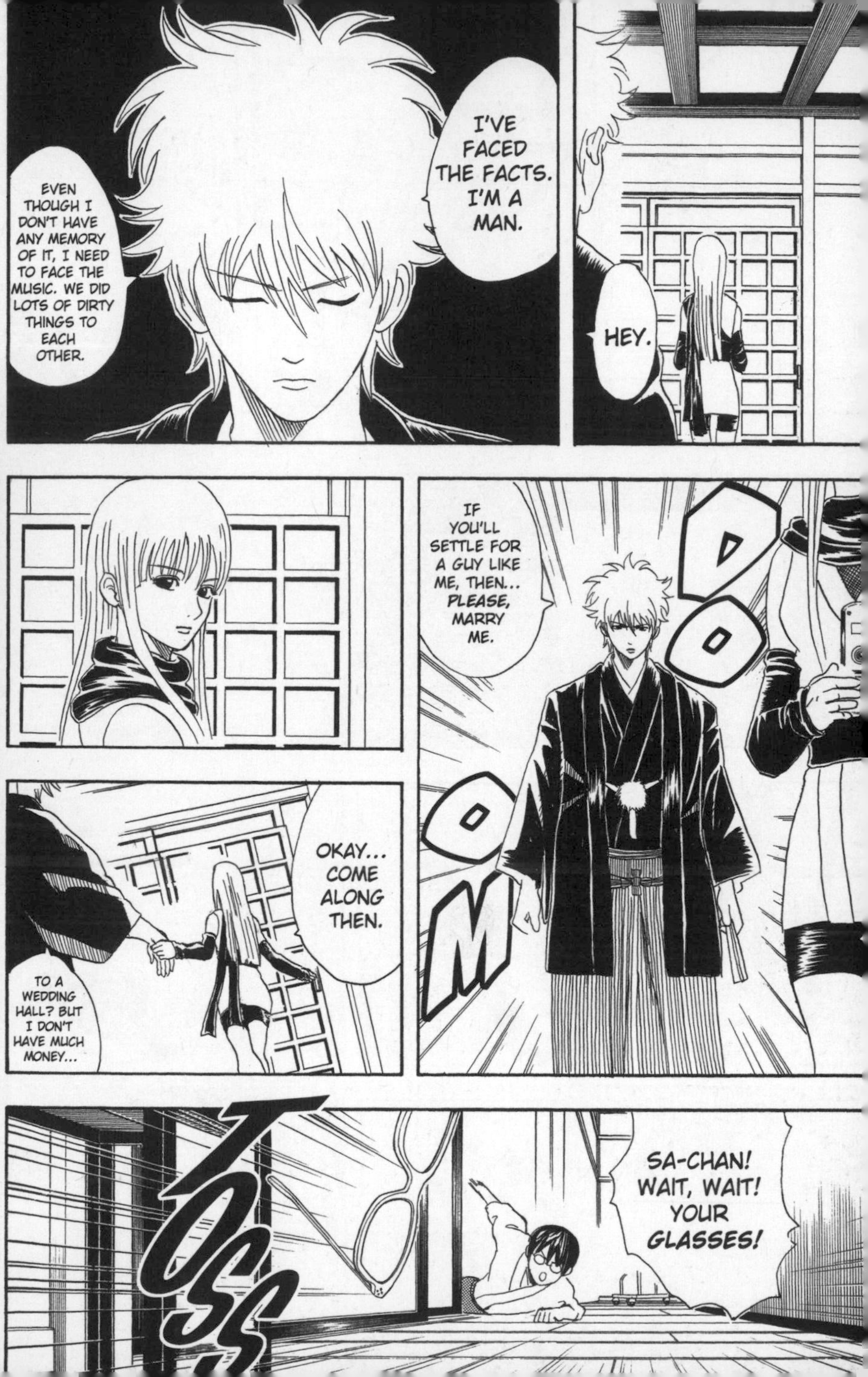
HEY.
I'VE FACED THE FACTS. I'M A MAN.
EVEN THOUGH I DON'T HAVE ANY MEMORY OF IT, I NEED TO FACE THE MUSIC. WE DID LOTS OF DIRTY THINGS TO EACH OTHER.
IF YOU'LL SETTLE FOR A GUY LIKE ME, THEN... PLEASE, MARRY ME.
DOOM
OKAY... COME ALONG THEN.
TO A WEDDING HALL? BUT I DON'T HAVE MUCH MONEY...
SA-CHAN! WAIT, WAIT! YOUR GLASSES!
TOSS

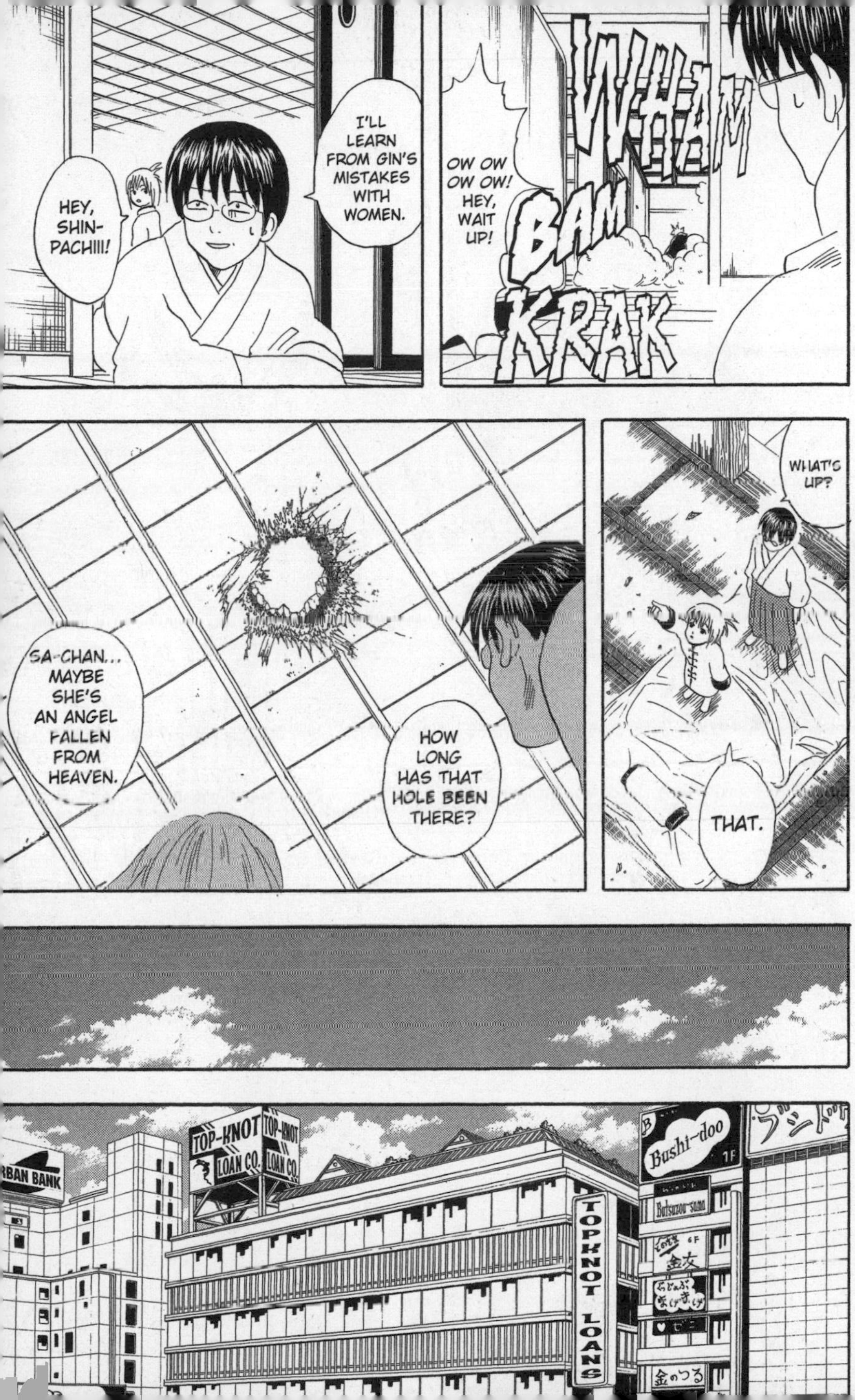
WHAM
OW OW OW OW! HEY, WAIT UP!
BAM
KRAK
I'LL LEARN FROM GIN'S MISTAKES WITH WOMEN.
HEY, SHIN-PACHIII!
WHAT'S UP?
THAT.
HOW LONG HAS THAT HOLE BEEN THERE?
SA-CHAN... MAYBE SHE'S AN ANGEL FALLEN FROM HEAVEN.
Bushi-doo
7F
Butsuzou-sama
金文
金のつる
TOPKNOT LOANS
TOP-KNOT LOAN CO.
TOP-KNOT LOAN CO.

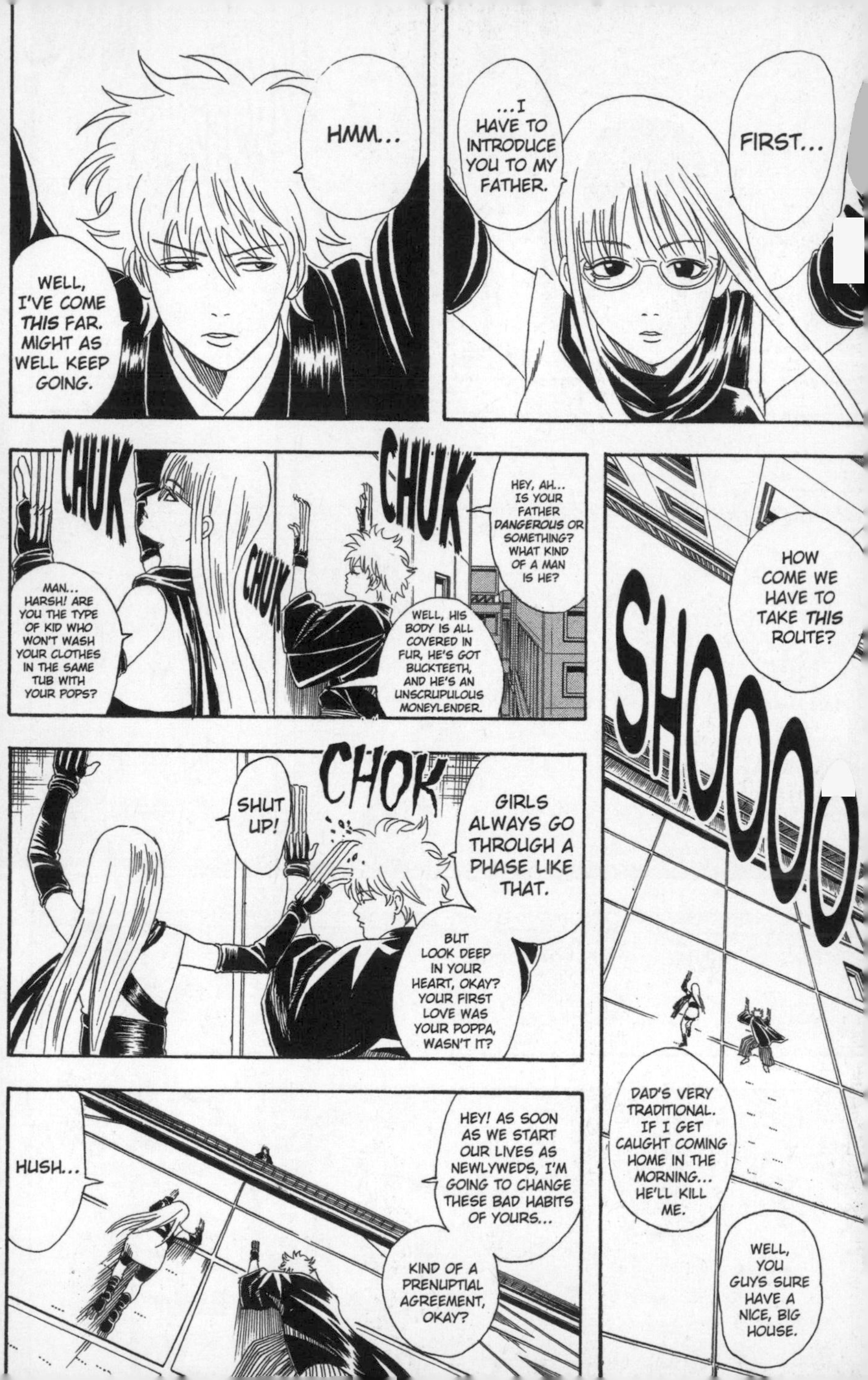
FIRST...
...I HAVE TO INTRODUCE YOU TO MY FATHER.
HMM...
WELL, I'VE COME THIS FAR. MIGHT AS WELL KEEP GOING.
HOW COME WE HAVE TO TAKE THIS ROUTE?
SHOOOO
DAD'S VERY TRADITIONAL. IF I GET CAUGHT COMING HOME IN THE MORNING... HE'LL KILL ME.
WELL, YOU GUYS SURE HAVE A NICE, BIG HOUSE.
CHUK
CHUK
CHUK
HEY, AH... IS YOUR FATHER DANGEROUS OR SOMETHING? WHAT KIND OF A MAN IS HE?
WELL, HIS BODY IS ALL COVERED IN FUR, HE'S GOT BUCKTEETH, AND HE'S AN UNSCRUPULOUS MONEYLENDER.
MAN... HARSH! ARE YOU THE TYPE OF KID WHO WON'T WASH YOUR CLOTHES IN THE SAME TUB WITH YOUR POPS?
GIRLS ALWAYS GO THROUGH A PHASE LIKE THAT.
BUT LOOK DEEP IN YOUR HEART, OKAY? YOUR FIRST LOVE WAS YOUR POPPA, WASN'T IT?
CHOK
SHUT UP!
HEY! AS SOON AS WE START OUR LIVES AS NEWLYWEDS, I'M GOING TO CHANGE THESE BAD HABITS OF YOURS...
KIND OF A PRENUPTIAL AGREEMENT, OKAY?
HUSH...

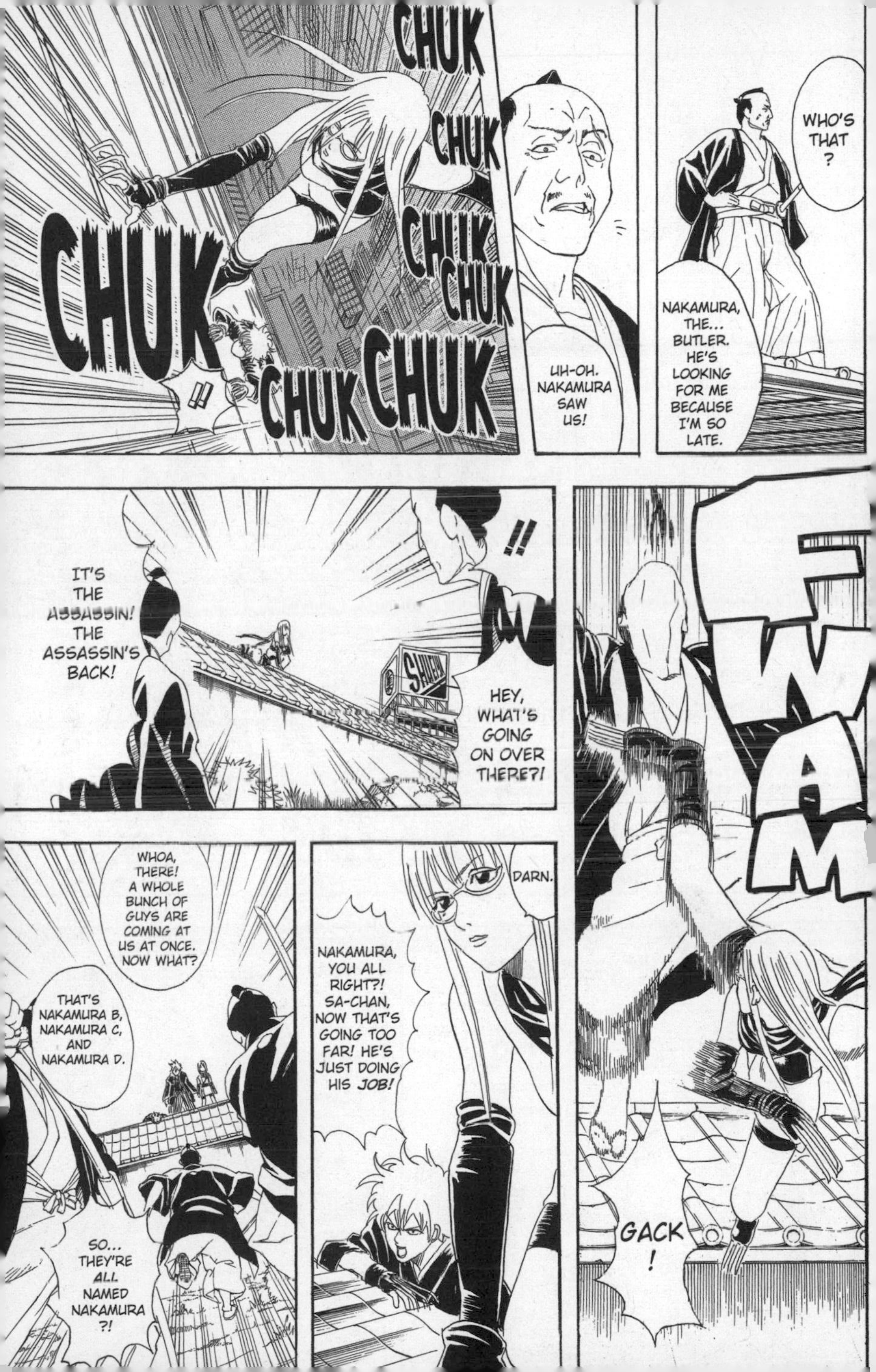
WHO'S THAT ?
NAKAMURA, THE... BUTLER. HE'S LOOKING FOR ME BECAUSE I'M SO LATE.
UH-OH. NAKAMURA SAW US!
CHUK
CHUK
CHUK
CHUK
CHUK
CHUK
CHUK
!!
FWAM
GACK !
!!
HEY, WHAT'S GOING ON OVER THERE?!
IT'S THE ASSASSIN! THE ASSASSIN'S BACK!
DARN.
NAKAMURA, YOU ALL RIGHT?! SA-CHAN, NOW THAT'S GOING TOO FAR! HE'S JUST DOING HIS JOB!
WHOA, THERE! A WHOLE BUNCH OF GUYS ARE COMING AT US AT ONCE. NOW WHAT?
THAT'S NAKAMURA B, NAKAMURA C, AND NAKAMURA D.
SO... THEY'RE ALL NAMED NAKAMURA ?!

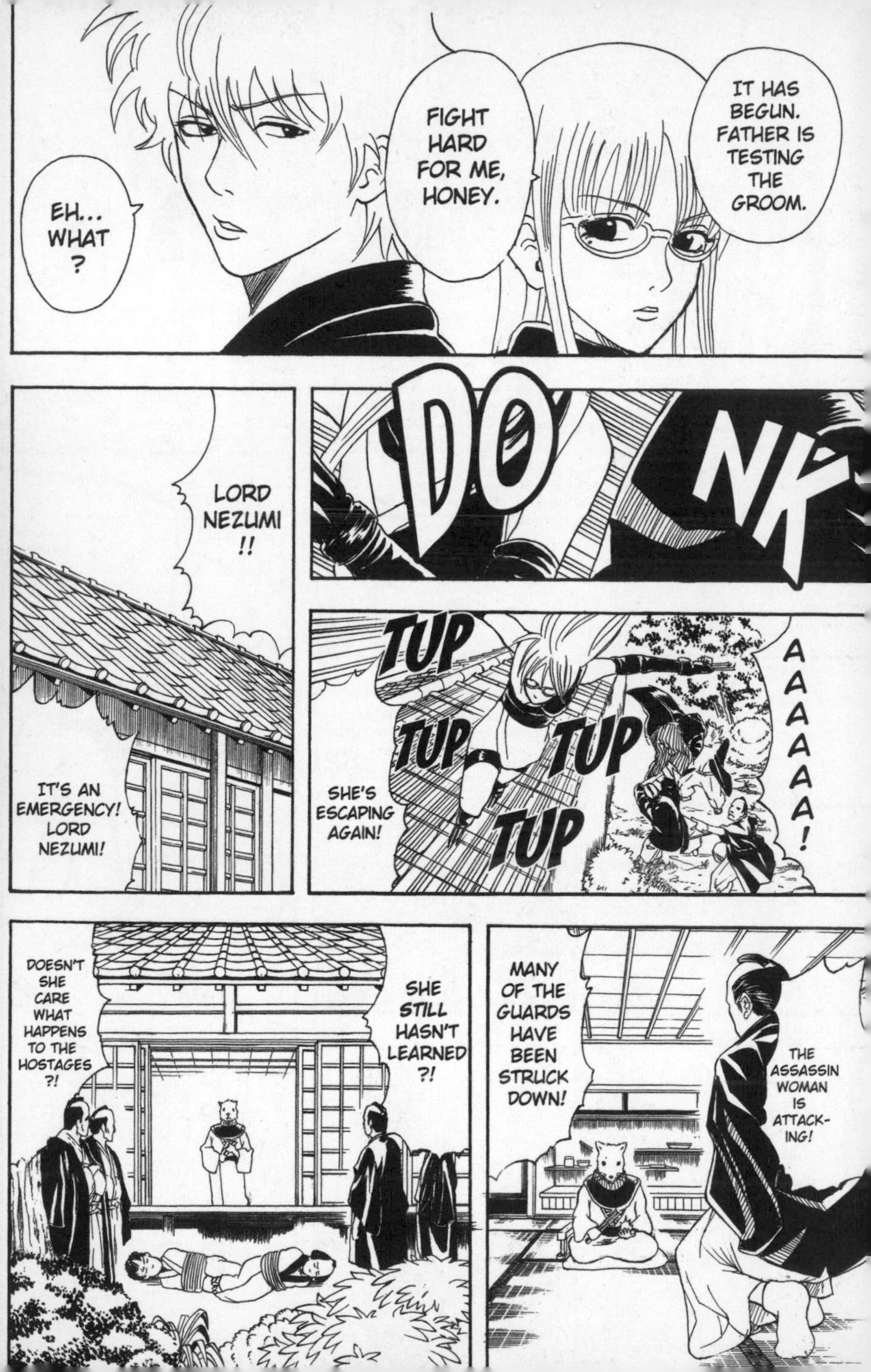
IT HAS BEGUN. FATHER IS TESTING THE GROOM.
FIGHT HARD FOR ME, HONEY.
EH... WHAT?
DONK
AAAAAA!
TUP TUP TUP TUP
SHE'S ESCAPING AGAIN!
LORD NEZUMI!!
IT'S AN EMERGENCY! LORD NEZUMI!
THE ASSASSIN WOMAN IS ATTACK-ING!
MANY OF THE GUARDS HAVE BEEN STRUCK DOWN!
SHE STILL HASN'T LEARNED?!
DOESN'T SHE CARE WHAT HAPPENS TO THE HOSTAGES?!

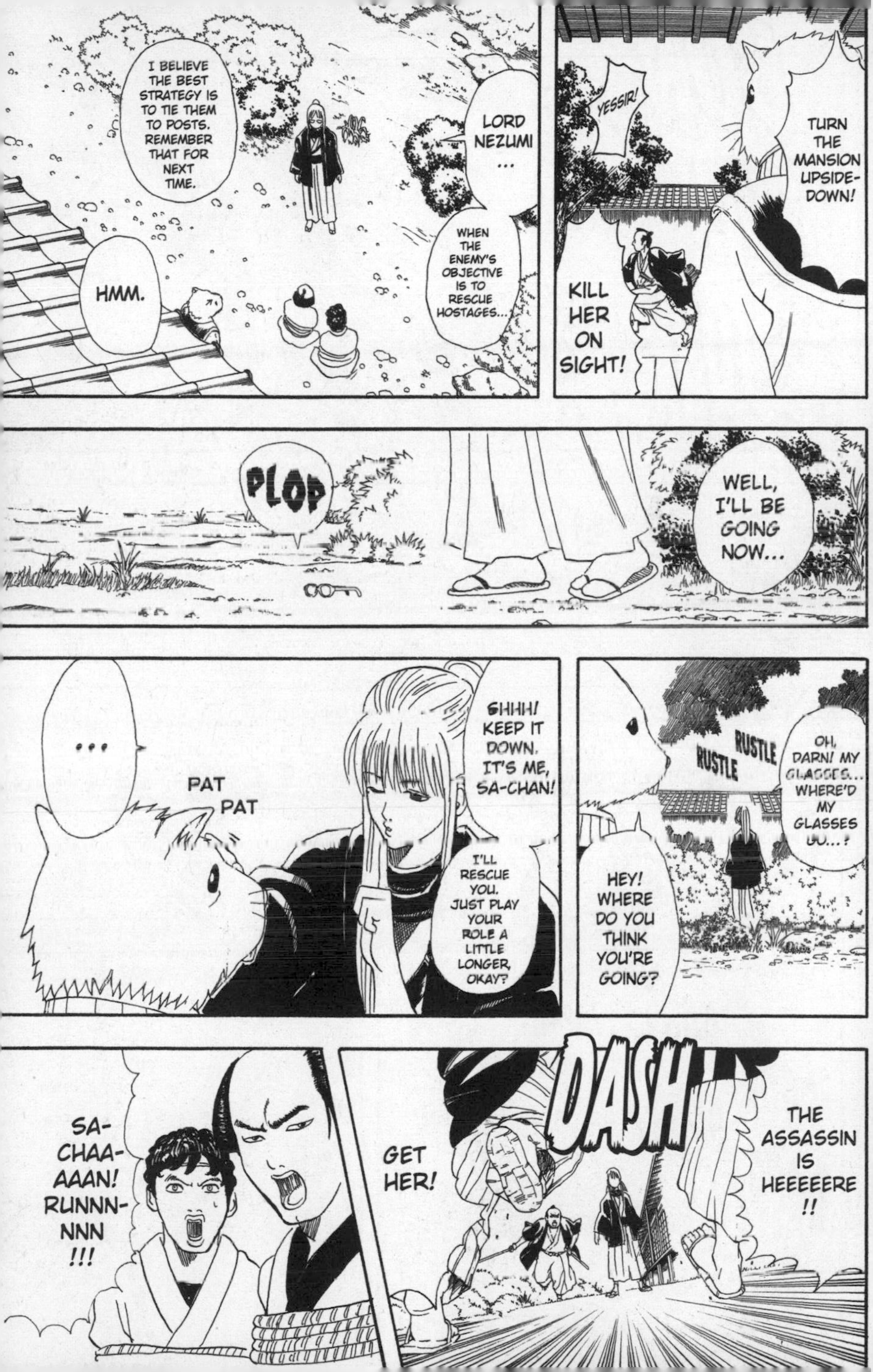
TURN THE MANSION UPSIDE-DOWN!
YESSIR!
KILL HER ON SIGHT!
LORD NEZUMI ...
WHEN THE ENEMY'S OBJECTIVE IS TO RESCUE HOSTAGES...
I BELIEVE THE BEST STRATEGY IS TO TIE THEM TO POSTS. REMEMBER THAT FOR NEXT TIME.
HMM.
WELL, I'LL BE GOING NOW...
PLOP
OH, DARN! MY GLASSES... WHERE'D MY GLASSES GO...?
RUSTLE
RUSTLE
HEY! WHERE DO YOU THINK YOU'RE GOING?
SHHH! KEEP IT DOWN. IT'S ME, SA-CHAN!
I'LL RESCUE YOU. JUST PLAY YOUR ROLE A LITTLE LONGER, OKAY?
...
PAT PAT
DASH
THE ASSASSIN IS HEEEEERE !!
GET HER!
SA-CHAAAAAN! RUNNNNNN !!!

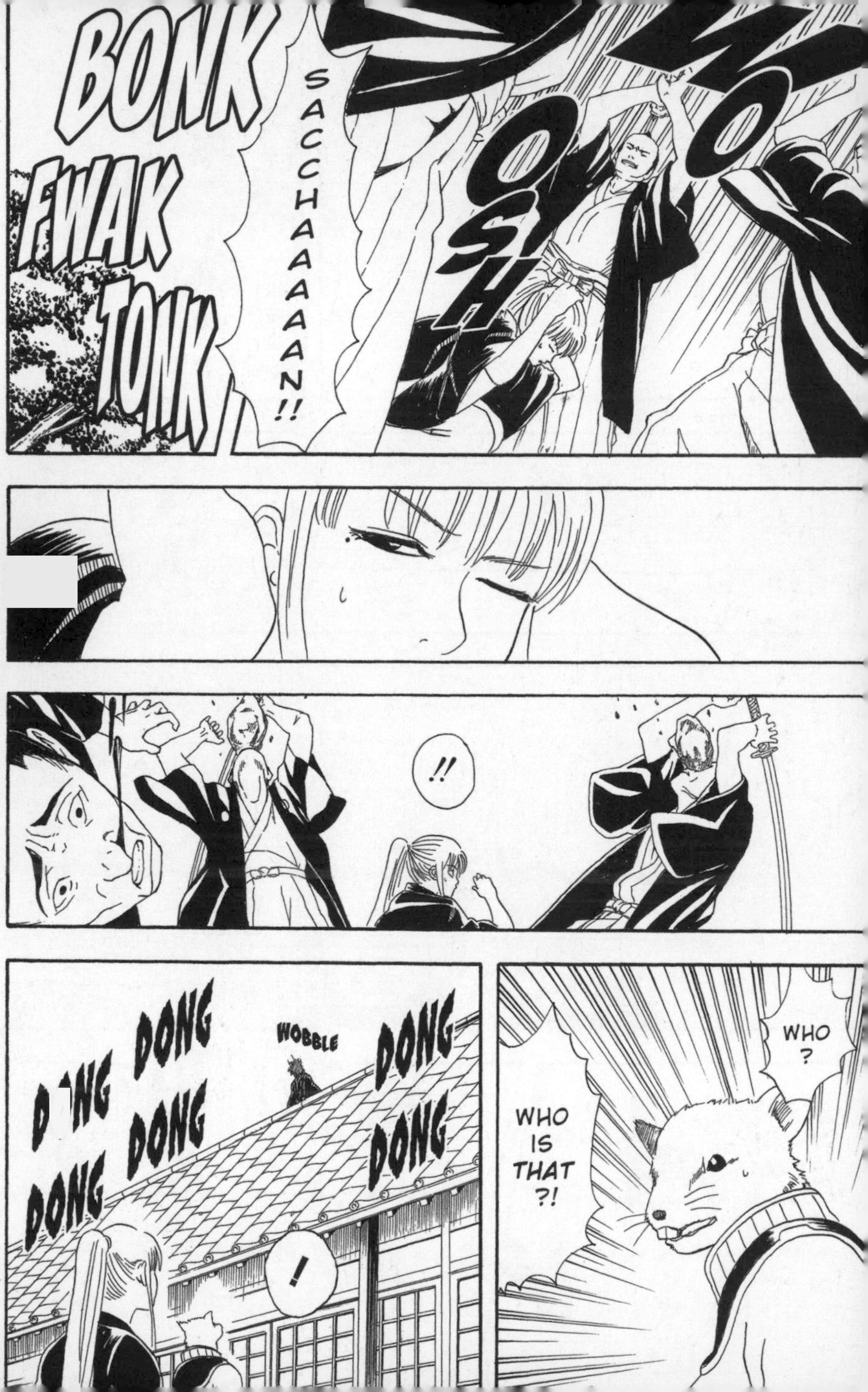
WOOSH
SACCHAAAAAAN!!
BONK
FWAK
TONK
!!
WHO?
WHO IS THAT?!
DONG DONG DONG DONG
DONG DONG DONG
WOBBLE
!

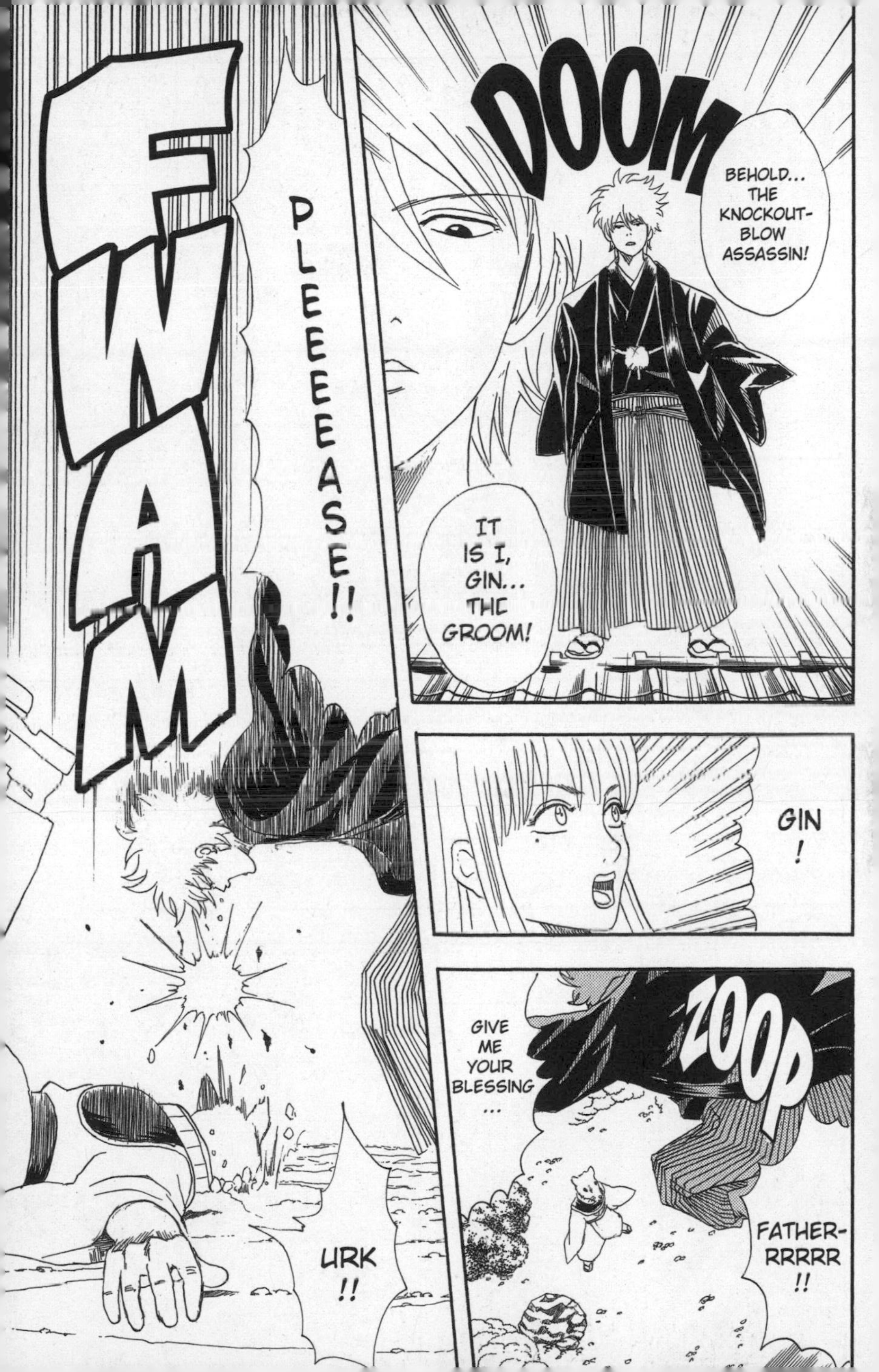
DOOM
BEHOLD... THE KNOCKOUT-BLOW ASSASSIN!
IT IS I, GIN... THE GROOM!
GIN!
ZOOP
GIVE ME YOUR BLESSING...
FATHER-RRRRR!!
PLEEEEASE!!
FWAM
URK!!

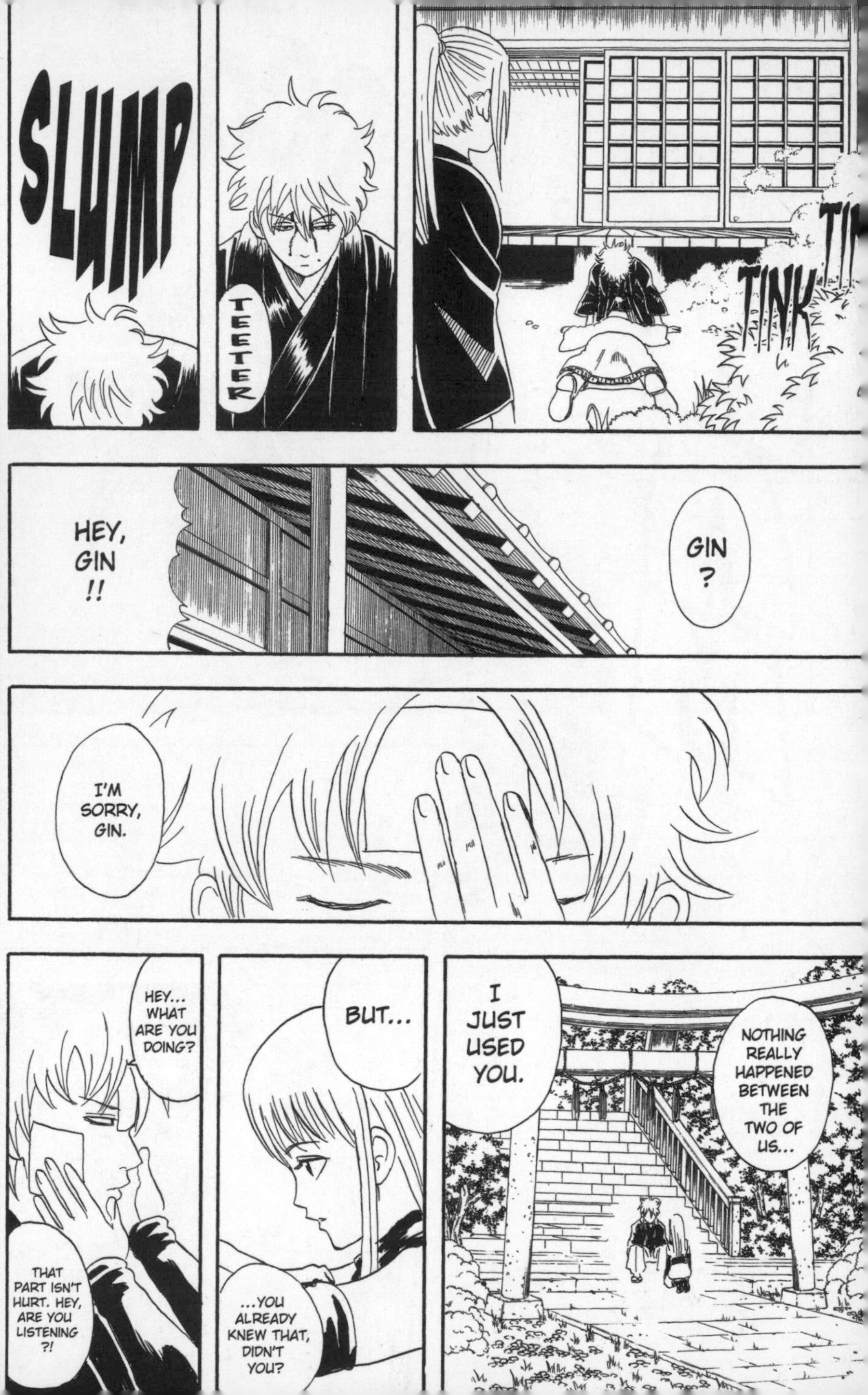
TINK
TEETER
SLUMP
GIN ?
HEY, GIN !!
I'M SORRY, GIN.
NOTHING REALLY HAPPENED BETWEEN THE TWO OF US...
I JUST USED YOU.
BUT...
...YOU ALREADY KNEW THAT, DIDN'T YOU?
HEY... WHAT ARE YOU DOING?
THAT PART ISN'T HURT. HEY, ARE YOU LISTENING ?!

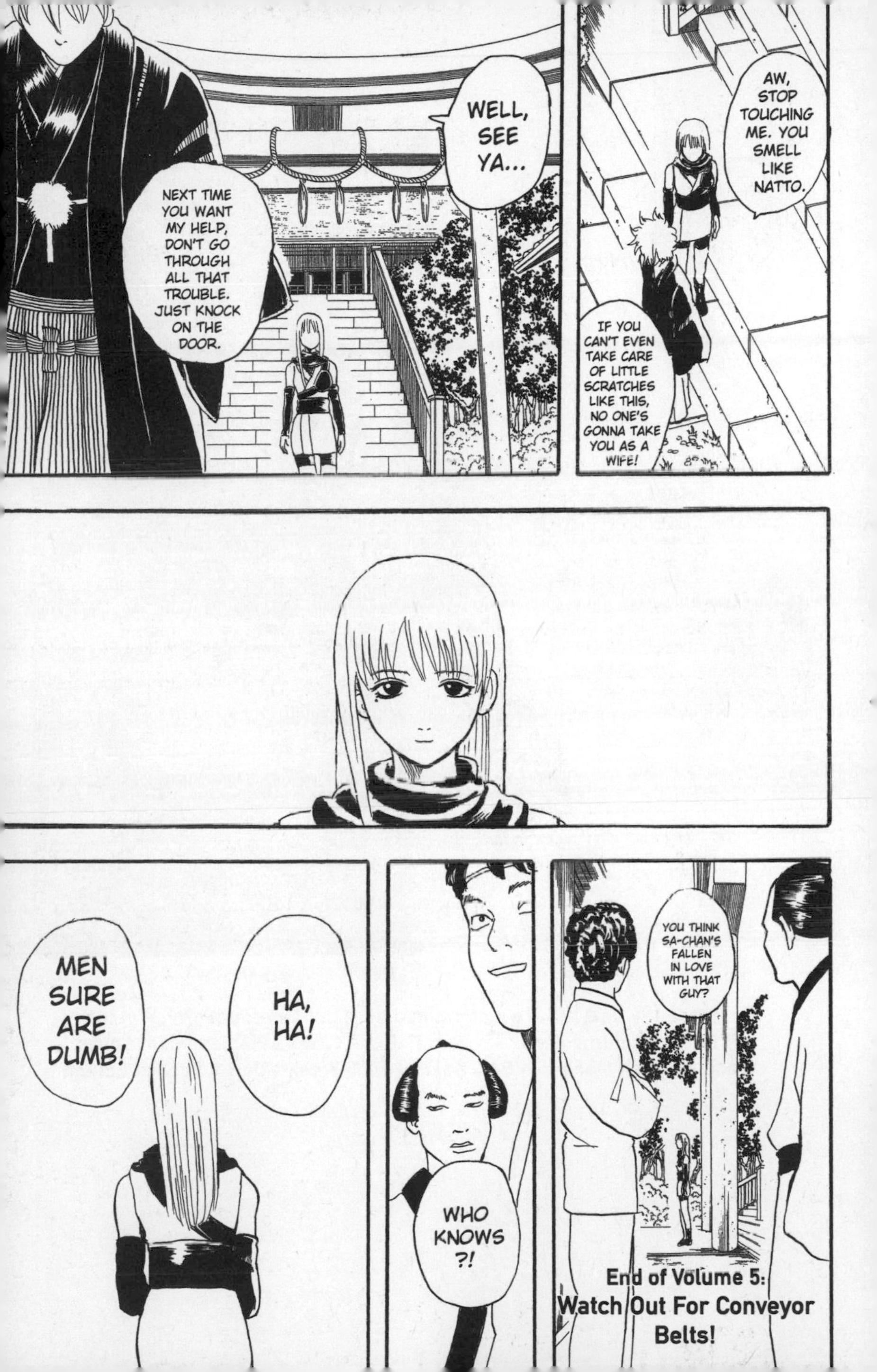
AW, STOP TOUCHING ME. YOU SMELL LIKE NATTO.
IF YOU CAN'T EVEN TAKE CARE OF LITTLE SCRATCHES LIKE THIS, NO ONE'S GONNA TAKE YOU AS A WIFE!
WELL, SEE YA...
NEXT TIME YOU WANT MY HELP, DON'T GO THROUGH ALL THAT TROUBLE. JUST KNOCK ON THE DOOR.
YOU THINK SA-CHAN'S FALLEN IN LOVE WITH THAT GUY?
End of Volume 5: Watch Out For Conveyor Belts!
WHO KNOWS?!
HA, HA!
MEN SURE ARE DUMB!

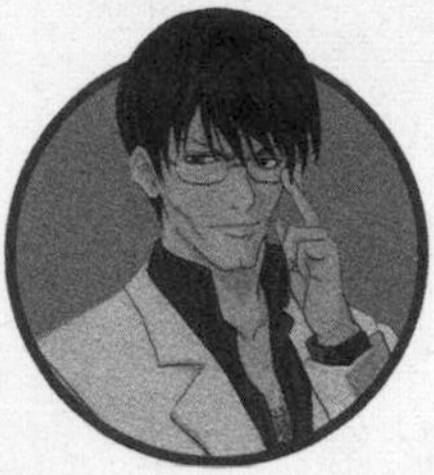

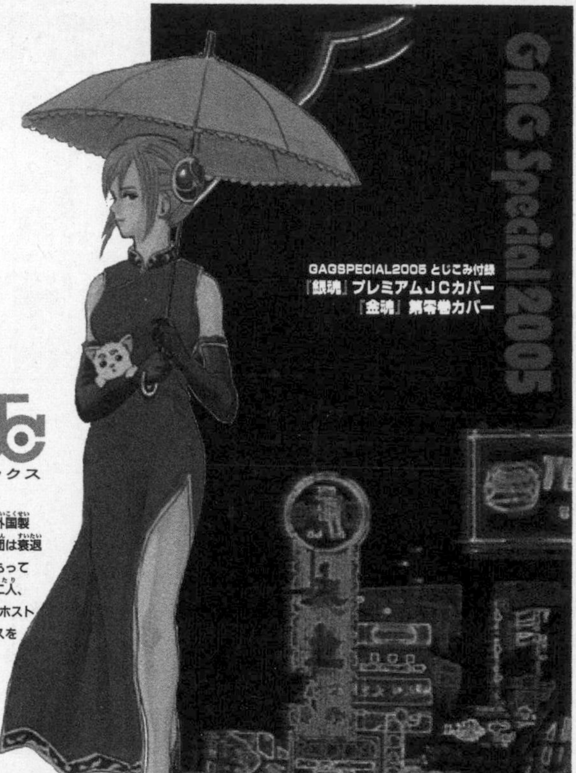

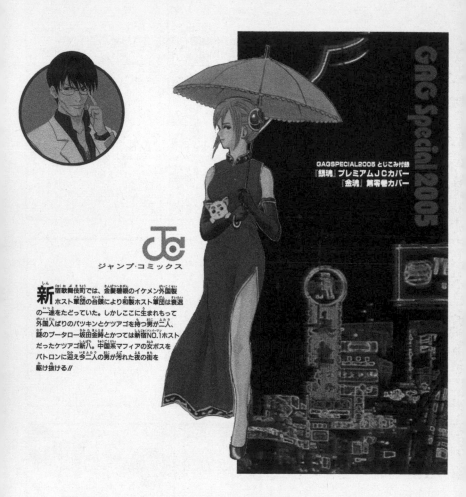

GAG Special 2005
GAGSPECIAL2005 とじこみ付録
『銀魂』プレミアムＪＣカバー
『金魂』第零巻カバー

ジャンプ·コミックス

新宿歌舞伎町では、金髪碧眼のイケメン外国製ホスト軍団の台頭により和製ホスト軍団は衰退の一途をたどっていた。しかしここに生まれもって外国人ばりのパツキンとケツアゴを持つ男が二人、謎のプータロー坂田金時とかつては新宿NO.1ホストだったケツアゴ新八。中国系マフィアの女ボスをパトロンに迎え今二人の男が汚れた夜の街を駆け抜ける//

● Pages 194 and 195 are a combined spread of a reduced copy of the Premium Volume Zero "Gin Tama" Jump Comics Replacement Cover, included as a freebie in GAG Special 2005 Weekly Jump Special Edition

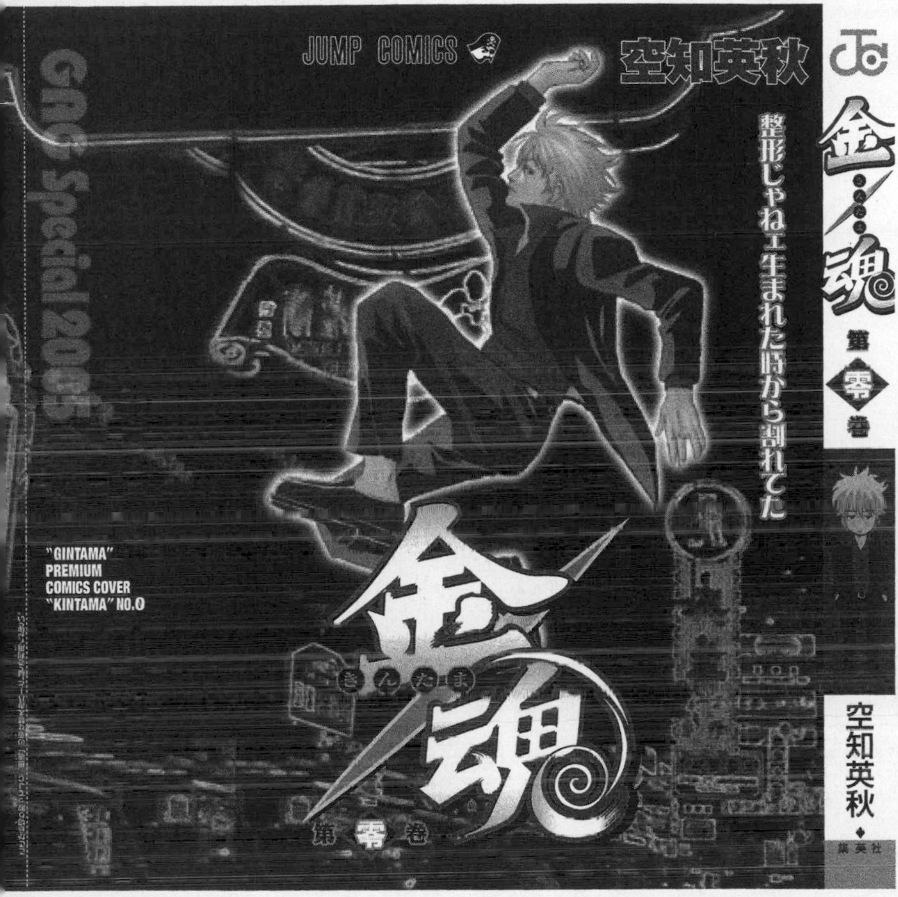
JUMP COMICS
空知英秋
整形じゃねェ生まれた時から割れてた
金魂
きんたま
第零巻
"GINTAMA"
PREMIUM
COMICS COVER
"KINTAMA" NO.0
GAG Special 2005
JC
金魂
第零巻
空知英秋
集英社

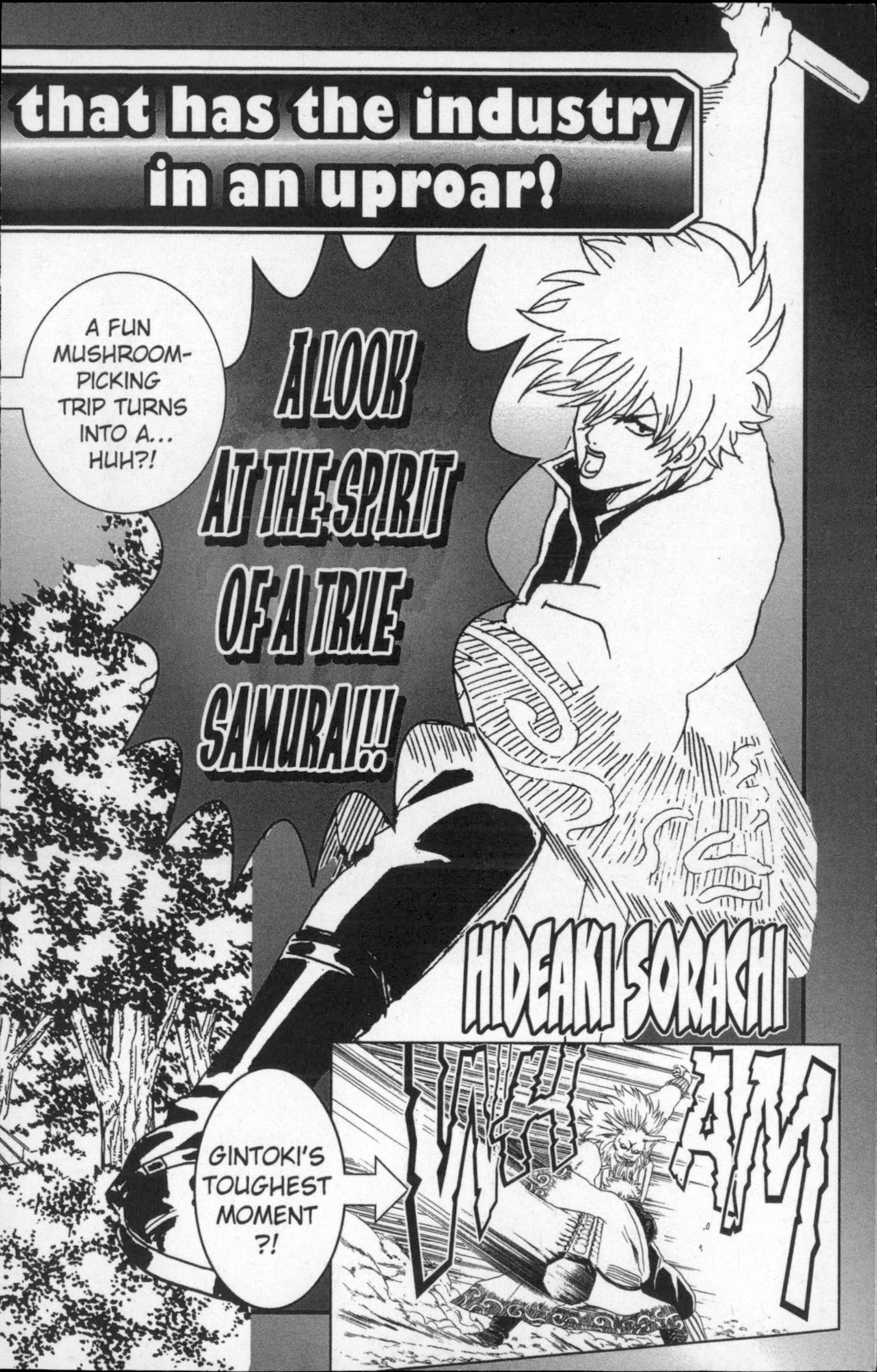
that has the industry in an uproar!
A LOOK AT THE SPIRIT OF A TRUE SAMURAI!!
A FUN MUSHROOM-PICKING TRIP TURNS INTO A... HUH?!
HIDEAKI SORACHI
GINTOKI'S TOUGHEST MOMENT ?!

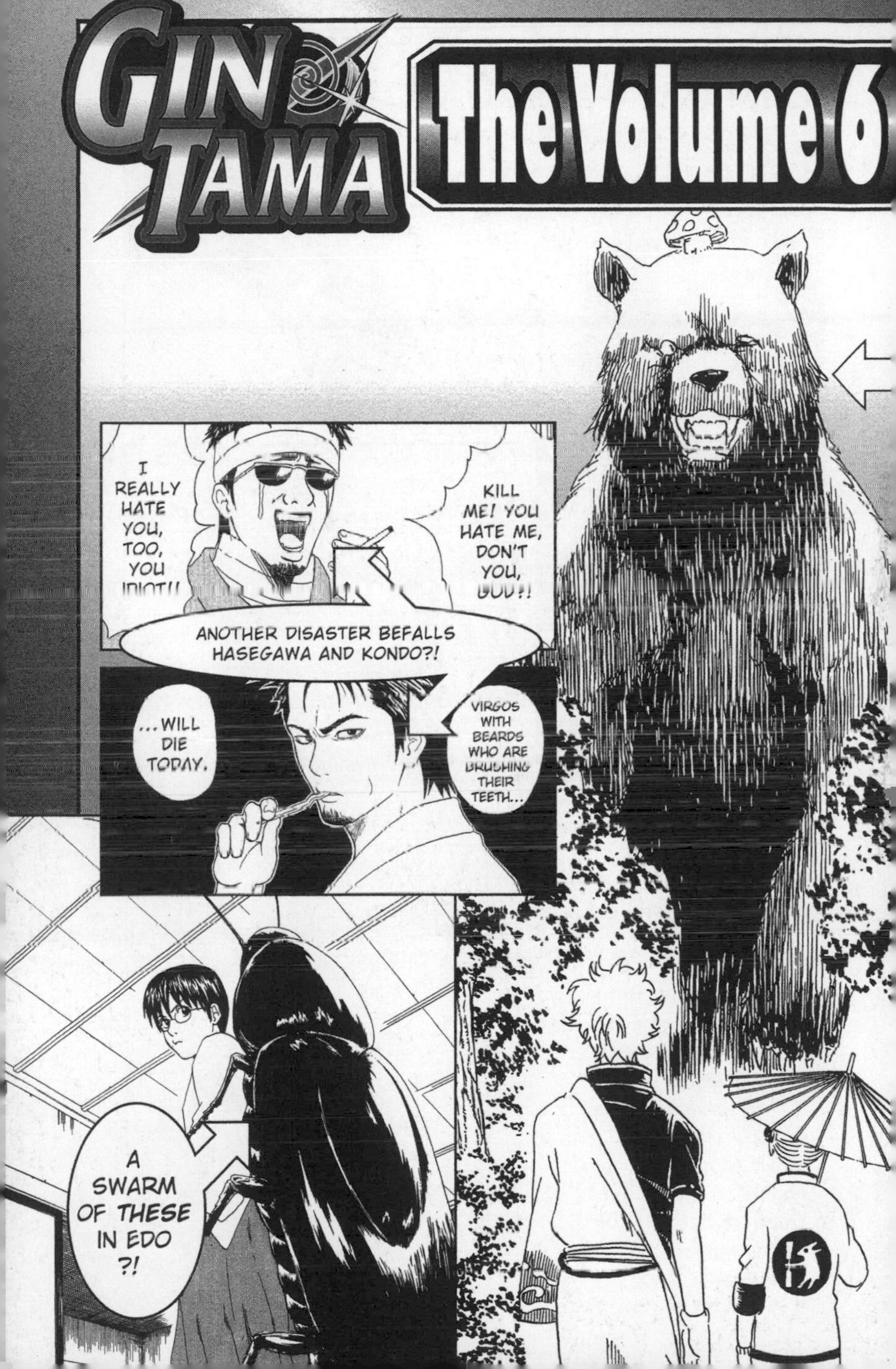
GIN TAMA
The Volume 6
KILL ME! YOU HATE ME, DON'T YOU, DUD?!
I REALLY HATE YOU, TOO, YOU IDIOT!!
ANOTHER DISASTER BEFALLS HASEGAWA AND KONDO?!
VIRGOS WITH BEARDS WHO ARE BRUSHING THEIR TEETH...
...WILL DIE TODAY.
A SWARM OF THESE IN EDO ?!

Next volume, the Odd Jobs Trio finds the stuff of adventure!

Yoruzuya Trio Hunting and Gathering List

1. Zombie bear with mysterious mushroom growing out of head (magic?)
2. Crab chock-full of food poisoning (yum!)
3. Hot nurse in hospital (where we wind up due to #2)
4. Goro, queen of the human-size cockroaches (yuk!)
5. 100 ice cream mini-cups (yum!)
6. The truth behind a cult that promises to make your dreams come true (dream on...)

AVAILABLE NOW

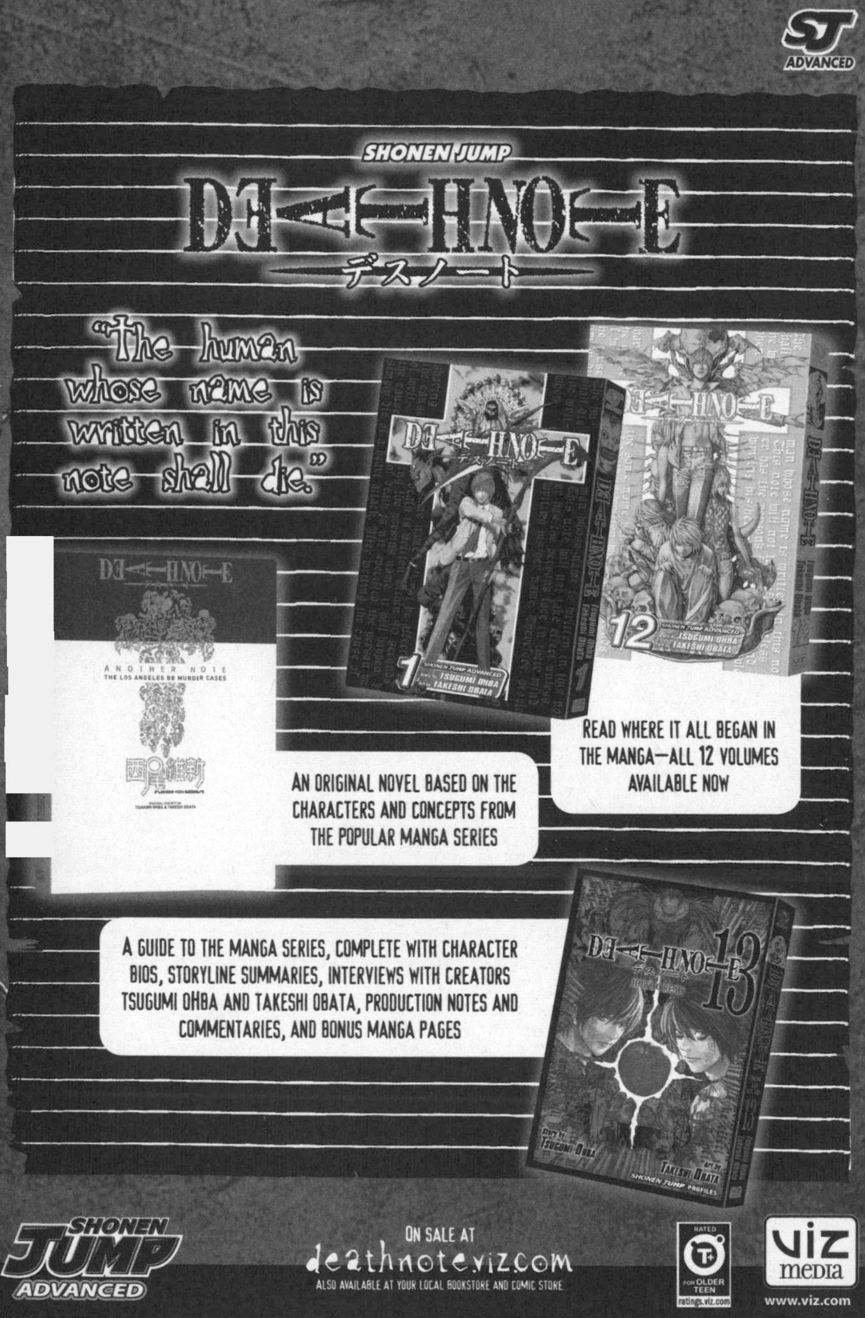
SJ ADVANCED
SHONEN JUMP
DEATH NOTE
"The human whose name is written in this note shall die."
READ WHERE IT ALL BEGAN IN THE MANGA—ALL 12 VOLUMES AVAILABLE NOW
AN ORIGINAL NOVEL BASED ON THE CHARACTERS AND CONCEPTS FROM THE POPULAR MANGA SERIES
A GUIDE TO THE MANGA SERIES, COMPLETE WITH CHARACTER BIOS, STORYLINE SUMMARIES, INTERVIEWS WITH CREATORS TSUGUMI OHBA AND TAKESHI OBATA, PRODUCTION NOTES AND COMMENTARIES, AND BONUS MANGA PAGES
SHONEN JUMP ADVANCED
ON SALE AT
deathnote.viz.com
ALSO AVAILABLE AT YOUR LOCAL BOOKSTORE AND COMIC STORE
RATED T+ FOR OLDER TEEN
ratings.viz.com
viz media
www.viz.com

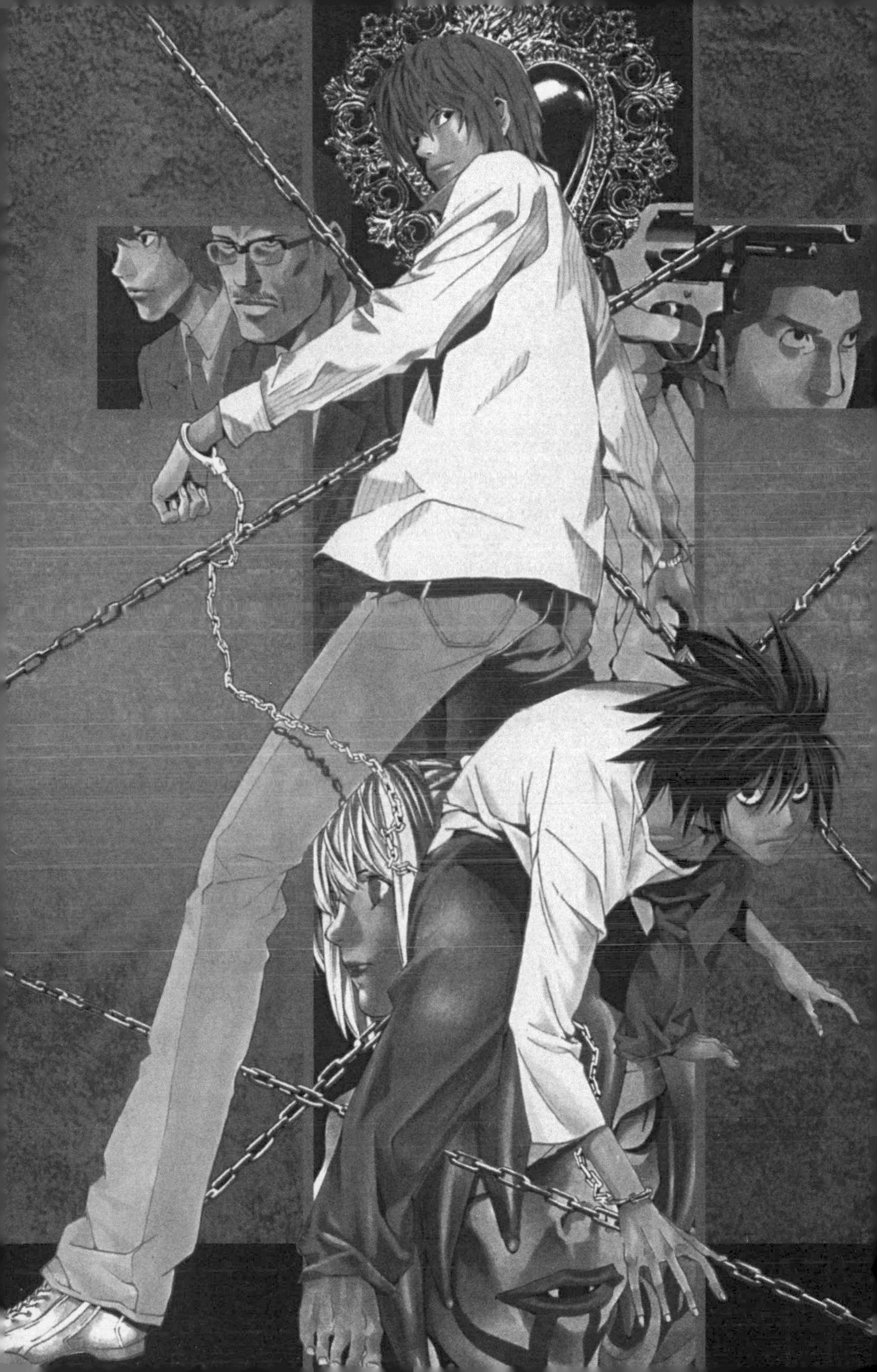

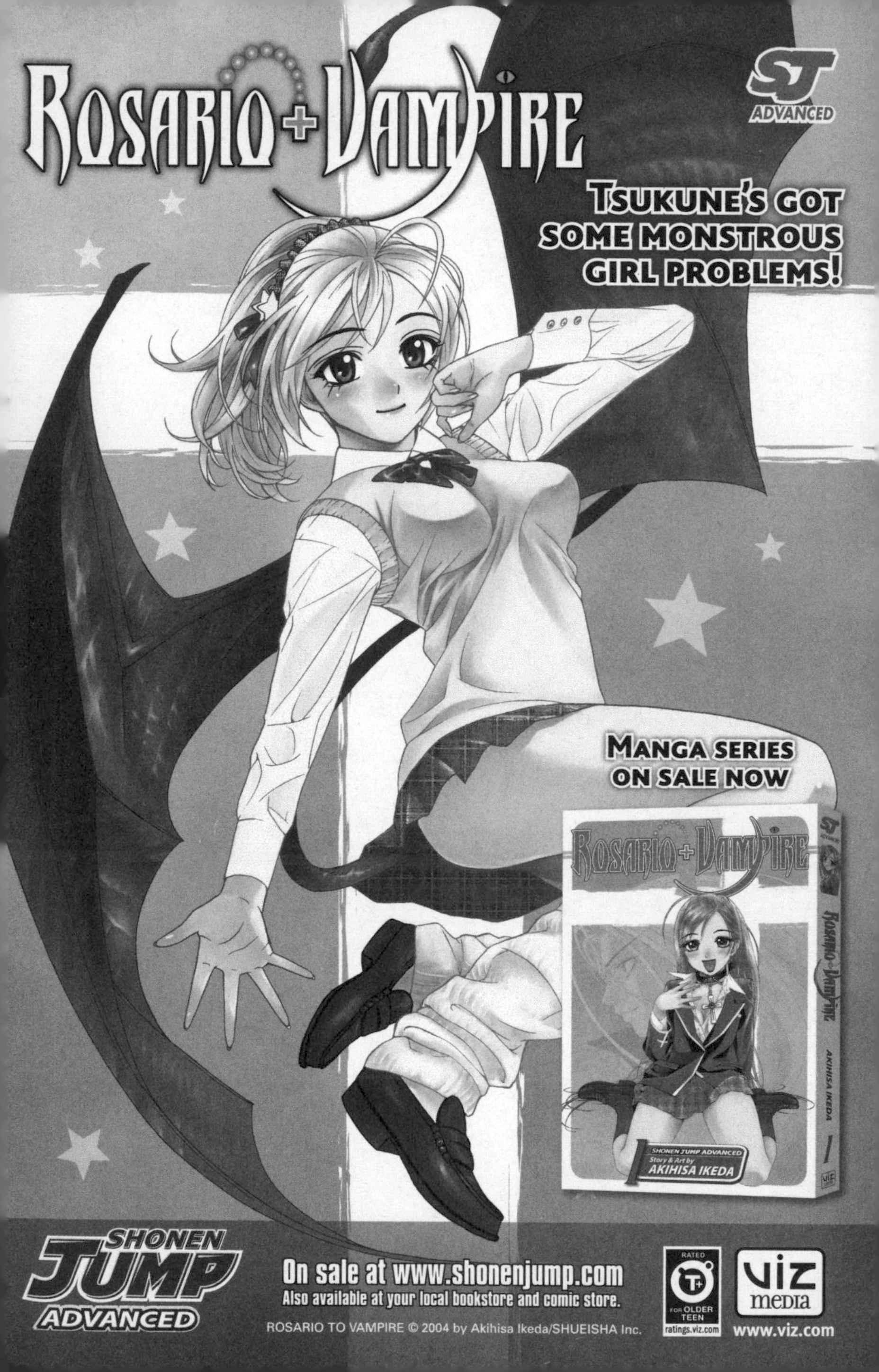
ROSARIO+VAMPIRE
SJ ADVANCED
TSUKUNE'S GOT SOME MONSTROUS GIRL PROBLEMS!
MANGA SERIES ON SALE NOW
ROSARIO+VAMPIRE
SHONEN JUMP ADVANCED
Story & Art by
AKIHISA IKEDA
SHONEN JUMP ADVANCED
On sale at www.shonenjump.com
Also available at your local bookstore and comic store.
ROSARIO TO VAMPIRE © 2004 by Akihisa Ikeda/SHUEISHA Inc.
RATED T+ FOR OLDER TEEN
ratings.viz.com
VIZ media
www.viz.com

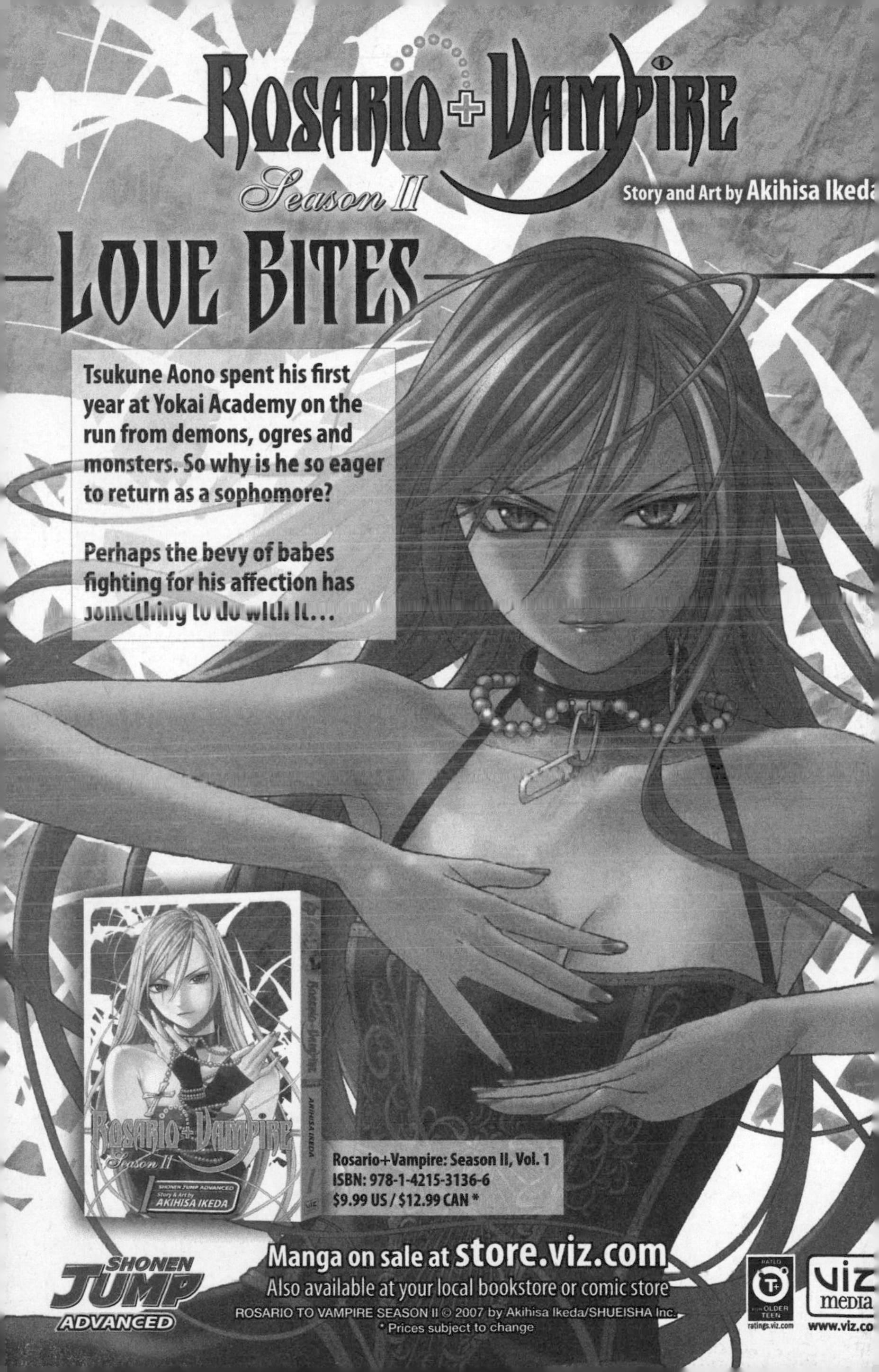
ROSARIO+VAMPIRE
Season II
Story and Art by Akihisa Ikeda
LOVE BITES
Tsukune Aono spent his first year at Yokai Academy on the run from demons, ogres and monsters. So why is he so eager to return as a sophomore?
Perhaps the bevy of babes fighting for his affection has something to do with it...
ROSARIO+VAMPIRE
Season II
SHONEN JUMP ADVANCED
Story & Art by
AKIHISA IKEDA
Rosario+Vampire: Season II, Vol. 1
ISBN: 978-1-4215-3136-6
$9.99 US / $12.99 CAN *
SHONEN JUMP ADVANCED
Manga on sale at store.viz.com
Also available at your local bookstore or comic store
ROSARIO TO VAMPIRE SEASON II © 2007 by Akihisa Ikeda/SHUEISHA Inc.
* Prices subject to change
RATED
OLDER TEEN
ratings.viz.com
viz media
www.viz.co

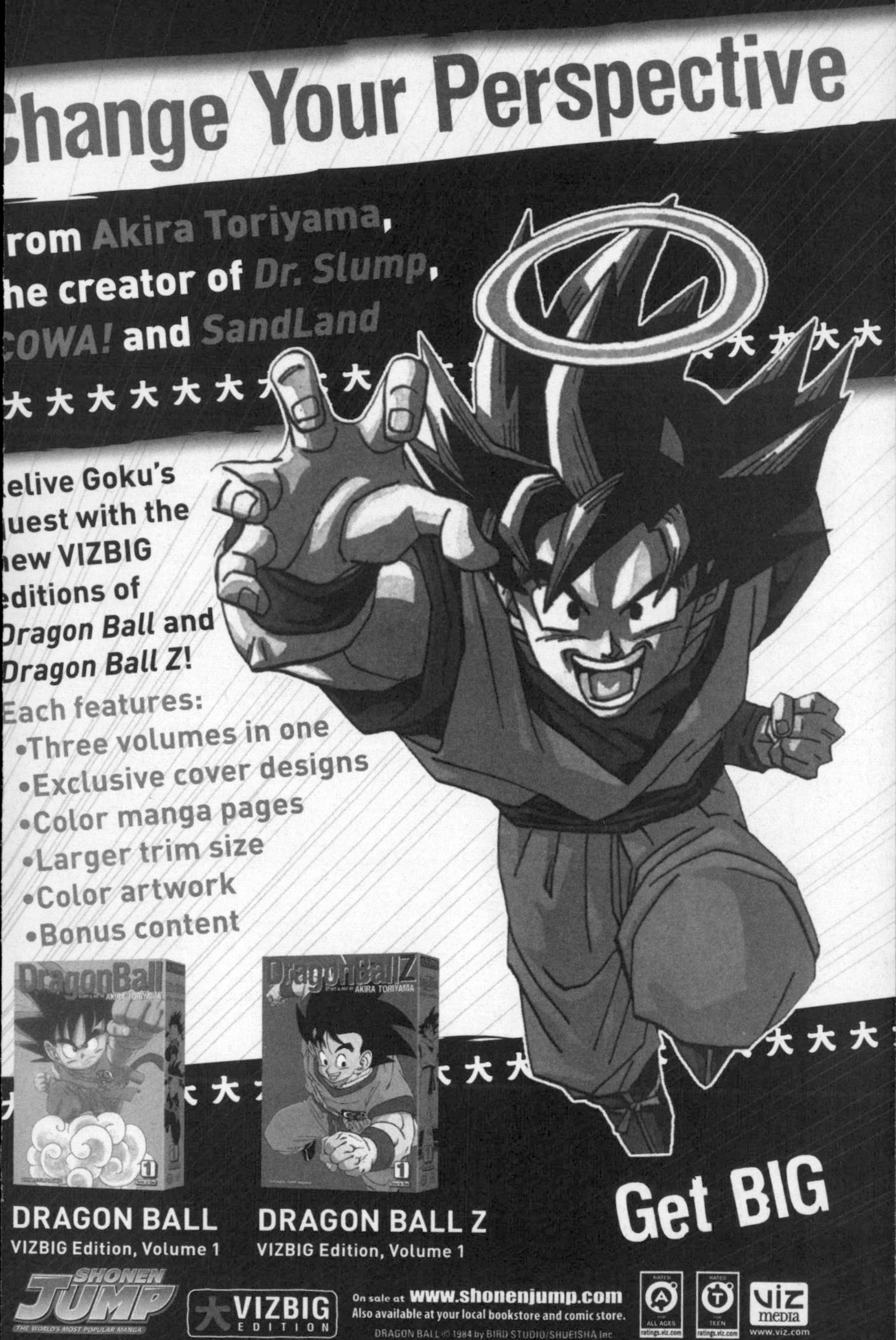
Change Your Perspective
rom Akira Toriyama,
he creator of Dr. Slump,
COWA! and SandLand
elive Goku's
uest with the
ew VIZBIG
ditions of
Dragon Ball and
Dragon Ball Z!
Each features:
•Three volumes in one
•Exclusive cover designs
•Color manga pages
•Larger trim size
•Color artwork
•Bonus content
DRAGON BALL
VIZBIG Edition, Volume 1
DRAGON BALL Z
VIZBIG Edition, Volume 1
Get BIG
SHONEN JUMP
THE WORLD'S MOST POPULAR MANGA
VIZBIG EDITION
On sale at www.shonenjump.com
Also available at your local bookstore and comic store.
DRAGON BALL © 1984 by BIRD STUDIO/SHUEISHA Inc.
RATED A FOR ALL AGES ratings.viz.com
RATED T FOR TEEN ratings.viz.com
VIZ media
www.viz.com

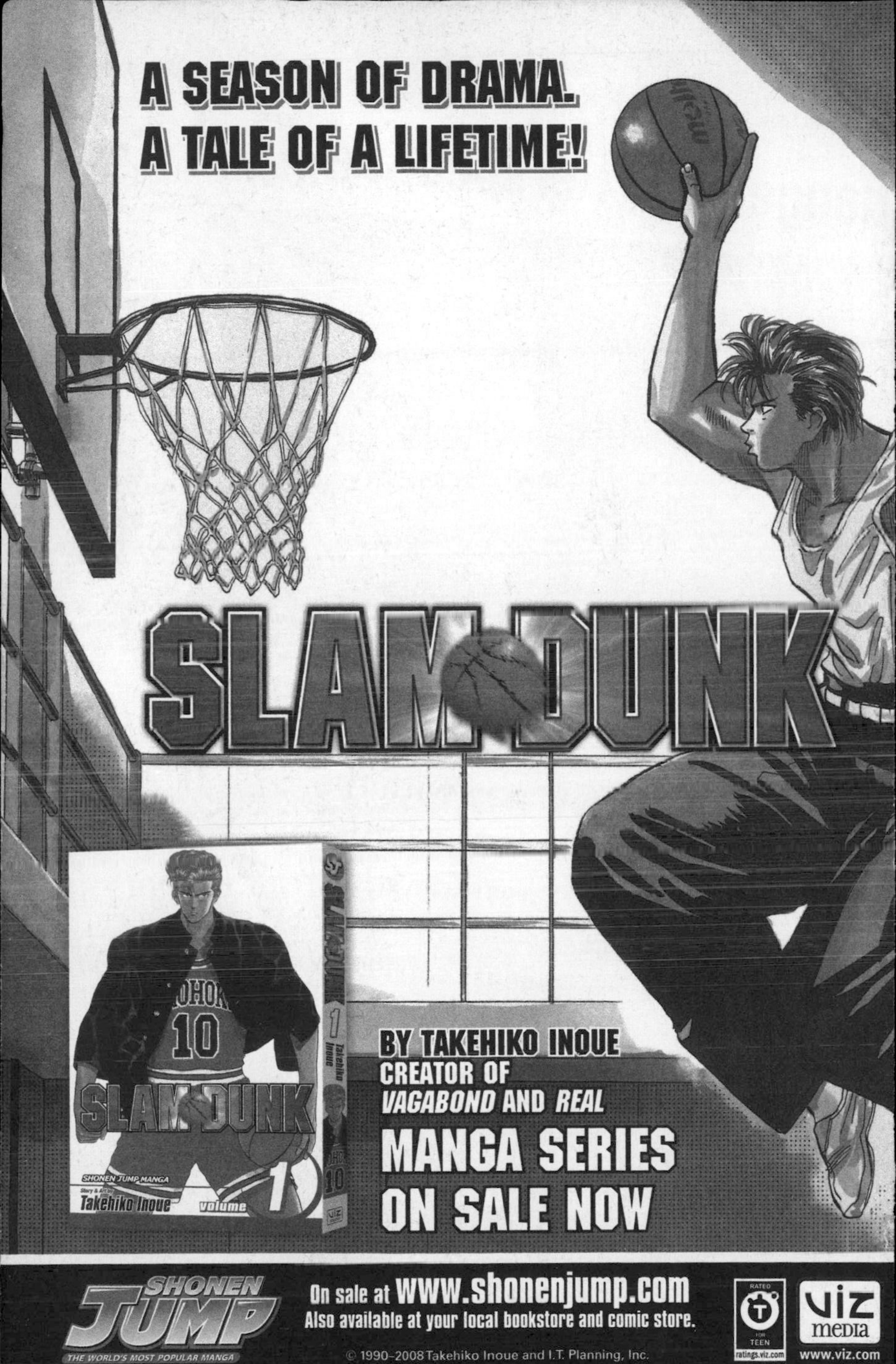